Patient Safety

For Ellen

Patient Safety

Perspectives on Evidence, Information and Knowledge Transfer

Edited by
LORRI ZIPPERER

Routledge
Taylor & Francis Group

LONDON AND NEW YORK

First published 2014 by Gower Publishing

2 Park Square, Milton Park, Abingdon, Oxon OX14 4RN
711 Third Avenue, New York, NY 10017, USA

Routledge is an imprint of the Taylor & Francis Group, an informa business

First issued in paperback 2016

British Library Cataloguing in Publication Data
A catalogue record for this book is available from the British Library

Library of Congress Cataloging-in-Publication Data
Zipperer, Lorri A., 1959-
  Patient safety : perspectives on evidence, information and knowledge transfer / by Lorri Zipperer.
      pages cm
  Includes bibliographical references and index.
  ISBN 978-1-4094-3857-1 (hbk)
1. Hospital patients--Safety measures. 2. Medical errors--Prevention. I. Title.
  RA965.6.Z57 2014
  610.28'9--dc23
                                                                    2013028766

ISBN 978-1-4094-3857-1 (hbk)
ISBN 978-1-138-24916-5 (pbk)

Contents

List of Figures

List of Tables

About the Editor

Lorri Zipperer, Cybrarian, is the principal at Zipperer Project Management, in Albuquerque, New Mexico. Lorri has been in the information and knowledge management field for over two decades, over half of which have been focused on patient safety. She was a founding staff member of the National Patient Safety Foundation as the information project manager. Lorri currently works with clients to provide patient safety information, knowledge-sharing, project management and strategic development guidance. Lorri has recently led projects in patient safety educational tool development, publication evidence identification and organizational knowledge access improvement. She currently serves as the Cybrarian for the Agency for Healthcare Research and Quality's Patient Safety Network collaborating with the multidisciplinary editorial and production team since the launch of the site in 2005. She was recognized that same year with a 2005 Institute for Safe Medication Practices Cheers Award for her work with librarians, libraries and their involvement in patient safety. She has initiated and published two national surveys of librarians on their role in patient safety work to map the evolution of that role over time. Ms Zipperer's expertise was highlighted in the June 2009 Medical Library Association policy on the role of librarians in patient safety. She has launched blogs, online groups and communities of practice to support sharing of information and knowledge to facilitate safety and quality improvement among her peers.

Ms. Zipperer was a 2004–2005 Patient Safety Leadership Fellow where she explored how information and knowledge transfer behaviours affect a learning culture. She has participated in research to explore the process of knowledge-sharing both at the bedside and with clinical teams. In 2007 and 2009, she was funded by regional offices of the National Network of Libraries of Medicine to work with her colleagues in acute care environments to facilitate avenues for implementation of knowledge-sharing initiatives. More recently Lorri has participated in a series of workshops looking at systematic and cognitive impacts that evidence, information and knowledge can have on decision-making in diagnostic error. She has designed and co-facilitates an interprofessional workshop on knowledge-sharing in hospitals which has been noted by attendees as being "transformational".

Lorri earned her Masters of Arts in library and information studies from Northern Illinois University. She has served as an adjunct professor for library management at the university level. Lorri has received honours from the library and information science community and has been published on topics such as alternative roles for librarians, patient safety, collaboration, systems thinking and knowledge management.

About the Contributors

Elaine Alligood, MLS   Elaine is the Chief, Library Service for the Boston Veterans Affairs (VA) Healthcare System's three campuses. A member of the New England VA Library Re-design Task Force, she helped develop a consolidated network-wide 24/7 virtual knowledge library accessible across VA New England. She provides client-focused service for clinicians and researchers. She's a member of several research teams, care coordination, mental health, and service line management. Working directly with clinicians and researchers at the frontlines she attends rounds and morning reports. She partners with clinical staff to integrate e-resources into teaching and research. One of the co-developers of the Medical Library Association (MLA) continuing education program entitled "Diagnostic Error and the Librarian's Role in Patient Safety," Elaine believes librarian's transforming roles perfectly align us with the clinical and research staff's ever-changing information needs. Moving librarians out of the library "place" to where information needs occur – at the point-of-care where research benefits everyone: clinicians, researchers and patients.

James P. Bagian, MD, PE   Jim is the Director of the Center for Healthcare Engineering and Patient Safety, the Chief Patient Safety and Systems Innovation Officer, as well as a Professor in the Department of Anesthesiology and College of Engineering at the University of Michigan. Dr. Bagian is a member of the National Aeronautics and Space Adminitration (NASA) Aerospace Safety Advisory Panel and was a NASA astronaut and veteran of two space shuttle flights. He serves as a member of the Board of Governors of the National Patient Safety Foundation, was the founding Director of the National Center for Patient Safety and the first Chief Patient Safety Officer at the US Department of Veterans Affairs. Dr. Bagian was elected as a member of the National Academy of Engineering and the Institute of Medicine in 2000 and 2003, respectively.

Jeff Brown, MeD   Jeff is a senior member of the Cognitive Systems Engineering Group and Cognitive Solutions Division of Applied Research

Associates (ARA), based in Fairborn, Ohio. He holds a faculty appointment with Parks College of Engineering, Aviation, and Technology at St. Louis University. His work is focused on supporting improvement in the management of risk and safety in domains where there is high consequence for failure. Although he has worked in a variety of high-risk domains, he is especially interested in supporting improvement in the safety of patient care. He has engaged in numerous patient safety improvement efforts in US hospitals since 1999 and, in 2002, joined a cardiac surgery care team from Concord, NH in receiving a John M. Eisenberg Patient Safety Award for System Innovation from the Joint Commission and National Quality Forum. Jeff has authored and co-authored articles, books, book chapters, and technical reports on patient safety and system safety topics. He is a co-author of *Safety Culture: Building and Sustaining Safety Culture in Aviation and Healthcare* (Ashgate, 2012), *Safety Ethics: Cases From Aviation, Healthcare, and Occupational and Environmental Health* (Ashgate, 2005), and a contributing author to *Improving Healthcare Team Communication: Lessons From Aviation and Aerospace* (Ashgate, 2008). Prior to 1996, Jeff served as a faculty member and department chair in collegiate aviation programs. He earned his Master's and Bachelor's degrees from the University of Maine.

Susan Carr   Susan is editor of *Patient Safety & Quality Healthcare*,[1] a bi-monthly publication and website she developed with Lionheart Publishing in 2004. Susan also works as a freelance editor and writer for organizations including the Society to Improve Diagnosis in Medicine (SIDM), Institute for Healthcare Improvement (IHI), Medically Induced Trauma Support Services (MITSS), the Association of Educators in Imaging and Radiological Sciences, and the Scleroderma Foundation. Susan's interests include the use of social media to improve patient safety and efforts to engage patients as active partners in care. She is a member of the Society for Participatory Medicine, the American Society of Professionals in Patient Safety, and the Association of Health Care Journalists. Susan lives and works in Concord, MA.

Melissa Cole, BSN, MSW, FACHE   Melissa is a Quality Consultant at the University of New Mexico Hospitals. As a healthcare leader for over 25 years, Melissa builds bridges to leverage low- and high-tech solutions to create high performing, quality care environments. Ms. Cole was named as one of the "12 Powerful Voices in Healthcare Innovation" by *Medcity News* in October 2012 and is listed in *Healthcare IT News'* top 100 to follow on Twitter for health information technology information. Ms. Cole is a contributor to Frankie Perry's

---

1   See www.psqh.com

second edition, *The Tracks We Leave: Ethics in Healthcare Management Dilemmas in Healthcare* (Health Administration Press, 2013). Ms. Cole currently serves as a Past-President of New Mexico Healthcare Executives and is an active member of Health Information Management Systems Society (HIMSS). Melissa holds a master of social work degree from The University of Michigan and earned her bachelor's degree in nursing at Hope College, Hope-Calvin Department of Nursing.

Catherine K. Craven, PhD MLS, MA   Catherine is a doctoral candidate in health informatics at University of Missouri, where she is a REDCap developer and system administrator for the School of Medicine, and has been a National Library of Medicine Biomedical and Health Informatics Research Fellow. Her research interests involve human and socio-technical factors. She has most recently published on planning and preparation processes for electronic health record (EHR) system implementation in critical access hospitals and a task analysis of intensive care unit (ICU) physicians examining technology, interruptions and clinical team communication. Catherine was a clinical informationist at Welch Medical Library, Johns Hopkins Medical Institutions, from 2007–2010, where she helped develop the embedded informationist service model in practice there. She was a core course-development team member for a new course, "Transitions to the Wards," in the new "Genes to Society" medical curriculum, participated on research teams leading to co-authored publications, managed a clinical research informatics project for the School of Medicine's Vice Dean of Clinical Research, and earned a graduate certificate in the business of medicine at the Carey Business School, Johns Hopkins University. Catherine has been an active member of the American Medical Informatics Association (AMIA) for 10 years, serving in leadership roles including on the AMIA Board (2008–2009), as Chair, Membership Committee (2008–2011), and the 2013–2014 Chair, Evaluation Working Group.

Prudence W. Dalrymple, PhD, MS, AHIP   Prudence is the Director of the Institute for Healthcare Informatics at Drexel University, an interdisciplinary center devoted to the intersection of people, information and technology in the service of health communication and information. In addition to her earlier work in cognitive models of information system design, she has more than 20 years of experience in the field of health information and health communications, and holds a master's degree in health informatics from Johns Hopkins University School of Medicine and a certificate in health communications from its Bloomberg School of Public Health. She uses both qualitative and quantitative methods to examine how both patients and professionals seek and apply evidence, information and knowledge, and how information seeking and health literacy affect patient engagement and health outcomes. The author of over 50 articles and book chapters, Prudence has held leadership positions in professional associations and is the recipient of numerous academic honors.

Amy E. Donahue, MLIS, AHIP   Amy is the User Education and Reference Librarian at the Medical College of Wisconsin where she provides library and information services education to students, faculty and staff. Prior to this role, she worked at the Aurora Medical Center in Grafton, Wisconsin as the new hospital's first librarian and provided information services to the hospital's clinical staff as well as patients in support of patient-centered care and evidence-based practice. She received her master's degree in library and information from the University of Washington's iSchool in 2007, and was accepted into the National Library of Medicine's prestigious Associate Fellowship Program from 2008–2010. She is a member of the Academy of Health Information Professionals (AHIP) and is active in the Medical Library Association and the Special Libraries Association.

Julia M. Esparza, MLS, AHIP   Julie is an Associate Professor of the Department of Medical Library Science and Clinical Medical Librarian working at Louisiana State University Health Sciences Center in Shreveport, LA. Ms. Esparza is on the Institutional Review Board of the health sciences center. She has over 16 years of experience in the healthcare field. As a hospital librarian she was trained as a Six Sigma Green Belt and has worked on Failure Modes and Effects Analyses teams. She specifically teaches a course called "Searching for Quality" with the emphasis on searching for quality improvement information. Ms. Esparza is a Distinguished Member of the Academy of Health Information Professionals (AHIP) and currently serves on the Board of Directors for the Medical Library Association. She graduated from Indiana University with a Master of Library Science.

Margo S. Farber, BS, PharmD   Margo is currently the Director, Drug Information Service at the University of Michigan Health System. In this role, Farber oversees drug use policy and formulary management for the University of Michigan Health System as well as drug information experiential training for pharmacy students and residents. Prior to this appointment, Farber served as the Director, Drug Information/Drug Use Policy at the Detroit Medical Center (DMC). Primary responsibilities included overseeing the development, standardization and maintenance of drug use guidelines, formulary and medication safety initiatives at the DMC, an eight-hospital health system.

Integrating medication safety principles into the electronic health record became a primary focus while at the DMC position. Farber maintains didactic teaching responsibilities at the Wayne State University School of Medicine in the areas of medication safety and psychotherapeutics. Margo Farber received her Bachelor of Science and PharmD degrees from the University of Michigan and completed a residency in pharmacy practice at the National Institutes of Health, Bethesda, MD.

Howard Fuller, MLS   Howard is currently the Director of Library Services for the Heald College Library & Learning Resource System. His primary function is to provide 12 on-ground and one online campuses with strategic guidance and initiate and lead projects that support their fiscal, operational, and academic operations. Howard holds a master's degree in Library and Information Science and a baccalaureate in health education/cardiac rehabilitation from the University of Wisconsin in Milwaukee. Howard was a National Library of Medicine fellow in Medical Informatics; completed a post-graduate program in Leadership at Stanford University; is a certified project manager; and accredited Cognitive Edge practitioner in complex adaptive systems. He's published in professional and peer-reviewed journals.

Mark L. Graber, MD, FACP   Mark is a Senior Fellow at RTI International and Professor Emeritus of Medicine at the State University of New York at Stony Brook. Dr. Graber has an extensive background in biomedical and health services research and has authored over 70 peer-reviewed publications. He is a national leader in the field of patient safety and originated Patient Safety Awareness Week in 2002, an event now recognized internationally. Dr. Graber has also been a pioneer in efforts to address diagnostic errors in medicine, and his research in this area has been supported by the National Patient Safety Foundation and the Agency for Healthcare Research and Quality. In 2008 he convened and chaired the Diagnostic Error in Medicine conference series, and in 2011 he founded the Society to Improve Diagnosis in Medicine (SIDM). Dr. Graber has participated in several different events targeted at medical librarians with the goal of applying their expertise to the improvement of the diagnostic process at their local sites.

Suzanne Graham, RN, PhD   Suzanne is Executive Director of Patient Safety and Patient and Family-Centered Care for Kaiser Permanente California Regions. She has served in multiple roles within Kaiser Permanente at the medical center, regional and national levels. Her educational background includes a Bachelor of Science in nursing as well as master's degrees in school health and developmental disabilities and a doctoral degree in allied health administration and education. Suzanne is a graduate of the University of North Carolina Kenan-Flager Business School Kaiser Permanente Advanced Leadership Program and the AHA Health Forum Patient Safety Leadership Fellowship Program, and completed the IHI Patient Safety Officer Executive training program. Suzanne is a member of several national patient safety groups including the Joint Commission Patient Safety Advisory Group. In 2006 Suzanne received the first National Patient Safety Foundation Chairman's Medal in recognition of leadership in patient safety.

Barbara Jones, MLS   Barbara is a health sciences librarian with the National Network of Libraries of Medicine, MidContinental Region. She is the Missouri Coordinator and represents the six-state MidContinental Region as Library Advocacy Project Coordinator. Her work experience includes clinical librarianship in both hospital and clinic settings as well as program development, teaching and training in academic hospital and public library settings. She actively writes, presents and encourages the expanded involvement of librarians in patient safety and knowledge management work. Barbara designs methods for teaching business practices to librarians and develops tools to advocate the value of librarian engagement in the work of healthcare. In addition, Barbara is a co-developer of the Library Valuation Calculators that have application in a variety of library settings. She provides instruction for librarians on business practices in the library. Barbara has a master's degree in library science from the University of Arizona. She is based at, and serves on the staff at the J. Otto Lottes Health Science Library at the University of Missouri.

Gunjan Kahlon, MD   Gunjan, a board certified internist, is Assistant Professor of the Department of Medicine and serves as the Section Chief of Internal Medicine at Louisiana State University Health Sciences Center in Shreveport, LA. She currently is course director for Foundations of Clinical Medicine which is for first-year and second-year students. Dr. Kahlon serves as director of the Internal Medicine Board Review. She has written on teaching evidence-based medicine to medical students. Gunjan graduated from Government Medical College and Rajindra Hospital in Patiala, Punjab, India and her residency at St. Luke's Hospital in Bethlehem, Pennsylvania.

Linda Kenney   Linda is the Executive Director and President of MITSS (Medically Induced Trauma Support Services, Inc.). She founded the organization in 2002 as the result of a personal experience with an adverse medical event, when she identified the need for support services in cases of adverse events and outlined an agenda for change. Since that time, she has been a tireless activist for patient, family, and clinician rights. She has become a nationally and internationally recognized leader in the patient safety movement and speaks regularly at healthcare conferences and forums. In 2006, Linda was the first consumer graduate of the HRET/AHA Patient Safety Leadership Fellowship. That same year, she was the recipient of the National Patient Safety Foundation's esteemed Socius Award, an annual award given in recognition of effective partnering in pursuit of patient safety. She has authored and contributed to a number of publications on topics including the emotional impact of adverse events on patients, families, and clinicians. Linda serves on the boards of the Massachusetts Coalition for the Prevention of Medical Errors, National Patient Safety Foundation and Planetree.

Ross Koppel, PhD, FACMI   Ross is a leading scholar of healthcare IT and of the interactions of people, computers and workplaces. His articles in the *Journal of the American Medical Association (JAMA)*, *Journal of the American Medical Informatics Association (JAMIA)*, *New England Journal of Medicine (NEJM)*, *Health Affairs*, etc are considered seminal works in the field. Professor Koppel is on the faculty of the Sociology Department, University of Pennsylvania (UPenn) and on the faculty of the Medical School at UPenn, where he is the Principal Investigator of the "Study of Hospital Workplace Culture and Medication Error." Koppel is also a Senior Fellow of the Leonard Davis Institute at Penn's Wharton School. In addition, Dr. Koppel is also the Internal Evaluator of Harvard Medical School's project to create a new HIT architecture, and is a co-investigator of the National Science Foundation Project on Safe Cyber Communication and Smart Alerts in Hospitals. At the American Medical Informatics Association, he is past chair of the Evaluation Working Group and a member of the Usability Task Force. Professor Koppel focuses on the use of computer system *in situ*. His work combines ethnographic research, extensive statistical analysis, surveys, and usability studies. Recently he co-authored the Agency for Healthcare Research and Quality (AHRQ) online resource *Guide to Reducing Unintended Consequences of Electronic Health Records*.[2] His newest book, *First Do Less Harm: Confronting the Inconvenient Problems of Patient Safety* (Cornell University Press) was published in May of 2012.

Kathryn K. Leonhardt, MD, MPH   Kathy is the Vice President, Patient Experience and Patient Safety at Aurora Health Care in Wisconsin. In this role, she leads patient safety and patient experience throughout Aurora, a large integrated health system including 15 hospitals, 150 clinics and over 80 retail

---

2   See http://www.healthit.gov/unintended-consequences/

pharmacies. Dr. Leonhardt has worked in a variety of healthcare settings, including the public and private sector. She has held clinical, administrative and research positions in California, Guam and Wisconsin. Her research, publications and national presentations have included epidemiologic investigations, Phase III clinical trials, quality improvement, patient safety and patient experience. Research topics have included patient-and family-centered care, women's health, medication safety, and infection prevention in both ambulatory and hospital settings. She was the Principal Investigator and author of an AHRQ-funded guide on patient advisory councils. Her patient safety projects have been recognized nationally, including the Institute for Safe Medication Practices Cheers Award in 2004 and 2007. Dr. Leonhardt is a preventive medicine/public health physician, with a Bachelor of Arts from Williams College, an Doctor of Medicine from the University of Michigan and an Master of Public Health in Epidemiology from the University of California-Berkeley.

Della M. Lin, MD   Dr. Lin is a Senior Fellow with the Estes Park Institute[3] with a passion for patient safety and collaborative systems thinking. She was an inaugural National Patient Safety Foundation/Health Forum Patient Safety Leadership Fellow[4] (2002) and continues as core faculty for the program, now in its twelfth year. Dr. Lin is adjunct faculty with the Institute for Healthcare Improvement (IHI), and faculty with the Jefferson School of Population Health Quality Safety Leadership Series (QSLS). She is a frequent speaker and author on issues relating to physician, executive leadership and board engagement around quality; patient safety and patient-centered care; organizational and safety culture; surgical and anesthesia safety; and multidisciplinary team simulation/near miss debriefing. Dr. Lin is currently the Hawaii Physician Lead for the Surgical Unit Safety Program (SUSP), dedicated to improving patient safety and surgical site infections in the perioperative environment. Dr. Lin continues an active practice in anesthesiology, has several committee appointments with the American Society of Anesthesiology, and has been a board examiner for the American Board of Anesthesiology.

Judith Napier, BSN, MSN, RN   Judith is the Vice President for Risk Services for Allina Health in Minnesota. Before joining Allina Health, Napier was a Senior Director for Patient Safety and Risk Management for Children's Hospitals and Clinics of Minnesota. Napier has held past positions of Senior Vice President for MMI Companies, an international healthcare risk

---

3   See www.estespark.org
4   This program has changed its name over time. It is now called: AHA-NPSF Comprehensive Patient Safety Leadership Fellowship. See http://www.hpoe.org/PSLF/PSLF_main.shtml

management company where she was a Senior Consultant and Healthcare leader working with domestic and international hospitals and healthcare systems on risk management tools and patient safety techniques for clinical and administrative performance improvements. Before her work with MMI Companies, Napier held positions in perinatal clinical care and academics where she led the maternal child nursing curriculum for the associate nursing degree program in a community college setting. Napier is a Registered Nurse with a Bachelor of Science in Nursing from Niagara University in New York State, and a Masters in Nursing from California State University at Los Angeles. She has a certificate of completion from HRET and the Health Forum Patient Safety Leadership Fellowship 2004–2005 and completion of the Institute for Healthcare Improvement's (IHI's) Patient Safety Executive Development Program. Judith has been a national and international speaker in the areas of patient safety, quality and risk management.

Barbara L. Olson, MS, RN, FISMP   Barbara is Senior Patient Safety Officer at LifePoint Hospitals, Inc., serving 57 non-urban hospitals in 20 states. She received her BSN from Emory University, Atlanta, GA, and completed a master's degree in Nursing Leadership in Healthcare Systems at Regis University in Denver, CO. Barbara completed a one year post-graduate Safe Medication Management fellowship with the Institute for Safe Medication Practices. She serves on the Executive Board of the American Society of Medication Safety Officers. Barbara is a Certified Professional in Patient Safety and a Fellow of the American Society of Medication Safety Officers. In 2009, Barbara received ISMP's Cheers Award for her contributions to medication safety using emergent social media platforms. You can find her on Twitter (@safetynurse) and on the Medscape platform where she hosts a blog, "On Your Meds: Straight Talk about Medication Safety."

Grena Porto, BSN, MS   Grena is a nationally recognized expert, leader and author in patient safety, risk management and quality improvement. She is a consultant specializing in providing customized consulting support to healthcare organizations with a focus on implementation of patient and worker safety practices and programs, clinical teamwork, culture of safety implementation and sustainment, disclosure of error to patients and families, critical incident response and other areas of clinical risk management and patient safety. In the past, Ms. Porto served as Client Executive and Sr. Vice President with Marsh USA, Inc., as Senior Director of Clinical Consulting and Director of Clinical Risk Management at VHA, Inc., as a regional claims manager for a surplus lines insurance carrier, and as director of risk management for an academic medical center. Ms. Porto has over 25 years' experience in all areas of risk management, including loss prevention, risk financing and claims management. She served as President of the American Society for Healthcare Risk Management (ASHRM) in 1999 and on the Board of Directors of the National Patient Safety Foundation from 1998 to 2001. She currently serves on The Joint Commission's Patient Safety Advisory Group. Ms. Porto is a Distinguished Fellow of ASHRM and has also attained the designations of Associate in Risk Management (ARM) from the Insurance Institute of America, and Certified Professional in Healthcare Risk Management (CPHRM) from the American Hospital Association. She holds a Bachelor of Science in Nursing and Master of Science in Health Administration from the State University of New York at Stony Brook.

Sumant Ranji, MD   Sumant is an Associate Professor of Medicine at the University of California, San Francisco (UCSF). Sumant has a strong interest in quality improvement research in both the inpatient and outpatient settings. He has completed systematic reviews of quality improvement strategies for diabetes care, outpatient antibiotic use, and prevention of healthcare-associated infections for the Agency for Healthcare Research and Quality and is actively involved in quality improvement efforts at UCSF Medical Center. He maintains an active clinical and teaching role, including serving as the faculty advisor for the categorical Internal Medicine Residency program journal club and attending on the ward and medical consult services at Moffitt-Long Hospital and Mount Zion Hospital. Sumant received his medical degree from the University of Illinois at Chicago. He completed his Internal Medicine residency training at the University of Chicago and subsequently served as Chief Medical Resident at Cook County Hospital. He joined the UCSF Hospitalist Group in 2004 after completing a two-year fellowship in Hospital Medicine and Clinical Research at UCSF.

Amanda Ross-White, MLIS, AHIP   Amanda is the Nursing Librarian at the Bracken Health Sciences Library at Queen's University in Kingston, Ontario, Canada and library scientist for the Queen's Joanna Briggs Collaboration, which produces systematic reviews in patient safety topics. Her interest in patient safety began on her first week on the job, helping a pregnant woman with low literacy find resources to explain her unborn child's genetic condition. Since that time, she has explored how connecting both healthcare professionals and patients with the right information is critical for optimum patient care. She is a recognized patient safety trainer through Northwestern University and the Canadian Patient Safety Institute and a Patient Advisor for the Obstetrics and Gynecology Program at Kingston General Hospital. She is also an active public speaker on healthcare from the patient's perspective and is authoring a book on guiding patients through a subsequent pregnancy after a loss.

Debora Simmons, PhD, RN, CCRN, CCNS   Debora is Senior Vice President and Chief Quality Officer St. Luke's Health System. Ms Simmons is formally the Executive Operations Director, National Center for Cognitive Informatics and Decision Making in the Healthcare School of Biomedical Informatics, University of Texas Health Science Center at Houston.

Kathleen M. Sutcliffe, PhD   Kathleen is the Gilbert and Ruth Professor of Business Administration and Professor of Management and Organizations at the Stephen M. Ross School of Business at the University of Michigan. Before receiving her doctoral degree she worked in urban and rural Alaska, directing a health program for the State of Alaska and as chief health director for the Aleutian/Pribilof Islands Association, one of the Alaska Native Health Corporations. Her research is aimed at understanding how organizations and their members cope with uncertainty and unexpected events, and how complex organizations can be designed to be more reliable and resilient. Her research has appeared widely in organization studies and healthcare publications. Two books include: *Medical Error: What Do We Know? What Do We Do?*, co-authored with Marilynn Rosenthal (Jossey-Bass, 2002) and *Managing the Unexpected: Resilient Performance in an Age of Uncertainty*, co-authored with Karl E. Weick (Jossey-Bass, 2007, second edition). Sutcliffe recently was named by the National Academy of Sciences Institute of Medicine to a research panel on the Department of Homeland Security.

Affaud Anaïs Tanon, PhD   Anaïs holds a bachelor degree from École Nationale Supérieure de Statistique et d'Économie Appliquée (ENSEA), Ivory Coast, with a concentration in Health Information systems. She completed a Masters degree in Healthcare Administration at the University of Montreal with a merit scholarship awarded by the Canadian International Development Agency through the Canadian Francophonie Scholarship Program. She also holds a PhD in Public Health from the University of Montreal with a concentration in Program Evaluation. She launched the official chapter of the Open School of the IHI (Institute for Healthcare Improvement) at Montreal University to bring together students and faculty members interested in quality and patient safety. As part of her PhD project, she designed bibliographic search filters to retrieve patient safety papers on the MEDLINE®, EMBASE and CINAHL databases. She is an alumni of the Takemi Fellowship Program in International Health at Harvard University. While there she deepened her interest in using information sciences to better support decision-making in healthcare and improve quality and patient safety. She is currently working as the scientific coordinator and manager of the McGill Centre of Excellence in Aging and Chronic Disease, Montreal, Quebec.

Sara Tompson, BS, MLS   Sara is the Manager of the Library, Archives & Records Section of the NASA Jet Propulsion Laboratory (JPL) in Pasadena, CA. She recently finished a three-year term as a Director at Large on the Board of the international Special Libraries Association (SLA). She has written and taught with Lorri Zipperer and others on the applications of systems thinking to libraries and information centers. Tompson is an instrument-rated private pilot who is a member of the Southern California Chapter of the Flying Samaritans, and as such flies dental and medical practitioners to Guerrero Negro, Baja Sur, Mexico, to provide services at a small medical clinic.

Eric Van Rite, PhD   Eric completed a PhD in Sociology from the University of California, San Diego (UC-San Diego) in 2011. His doctoral thesis, *The Challenge of Patient Safety and the Remaking of American Medicine*, employed discourse analysis to trace the history of patient safety in the United States. Through reviews of technical reports, media narratives, and advocacy campaigns, his dissertation research analyzed shifts in the conceptualization of medical error over the course of the 1990s and 2000s. He concluded that conceptual shifts in medical error, understood within the context of broader changes to the medical profession, help to explain the development of the patient safety movement. He has presented his doctoral research at conferences for the American Sociological Association and for the Law and Society Association. While at UC-San Diego, he taught courses in sociology, law and society, and public health. He currently works as a Sociology Editor, focusing on research in medical sociology, at the American Institutes for Research in Washington, DC.

Robert M. Wachter, MD   Dr. Wachter is Professor and Associate Chair of the Department of Medicine at the University of California, San Francisco, where he directs the 60-physician Division of Hospital Medicine. Author of 250 articles and six books, he coined the term "hospitalist" in 1996 and is generally considered the "father" of the hospitalist field, the fastest growing specialty in the history of modern medicine. He is past president of the Society of Hospital Medicine, and is currently the chair of the American Board of Internal Medicine. In the safety and quality arenas, he edits the US government's two leading websites on safety (they receive about one million yearly visits) and has written two bestselling books on the subject, including *Understanding Patient Safety* (McGraw Hill), whose second edition was published in 2012. In 2004, he received the John M. Eisenberg Patient Safety Award for System Innovation, the nation's top honor in patient safety. For the past five years, *Modern Healthcare* magazine has named him one of the 50 most influential physician-executives in the US (#14 in 2012). He has served on the healthcare advisory boards of several companies, including Google. His blog,[5] is one of the nation's most popular healthcare blogs.

Robert L. Wears, MD, MS, PhD   Dr. Wears is an emergency physician, Professor of Emergency Medicine at the University of Florida, and Visiting Professor in the Clinical Safety Research Unit at Imperial College London. He serves on the board of directors of the Emergency Medicine Patient Safety Foundation, and multiple editorial boards, including *Annals of Emergency Medicine, Human Factors and Ergonomics,* the *Journal of Patient Safety,* and the *International Journal of Risk and Safety in Medicine.* He has co-edited two books, *Patient Safety in Emergency Medicine* (Lippincott Williams and Wilkins 2009), and *Resilient Health Care* (Ashgate 2013). His research interests include technical work studies, resilience engineering, and patient safety as a social movement.

Mark G. Weiner, MD, FACP, FACMI   Mark is the Chief Medical Information Officer and a practicing primary care clinician at Temple University Health System, and the Assistant Dean for Informatics and Professor of Clinical Sciences at the Temple University School of Medicine. A medical informatician and health services researcher with 15 years of practical experience in electronic health record use and implementation, his work enables the integration of large datasets in support of the clinical and research enterprises. His research focuses on clinical trial simulation, quality measurement and exploring the contributing factors and outcomes of diagnostic and therapeutic decisions by patients and clinicians. He has been an Associate Professor of Medicine at the University of Pennsylvania School of Medicine, the Senior Director of R&D Informatics at AstraZeneca Pharmaceuticals, and a Senior Fellow of the Leonard Davis Institute of Health Economics. He has served as the Co-Chief of the Biostatistics and Informatics Core of the Philadelphia Veterans Affairs (VA) Center for Health Equity and Promotion, and Co-Director of the Data Core of the Food and Drug Administration (FDA) mini-Sentinel Initiative.

Linda C. Williams, RN, MSI   Linda is a member of the team at VA National Center for Patient Safety, serving initially as computer specialist, now part of program operations with the central focus of development and implementation of patient safety curriculum for physicians. Linda teaches an introductory human factors engineering session at faculty development workshops and is co-director of the patient safety fellowship program. She also is involved in the practical application of usability principles to medical devices, software and education. Linda holds an undergraduate nursing degree from the University

---

5   See www.wachtersworld.org

of California-Los Angeles (UCLA) and an MSI degree from the University of Michigan's School of Information, a degree tailored to medical informatics with emphasis in human computer interaction. After discovering the locus of like-mindedness in librarians, her motivation has been to involve medical and clinical librarians in the problem-solving work of patient safety.

Foreword

Robert M. Wachter, MD

Although it is customary to date the birth of the modern patient safety movement to the December, 1999 release of the Institute of Medicine's report, *To Err is Human* (Kohn, Corrigan, and Donaldson, 2000) one can mount a credible case that the movement really began a decade earlier, in a conversation between a pediatric surgeon and health policy expert, and a librarian.

The surgeon/policy expert was, of course, Dr. Lucian Leape. In my 2006 interview with Leape (Agency for Healthcare Research and Quality, 2006) I asked about his 1990 Harvard Medical Practice study (Leape et al. 1991) from which the now famous estimate of 44,000–98,000 deaths per year from medical errors was drawn, and the evolution of his interest in safety. He responded:

> We always were convinced it was an important study, if nothing else, because of its magnitude. Looking at 30,000 patients gives you some clout. None of us had really thought much about the preventability issue, and nobody knew anything about systems, of course. We weren't completely surprised by our results, because earlier work had shown similar findings. But we were, shall we say, dismayed to find that 4 percent of patients had adverse events. The surprise for me was that two thirds of them were caused by errors. I'll never forget – I went to the library one day and did a literature search on what was known about preventing errors, and I didn't find anything. And I went to the librarian and said, "I'm interested in how you prevent medical errors, and I've found papers about complications, but nothing much about errors."... She looked at [my search strategy] and she said, "Well, your strategy looks all right. Have you looked in the humanities literature?" And I sort of looked at her and said, "The what?" I know what humanities are, mind you. But it really never occurred to me. So she tried the same

*search strategy in the humanities literature, and boom, out came 200
papers. I started to read them and discovered James Reason and Jens
and all those people. A year later, I came up for air and realized that we
in health care could use this. If I didn't know how errors happen, most
other people wouldn't know it either. So I decided to write a paper.*[1]

That paper was the 1994 *JAMA* classic, "Error in Medicine," which introduced
the concept of systems thinking to a broad medical audience (Leape 1994). So
one can make the case that the patient safety field was launched by a medical
librarian!

I love Leape's story on many levels. First, it vividly illustrates the kind of
cross-disciplinary learning necessary to move a field like patient safety forward.
Surely, the input and engagement of experienced clinicians and clinical leaders
have been crucial. But so have been the lessons from many other industries
– aviation, logistics, the military, nuclear power – and the wisdom and
experience from many disciplines, such as psychology, engineering, human
factors, education, business, and informatics.

The story also demonstrates the centrality of information sharing to
improvement. One thing we have learned in the first 15 years of the patient
safety movement is that improving safety is not easy. Instead, it feels like one
of those icy late December NFL football games. There are no long touchdown
passes; it's all about the ground game and little victories. A good play is one in
which the team gains two or three yards. Then – just when they think they're
getting somewhere – they give back a yard. The good teams brush themselves
off and go at it again, now just a little bit smarter.

And so it is in patient safety. The only way we will ultimately reach our
goal of a safer healthcare system is by learning from both our successes and our
failures, moving forward in bite-size steps.

Once the safety field began, we needed to ask some fundamental questions.
Where can we find answers to the challenges of patient safety? And once
we find them, what is the best way to share what we've learned – across
disciplines, organizations, countries? And there was an underlying, even more
fundamental question: what exactly *is* evidence?

---

1   Reprinted with permission of *AHRQ WebM&M*. In conversation with Lucian Leape, MD
    [interview]. *AHRQ WebM&M* [serial online], August 2006. Available at: http://www.webmm.
    ahrq.gov/perspective.aspx?perspectiveID=28

This latter question is particularly complex when it comes to patient safety. No sophisticated observer would claim that the correlation between taking a single pill and improved symptoms constituted evidence. In clinical medicine, we have discovered ways to test questions like this, with strategies such as randomized clinical trials, which allow us to standardize the intervention, account for the placebo effect and for confounding and biases.

But patient safety presents several very different challenges when it comes to evidence. I first stepped into this area of controversy after my colleagues and I published the first evidence report on patient safety, *Making Health Care Safer*, for the Agency for Healthcare Research and Quality in 2001 (Shojania et al. 2001). To produce the report, we reviewed the world's literature and rated practices on a set of metrics that had been vetted by experts. While the report found strong evidence for many safety practices, others – including some with high face validity like computerized provider order entry – did not fare as well. Three of the most prominent leaders in patient safety, Drs. Don Berwick, David Bates, and yes, Leape himself, took us to task, arguing that for many safety practices, a policy of waiting for firm scientific evidence (at least in the traditional sense) would be a recipe for inaction (Leape, Berwick and Bates 2002). Instead, they favored an approach that also considered things like experience from other industries, human factors principles, and common sense.

In our response, we highlighted a section of the AHRQ report in which we addressed the need for evidence in patient safety (Shojania et al. 2001: 26–7):

> *Healthcare clearly has much to learn from other industries. Just as physicians must learn the "basic sciences" of immunology and molecular biology, providers and leaders interested in making healthcare safer must learn the "basic sciences" of organizational theory and human factors engineering. Moreover, the "cases" presented on rounds should, in addition to classical clinical descriptions, also include the tragedy of the Challenger and the successes of Motorola. On the other hand, an unquestioning embrace of dozens of promising practices from other fields is likely to be wasteful, distracting, and potentially dangerous. We are drawn to a dictum from the Cold War era – "Trust, but verify."*

This tension, of course, will always exist, as will others – including how best to present evidence so that it influences clinicians and policymakers appropriately. We know that much evidence never makes it into practice, or does so only after long – sometimes immorally long – delays. On the other hand, because of the high level of concern on the part of policymakers and patients, patient safety practices are sometimes turned into regulatory or accreditation standards before the evidence has had an opportunity to ripen, which can cause its own harm. For example, a four-hour "door-to-antibiotics" mandate for patients with pneumonia in the Emergency Department led to many cases in which antibiotics were given to patients later proven not to have an infection (7).

Finally, how the information is presented can be hugely influential. One of the things that drove the patient safety field to the top of the healthcare agenda was its drama: a "jumbo jet a day" worth of patients dying from medical mistakes, the death of the *Boston Globe* healthcare columnist from a chemotherapy error, a near-fatal heparin overdose in actor Dennis Quaid's twin newborns. Yet, as important as storytelling is, using stories exclusively can become hyperbolic and skewed: amounting to arguing by anecdote. On the other hand, I attend many safety and quality presentations these days in which the field has been stripped of its drama; harms are depicted on PowerPoint slides crammed full of run charts, spider plots, and green and red dots. Neutered by this numbing detail, the stories lose their power to influence emotions, to shock … and thus to motivate change.

Such tensions – determining what constitutes evidence, balancing the single case with more aggregate forms of data – have always been with us, but today we find ourselves in an environment in which the game is changing before our eyes. In the old days, evidence resided in journals and books, these collections lived in buildings we called libraries, one accessed them by going to a physical building and flipping through hundreds of pages of dusty indices. If one needed help, there were experts in this information gathering and storage process. They were known as librarians.

How the world has changed! Evidence is ubiquitous; we are awash in it. I haven't gone to my university's library to look up information for several years, and we've begun to convert floors of the majestic building into other functions, such as our organization's simulation center. Expertise has also been diffused and democratized – it no longer simply lives in journals and in the minds of certified experts. In many cases, patients know more about their diseases than their doctors do. Social media allows this information to be spread and accessed using tools, such as Twitter, that had not been invented a decade ago.

This book, to its great credit, considers all these questions from a broad perspective. It recognizes that the railroad companies failed by not realizing they were in the transportation, not the railway, business, and Kodak failed by steadfastly remaining a photography, not an imaging, company. In patient safety and healthcare more generally, both the consumers and purveyors of information are not in the library, or journal, or book business. They are in the evidence, information and knowledge (EI&K) business. It seems clear that from this point forward, this business will have an address that begins with "www", "@" or "#", not 530 Parnassus Avenue.

I have had the opportunity to work with Lorri Zipperer, the editor of this volume, over the past decade. When my group at UCSF won the contract from AHRQ to produce two patient safety websites (a web-based journal, *AHRQ WebM&M*,[2] and a patient safety portal and information resource, AHRQ Patient Safety Network),[3] we needed help in information retrieval, analysis, and presentation, with a focus in the field of patient safety. Luckily, we didn't need to search very far to find all of these skills rolled up in a single individual, Lorri Zipperer, a self-described "patient safety cybrarian." Not only were her credentials ideal, so was she.

So, as I read this book, I was not surprised that Lorri was able to assemble a formidable team, that she chose to cover all the right topics, and that she and her colleagues were able to blend an appropriate reverence for history and core knowledge with a forward-thinking, even futuristic, point of view. The book doesn't answer every question, because the questions it tackles are evolving so rapidly. But it does something far more important, which is to offer readers a strong foundation and the tools to answer many of them themselves, as the environment changes.

Although this book will be widely read by librarians and patient safety professionals, it deserves a broader readership: of clinicians and others interested in patient safety and quality, of those interested in the use of and access to data, of those grappling with change management, and of those interested in informatics. I for one will keep this volume well within reach.

Robert M. Wachter, MD

2   See www.webmm.ahrq.gov
3   See www.psnet.ahrq.gov

Preface

The scene opens on a busy healthcare library where the only senior research librarian is out for the day and a library student – new to the department and to medicine – is covering the service.

[Phone rings]

Patron: [Panic in her voice] "I have a surgeon who has a patient on the table and he wants information on a curious growth in the large colon. He was operating and saw something he had never seen before. He has stepped out of the OR and needs me to find an article on unexplained masses in the large colon – right now!"

Library student: [After a "text book" reference interview that yielded no clear direction] "Have you done a search on MEDLINE®. What MeSH heading did you use?"

Patron: "What is a MeSH Heading?" [the library student gasps!] "I am in charge of the library, but am not a librarian. I am a secretary. [Patron voice rising] There is no one else here!"

Library student: [Her supervisor who had more experience in searching the clinical literature was out of the office] She places the phone on her desk and goes to other non-librarian but senior staff to ask for clarification as what exactly the "large colon" is and how it is represented in MeSH. She gets no conclusive answer. Upon picking up her phone she says "Why not call the National Library of Medicine, I am sure there would be expertise on staff there and someone can help you."

[Two weeks later]

Doorbell rings. The Cook County Sheriff at the apartment door serves the library student a summons.

The library student's heart stops for just a second.

This moment for me was significant. When I realized that the summons was not associated with my failure to help a panicked, under-skilled and overwhelmed patron find information needed in an emergent medical situation – but instead to appear to be selected as a member of a grand jury in Cook County, IL – it gave me time to reflect. I considered how I inherently knew that a lack of information retrieval expertise could contribute to poor care. If it could happen in my practice, could it happen to others with less training? I now believed that it was possible.

Several years later I knew it could. An incident took place to illustrate this point in a tangible, tragic way. With the death of Ellen Roche in 2000, I was sure that failure in evidence seeking could affect patient safety. I felt that this example would mobilize the patient safety and the library science communities to infuse the lessons from this incident to a distinct and important facet of patient safety improvement research, strategic development, and intervention. Yet despite this loss of Ellen Roche no concerted inter or multidisciplinary effort to fully understand and learn from the evidence, information and knowledge (EI&K) factors contributing to that failure has been mounted.

Over a decade later – this text aims to motivate work to close that chasm.

Patient safety is as others have said before me not a solo endeavor. Much has been heralded of engaging multidisciplinary teams to address both latent and evident failures contributing to not only unsafe frontline conditions and care, but blunt end services. The existence of under informed, non-evidence or knowledge enhanced work in safety needs to be addressed with a team as well. The systematic nature of failure of clinicians, patients, and administration to use information, evidence, and knowledge to enable individuals, teams, and the organization to learn from errors begs for robust consideration and examination.

The change in seeing and demonstrating the role of EI&K as a safety element requires hard thinking, focus, courage, and a stance toward commitment and accountability across the spectrum of expertise in healthcare. Yet members of my profession – despite educational efforts presented at both the regional and national levels – have not been collectively and visibly engaged in this work. The representation of highly developed information, evidence, and knowledge skills into safety, culture, and skill assessments is lagging behind work in other frontline sectors. This omission weakens healthcare's arsenal to understand how to optimize the use of externally developed, published materials to deliver safe care and build a culture to support this behavior. The gap has yet to be researched and measured in the context of patient safety. This lack of engagement detracts from efforts to fully understand how evidence use and access can affect safety through organizational learning, proactive failure mitigation, and root cause analysis. These ideas have yet to robustly appear together in the dialogue to improve safety.

We don't yet know about the impact of EI&K failures. But can healthcare afford to not know? Should patients be comfortable with ineffective EI&K use to support their care? In times when resources are tight, schedules full and demands intense, this lack of engagement can be misunderstood as inertia or indifference. It raises the question, if working with incomplete evidence and information has become a normalized deviance in healthcare. Has "good enough" been accepted and worked around to create a culture dependent on easy, immediate access to some material rather than reliable access to the best material? It is hoped that the arguments submitted herein will provide those who want to be involved in changing this paradigm with evidence and expert opinion that will help garnish new levels of interest and engagement in learning what to do and when to remedy the current situation.

How to Use this Text

This publication sets the stage for moving forward. It provides background on patient safety as a movement. It introduces systems safety, human error and other key philosophies to support change and advances in the EI&K arena to help reduce medical error. The contributors were invited to participate and share expertise to encourage innovation in identifying problems, designing initiatives and implementing new ways of approaching this area of improvement in healthcare. They juxtaposed their perspectives onto the challenge of seeing evidence, information, and knowledge use through the spectrum of safety.

The text seeks to inform dialogue and innovation within the multidisciplinary acute care environment to envision proactive changes in how team-based improvement efforts can affect the EI&K provision necessary to support safe care delivery. The publication is rooted in the tenets of safety sciences as the strategy of employing distinct initiatives has to be moored in that foundation to successfully apply fresh thinking to the field.

The objectives of the book are to:

- Inform healthcare leadership, clinical directors, clinicians, risk managers and librarians of the intersection between key patient safety philosophies and information, evidence and knowledge delivery mechanisms that support medical error reduction.

- Raise awareness of the potential for systemic and individual information and knowledge-sharing failures that is latent in the healthcare delivery process.

- Explore the application of systemic improvement processes and tactics to identify opportunities to reduce risk and potential for EI&K failure.

- Illustrate how the expertise from the information and knowledge domains folds into the elements and language of the safety sciences.

- Submit innovative activities and measures in the EI&K spectrum to illustrate a tangible contribution to patient safety.

- Spawn thinking on avenues for research to take these ideas from what is *thought* to have benefit to what is *known* to have benefit in medical error reduction work.

Notes on Context and Scope

Patient Safety vs Quality: The conversation about EI&K as an element of safe care could translate into other areas of work to improve healthcare quality. To align the writers and readers alike, the designation of safety as an element of quality as noted by the Institute of Medicine Quality Chasm report served as a standardizing force.

Acute Care vs Ambulatory: EI&K obviously affects care delivered at home, in community settings and in clinics. The opportunity to explore its improvement in those environments is needed; yet beyond the scope of this text.

Health Information, Patient Information, and EI&K: Plenty has been written and reported on health information technology as a mechanism to sharing patient care-related data and information. Although these concepts are very valid and important – it is not that type of information that is the primary concern of this text. Information and the expanded concepts of "evidence" and "knowledge" are defined for this book as follows:

- Evidence: "Evidence refers to the scientifically sound, fully researched and validated information and data collected during the pursuit of the understanding and validation of a hypothesis. In other views, evidence can refer to what someone's experience has been."

- Information: "Data that is processed and repurposed and printed for distinct use."

- Knowledge: "What an individual knows [sic]" It is dynamic in nature and embedded in the actions of experts" (Zipperer 2011: 302).

It's Not About Marian the Librarian Anymore: Recognizing a Gap in Expertise: A prominent theme throughout the text is that established skills in the identification, acquisition and dissemination of EI&K could enhance the reliability and effectiveness of care and organizational learning. One explicit source of that expertise is a librarian. Medical librarians are professionals with degrees who have been visibly absent from the deep conversations around improving blunt and sharp end decision-making, point-of-care evidence failure and use of knowledge generated from incidents and near misses to enhance healthcare's quest to engage in organizational learning from both error and success. For example, in nine of the primary publications in the IOM's series of books related to patient safety and quality care improvement, the word "librarian" appears five single times: in only three of the books. The lack of the term from this discourse minimizes opportunities for librarians to be invited to the table or to see themselves there despite their long standing history in providing access to such resources. Yet the texts talk about evidence, information and knowledge, and their role in improving safety and quality throughout. This lack of the application of this unique expert community could in fact have ramifications we have yet to understand – the gap perhaps has been normalized.

Organizing Principles: Diving In

The book takes into account that its readers will be expert or at least acquainted with some of the concepts discussed herein. However, it is assumed that the juxtaposition of the various mindsets will be new to them – hence some of the material will be introductory. It is recognized that the chapters cannot fully cover the topics they discuss – their goal instead is to stimulate in-depth discussion and to motivate research and improvement activities folding together the concepts to define initiatives to engage healthcare in becoming more concrete in designing and testing actions to inform improvements. The six-part text is organized as follows:

Part 1: Context for Innovation and Improvement: This section provides introductory information for readers who are new to either the emergent field of patient safety or who have not really considered the field of information, evidence or knowledge as a professional practice area. The three chapters here offer background and definitions from which to situate the thinking to follow – anchored by a discussion of failure that places the concern voiced by chapter contributors in the context of reality.

Part 2: The Role of Evidence, Information and Knowledge: Core elements of success in improving the use of EI&K are touched on by the chapters exploring the complexity of the frontline EI&K sharing environment, the unstated role of leadership in this particular piece of the patient safety continuum and the latent problem of the weaknesses in the evidence base that are often superficially discussed yet not deeply considered as a contributor to system safety.

Part 3: Building Blocks of Safety that Affect Information, Evidence and Knowledge-sharing: Despite their seeming lack of application in frontline discussions of improvement, these foundational concepts need to be seriously applied to devise lasting safety improvements. These theories and models – generally seen as external to healthcare – provide insights for generating breakthrough thinking in healthcare. The two chapters in this section share introductory thinking about how to bring the schools of high-risk industries, complexity, and systems thinking to the table of safety improvement through robust and reliable EI&K processes.

Part 4: Practical Applications to Drive EI&K Progress in the Acute Care Environment: Considerations of how care happens and how EI&K are currently shared can offer foundations for moving forward. The chapters in this section derive from the current state of technologies, teams and the human condition to explore a reality base from which to drive explorations to generate improvement, innovation and personal responsibility. From the use of social media to the personal interaction between patient and their physician and the flaws inherent due to the human interface of the process, the material here places the concepts coming before it in the context of daily work both at the individual and system level.

Part 5: Future States: This section introduces approaches to think about the use of EI&K to learn and enhance the reliability of EI&K processes by looking inward to identify failure. It illustrates that taking failure and learning from it – through effective spread and leadership – can pave the way to generate interest to do research and ask questions both of individuals and organizations to devise systems that are safer because the five rights of EI&K use were addressed: the *right resource* (whether evidence, information or knowledge), to the *right person*, for the *right patient or place*, through the *right modality*, at the *right time*.

At the end of the book several resources have been provided to assist with the translation of the concepts introduced in the text:

- Glossary: over 40 terms are explicitly listed. Readers will be directed to definitions that appear in the text from the index. A more complete glossary of key terms related to patient safety is available from AHRQ's Patient Safety Network website.[1]

- A substantial reference list: the value in the in-depth use of references is that it illustrates the existent scholarship base to draw from to begin to design research to fully explore the issues and opportunities to leverage. It confirms that evidence exists for design opportunities to seek new applications of what is known to inform action.

- Appendices: Several appendixes flesh out concepts related to human factors, cognition and resources, strengths and weaknesses that represent a selection of deeper explorations on how EI&K and overarching concepts may merge to delineate areas of improvement and learning.

These resources are included to fuse the concepts discussed in the five primary sections and multi-chapter sections of the text.

Given the newness of some of the material for readers, it is suggested that the book be first approached sequentially despite assumed familiarity with

---

1   Available at: http://psnet.ahrq.gov/glossary.aspx

the content. For example, patient safety officers are likely to be familiar with the history discussed in Chapter 1, but they may not have thought about that history with EI&K milestones in mind. Librarians may gloss over chapters that don't seem to be directly related to their frontline practice, when in fact a sensitivity to human factors, cognition and systems safety are what need to be brought to bear on scoping a vision to reform such practice to contribute to process design focused on safety improvement.

An Engaging Passion, a Worthy Pursuit, a Possible Passageway

Those with whom I have worked in patient safety have a passion for this work: the leaders participate consistently at that level and those who encounter them know it. The pursuit toward reduced harm, reduced pain, and reduced anxiety are worthy exercises toward improving patient safety. Until we know more – after the initial conversations have happened, concerns have been raised and gaps have been determined – the experiences of faltering due to ineffective use of EI&K remain under a bushel, where they do no one any good at all.

List of Abbreviations

AHCPR	Agency for Health Care Policy Research
AHRQ	Agency for Healthcare Research and Quality
BMJ	*British Medical Journal*
CDDS/CDS	Computerized Clinical Decision Support Systems
CEO	Chief Executive Officer
CLASBI	Central Line Associated Blood Stream Infections
CMA	US Centers for Medicare and Medicaid Services
COWS	Computers on Wheels
CRM	Crew Resource Management
CS	Complex Systems
CVR	Cockpit Voice Recorder
D2B	Door to Balloon
EHR	Electronic Health Record
EI&K	Evidence, Information and Knowledge
EBM	Evidence-based Medicine
ED	Emergency Department
FDA	US Food and Drug Administration
FMEA	Failure Modes and Effects Analysis
HAMP	High Alert Medication Program
HCA	Hospital Corporation of America, Inc.
HFE	Human Factors Engineering
HIT	Health Information Technology
HMPS	Harvard Medical Practice Study
HRO	High Reliability Organization
ICU	Intensive Care Unit
IHI	Institute for Healthcare Improvement
IOM	Institute of Medicine
IRB	Institutional Review Board
ISMP	Institute for Safe Medication Practices
IV	Intravenous

JAMA	*Journal of the American Medical Association*
KPNC	Kaiser Permanente Northern California
MBWA	"Management by Walking Around"
MeSH	Medical Subject Headings
MRSA	Methicillin-resistant Staphylococcus Aureus
NCPS	National Center for Patient Safety
NHS	National Health Service
NIOSH	National Institute for Occupational Safety and Health
NPSF	National Patient Safety Foundation
OHRP	Office for Human Research Protections
PI	Principal Investigator
RCA	Root Cause Analysis
SOC	Service Operations Committee
TCAB	Transforming Patient Care at the Bedside
UK	United Kingdom
UPI	Unique Patient Identifier
USP	United States Pharmacopeia
VA	US Veterans Administration
WHO	World Health Organization

Acknowledgements

Think left and think right and think low and think high.
Oh, the thinks you can think up if only you try (Dr Seuss:
http://quotations.about.com/od/bookquotes/a/seuss1.htm).

Since my involvement with patient safety began almost two decades ago, many interactions and experiences have shaped the thinking represented in these pages. To try and list each individual would not be effective – however gratifying it would be to put it on paper here. I have benefited from conversations on the issues raised in this text over the years with clinicians, administrators, librarians, and patients. Hearing their stories has repeatedly confirmed that the concepts have value and has helped me to insist on change. I am thankful for the time spent discussing the important work of safety.

I must "en masse" acknowledge the contributors. All had little room in their scheduled for an additional commitment yet signed on to participate. When they came on board, they were instructed to approach the topic with "one foot in their box, one foot outside it." This served as a metaphor to have them apply what they know and work with regularly to an area that was potentially outside their thinking at the time of joining the project. Several of the chapters were co-written by individuals who had never met yet collaborated despite that. It is my hope that this small assignment planted seeds that would sprout into relationships of lasting vitality. I would be pleased to see that the authors seek to work together in the future on projects that apply the concepts covered in the book to the frontlines of care or EI&K delivery. I am grateful for the energy they brought to the effort.

As would be expected by any task of this sort, there were individuals who helped to bring the project closer to its intended course: Vida Lynum,

Janice Molloy, Michael Moore, Pat Muller, John Jackson, Helen Haskell, Jessica Ochtera, James Green, Erin Hartman, and Gene Kim. I appreciate the time they took to fill in gaps in the development process. Also, thanks to my family, friends, and colleagues for patiently listening to me prattle on about the book as I worked through the kinks of getting it finalized.

However, there are several individuals who deserve a "call-out" as being instrumental in the book becoming a reality.

Gail Hendler – who planted the seed about my authoring a book on this topic in the first place and saw value in the multidisciplinary approach I wanted to take. Barb Jones – who has spent countless hours listening to me, whose energy and commitment to the theoretical aspects of the work has yet to wane, and who continues to be a nurturing and invigorating colleague. Joanne Turnbull, Tania Bardin, and Julie Lawell – who reviewed the draft and shared candid and effective comments to sharpen the language. Ross Vagnieres of Vagne Design – who developed the consistent and clear graphics for the text. Jeannine Gluck – who has been attentive to the nurturing role of librarians in patient safety for years and whose indexing expertise has brought value to the text. Jonathan Norman and his team at Gower – who expertly answered questions, weathered the process and was patient with delays. Linda Williams – who, from our chance meeting at the National Patient Safety Foundation Annenberg meeting in 2001 – has spawned a partnership that is fruitful and a blessing to me professionally and personally and is reflected in the concepts in the text. Sara Tompson – who embraces challenges, sees strengths in partnership and enjoys new avenues to apply her considerable expertise in librarianship. This mindset guided her to accept the assignment of copy editor for the text. Sara's level head, honesty, sense of adventure, reliability and candor have been an asset in my work since she and I first wrote together almost 20 years ago.

Lastly, my husband Ross provided much needed support and encouragement throughout. When the offer to accept the opportunity to do this text in tandem with a second publication for Gower on knowledge management in medicine[1] he said "go for it!" To him, I am thankful and am looking forward to coming back into the New Mexico sun to help our garden grow.

---

1 See http://www.gowerpublishing.com/isbn/9781409438830

PART 1

Context for Innovation and Improvement

Chapter 1 Synopsis – Patient Safety: A Brief but Spirited History

The authors provide a review of the evolution of the patient safety movement through three primary periods of development. The chapter challenges readers to think about how the movement lagged despite evidence of medical error and how it has subsequently grown into an influential movement. The narrative highlights evidence, information and knowledge evidence, information and knowledge (EI&K) episodes that contributed to this evolution.

Chapter 2 Synopsis – Concepts, Context, Communication: Who's on First?

Conceptual murkiness has the potential to compromise patient safety efforts. In an effort to reduce that potential, the authors highlight differences between key terms that must be understood across professional groups, task teams and organizational levels in order to support reliable EI&K processes. They argue a consistent terminology and a shared understanding of its use is critical for establishing a solid EI&K sharing process for patient safety.

Chapter 3 Synopsis – Potential for Harm Due to Failures in the EI&K Process

This chapter discusses the need to improve EI&K identification, acquisition and transfer. The argument is made through a discussion of an accidental death in which failures in evidence identification during a clinical trial was identified as a contributing factor. The authors advocate for an exploration into EI&K seeking and sharing behaviors as an element of safe care from the systems safety perspective. This approach is an innovation for EI&K service design yet to be capitalized on in patient safety circles.

1

Patient Safety: A Brief but Spirited History

Robert L. Wears, Kathleen M. Sutcliffe and Eric Van Rite

> *Experience is by industry achieved and perfected by the swift course of time.*
>
> *William Shakespeare,* Two Gentlemen of Verona,
> *Act 1, Scene 3*

The Emergence of a Field of Focus

Conventional wisdom regards the publication of the Institute of Medicine's (IOM) *To Err is Human* (Kohn, Corrigan and Donaldson 2000) as the watershed moment for the field of patient safety – when harm from medical care was suddenly recognized as a large-scale problem and patient safety was propelled to the top of the national healthcare reform agenda. Indeed, as Figure 1.1 shows, since 2000 there has been a dramatic increase in attention paid to patient safety.

Yet, this pattern of attention is not evidence that *To Err Is Human* marked the start of patient safety reform. The report itself rests upon a series of other historical episodes, as shown in the timeline in Appendix 1.1. These episodes contributed basic information, and also fueled the social processes through which that information was: validated and accepted as evidence; interpreted and given a moral dimension; and, ultimately transformed into taken-for-granted knowledge (Latour 1987) that was used to justify reform (Hilgartner and Bosk 1988).

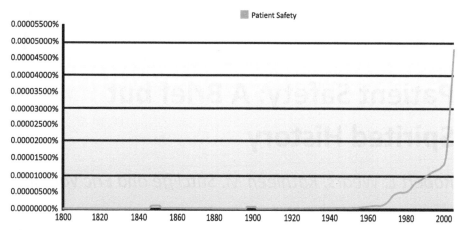

Figure 1.1   Relative Frequency of the Phrase "Patient Safety" in English
               Language Books Over Time: 1800–2008

Source: Google, 2013. Ngram Viewer. Available at: http://books.google.com/ngrams
[accessed: 1 April 2013].

This chapter traces the historical development of patient safety as it evolved
from a set of sporadic concerns to a sustained social movement. Three periods
are examined:

1.   The sporadic period, where isolated evidence appeared but did not
      coalesce into a coherent body of thought.

2.   The cult period, characterized by the development of a small group
      of vocal and passionate believers.

3.   The breakout period, in which patient safety became established as
      a legitimate area of activity and enquiry in healthcare at large and
      in the broader society.

The goal is to examine a few illustrative episodes in each period, but not to
comprehensively discuss every element on the timeline; in addition, events in
the past five years are not covered in great detail, as it is not currently knowable
which are truly influential and which are merely passing. More detailed and
comprehensive histories are available (for example in Sharpe and Faden
1998 and Vincent 2010). The chapter concludes by addressing two additional
questions: Why did patient safety emerge as an organized social movement in
the 1990s when fundamental evidence about hazards in healthcare had been
known and discussed for at least the previous 150 years? And, once the patient

safety movement emerged, what explains its subsequent continuation and evolution?

Three Periods of Patient Safety History

PERIOD ONE: THE SPORADIC ERA

The sporadic period, which ranges from ancient Greeks to about the 1950s, is characterized by intermittent insights into the hazards of healthcare, some of which have endured in specific practices. Yet, for the most part they were "one-off" processes, which were not mutually informative and did not result in a comprehensive or sustained sphere of activity. Figure 1.1 illustrates the sporadic nature of this period by showing appearances of the term "patient safety" in English language books; note prior to about 1950 there are long periods where the phrase never appears.

The famous dictum "First, do no harm" is commonly attributed to Hippocrates, but does not appear verbatim in his writings. Still, Hippocrates advises physicians to "abstain from harming or wronging any man" (Vincent 2010: 3), indicating that concern for the safety of medical care dates to classical times. Doubts about the safety of medical practices continued to be expressed, albeit occasionally, as medicine came of age in the modern era. A medical student graduating in 1835 noted "… that medicine was not an exact science, that it was wholly empirical and that it would be better to trust entirely to nature than to the hazardous skill of the doctors" (Sharpe and Faden 1998: 8). Similarly, Florence Nightingale in 1863 wrote, "the very first requirement of a hospital [is] that it should do the sick no harm" (Sharpe and Faden 1998: 157).

In 1847 Semelweiss provided the earliest organized, empirical evidence about the risks of healthcare. He based his insights into the origin and prevention of puerperal sepsis on empirical observations. Similar to present day healthcare researchers, Semelweiss was motivated by a personal situation

---

INFOBOX 1.1: THE SPORADIC ERA – HIGHLIGHTS

4 BCE: Hippocrates writes "abstain from harming or wronging any man."
1847: Semelweis documents the risks of medical treatment.
1860: Nightingale states "A hospital should do the sick no harm."
1915: Codman designs classification of reporting of surgical errors.

– the rapid death of a beloved colleague who had cut his finger during an autopsy (Vincent 2010). This prefigures the prominent role that dramatic, morally imbued narratives will play later in the evolution of patient safety.

In the early twentieth century, Ernest Amory Codman, a surgeon inspired by Taylor's "scientific management" theories, argued for routine recording and scientific assessment of surgical outcomes and for making results publicly available (Timmermans and Berg 2003). He developed a seven-category causal classification scheme to categorize unsuccessful cases. Four were labeled "errors" (of skill, judgment, equipment, diagnosis), and a fifth "calamities of surgery" over which there were no control. Codman's efforts were partially adopted by professional organizations and also became part of the hospital standardization movement in the US, playing an important role in the development of an accreditation system that ultimately became The Joint Commission (Timmermans and Berg 2003: 9).

PERIOD TWO: THE CULT ERA

The modern patient safety movement took shape as bits of data and evidence began to coalesce into a more related whole, and through the formation of a self-selected group that was interested in advocating for safety in healthcare. This small group of passionate believers was little known outside of their own circles.

Evidence, information and knowledge in this period came from a variety of sources. Some sources were scientific in nature and some were based in

---

INFOBOX 1.2: THE CULT ERA – HIGHLIGHTS

1959: Moser's book *Diseases of Medical Progress*.
1978: Cooper: *Preventable Anesthesia Mishaps* published.
1982: *20/20* "The Deep Sleep" airs.
1984: Libby Zion dies.
1985: Anesthesia Patient Safety Foundation formed.
1991: Harvard Medical practice studies published in the *New England Journal of Medicine*.
1994: Leape: "Error in Medicine" in the *Journal of the American Medical Association* published.
1995: *Boston Globe* Columnist Betsy Lehman dies.
1996: First Annenberg Patient Safety Conference held.
1997: National Patient Safety Foundation formed.

narrative; some rested in healthcare and some were taken from the social and safety sciences.

Evidence Raises Awareness

Developments in healthcare began with physician David Barr's 1955 Billings Memorial Lecture entitled "The Hazards of Modern Diagnosis and Therapy – The Price We Pay" (Barr 1955) in which he identified risks posed by medical care, and argued that this was an inevitable (and mostly worthwhile) price to pay for therapeutic advances. Nonetheless, he concluded that physicians had a responsibility to avoid incurring unnecessary harm to minimize the price that physicians and patients both pay for modern disease management (Barr 1955).

By 1959, the ground had shifted a bit; military internist and educator Robert H. Moser's book, *Diseases of Medical Progress*, promoted the perspective that harm was not an entirely unavoidable byproduct of medical success but also a consequence of unsound practice without due regard for the balance of risk and benefit (Moser 1959). In the ten years between editions, the text increased in size eight-fold (Moser 1969).

Gastroenterologist Elihu Schimmel expanded this line of thinking by focusing on episodes of harm (but excluding potentially harmful situations) in his 1964 paper on the hazards of hospitalization (Schimmel 1964). Schimmel reported that 20 percent of hospitalized patients suffered one or more adverse events, and 1.6 percent died as a result. However, he also noted that modern medicine cannot always be used harmlessly, and worried that a focus entirely on safety would produce a therapeutic nihilism: "... the dangers of new measures must be accepted and are generally warranted by their benefits" (Schimmel 2003, reprint of 1964 article: 63).

Geriatrician Knight Steel and his colleagues replicated Schimmel's work in showing roughly similar results: 36 percent of patients suffered some sort of adverse event; 9 percent were major and 2 percent fatal (Steel et al. 1981). Steel's research team did not try to assess preventability, or balance risk and benefit, but concluded that technical, educational and administrative means should be sought to reduce the number and severity of adverse events caused by care.

Periodic crises in the availability and affordability of malpractice insurance, starting in the 1970s and continuing to the present, led to studies of medical harm to inform the development of alternative compensation systems. The *Medical Insurance Feasibility Study* was the first to establish a statewide (California) estimate of the burden of medical harm (Mills 1978; Mills, Boyden and Rubamen 1977). It was followed about a decade later by the *Harvard Medical Practice Study*, which used a roughly similar methodology to estimate harm in New York hospitals and obtained similar results. From a review of 1984 medical records, the study found that 2,550 patients were permanently disabled and over 13,000 died from causes related to adverse care events (see Brennan et al. 1991; Leape et al. 1991 and Localio et al. 1991). In these studies, approximately 4 percent of hospitalizations showed evidence of injuries from care, and about 1 percent of hospitalizations were attributed to negligence.

The 1991 Harvard study received brief national publicity and was more influential than earlier studies for several reasons (Van Rite 2011). First, the authors extrapolated the results to the entire state of New York, giving a specific number of deaths, which was more dramatic and impactful than a rate. The authors also drew different conclusions from roughly the same empirical results. They implied that adverse events were not a reasonable price to pay for medical progress, but rather argued that the burden of iatrogenic injury was "large" and "disturbing." Finally, the authors differentiated negligence from error or safety; this justified targeting medical error as a legitimate field for research and policy, independent of – and perhaps even more important than – negligence and malpractice (Van Rite 2011).

PERIOD THREE: BREAKOUT ERA

As patient safety moved into the larger public sphere, it faced a bit of opposition and denial; but that was quickly replaced by a scramble by the healthcare industry to say, in effect, "We're on it." Three episodes (among many) stand out as highly influential in bringing about this change:

1.   Publication of *To Err is Human*;

2.   The *British Medical Journal* special issue on safety; and

3.   The National Health Service (NHS) report, *An Organisation with a Memory*, which appeared within a few months of each other (Department of Health 2000; Kohn et al. 2000; and *British Medical Journal* issue on patient safety, 18 March 2000).

These publications were influential not because they contained new information, but because of the venues in which the information appeared, and the legitimacy granted by such appearance. That is, these publications were not causal influences by themselves, but instead were the effects of previous causes (such as those described in this chapter). Each publication amplified what had been previously known, brought it to a much larger audience, and gave it an *imprimatur* with greater credibility and legitimacy that derived from the distinction and reputation of the publishers.

> *"After these reports, no government or care delivery organization could ignore patient safety."*

The 2000 IOM report *To Err is Human* received massive publicity that surprised even its authors. The report was a rhetorical triumph; it combined the estimate of 44–98,000 US deaths from previous studies with the personal stories of Betsy Lehman (discussed elsewhere in this text), medication misadministration casualty 8-year-old Ben Kolb, wrong site surgery victim Willie King, and others. The principal aim of the report, which was based on more than just the Harvard study, was to establish patient safety as a major required activity of modern healthcare (Kohn et al. 2000). It concluded with a call for a national effort, including establishing a "Center for Patient Safety" within the Agency for Health Care Policy and Research (AHCPR; now the Agency for Healthcare Research and Quality, AHRQ). Curiously, there seems to have been little or no discussion of the appropriate home for the government's safety research portfolio. President Clinton promptly ordered a government-wide study on the feasibility of the recommendations. A series of hearing and public meetings with stakeholders followed, from which AHCPR/AHRQ eventually developed a safety research program (Quality Interagency Coordination; QuIC Task Force 2000).

The March 18, 2000 issue of BMJ, the *British Medical Journal*, was a special issue, "Reducing error, improving safety," edited by US-based patient safety

---

INFOBOX 1.3: THE BREAKOUT ERA – HIGHLIGHTS

2000: Institute of Medicine publishes *To Err Is Human*.
2000: The *British Medical Journal* publishes a Special Issue on Patient Safety, Leape, Berwick editors.
2000: The British National Health Service publishes *An Organisation with a Memory*.
2001: Josie King dies at Johns Hopkins.
2004: World Alliance for Patient Safety is formed by the World Health Organization.

visionaries Lucian Leape MD and Donald Berwick MD, and included a dramatic cover of a plane crash. It is interesting to note that in their opening editorial, Leape and Berwick cite information as critical: "...the safety of our patients and the satisfaction of our workers require an open and non-punitive environment where information is freely shared and responsibility broadly accepted" (Leape and Berwick 2000: 726).

In the United Kingdom, *Organisation with a Memory* (Department of Health 2000) had similar impact. It was issued by the Department of Health, and since it was critical of safety in the National Health Service, this took some degree of fortitude. A similar flurry of government activity followed, resulting in the establishment of the UK's National Patient Safety Agency in 2001 (Department of Health, National Health Service 2001).

These reports clearly changed the safety conversation, pushing the door wide open, bringing patient safety out of the domain of a few researchers and committed activists and placing it clearly on national agendas (Sheridan 2003). After these reports, no government or care delivery organization could ignore patient safety.

Two Forms of Resistance

The widespread public attention and governmental activities that followed were not uniformly well received; resistance took two forms. First, those who had been working in the quality movement (discussed further, below) argued that many safety concepts were simply a reworking of long-standing quality improvement ideas. They asked: if safety is a core dimension of healthcare quality, then why is patient safety a special case? How is the "search for error" different from the past two decades of effort to understand, profile, and improve the quality of care (Hofer, Kerr and Hayward 2000)?

The second form of resistance was more important, as it amounted to a denial of the magnitude of the problem of *iatrogenic injury*. For example, some criticized the "loose language" about "errors" and the hindsight bias issues entailed in the IOM report and its supporting studies (Fisher and Welch 2000). The ambiguity or murkiness of "error" as a framing concept had figured prominently in studies of human performance outside of healthcare (Hollnagel 1991), but had not been incorporated into the developing patient safety orthodoxy along with other concepts from cognitive psychology. Other concerns related to the potentially misleading rhetorical conflation of deaths in chronically ill, debilitated patients (even if inadvertently hastened by medical care), with the unexpected deaths of healthy innocents.

These arguments resonated with the *evidence-based medicine* (EBM) movement (Evidence-Based Medicine Working Group 1992), a strongly positivist, normative, empiricist approach to research quality, which challenged both the vague definitions of "error" in the IOM report and the interpretivist philosophy of science that infused much of the safety sciences (Dekker 2011). This conflict led to a small, and ultimately unproductive, debate about defining errors and getting the numbers right (Leape 2000; McDonald, Weiner and Hui 2000). Similar debates about what constitutes legitimate scientific activity have continued to bedevil discourses on research and implementation in patient safety (Shekelle et al. 2001; Shojania et al. 2002; and Wears and Nemeth 2007).

Leaders and Outside Influences During the Eras

A LEADER SURFACES

Even with evidence accumulating, healthcare at large still did not collectively perceive that medical harm was an important problem during the "cult" era. But this was not the case in all of medicine, *"... although great progress was made in anesthetic safety, the evidence, information and knowledge gained there stayed encapsulated inside anesthesia."* particularly anesthesia. In the spring of 1982, the popular ABC program *20/20* aired a story of a patient who suffered severe brain damage when the nitrous oxide was turned up and the oxygen turned off (rather than the reverse) at the end of a procedure (American Broadcasting Service 1982).

The *20/20* broadcast brought together anesthesiologists such as Ellison "Jeep" Pierce, and biomedical engineers such as Jeff Cooper, who had separately developed interests in anesthetic accidents. Pierce, elected president of the American Society of Anesthesiologists in 1982, used these stories to persuade the profession that it was possible to mount a sustained effort to reduce the death rate from anesthesia. This led to the founding of the Anesthesia Patient Safety Foundation in 1985, and foreshadowed the wider patient safety movement that developed a decade or so later. Curiously, although great progress was made in anesthetic safety, the evidence, information and knowledge gained there stayed encapsulated inside anesthesia (Eichhorn 2010).

QUALITY EMERGES

Another development in healthcare was the quality improvement movement, beginning in the late 1980s, also in the "cult" era timeframe. Improvement activities initially were sporadic and unsystematic and were regarded by clinicians either with disinterest or active hostility. By the mid-1990s, however, improvement efforts took hold and became legitimate.

In contrast to patient safety, the quality movement did not explicitly focus on harm. Rather, it aimed at standardization, identification, and implementation of best practices while improving access and decreasing costs. Substandard or less effective care was discouraged more because it was economically or clinically inefficient than because patients were (or might be) harmed. The quality movement differed from the later patient safety movement in other ways as well. Although both were grounded in ideas from fields outside of healthcare, they looked to different fields for evidence, information, and knowledge.

Quality improvement took guidance from operations research and industrial process control for exemplars; its "heroes" were W. Edwards Deming, Walter Shewhart who conceptualized Total Quality Management, and Joseph M. Juran and the Toyota production system model spawned by his work (Thompson, Wolf and Spear 2003). In contrast, patient safety looked to high-risk industries such as aviation, chemical, and nuclear power as its models, and psychology, ergonomics, and organization behavior as its "basic sciences;" its "heroes" were Charles Perrow, James Reason and Karl Weick (Perrow 1984; Reason 1990; Weick 1987). Quality advocates tended to focus on the central tendency of the distribution of performance (making sure normal care went normally), while safety advocates tended to focus on the "tales" – dramatic accidents or heroic rescues (Cardiff 2008; Cardiff et al. 2008). Despite these differences, and tension between proponents, the quality movement provided scaffolding for the safety ideas and activities that followed. For example, quality advocates introduced the idea of system rather than individual performance as the relevant (or at least, more useful) unit of analysis, and the notion that conscientious work by qualified individuals is not sufficient to assure quality or safety.

SOCIAL EXPLORATIONS PROVIDE INSIGHT

Studies on injuries and harm in medicine continued to accumulate in the 1970s and 1980s. Scholars from the social sciences independently added information and knowledge to the field that was to become patient safety.

Sociology and medical ethics professor Charles L. Bosk's classic ethnography *Forgive and Remember* documented the emphasis that surgeons place on the process of clinical work in the face of uncertainty, and noted that technical and judgmental errors could be "forgiven" if not repeated, but that normative errors were inexcusable,

"New thinking about system safety and organizing with regard to high-hazard work and technologies in the 1980s–1990s, as the 'cult' era was morphing into the 'breakout' era, came from many social science disciplines."

as they reflected upon the character of the agent (Bosk 1979). At about the same time, sociologist Marianne Paget presented an analysis of professional interpretations of failure. Paget argued that things go wrong in medical work as a matter of course, but that mistakes only become apparent as events unfold: "an act is not a mistake in itself – the end product is a mistake" (Paget 1988: 45). These descriptive studies foreshadowed a genre of investigation in patient safety that was to come, one that was distinctively different from traditional biomedical or health services research (Greenhalgh et al. 2011).

Philosopher and social critic Ivan Illich advanced a provocative view that triggered outrage in the medical community. Illich argued that medicine had sought to move beyond its proper boundaries and by doing so was causing harm. He posited that harm to patients was not just an unfortunate side effect of medical treatment that would eventually be resolved by technological advances, but rather saw harm as inherent in healthcare. The only solution was for people to resist unnecessary therapeutic intervention in the medicalization of life (Illich 1977).

In 1983, British philosopher and economist Sir Karl Popper joined with a prominent physician Neil McIntyre to apply his philosophy of science (that greater advances come from recognition of flaws in existing thinking than from the steady accumulation of new facts) to the issue of errors in medicine. Their paper suggested errors should be actively sought and broadly disclosed in order to improve both personal and general knowledge about hazards and how to prevent or mitigate them (McIntyre and Popper 1983). Through this framing, human error becomes something of value, a resource to be treasured, both scientifically and clinically.

While understanding about patient safety in healthcare was quietly incubating, understanding about safety in complex work systems in other disciplines was advancing. The explanatory power of early accident models (e.g., the domino model (Heinrich 1931), which assumed sequential causal chains that were triggered by "unsafe acts") was fundamentally challenged by complex events such as the 1977 Tenerife disaster, and the 1979 accident at Three Mile Island (Nance 2008). These events were inexplicable or, unsatisfyingly explicable using prior models. These disasters, and their associated information failures, triggered a series of meetings, analyses, books, papers, and discussions that resulted in newer and more appreciative ways to look at human performance in complex, uncertain, ambiguous and volatile work environments. These ideas would become critical to the collective recognition of patient safety as a significant issue, in part because a "system's willingness to become aware of problems is associated with its ability to act on them" (Westrum 1993: 340).

New thinking about system safety and organizing with regard to high-hazard work and technologies in the 1980s–1990s, as the "cult" era was morphing into the "breakout" era, came from many social science disciplines. Sociologist Charles Perrow's Normal Accident theory grew out of his understanding of the disaster at Three Mile Island (Perrow 1984). The technology at Three Mile Island was *tightly coupled* (i.e., it had time-dependent processes, invariant sequences) and interactively *complex* (i.e., different elements could affect each other in unforeseen ways). Perrow hypothesized that the combination of these two factors allowed events to spread throughout the system by way of connections that were impossible to anticipate, and with a speed that precluded understanding, much less response. Thus, regardless of the effectiveness of management and operations, accidents in these systems will be "normal" or inevitable.

At about the same time, proponents of High Reliability Organization theory (or HRO) – an increasingly popular perspective in patient safety today – took a more appreciative view arguing that some high-risk, high-hazard organizations can and do function safely despite the hazards of complex systems (Roberts 1993; Rochlin, La Porte and Roberts 1987; Weick 1987 and 1990). Normal Accident and High Reliability Organization theory share a focus on the social and organizational underpinnings of system safety and accident causation/prevention, paying little attention to technical and engineering aspects, which are assumed to be relevant but insufficient as explanatory factors.

Psychologists and engineers, particularly in Europe, questioned whether the idea of errors was even relevant for understanding accidents (Rasmussen 1990; Rasmussen, Duncan and Leplat 1987; Senders and Moray 1991). Consistent with HRO researchers, psychologists and engineers also viewed human performance as continuously making sense of a jumbled stream of phenomena with attempts to maintain cognitive control, and they tended to view normative, top down, prescriptive direction with some suspicion (Klein et al. 1993; Reason 1990).

Thus, a rich arena of somewhat related ideas about both successful and unsuccessful human performance developed outside of healthcare from the 1970s through the 1990s. These ideas offered greater insight into the problems of safety in complex work, held out the possibility of more effective methods of managing hazards, and would later inform thinking about safety in healthcare.

In addition to accumulating evidence and information from outside of healthcare, dramatic stories of individual patient's tragedies brought patient safety from the periphery into the public arena. The tragic stories of Betsy Lehman, Willie King, Ben Kolb, Libby Zion, Ellen Roche in the "cult" era, and Dennis Quaid's twins and Josie King in the "breakout" era generated both popular and professional interest (Cook, Woods and Miller 1998; Ramsey 2001; Grant 2010; King 2009). In addition, formal inquiries into children's deaths at the Bristol Royal Infirmary and the Winnipeg cardiac surgery programs, put faces on the dry, technical statistics of the Harvard Medical Practice Study (Weick and Sutcliffe 2003; Davies 2001). Drama is critical in contests for attention and legitimacy in the public arena; success often comes from a strategy of coupling cold, hard facts with vivid, emotional rhetoric (Hilgartner and Bosk 1988).

KNOWLEDGE OF HARM: THE POWER OF STORY

During the "cult" era, Betsy Lehman's riveting story heightened media coverage and public awareness of system causes of medical errors. Lehman died in 1994 after receiving a four-fold overdose of a chemotherapeutic drug, and her death was significant for several reasons (Knox 1995). First, the incident occurred at a prestigious, cutting-edge research facility widely considered one of the world's best cancer centers. Second, Lehman's husband worked as a cancer researcher at the very institution where she was killed by medication error. Third, Lehman was a respected health columnist for the *Boston Globe*. Finally, Lehman's story emerged in a context of other reports of medical mistakes around the country. Because the reputation of the institution, the patient's personal connection to it, and her profession are all factors that generally would have been thought to result in above

"... Betsy Lehman's riveting story heightened media coverage and public awareness of system causes of medical errors."

average care, the incident left the strong implication that "ordinary people" – those in ordinary, local hospitals, without personal connections to the staff, and without the sophistication and knowledge of a health reporter – would be at even greater risk than someone like Lehman (Knox 1995).

The deaths of 18-month-old Josie King and of Ellen Roche (both at Johns Hopkins, as discussed in more detail elsewhere in this text) shortly after the release of *To Err is Human* in 2000 – which marks the beginning of the "breakout" era – brought further awareness to the impact of error and the question of how it could happen at the "best" institutions (King 2009; Ramsey 2001). Particularly, the moving story recounted by Josie King's mother Sorrel King reinforced the public face of medical error and provoked patient advocacy and comprehensive reform. Story, or narrative, is a particularly compelling format for information and knowledge delivery. In these instances, story as a sharing mechanism demonstrates a key ability to generate action. To illustrate, the Kings not only received a financial settlement for the hospital's role in the death of their daughter, but also attained a commitment from Johns Hopkins to implement policy changes promoting patient safety (King 2009).

Although public reporting of these and other celebrated cases was often superficial and sometimes inflammatory, media attention had two important effects. First, it kept patient safety on the public agenda in an easily digestible and viscerally important way. Second, the dramatic personalization in media narratives contrasted with the more complex understandings developed from the "new look" at safety coming from outside healthcare. This distinction was captured in the invited conference report (since widely disseminated) *A Tale of Two Stories*, one of the first outputs of the newly founded National Patient Safety Foundation (Cook, Woods and Miller 1998).

Narratives of celebrated cases were equally influential elsewhere in the English-speaking world, and had similar bi-dimensional impact (generating public support and academic understanding). The two most prominent examples are the 2001 Bristol Royal Infirmary inquiry in Britain, discussed in *Report of the Public Inquiry into Children's Heart Surgery at the Royal Bristol Infirmary: Learning from Bristol* (Public Inquiry into Children's Heart Surgery at the Bristol Royal Infirmary 2001; Smith 1998a, 1998b; Walsh and Offen 2001; Weick and Sutcliffe 2003) and the Winnipeg inquiry in Canada (Davies 2001; Sinclair 1998). Investigating excess deaths in pediatric heart surgery programs, both analyses took a very wide view, focusing not so much on individuals as on the broader problems of safety in care delivery organizations.

A FIELD OF STUDY COALESCES

These three streams of thinking about safety in healthcare – traditional medical studies of harm; new insights on safety from the social sciences and engineering and, dramatic narratives of individuals harmed by care – began to mingle and coalesce in the mid-1990s. Lucian Leape, one of the authors of the *Harvard Medical Practice Study*, published an influential paper in 1994 that marked this merging of thought (Leape 1994). In introducing to the medical literature safety concepts from the social sciences and engineering identified through the help of a Harvard reference librarian, Leape argued that "the literature of medical error is sparse," since most studies focus on injuries rather than on errors or the mechanisms of injury (Agency for Healthcare Research and Quality 2006). This lack of attention to error, according to Leape, was not because physicians and nurses do not experience error, but rather that "they have a great deal of difficulty in dealing with human error when it does occur" (Leape 1994: 1851).

Coalescence progressed because of a series of publications, meetings, and the establishment of institutions. For example, also in 1994, Bogner edited a multi-author text entitled *Human Error in Medicine* (Bogner 1994). Roughly half of its authors were not clinicians, and it made a rather strong statement that: "Human error in medicine, and the adverse events that may follow, are problems of psychology and engineering, not of medicine" (Senders 1994: 159).

The 1996 Annenberg conference on *Examining Errors in Healthcare: Developing a Prevention, Education, and Research Agenda* (Annenberg I) provides tangible evidence of coalescence. This was the first major meeting that gathered experts from a wide variety of disciplines, many of them non-clinical, to address the problem of harm due to care. Almost half of the plenary speakers were not clinicians, roughly equally divided between "safety experts" (from psychology, engineering, organizational behavior, etc.) and other important constituencies, such as ethics, the law, and advocates for patients and families (Wears, Perry and Sutcliffe 2005). The meeting had a similarly eclectic group of funding sources, including the American Academy for the Advancement of Science and the Robert Wood Johnson Foundation, as well as healthcare-related groups such as the American Medical Association, the Joint Commission on Accreditation of Healthcare Organizations.

The first Annenberg conference led to the 1997 founding of the National Patient Safety Foundation (NPSF) at the AMA, modeled after the highly successful Anesthesia Patient Safety Foundation. The success of Annenberg I led to a second Annenberg conference, *Enhancing Patient Safety and Reducing Medical Error* (Annenberg II) in 1998. This meeting was larger than the first, and featured an even wider proportion of non-clinical safety scientists as plenary speakers (Wears et al. 2005). Annenberg II strengthened the partnership between clinicians and safety scientists and suggested this association would become self-sustaining (Scheffler and Zipperer 1999). The establishment of the NPSF's listserv™ for patient safety issues in 1998 facilitated this self-sustaining community of interest. This early form of social networking support has continued to be an active resource for communication and connection, and furthered the coalescence of core ideas and the development of patient safety as a social movement (Dixon-Woods et al. 2011).

Patient Safety: Consolidation and Absorption

Objection and resistance to the one-two punches of the IOM report and the BMJ special issue did not last long; despite a failure to resolve issues about the validity of the science, the impact of the claims, and the distinction between safety and quality, patient safety did become mainstream fairly rapidly – no longer marginal, but rather a legitimate focus of effort within healthcare. Signifying this acceptance, the journal *Quality in Health Care* changed its name to *Quality and Safety in Health Care* in March 2002 (Barach and Moss 2001).

Yet, the more patient safety became mainstream, the more it risked losing its reformist edge – particularly the input from other scientific fields that originally made safety problems seem potentially tractable. Both the proportion and number of non-clinical safety scientists involved in patient safety began to fall (Wears et al. 2005). This decline in non-clinician involvement is important for two reasons. First, medical and healthcare education have been admonished for failing to equip learners with the abilities to interpret, understand, and value the knowledge, theories, tools, and literature of other disciplines (Kneebone 2002). Second, patient safety as a field has been criticized for having adopted the language of other fields without really understanding or being able to effectively apply their insights and methods (Kneebone 2006; Rowley and Waring 2011; Saleem et al. 2011).

In addition, safety became conflated with other (legitimate) healthcare agendas. For example, around 2003, the Agency for Healthcare Research and Quality (AHRQ) shifted the majority of its safety research

"... the more patient safety became mainstream, the more it risked losing its reformist edge ..."

portfolio into information technology related projects, which may have applied to safety, but left many areas struggling, particularly the development of human capital in the form of new safety researchers. Similarly, by 2013, just over 50 percent of the AHRQ safety budget request was directed at hospital-acquired infections – an important issue to be sure, but also one that had long been addressed and supported in other ways (Agency for Healthcare Quality and Research 2013).

Thus, the successful diffusion and adoption of patient safety in healthcare has been accompanied by a sort of "medicalization" of the field, in terms of who is active in it, and what methods and subjects are considered admissible. Patient safety was once an interdisciplinary community of safety researchers and advocates, but it now has become dominated by the medical community. This, regrettably, has resulted in a premature return to "normal science," closing off potentially more promising paths before their value could be established. For example, the use of qualitative methods, which are fundamental to understanding processes and mechanisms, are now discouraged rather than embraced in patient safety circles (Hoff and Sutcliffe 2006).

Although patient safety successfully gained credibility and legitimacy, and well-intentioned resources and reform efforts, progress on improving safety has been slow. Commentaries published at the five- and the ten-year anniversaries of *To Err is Human* have explored the failure to live up to the high hopes of 2000 (Leape and Berwick 2005; Wachter 2010). Critics have advanced multiple reasons: the hopes may have been too optimistic; healthcare is so large and diverse, it can only change slowly; the problems have proven much more difficult than anticipated; illness and death are inevitable, making adverse events essentially ambiguous; and, funding for research and implementation has not approached what was originally envisioned. A few voices have started to address deeper issues and express concern that efforts have used the wrong scientific models (Cook 2003; Vincent, Batalden and Davidoff 2011). Even more disconcerting are concerns that the opportunity for truly innovative change has passed, particularly now that safety activities have become bureaucratized and turned into marketable services (Cook 2013).

A Foundation Built on Collective Judgment

To understand the role of evidence, information and knowledge in patient safety, it is necessary to review the emergence of the field as a distinct set of ideas in a particular historical context (Vincent 2010). As this chapter has shown, concerns about the safety of healthcare have been omnipresent but scattered since medicine's inception. The emergence of patient safety as a concern seems to have come as much from a shift in social concerns about the acceptability of risk than from evidence about the level of risk, accompanied by knowledge about the workings of complex organizations from outside of medicine. This reflects the notion that social problems are "projections of collective sentiments rather than simple mirrors of objective conditions in society" (Hilgartner and Bosk 1988: 53–4).

"The emergence of patient safety as a concern seems to have come as much from a shift in social concerns about the acceptability of risk than from evidence about the level of risk, accompanied by knowledge about the workings of complex organizations from outside of medicine."

Certainly in society at large, there has been a general decrease in a fatalistic attitude towards risk or injury, less willingness to attribute harm to the mysterious workings of a divine providence, and decreased acceptance of what were once considered the inevitable ravages of age. In addition, the new understandings of safety stemming from scientific study of complex accidents such as Three Mile Island, and the fortuitous introduction of those ideas into healthcare, offered an explanation for the safety problems of care provision and afforded means of approaching them. The combination of generally lower willingness to accept the problems of safety, the possibility that they might be solvable, and the dramatic personal narratives all together created a collective judgment that injuries due to medical care were no longer acceptable; an effort to change that state of affairs – the patient safety movement – resulted.

KEY TAKE-AWAYS
- Patient safety is an evolving, and still young, discipline.
- Reliance of evidence and development and collection of information on medical error as well as on safety practices from other fields, have been critical in the development of the knowledge base of this emerging discipline.
- This multitude of ideas, perspectives and avenues for improvement and learning indicate a need for robust evidence, information and evidence application to generate and learn from both failures and success.

Suggested Reading

Berwick, D.M. and Leape, L.L., (eds) 2000. Reducing error, improving safety. *British Medical Journal*, 320(7237), Theme Issue (March 18, 2000).

Dekker, S.W.A. 2011. *Patient Safety: A Human Factors Approach*. Boca Raton, FL: CRC Press.

Department of Health. 2000. *An Organisation with a Memory* [Online: Department of Health]. Available at: http://www.dh.gov.uk/prod_consum_dh/groups/dh_digitalassets/@dh/@en/documents/digitalasset/dh_4065086.pdf [accessed: 24 June 2012].

Kohn, L.T., Corrigan, J.M. and Donaldson, M.S., (eds) 2000. *To Err is Human: Building a Safer Health System*. Washington, DC: Institute of Medicine.

Vincent, C. 2010. *Patient Safety*. 2nd edition. Chichester: Wiley-Blackwell.

Wachter, R. 2012. *Understanding Patient Safety*. 2nd edition [Paperback]. New York, NY: McGraw-Hill Professional.

2

Concepts, Context, Communication: Who's on First?

Lorri Zipperer and Linda Williams

> *The single biggest problem in communication is the illusion that it has taken place.*
>
> George Bernard Shaw, 1856–1950

The Importance of Shared Understanding

Healthcare is delivered through distinct service providers and departments. These disciplines and departments have their own lexicon that contributes to the maintenance of boundaries that can inhibit information and knowledge-sharing. These groups form barriers though competition, acquired specialty expertise, time pressures, and structural configuration that result in what might be referred to as organizational *silos*. Despite efforts to enhance teamwork, these silos still hamper effective care. Context, word use and meaning can vary and contribute to misinterpretation and misunderstandings. For example, *knowledge* could mean "data" to an information technician, "evidence" to a physician, "database" to a librarian and "intellectual capital" to an organizational development expert.

Safety and EI&K initiatives are particularly vulnerable to these misunderstandings as terminologies in both fields are in flux, and because the work in both areas is best accomplished through multidisciplinary efforts. Professional specialty disciplines have different vocabularies (Mason et al. 2012; Kothari 2011).

Bringing the vocabularies of safety and evidence/information/knowledge disciplines together without clarity of terminology can create a *perfect storm* for slowing down collective progress. Lack of shared understanding of terms can minimize the ability to implement, monitor, and study outcomes as evidence is applied to practice.

INFOBOX 2.1: PRIMARY TERMS – SAFETY AND EI&K

- Patient Safety: Promotes action that "avoid[s] injuries to patients from the care that is intended to help them" (Committee on Quality of Health Care in America 2001: 5).
- Evidence: "Evidence refers to the scientifically sound, fully researched and validated information and data collected during the pursuit of the understanding and validation of a hypothesis. In other views, evidence can refer to what someone's experience has been."
- Information: "Data that is processed and repurposed and printed for distinct use."
- Knowledge: "What an individual knows. [sic] It is dynamic in nature and embedded in the actions of experts" (Zipperer 2011: 302).

Teamwork and effective communication are essential to healthcare delivery (Pronovost and Freischlag 2010; Neily et al. 2010; Nembhard and Edmondson 2006; Baker et al. 2007). This approach aims to discourage silos in support of collective, team level decision-making. Unexpected juxtapositions of established concepts and terms can make work processes, team communications and initiative deliverables, complex. For example the core term *safe* is used and interpreted inconsistently. Safely, safer, safety and safe all connote different actions and relations to them (Hansson 2012). In healthcare, definitions of *safe* can morph depending on a patient's condition (Wear et al. 2000). It is therefore premature to proclaim absolute terms that describe the intersection of patient safety with EI&K because definitive terminology does not yet exist for either field. The languages of both fields are evolving as they investigate, apply and evaluate.

This chapter raises awareness of this vocabulary and meaning problem. It discusses the foundational terms used to frame this publication (see Infobox 2.1) as a pointed example to illustrate the conceptual *murkiness* that has the potential to compromise efforts to harness EI&K use as a patient safety improvement mechanism.

Much has been accomplished toward the development of robust taxonomies to apply to error reporting and other research efforts (Chang et al. 2005; World Alliance for Patient Safety 2009; Dovey et al. 2002; Runciman et al. 2010). However, these efforts may not be effectively broad-based and flexible enough to use across the spectrum of safety work and research at the frontline (Shekelle et al. 2010). It is the frontline use of terms related to the discussion that is the concern of this chapter.

Murky Terms Contribute to Complexity

'Safe' is an inherently inconsistent concept (Hansson 2012).

PATIENT SAFETY

The *patient safety* movement is now in its breakout period and gaining recognition as a valid area of activity and investigation (see Chapter 1). The change in the conversation launched by *To Err is Human,* today finds healthcare still working toward consensus on terminology (Leape and Berwick 2005; Kohn, Corrigan and Donaldson 2000). An agreed upon language for the discussion of patient safety is essential to reach shared understanding among the various stakeholders at both the sharp and blunt end. It is as yet unclear whether such understanding exists (Lin and Kumar 2012). The term *patient safety* and other safety words like checklist and teamwork, have also been used as buzzwords to draw readers to content that in reality is not about patient safety (Lin and Kumar 2012). This superficial use of terminology muddies the EI&K piece of the puzzle.

EVIDENCE

Discussions by clinicians, administrators and information professionals may include as *evidence* the full range from anecdotes and case studies, to randomized controlled trials. Scientific publishing offers an intellectual rigor that is designed to enhance use, credibility and applicability, but also tends to discount the value of experience (Greenhalgh 2010; Shekelle et al. 2010). Qualitative research – recognized in social, cultural and organizational circles – can and should be folded into empirical research to improve understanding of patient safety improvement work. If qualitative research is less valued by clinicians and scholars in patient safety, a *reinforcing loop* minimizing the contribution of that evidence base will develop and negatively influence interest in and funding of such studies (Hoff and Sutcliffe 2006).

While randomized controlled trials drive medical therapy decisions, qualitative studies are increasingly recognized as effective tools that provide insight into organizational behavior (Tamuz 2006). Socio-cultural and organizational studies provide evidence and insights into shared cognition for improving patient safety (Weick and Sutcliff 2007). Therefore, *all* forms of evidence generated by research are necessary to grasp the complexity of patient safety.

INFORMATION

When human beings lack the necessary knowledge to act, communicate, or make decisions, they seek *information* (Ans and Tricot 2009). And, when individuals resolve to fix an information deficit, they often focus on improving the availability of *more* information rather than *better* information. Misunderstanding and misinterpretation of information results from *context*, because context is a function of culture, gender, education, professional hierarchies, experience, socio-cultural environment, technical expertise, stress and even mood (Isaacs 1999).

KNOWLEDGE

The various meanings of *knowledge* and related terms are the focus of continuing debate (Barnard, Napier and Zipperer 2014; Wilson 2005). The lack of a common definition of knowledge in patient safety, let alone across disciplines, slows down progress in knowledge management initiatives (Kothari 2011). For example, in an interview study exploring drivers and influences on knowledge-sharing in hospitals, interviewees were unfamiliar with the meaning of *tacit knowledge* and how it differed from information or knowledge in general (Zipperer and Tokarski 2014). Assessing the use of EI&K in support of organizational learning is hampered by unfamiliarity with knowledge management-related concepts that differ for healthcare workers at sharp and blunt ends (Zipperer, unpublished data). This confusion is confounded by the incorrect use of knowledge and its variants (see Table 2.1) to market the robustness of care delivery, educational materials and websites.

Some common variably and interchangeably-used terms in EI&K and patient safety are listed in Table 2.1. These are representative of problematic terms; and are not an exhaustive listing for all that is murky.

Table 2.1   Collections of Murky Terms

Focus on Patient Safety
Just culture, safety culture, blame free, accountable, preventable harm.
Anonymous reporting, confidential reporting, voluntary versus mandatory reporting.
Human error, human factors, normal human performance, performance improvement.
Error, mistake, slip, failure, unintentional, inadvertent.
Close call, near miss, good catch.
Malpractice, risk management, enterprise risk management, over- or under-utilization, criminal activity, professionalism, peer review.
High reliability, reliable system, redundant safety design.
Sentinel event, adverse event, adverse reaction, never event, iatrogenesis.
Medication error, adverse drug event, adverse drug reaction, preventable adverse drug event, overdose, drug related problem, adverse effects, drug related morbidity (Pinto-Mármol et al. 2012).
Focus on Evidence/Information/Knowledge
Evidence: data, studies, research, best practice.
Information: communication, news media, television articles, reports, books, education, training.
Knowledge: explicit, implicit, tacit.
Wiki, blog, community of practice, community of interest, listserv; social media.
Learning, training, teaching, education.
Knowledge management, knowledge transfer, knowledge synthesis, knowledge translation, intellectual capital.
Electronic medical record, electronic health record, health information technology, personal health record, computerized physician order entry, computerize practitioner order entry, decision support, medication administration record, protected health information, reporting system, incident reporting system.
Classification, taxonomy, ontology, vocabulary (Bauder 2012), key words, subject headings.
Systems thinking, systems approach, system, systematic, systemic.

ONE MURKY EXAMPLE: PREVENTABLE VERSUS NON-PREVENTABLE HARM

> *[…] as a person with a lot of experience in human factors, cause analysis and behavioral engineering, my vote for the #1 confusing concept [in patient safety terminology] is what you should consider preventable versus non-preventable. To me, it's more about the depth to which you are willing and ready to redesign your system—and the typical healthcare leader seems more willing to abandon ship than really re-engineer. That mentality is a large part of the reason high reliability has taken so long to take hold in healthcare, in my opinion (Butler 2012).*

When the patient safety movement was driven by passionate believers in the "cult" era (see Chapter 1) and gathering momentum, experts and advocates resisted considering certain preventable problems as remedial or reducible, and instead accepted them as inevitable. There was an expected rate of dire outcomes as a result of the disease process, or as a side effect of treatment, or as a consequence of being hospitalized. Healthcare organizations might observe trends and aim to keep rates for below the established, expected range of dire outcomes, without aiming to prevent them altogether.

The use of the term *preventable* has varied over time. Nabahn and colleagues found a lack of valid and reliable definitions of the word in a systematic review of the evidence of its use over a decade (Nabahn et al. 2012). There is a new standard in North American hospitals that may help rectify this problem (Joint Commission 2011). Agreement is necessary so that adverse outcomes are seen as preventable, allowing collaborative work towards prevention of inadvertent harm.

An example of the expansion of meaning for *preventable* harm is found in psychiatry. Experienced clinicians expect that a certain percentage of patients with mental illness who want to end their lives will find a way to successfully do so. A decade ago, recommendations to consider outpatient and attempted suicides within a patient safety framework were met with resistance because suicide among depressed patients was labeled as a non-preventable, not unexpected outcome. However, Watts et al. have found that reduced wait times and effective, reliable treatment can reduce both suicide attempts and completed suicides – therefore making them preventable with use of proven patient safety strategies (Watts et al. 2012). As Wagner and colleagues (2011) sum up: "What was once thought to be an inevitable occurrence turns out to be completely preventable when the institutional culture is such that it expects solutions to patient safety problems and works tirelessly to make them a reality" (Wagner et al. 2011: e17).

The Contribution of Context to Murkiness

> *Who's on first. What's on second. I Don't Know is on third (Abbott and Costello, Baseball Almanac).*

Groups of professionals convey meaning through context, shortcuts, and jargon that is understood by the like-minded individuals who share their domains. This shared understanding also contributes to the group's knowledge being actionable, evidence being effectively applied, and information readily useful.

There is a dark side to specialized vocabularies. The use of jargon and the expertise it displays, keeps outsiders and others from fully understanding what is being discussed. It can keep novices quiet, newcomers confused and lay individuals silent. This situation can make those external to the silo loath to ask for clarification or explanation – for fear of creating an impression of professional disqualification, lack of knowledge or inferiority. The inability to request clarification contributes to misunderstanding.

The misunderstanding and unclarity of term and concepts can be exacerbated by the multidisciplinary nature of patient safety work. Care must be taken to navigate silos and other organizational boundaries that share EI&K in support of both patient safety and knowledge-sharing work. The multidisciplinary cohorts involved in patient safety can be:

- Intraprofessional (physician to physician across specialties).

- Interdisciplinary (physician to nurse or pharmacist).

- Sharp end (frontline workers).

- Blunt end (organizational administrators and executive staff).

- Blunt-blunt end (regulators, membership organizations and assessors) (Wu and Zipperer 2014).

- Professional/patient and family.

As already discussed, term usage varies across disciplines. Common terms and meaning that transcend silos must be developed in multidisciplinary fields like patient safety in order for the fields to be successful. Fields of study committed to improving patient safety must establish agreed-upon meanings of core terms such as those noted in Table 2.1.

Given the variety of professionals required to use EI&K in safety work, agreement on terminology is a significant issue. But it must be tackled, because a lack of clarity around terms can negatively impact the ability to:

- Measure: lack of alignment as to how metrics are defined can constrain effective measures to a level less than useful to both the organization and to the broader work of safety improvement through EI&K.

- Achieve consensus around efforts.

- Develop a shared mental model around concepts.

- Communicate reliably across silos.

- Translate the theoretical to apply EI&K effectively to the work of patient safety improvement.

- Reduce complexity of effort and simplify work.

- Communicate consistently within units and teams.

Sensitivity: Required for Definitional Clarity

"To listen well, you should get into the other person's movie." There is an admonition that to listen well, you should get into the other person's movie (Shafir 2003). Definitional disconnects and conceptual misperceptions that add to confusion need to be addressed at both the organizational and unit level. To do that, individuals and organizations must be aware that the variety of perspectives they interface with can affect understanding.

For example, Table 2.3 focuses on individual players in the risk management *silo*. It illustrates how the context of a role can contribute to misalignments around the activities and can influence word use and understanding.

It is recognized that in large healthcare systems, enterprise-wide risk management may be more likely to incorporate anticipatory problem-solving. At that level an eagerness to promote disclosure and fairness may support a robust EI&K strategy to reinforce patient safety efforts, as EI&K sharing principles align with transparency and organizational learning concepts rather than those that advocate concealing information to protect the institution (Zipperer and Amori 2011).

Table 2.2   Risk Management/Patient Safety (Adapted from Youngberg 2011: 9)

Focus – Organizational tactics Context: To fix problems	Focus – Culture of the organization Context: To drive change
Seeks to identify weakness associated with an individual case.	Seeks to identify systems failures.
Investigates events after the fact.	Identifies potential for error to proactively reduce harm.
Implements tactics to address the event rather than the system failures.	Respects human factors and their relationship to failures in the system.
Builds on the legal standard of care.	Builds work on identified systems themes and patterns.
Drives process of managing risk through response to unexpected outcomes.	Focuses efforts on good catches and "accident waiting to happen."
Uses stories as cautionary tales.	Embraces stories to provide context and deeper understanding.
Reactive.	Proactive.
Sequesters and protects evidence and information and knowledge.	Shares evidence and information and knowledge. to support transparency and learn from failure.
Evidence = data and numbers rule.	Evidence = stories and experience motivate.

TACTICS FOR IMPROVEMENT: TWO EXAMPLES

The difficulty in addressing the variance in terminology can be overcome by a concerted strategic interest in doing so. Two tactics, the employment of boundary spanners and consensus efforts are submitted as possible strategies for organizations seeking to address the problem of misaligned understanding due to murky vocabularies.

Boundary spanners can affect the use of EI&K and promote consistent term use and understanding. In the absence of shared language/cognition, a boundary spanner can interpret meaning until shared mental models are achieved. Boundary spanners are individuals that connect an informal network with other parts of the company or with similar networks in other organizations to nurture relationships, share information and knowledge and navigate silos (Cross and Prusak 2002). Evidence, information and knowledge use can empower individuals to span boundaries, translate terms and facilitate collaboration between various areas that have been siloed.

Dissolving silos entirely may not be possible. However, EI&K sharing may allow valuable characteristics of silos to continue (for example, development of expertise and specialized experience) while overcoming language and culture barriers to facilitate cooperative and collaborative work. Recognizing the impact of internal/external politics, stress, hierarchy, competition for funding and other organizational pressures can aid in the use of EI&K to overcome silos (MacIntosh-Murray and Choo 2005).

EI&K definitions developed through consensus efforts at the organizational level can be the result of boundary spanners and leadership committed to improving clarity of terminology through strategic improvement and awareness efforts. A variety of experts in information services, knowledge management, corporate communications, leadership, media and publishing are needed. They should hail from such diverse fields as high reliability, safety engineering, system redesign, librarianship and quality improvement in addition to medical, healthcare and business practitioners. Grasping the nuances between key terms from these distinct sets of specialists is required in order for the resulting understandings to contribute to the coalescence of patient safety efforts and mindsets. A facilitated conversation to raise red flags as to misunderstandings would be a helpful short term deliverable from such a multidisciplinary group.

Reducing Ambiguity is Complex Work

Data that articulates the collective potential of EI&K to enhance organizational learning and drive safety is nascent and bogged down by the same conceptual murkiness. There is no one overarching definition of the individual elements "evidence," "information" and "knowledge." The clarity of each element will improve understanding and awareness of EI&K failure; reporting of EI&K failure and understanding of the role of EI&K failure as a latent factor affecting safe care (see Chapters 3 and 14 for a discussion of an EI&K failure). In turn, a deeper understanding for the potential for failure will enable clearer articulation of EI&K's tangible support for innovation around patient safety. EI&K solutions can then be sustained and disseminated effectively.

Shared mental models are needed to reduce this murkiness and sustain cross-silo understanding of the conversation as teams, players and organizations work toward improving patient safety through EI&K initiatives. Mental models are framed by personal history and can slow or enhance progress. Differences in mental models can explain how two people can see the same thing in very different ways that are real to them (Senge 1990; Reason 1990).The examples of mental models in this chapter illustrate how murky terminology can derail progress in patient safety EI&K work. The lack of a shared understanding persists due to an unconfirmed definition of what both patient safety and EI&K mean in the context of the care environment. Consistent terminology is needed to engage actors at both the sharp and blunt end to drive improvement. Varying contexts also play a role in both misunderstandings and clarity. A lack of recognition of the importance of context will limit organizational and individual learning (Croskerry 2009).

The healthcare teamwork-focus as it is currently applied in healthcare is an opportunity to remedy this terminology disconnect. An openness to draw from broader experience can enable improved conceptual access to EI&K and can serve as an organizational learning strategy to enable patient safety improvement. A team approach supports dialog that will drive innovative application of EI&K. Patients will ultimately be safer when stakeholders are no longer talking at cross purposes and stumbling on misunderstandings that affect their use of evidence, information and knowledge.

KEY TAKE-AWAYS

- The language associated with describing and discussing both patient safety and evidence, information and knowledge improvements are in a state of flux.
- When applying the work of EI&K improvements to patient safety work, increased opportunities for confusion exist.
- To generate lasting commitment to the work of either area, care must be taken not to assume commonalities in understanding of concepts across professional and disciplinary lines.

Suggested Reading

Cooper, I.D. 2011. Is the informationist a new role? A logic model analysis. *Journal of the Medical Library Association*, 99(3), 189–92.

Kothari, A., Hovanec, N., Hastie, R. and Sibbald, S. 2011. Lessons from the business sector for successful knowledge management in health care: A systematic review. *Biomed Central, BMC Health Services Research*, 11(2), 173. Available at: http://www.biomedcentral.com/1472-6963/11/173 [accessed: 6 April 2013].

Weller, J., Boyd, M. and Cumin, D. 2014. Teams, tribes and patient safety: Overcoming barriers to effective teamwork in healthcare. *Postgraduate Medical Journal*, January 7 [Epub ahead of print].

Woods, D.D. and Cook, R.I. 2013. Mistaking error, in *Patient Safety Handbook*, edited by B.J. Youngberg. 2nd edition. Sudbury, MA: Jones & Bartlett Learning.

3

Potential for Harm Due to Failures in the EI&K Process

Catherine K. Craven, Barbara Jones and Lorri Zipperer

> *The questions are complex and no solution is perfect, and so the status quo drags on (Wachter and Shojania 2004: 346).*

A Loss, A Lesson, A Call to Think and Interact Differently

In the summer of 2001, a healthy 24-year-old clinical trial volunteer, Ellen Roche, died as a result of her participation as a subject in a clinical trial at Johns Hopkins University (Ramsey 2001; Kennedy 2001; Kolata 2001). Roche was an employee at Hopkins, a technician in the Allergy and Asthma Center, and her willingness to participate in clinical trials, as she had done a number of times, illustrated her, and thousands of others', confidence in the institution. This confidence is widely recognized. The Johns Hopkins School of Medicine is consistently ranked in the top five medical schools in the United States, often ranked only behind Harvard; Johns Hopkins Hospital has been voted the number one hospital in the United States for 21 years in a row (US News and World Report 2011). Johns Hopkins is a recipient of substantial research funding from the US National Institutes of Health (NIH RePORT 2013).[1] Until this incident occurred, no healthy volunteer had ever died in a clinical trial at Hopkins (Keiger and De Pasquale 2002; Steinbrook 2002).

Roche's death triggered an investigation into the Institutional Review Board (IRB) and research practices at Hopkins. Internal and external review

---

committees for the university, the US Food and Drug Administration (FDA) and the Office for Human Research Protections participated. The investigation findings and surrounding discussion uncovered multiple points in the IRB process, and the research process itself, where evidence, information and knowledge transfer had failed with tragic results. Roche's death illustrates the potential for failure and harm that can result from what might be considered a rarely surfaced evidence-identification failure. Although reforms were put into place at Hopkins, questions remain regarding critical junctures in the research process at all institutions in which organizationally accepted but unreliable information and evidence-identification practices may still put clinical trial participants, and more broadly, patients at risk.

Details of the Roche incident and the analysis of the event were shared with the interested public in a transparent manner (Becker et al. 2001). A brief summary of the trajectory of the failure is recapped below. Roche was participating in an asthma research study to "explore how the tubes that carry air into the lungs can stay open when irritants are inhaled" (Keiger and De Pasquale 2002: 1). Volunteers inhaled a chemical called hexamethonium, which was used in the 1950s and 1960s for treating high blood pressure (Savulescu and Spriggs 2001), but the FDA removed it from the market in 1972 because it was ineffective (Steinbrook 2002). The hypothesis was that in normal functioning lungs, a neural mechanism protects airways from obstruction, and that in people with asthma this mechanism is impaired or missing.

On April 23, 2001, the first study subject inhaled hexamethonium. Subject 1 experienced mild shortness of breath and a dry cough that resolved eight days later on May 3. Subject 2 inhaled the agent during that same period and did not report any symptoms. On May 4, Roche inhaled the agent. The next day, she developed a dry cough. On May 9, Roche was hospitalized at Hopkins' Bayview Medical Center with a fever, low blood oxygen, and abnormalities on a chest film. The IRB was notified of the adverse events in Subject 1 and Roche, and the study was halted. On May 12, Roche was transferred to the intensive care unit with progressive shortness of breath. On June 2, Roche died of progressive low blood pressure and multiple organ failure (Keiger and De Pasquale 2002; Steinbrook 2002).

IMMEDIATE RESPONSE TO FAILURE

The clinical impacts of the decision not to seek further information have not been rigorously evaluated, though it is reasonable to assume

that such impacts do occur (Committee on Identifying and Preventing
Medication Errors 2007: 229–30).

Johns Hopkins temporarily suspended all studies involving healthy volunteers while an internal review committee examined the issues involved. On June 28, 2001, the FDA identified problems in the study protocol. On July 16, an internal review committee at Johns Hopkins submitted a report on Roche's death. From July 16–18, the Office for Human Research Protections (OHRP) conducted an onsite review of the case and the IRB system, and found a "widespread lack of compliance with federal regulations" (Steinbrook 2002: 219). As a result, the OHRP suspended all federally funded projects at Hopkins and its Multiple Project Assurance, the federal agreement under which the research is conducted. Johns Hopkins submitted a corrective plan on July 21.

The following day, OHRP lifted the suspension, reinstated the Multiple Project Agreement, and accepted the corrective plan, "subject to significant restrictions, conditions and monitoring" (Steinbrook 2002: 719). An external review committee reported back with its findings on August 8, 2001. On October 3, the OHRP cited additional concerns following a progress report submitted by Johns Hopkins. Johns Hopkins responded to those concerns on December 12. As a result of the investigation, university officials agreed to many changes in IRB procedures, including "more resources; new procedures; more training for investigators and for IRB members, chairs and staff; and the appointment of a vice dean for clinical investigation to oversee the process" (Steinbrook 2002: 719). In addition, Johns Hopkins agreed to re-review approximately 2,600 protocols, which was completed as of January 2002 (Steinbrook 2002).

FURTHER EXPLORATION OF FAILURE

Whether rare events are costly or beneficial, looking back we are often
surprised at the failure of organizations to draw appropriate lessons
(Lampel, Shamsie and Shapira 2009: 835).

Although the Hopkins internal review committee found the study to have a scientifically sound basis, it criticized the principal investigator (PI) for not reporting Subject 1's symptoms immediately, and for going ahead and giving the agent to Subject 2 while Subject 1 was experiencing symptoms. The internal review committee, and FDA reviewers in particular, were critical of the program for not submitting a new drug application for the use of the agent to the FDA, which "might have led to a more intensive review of hexamethonium, as well as the discovery of more information about its potential toxicity"

(Steinbrook 2002: 718). The harshest criticism of the OHRP review team was the conclusion that the two medical school IRBs did not "provide proper review of new protocols or 'substantive and meaningful review' of ongoing projects" (Steinbrook 2002: 719).

An external team hired by Johns Hopkins gathered additional insights on what went wrong. The team found that the consent form was misleading about the safety of the agent involved. Disapproval of the IRB protocol review process

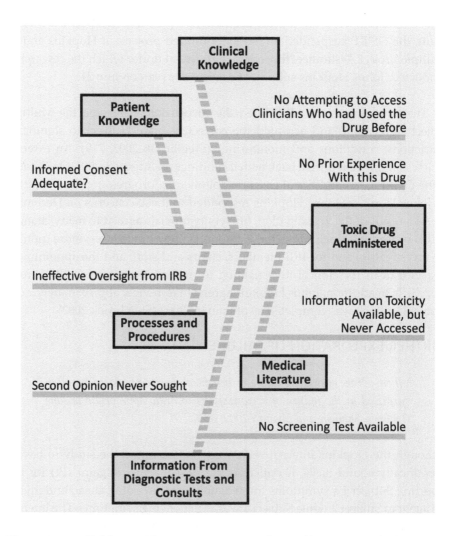

Figure 3.1   **Fishbone Diagram Deconstructing Failures Potentially Contributing to the Roche Incident**

Note: Original by Mark Graber (2012).

was made explicit; it was called "grossly inadequate ... not conform[ing] to current standards," and noted that "Until June 2001 there had been only one IRB committee, meeting once every two weeks...responsible for the review of 800 new proposals and the annual reviews resulting from them" (Steinbrook 2002: 719). In addition, and especially noteworthy for this text, the project PI was criticized for not conducting a more comprehensive literature search for previously published articles on hexamethonium and pulmonary toxicity. An evidence discovery failure had occurred.

The Roche case offers a rich opportunity to learn from a critical incident. This incident provides a well-documented failure with specific changes enacted to improve the reliability and validity of a clinical trial program. In addition, the EI&K failures inherent in several aspects of this incident are available for deconstruction toward the goal of learning from tragic human error and systemic incidents (see Figure 3.1 for one example and Chapter 14 for a more in-depth discussion). This analysis can inform others of the historical processes that still may be present in other institutions (March, Sproull and Tamuz 2003).

System Approaches to Minimizing Reoccurrence of Similar Failures

Finding a solution to ensure that only the highest quality literature searches would be conducted moving forward, however, was only partially addressed at the time of the investigation. The internal review report stated that "in good faith" the investigator had "performed a standard PubMed® search for potential hexamethonium-related pulmonary toxicity and consulted other standard, current edition textbook sources" (Perkins 2001: 3). None of the sources searched, including the free (non-subscription) Internet-based resources the PI reviewed, led to results indicating that toxicity (Perkins 2001). The external review said that the PI's search had been "reasonable and consistent with most institutions' standards" (Keiger and De Pasquale 2002: 10). Perhaps this was consistent with the skills of non-expert, non-medical librarian searchers, but medical librarians from around the country demonstrated that expertise applied to this work could have determined a different course (Perkins 2001).

Medical librarians searching for the same information were able to identify relevant citations that would have signaled potential problems with hexamethonium and drug toxicity; in fact, several citations showed the dangers of hexamethonium

"The notion of a literature review serving to fill a hole in the Swiss Cheese – a stop function to mitigate overuse and misdiagnosis – is hardly documented or talked about."

as being noted in the literature as far back as the 1950s (Perkins 2001). These citations were found in online resources that medical librarians consider standard and widely available; medical librarians – particularly those in research and academic settings at the time – used these resources regularly as a standard part of their practice.

In addition to tool identification, the librarians knew how to search MEDLINE®, the US government electronic biomedical literature citation database, to access older citations from before 1960, something not readily apparent to end-users. At the time of the Roche incident, the Internet-based PubMed® version of the MEDLINE® database only went back through 1966, although even that took "a double-search of a divided database" (Perkins 2002: 2). Librarians, however, knew that some of the other available versions of MEDLINE®, allowed access to older citations back through the late 1950s. Thus, librarians knew that multiple, separate searches would have been necessary to thoroughly cover all possible MEDLINE® records. In addition, librarians knew that they should also search the historical paper-based medical literature citation index, *Index Medicus*, which includes literature that predates what is included in the MEDLINE® database. *Index Medicus* goes back to pre-1900; using it would have been another avenue to older, relevant articles needed to address the gap, filling the hole in the "Swiss Cheese" (Perkins 2002: 2).

At Johns Hopkins, in the wake of Ellen Roche's death, it was stated "The university is strengthening and standardizing its procedures for literature reviews …" (Steinbrook 2002: 720). At the time of writing there is no literature supporting the strengthening and standardization of literature review processes that has been accepted as a patient safety requirement. However, the knowledge and expertise of librarians has begun to be recommended for incorporation into IRB and systematic review procedures (Committee on Standards for Systematic Reviews of Comparative Effectiveness Research, Board on Health Care Services 2011).

In the short term, the applied system-level fixes to make the process more reliable included:

- creation of a new School of Medicine Vice Dean position specifically for clinical research;

- formation of four additional IRB boards to deal with study oversight and review;

- retention of an external IRB to evaluate selected studies;

- introduction of an electronic IRB system to coordinate and streamline the review process; and

- enhancement of funding for IRB activities and staffing (Steinbrook 2002: 219–20).

The other important steps that have been taken at Johns Hopkins are longer-term service model and cultural shifts. Library leadership began to develop ideas for taking searching expertise to where it is needed most, that is, where clinicians, researchers, staff and students work: in the hospital and research offices (Oliver and Roderer 2006). The idea of the informationist (Davidoff and Florance 2000) was already percolating and beginning to gain traction at other institutions (Florance, Giuse and Ketchell 2002). Yet evidence that this shift was seen as a patient safety strategy is basically absent from the arguments justifying its value. The notion of a literature review serving to fill a hole in the Swiss Cheese – a stop function to mitigate overuse and misdiagnosis – is hardly documented or talked about.

Evidence and Expertise at the Sharp End: A Need for a Safety Context for the Work

> *Health care clinicians successfully apply proven medical evidence in common acute, chronic, or preventive care processes less than 80 percent of the time (Resar 2006: 1677).*

To push the bar for patient safety higher, the field of medical librarianship must advocate for an expanded role in healthcare institutions (Zipperer 2004). For example, the informationist can be shaped as a contributor to safety in the systems context of EI&K improvement and reliability. Librarians are becoming integrated as part of the care and research teams at their institutions. Yet, such changes have yet to result in increased engagement of, and study by, the medical librarian and informationist professions in failure analysis work to uncover poor, incomplete, biased, and misguided EI&K processes, protocols, and frontline use (Zipperer and Sykes 2009) from a system perspective as a contributor to failure. Clinicians and safety teams should see the integration of librarians and information professionals as a tactic akin to teamwork improvement and checklists.

As a broader medical librarian construct expands to embrace the informationist concept (Cooper 2011), a primary question to consider will be what level of informationist staffing is the optimum for safe searching? Not every clinician or administrator will need searching assistance at the same time. Many have jobs in which they will never need it. However, one can compare the number of *informationists* at an institution with the number of research protocols that go before its IRB. Then, carry those sorts of numbers across every academic biomedical institution and large academic or community hospital in the country, and it will become apparent that enhanced searching in a safe, reliable fashion, like IRB oversight safety, will not be free. The ultimate question is how many lives is that enhanced safety worth?

INFOBOX 3.1: A DEARTH OF EXPERTISE – A SAFETY ISSUE?

The Johns Hopkins Welch Medical Library, has ten informationists, three of whom have supervisory duties, and for the rest about 20 percent of their time is spent on internal library operations duties. There are more than 80 major departments and units in the Johns Hopkins Medicine organization, comprising around 30,000 people and producing 2,600 IRB protocols (Personal communication, Craven 2012).

Extrapolate that out to the number of hospitals and research teams doing human-subjects study and then beyond going to the daily care that requires expert searching and there is a dearth of expertise in this regard.

Could this then be presented as a patient safety issue?

The reality on the ground, however, is that since the mid-1990s, librarians have worked hard to purchase and push out to their users the ever-increasing number of electronic resources that publishers have been producing. Although this has allowed greatly enhanced, 24/7 access for end-users to full-text electronic access to information and evidence, this end-user based approach has minimized the opportunity for the librarians' search expertise to mitigate error in evidence identification. As end-user searching increased and began to take place during daily work contexts not associated with the library, end-users became increasingly distanced from the experts still needed to effectively search many of those resources – their medical librarians. Could this lack of access to experts and end-user use of point-of-care or free tools result in normalization of access to materials that provide answers that are "good enough" rather than the best resources that are highly reliable?

Also, with the increasing development and sophistication of the Internet, healthcare professionals increasingly engaged in online information and evidence-seeking practices that include using websites, not all of which would be considered refereed (Bennett et al. 2004). This, too, could represent a normalized deviance from expert practices (Banja 2010). Barriers to finding needed information continue to include "too much information, lack of specific information, and navigation or searching difficulties" (Bennett et al. 2004: 31), which "indicates that searching skills are not often adequate to answer important clinical questions" (Bennett et al. 2004: 37). Some physicians have acknowledged a discomfort in their own level of searching expertise (Bennet et al. 2004, 2005; Younger 2010).

A potentially dangerous state of affairs has arisen wherein end-users have started to overestimate the ease of searching – their own expertise – and the quality and completeness of the information they are able to find by themselves. Library budgets, too, are increasingly going toward electronic resources and away from funding to hire librarians as full time staff members (Kronenfeld 2005; AAAHL 2013). For example at academic health sciences libraries, "the proportion of total library expenditures allocated to personnel salaries decreased between 1978 and 2001, while relatively more was allocated to collections, and funding for professional librarian staff remained flat although salaries in constant dollars for such had decreased by 12 percent" (Bryd and Shedlock 2003: 189).

EI&K seeking and sharing behaviors need to change to ensure safety. Given the ease of access to electronic materials and search tools, it is appropriate that all staff become accountable for assuring that their searches are appropriate, complete, and thus safe, to inform decision-making and the application of information and evidence to care actions (Tomlin 2008). Similar to the recognition of the washing of hands as a routine and important safety mechanism, the need to be accountable and accurate as to when and how the evidence base is accessed must be required to engender reliability in its effective and safe use.

Like other safety issues, effective literature searching skills should be integrated in how care happens as an important element of safety. Leadership and management can partner with librarians and other information professionals to identify flaws in the evidence and information identification process whether at the sharp or blunt end (Zipperer 2004). Poor or incomplete work in this area with error and biases unchecked can be catastrophic (Tomlin

2008). In addition, practitioners – expert searchers as well as lay searchers – should recognize the importance of the application of reliability principles to this portion of the care and decision-making process.

A Real Gap, with Real Consequence for Safety

Some might say the Roche incident is not relevant to patient safety and instead is more about research ethics, volunteer selection, and blunt end problems. Evidence from other complex industries and settings such as nuclear power and aircraft carriers, begs the question as to why the Roche story has not engaged the variety of disciplines involved as a call to rethink evidence access and use and its implications for failure and patient harm. The opportunity for learning from the Roche incident has not been embraced by safety leadership to improve practice and design in the robustness required to make EI&K a strong factor in achieving patient safety.

At the time of the Roche incident, medical librarians voiced concern over its impact on the role of access to evidence in the clinical environment, yet there is a lack of documented concern that it went far beyond the profession. However some awareness is percolating from the diagnostic error and learning communities (Graber et al. 2012; Dhaliwal 2013) as is evidenced by the following quote.

> *Medical librarians are far more adept at navigating the entire canon of medical knowledge than are physicians, but their skills have not been leveraged for POCL (Point of Care Learning). While a librarian on staff in every office or on every medical team may be fanciful, a remote librarian service is not. In one study, a just-in-time information consultation service was shown to deliver useful answers in less than 15 minutes to clinicians' real-world questions submitted via smartphone (McGowan et al. 2008). Health care systems should consider investing in informaticians who search the medical literature, patient records, and the system's own 'big data' to provide answers to clinicians' real-time inquiries (Dhaliwal 2013: 1960).*

There has been – at the time of writing – no call for research papers or grants to enable study on the information and evidence research access piece of the safety continuum as defined for this text. This gap could be the result of a lack of understanding about failures, a lack of leveraging the expertise base involved, or the normalizing and latency of the problems. Research and activism can help bring an awareness of the potential for EI&K failure front and center. As with many safety incidents there were multiple small missteps that contributed to the loss of Ellen Roche. The evidence gap revealed, and the lack of object learning this case has presented thus far to the safety community, represents a systems failure (Zipperer 2004).

"The opportunity for learning from the Roche incident has not been embraced by safety leadership to improve practice and design in the robustness required to make EI&K a strong factor in achieving patient safety."

KEY TAKE-AWAYS

- Incomplete and erroneous literature review processes have the potential to contribute to both system failure and patient harm.
- Healthcare should utilize the Ellen Roche incident as an opportunity to learn more about making published evidence and information access methods highly reliable.
- Medical librarians and informationists are likely experts to assist in reducing EI&K failures while designing future opportunities to drive change and EI&K process improvement.
- Healthcare should consider the acceptance of using only EI&K resources on hand or through inexpert access and searching of resources as potentially normalized behavior that could reduce the safety of healthcare.

Suggested Reading

Banja, J. 2010. The normalization of deviance in healthcare delivery. *Business Horizons*, 53(2),139–48.

Davidoff, F. and Florance, V. 2000. The informationist: A new health profession? *Annals of Internal Medicine*, 132(12), 996–8.

March, J.G., Sproull, L.S. and Tamuz, M. 2003. Learning from samples of one or fewer. *Quality & Safety in Health Care*, 12(6), 465–71 (discussion 471–2). [Reprint of a 1991 paper that appeared in *Organization Science*, (2), 1–13].

Perkins, E. 2001. Johns Hopkins' tragedy: Could librarians have prevented a death? *Information Today, Inc.*, August 7 Available at: http://newsbreaks.infotoday.com/nbreader.asp?ArticleID=17534 [accessed: 15 March 2013].

PART 2

The Role of Evidence, Information and Knowledge

Chapter 4 Synopsis – Information and Evidence Failures in Daily Work: How They Can Affect the Safety of Care

This chapter discusses the prospect of failure and unintended negative consequences in healthcare evidence and information use and how it might affect the individual practitioner, patient and their families at the sharp end as a primary concern. The authors place the discussion in the context of healthcare information technologies and intensive care unit rounds. They share recommendations to address gaps in evidence, information and knowledge (EI&K) junctures as seen in the context of direct care delivery.

Chapter 5 Synopsis – Leadership, EI&K and a Culture of Safety

This chapter introduces organisational cultural concepts which healthcare leadership should consider in order to best use evidence, information and knowledge to drive safety-supportive behaviors, such as transparency, error/ incident reporting, communication, teamwork and learning. Challenges in implementing EI&K efforts are mapped to these concepts to underscore the role of administrative leaders and champions in resourcing EI&K programs and patterning EI&K behaviors.

Chapter 6 Synopsis – Weakness in the Evidence Base: Latent Problems to Consider and Solutions for Improvement

This chapter explores latent conditions that minimize the effectiveness and reliability of the information, evidence and knowledge gathering process in healthcare and the tools supporting it. The authors reveal gaps in the evidence base itself, weakness in the primary research publication and dissemination processes, and problems with research tools from a systems perspective. Some solutions will be proposed to aid those seeking evidence in the patient safety field.

4

Information and Evidence Failures in Daily Work: How They Can Affect the Safety of Care

Catherine K. Craven, Ross Koppel and Mark G. Weiner

> *For better or worse, error is already our lifelong companion. Surely then, it's time we got to know it (Kathryn Schultz 2010: 17).*

Errors and Gaps

To achieve the safest possible healthcare for patients, one must look at all processes that affect patients, at macro and micro levels, to find the critical gaps or junctures that allow, if not ensure, that errors will occur. Humans make errors of all sorts – of omission, commission, and more insidiously, errors that aren't even recognized. So many errors are unknown because practices or systems, although standard and part of the culture within the organization, profession, industry, or unit, are not optimized for safety. Each individual in healthcare must examine his or her own practices to try to "re-see" those processes and to identify what changes can be made to close evidence, information and knowledge (EI&K) transfer gaps. EI&K strategies to improve communication, between computer systems and humans, and to make use of the best resources possible could help prevent errors and patient harm. In this chapter, common occurrences of EI&K transfer gaps identified in the literature and from the authors' research and professional experiences illustrate this point.

Scenarios involving an intensive care unit (ICU) in a teaching hospital, open the chapter to identify potential EI&K failure opportunities, referred to as "junctures." The specifics of those junctures are discussed, the issues then further delineated, and potential solutions are provided. Although set in a teaching hospital ICU, these scenarios illustrate the pervasive opportunity for EI&K failures in the process of healthcare delivery in a variety of hospital settings.

Unintended Consequences, Trust and Health Information Technology

The following sharp-end example, adapted from a case report for the Agency for Healthcare Research and Quality (AHRQ), illustrates serious unintended consequences caused by health information technology (HIT), demonstrating that the speed and convenience of electronic systems linked to the transfer clinical information does not guarantee their accuracy (Koppel 2009).

A 47-year-old man with AIDS was admitted to an ICU in an academic medical center. His major complaint was shortness of breath. He was diagnosed with pneumonia and started on antibiotic therapy. In addition to his respiratory difficulties, the patient had multiple flat purple skin lesions on his thighs and several perianal lesions. Given his advanced AIDS, the medical team was concerned about Kaposi's sarcoma and human papillomavirus (HPV) infection. Biopsies were performed on thigh and perianal lesions. The patient continued to receive antibiotics over the course of a few days for the pneumonia and was slowly improving. A few days later, the physician, an intern, reviewing the results of the biopsies on the patient's electronic health record (EHR) learned that the thigh lesion was Kaposi's sarcoma, and the perianal biopsy showed squamous cell carcinoma *in situ*. The physician found a third biopsy report in the electronic record, labelled "right neck" and reported as "basal cell carcinoma." The intern didn't recall any neck lesions, but she questioned her memory, as it had been a busy call night when she conducted the biopsies. She made a note of the results and went to see other patients (Koppel 2009).

The patient's primary care doctor was not providing direct care in the hospital, but during a hospital visit, reviewed the medical record before visiting the patient. He noted the pneumonia diagnosis, a low white blood cell (CD4) count, and biopsies of three separate cancers. Given the patient's AIDS and new diagnoses, the primary care doctor recommended hospice care. He told the patient that with "cancer in three places," he would probably die soon.

However, the hospital's medical team – especially the intern – wondered about that neck biopsy, which had not been ordered by the team. Upon investigation, it emerged that the neck biopsy had been performed on another patient and accidentally entered into this patient's medical record. The team and the primary care doctor all met with the patient to disclose the mistake, but clearly the error had caused the patient tremendous pain and mental anguish.

During the investigation, it became clear that the dermatopathology department was unaware of the error. A standalone program to track and report biopsy results was in use that electronically "dumped" the results into the hospital's EHR system, but the dermatopathology department's physicians and staff did not have access to that system. In fact, when called and asked if they had seen the error in "X" (the name of the EHR), the pathologist responded, "What is 'X'?" Eventually, it was determined that the third biopsy result was from a different patient, but it had been entered into the pathology software under the wrong patient identifier and then uploaded into the hospital's EHR.

Clearly the information transfer between departments failed. Did the failure have anything to do with EHRs? Yes, to a minor extent. However, the EHR had not failed *per se*. It was the process that failed. The situation illustrates the following points:

- The risks associated with weak linkages *between* computer systems. Sending data across computer systems is often a perilous journey, with possible distortions and uncertain arrivals. These types of errors are difficult to track, and rarely is there an alert for information either *not* received or information that is received but inaccurate.

- Insufficient safeguards against patient misidentification introduce weaknesses. For example, the other patient in this example might have suffered because his or her lab results were sent to the wrong patient. No technical fix can eliminate the need for careful name and patient identification. The United States Congress prohibits creation of a unique medical ID; it even prohibits discussion of the creation of a unique ID by any federal or federally funded entity (Collins and Peel 2012). As the use of EHRs and interoperability grows, identity errors will increase, causing more avoidable errors and death. There is no simple solution for this dilemma.

- Privacy advocates offer excellent arguments about the dangers of a unique medical or patient identifier (sometimes known as an UPI). Given the number of data breaches, stolen access codes, and so on, we are reminded weekly of those concerns. On the other hand, UPI errors kill, injure and cost billions of dollars. A reasonable solution must be sought.

- Data displayed in electronic records appears neat and tidy, lending veracity to the information whether it is accurate or not, in terms of patient identification or other factors. For example, data displayed in the chart rarely include additional identifying information such as room number, referring physician, or other illnesses – items that might trigger a viewer's questions. (Note, remember that paper-based records came with many problems, too.)

That the medical team found the error in the AIDS patient's diagnoses is perhaps the most encouraging part of this example. It illustrates the caring and professionalism of dedicated clinicians – despite, or in addition to, the many benefits, efficiencies and promises of electronic health records and other health information technologies.

Global HIT Issues to Consider

Going from the specific to the more general regarding HIT raises other issues that could affect the safety and effectiveness of information sharing and contribute to gaps. For example:

Poor hospital work processes: EHRs must accurately share information with many other computer systems in the hospital, which are often implemented and updated on overlapping schedules. As implementations and updates proceed in parallel, software and work processes change in ways that create barriers to smooth and fail-safe communication. In a complex environment with multiple systems, re-programming or software changes to fix one issue can easily create more problems. Also consider that the average hospital has *several hundred* IT systems. Clinicians are inventive creators of workarounds when faced with system barriers – their need to help patients supersedes healthcare IT protocols (Koppel et al. 2008). Clinicians, for example, will reach into one patient's medication supply to grab a prepared IV bag for another patient in urgent need. While the clinicians undoubtedly feel that they are supporting their patient's needs, this type of "swap" can play havoc with the EHRs and other record-keeping systems, which are often, and increasingly will be, integrated with the hospital's computerized physician/practitioner order entry (CPOE), the pharmacy dispensing system, and the medication barcoding system (Koppel et al. 2008).

Data fragmentation: Unintended consequences in complex systems are the rule, not the exception. There is no map of the myriad hospital and office processes that affect and are affected by EHR use, data input, and data output. Most EHRs undergo massive customization during implementation, involving how information is displayed, order sets, warnings on drug–drug interactions and dosages, permission requirements, and linkages to other hospital IT systems (Harrison, Koppel and Bar-Lev 2007; Koppel et al. 2008; Dixon and Zafar 2009; Koppel and Kreda 2010; Kannry, Kshniruk and Koppel 2011; Koppel and Gordon 2012). With millions of lines of computer code, error possibilities are staggering. Linkages with other new systems escalate error odds further.

Lack of standardization: Another problem with IT systems, but especially within the fragmented healthcare system, involves the absence of standard definitions and processes. For example, there may be more than 32 ways of writing the same patient's name in any one hospital (Craven, Catherine; Catherine Craven; C. Craven; Craven, C.; Catherine K. Craven; C.K. Craven; Craven, C.K.; and so on). To a computer, these are all different names. In addition, long names may be truncated by EHRs, patient record numbers or room numbers may be attached to names as suffixes, and innumerable misspellings and transliterations are commonplace in EHRs and can set up medical mistakes. The variety of identification (ID) numbers for each patient is also disconcerting. Name and identification matching errors are common.

Proprietary interests: In a busy institution, there are many cooks in the software kitchen; a user interface designed to serve one dish becomes a smorgasbord or pot luck. Proprietary vendor interests and code can interfere with rapid response from the vendor or solutions via easy add-ons.

Under-reporting of HIT problems: Reports of problems probably reveal only a miniscule fraction of the actual problems. Clinicians are busy, resourceful, and don't want to take time to report difficulties that may reflect poorly on their own competencies. HIT leaders who are satisfied with few problem reports are too easily satisfied.

Difficult interfaces combined with user training issues: People are poor reporters of their own computer use (Koppel and Gordon 2012; Koppel 2013). One must shadow users and ask them what they are doing and why they are doing it (Koppel and Gordon 2012; Koppel 2013). Often, one discovers people are repeating a workaround handed down from a vestigial computer system or from a different institution's processes. Or, what is ordinarily a simple process is obscured by the vendor or the implementation process in a labyrinth of submenus and hidden instructions.

Although there are no simple or quick fixes to these issues, there are established, sensible methods to improve the odds of preventing, finding and correcting problems. Involvement on hospital information systems teams by those with the education and experience necessary to understand these issues, including health informaticists, is key. Informatics knowledge is required to understand and maintain constant vigilance over the complex interactions among the vendor's software, the institution's implementation, and the institution's personnel along with its culture and information and evidentiary resources.

Critical EI&K Junctures in Rounding: Herding COWs

There is a classic image of a doctor on rounds: a mature male in a white coat, accompanied by a female nurse and young doctors visiting patients in the hospital. The team goes from patient to patient. The verb of that process is called, reasonably enough, "rounding." The current reality of that process, however, is very different from the older image. Many of the changes reflect the increasing complexity of medical care, the number of participants, the amount of information to be coordinated, and technology. But the basic function remains: rounding is about information transfer and also about teaching. An illustration of rounding in a sophisticated ICU in a tertiary care teaching hospital is provided below.

A rounding team is analogous to a herd. The pun is intended because of the number of participants and because most are rolling their COWS (computers on wheels – a very small table on wheels with a laptop) from room to room as the rounding proceeds. Up to 18 clinicians and students participate: the attending doctor (the chief); the nurse for the particular patient under review; a few fellows from various specialties; some third-year residents, some medical students on rotation, a pharmacist, assorted specialists to deal with co-morbidities, and sometimes additional persons. Often, there are also some "groupies," that is, MDs with a few free minutes seeking to add to their knowledge. Those without COWS have papers. Everyone has a cell phone.

By thinking through the process of how rounds take place in an academic medical center, several critical junctures in evidence and information transfer are revealed. These points of interaction are necessary in building individual healthcare professionals' knowledge and providing them the information needed to provide care. When failures occur at these junctures, patient safety is jeopardized.

INFOBOX 4.1: CRITICAL EI&K JUNCTURES DURING ACADEMIC MEDICAL CENTER ROUNDS

- Juncture 1: Presentation of case.
- Juncture 2: Attending Q&A.
- Juncture 3: Unofficial E&I gathering in response to Q&A.
- Juncture 4: Nurse shares data/lab values.
- Juncture 5: MD/Nurse exchange.

CRITICAL EI&K JUNCTURE 1: PRESENTATION OF CASE

The herd arrives in front of a patient's room. A third-year resident or a fellow presents the case. The attending questions the presenter to learn more about the case and to help teach the other physicians. Some of the questions are very specific. For example, although the hospital has a modern integrated CPOE system, three or so unknown and additional medications can emerge in this conversation. Often this is because one drug was substituted for another, sometimes it is a dosage change, and often there are inexplicable changes.

CRITICAL EI&K JUNCTURE 2: ATTENDING Q&A

Some of the attending's questions are clearly didactic, obliging team members to think and to consider new information. In addition to what is transpiring between the attending and presenter in front of the team, much of the real action is within the herd. This is "parallel play" – where each person is doing his/her own thing with occasional interaction. There are many side conversations in a typical day's rounding, and at only one point in the example observed did everyone look at the same screen. Once, a doctor found the patient's chest (lung) x-ray on her COW and displayed it to another by turning around the COW. At the same time, another resident was looking at lab results, and one was using his COW to examine the patient's medication on the CPOE screen. Another was looking at the list of patients in the unit. One doctor, who was about to present the next case, was preparing that presentation. One was looking up an article on the medication that just emerged in conversation between the nurse and the doctors. A few were reading and sending emails, and some were talking on cell phones, calling the patient's cardiologist, the pharmacy, and the radiologist. One was arranging a date for later that evening. Clearly there were large gaps in the sharing of evidence and information in this scenario, and few if any of the herd gained new knowledge.

CRITICAL EI&K JUNCTURE 3: UNOFFICIAL E&I GATHERING IN RESPONSE TO Q&A

During periods of parallel play, situations can be observed in which one of the clinicians discovers information that is useful to all. In once such instance, the information was conveyed to the attending and the team via a call out (a raised hand or interruption), and then in a follow-up step by sending the information to the team via the Internet. However, a special effort had to be made to gain everyone's attention, so information about the evidence could be communicated to all. It was accepted behavior to not necessarily share all information amongst the herd.

CRITICAL EI&K JUNCTURE 4: NURSE SHARES DATA/LAB VALUES

The patient's nurse comes to the rounding group from the patient's room, and the attending commences a series of questions: Any special events? What medications and treatments is the patient receiving? What are the patient's vitals, the recent labs? In this instance, the nurse had not been a full participant in the rounding team, and had to be pulled in to provide more evidence as a consultant on the case. If the nurse had not been available, a larger gap in the evidence and information chain would have resulted.

CRITICAL EI&K JUNCTURE 5: MD/NURSE EXCHANGE

As an attending is listening to a nurse's reading of numbers from her paper notes, the information is sometimes dropped or lost, which can also happen in verbal exchanges that are not documented. In this case, the attending, while listening to a colleague, at one point said: "Oh she has MRSA" (methicillin-resistant *Staphylococcus aureus*). The attending noted this three seconds after the infection was read aloud from the nurse's list. This verbal mention of MRSA likely was not heard by some of the other physicians present either, and it easily could have been missed altogether.

This analysis highlights several characteristics about information transfer during rounds. Rounds no longer match the traditional image of one speaker and a quiet audience. At any point there could be 12 to 14 separate investigations and conversations. Clearly there are numerous critical junctures where evidence and information might be partially, if not totally, lost. Such gaps can have consequences for patient safety.

Improvement or Not?

It's worth considering whether the newer, large team, COW-focused rounding process represents an improvement or not. The authors believe it is both. Much more information is being discovered and presented than under the traditional approach. Most participants were actively involved in seeking evidence, information to increase their knowledge and contribute to the organization's knowledge base. In this illustration, the pharmacist and the specialists were consulted often in order to fold their knowledge into the process and further facilitate safe and effective care. Sometimes, however, a rounding team participant walked a few steps away to make a phone call to get needed information. The sense of a coherent and coordinated presentation of all of the information and data and evidence was missing.

As information is increasingly available and exchangeable without the intervention or mediation of the "wise" physician/professor during a day's typical rounding, a larger question emerges:

Is healthcare encouraging a chaotic autodidactic form of learning that is ultimately counter-productive because it discourages a theoretically guided integration of knowledge and understanding? This large team, technology-driven rounding speeds the creation or finding of puzzle pieces but not of a synthetic appreciation of the patient or the care plan.

OR

Is such rounding enhancing the accumulation and exchange of information at a speed previously unimaginable; more building a knowledge base for the benefit of both patients and medical education? Is this approach encouraging discovery of new information and connections via a wider net of young professionals and diverse knowledge and skills?

Presumably, such rounding can have both positive and negative aspects. More important, perhaps, is how an effective balance is established between these methods of information and evidence transfer in support of safe patient care.

Learning from the Analysis of Critical Junction EI&K Failures

The following discussion provides further insights about the EI&K failure junctures introduced in the previous ICU case.

CRITICAL EI&K JUNCTURE 1: PRESENTATION OF CASE

How is it possible that at least three medications are not clearly known or recorded in the patient's record? What are the implications of this problem? Sometimes, one drug was substituted for another, but the record of this change was not altered in *both* the nurse's paper record *and* in the CPOE. The same information failure can happen when a dosage is changed or when the medication administration schedule is altered. Any system that requires manual double entry is inherently problematic because the information is not automatically reconciled. Moreover, there may be a complex set of changes, where altering one medication necessitates a cascade of changes to others. The order-sets, groups of orders that go together, within the computer system may facilitate these multiple changes in the electronic record, but the paper records may not follow with the same process (Salanitro et al. 2012; Agency for Healthcare Research and Quality 2012).

In addition, medications might have been ordered by a number of clinicians, many of whom might not even be associated with that unit of the hospital, for example, consulting experts, radiologists ordering contrast dyes, etc. (Koppel et al. 2008).

The automatic integration of the information is assumed to be a wonderful and predictable benefit of the CPOE system. But even with this system, orders can be placed in areas of the CPOE and not be found for days, if ever (Koppel et al. 2005). This happens sometimes with off-formulary medications or with medications a patient brings from home. In addition, almost all orders in a teaching hospital or academic medical center are placed by first-year residents (interns) who might not be familiar with the CPOE system or with the medications of that service, especially when they are rotating in and out of service units every 30 days.

A physician's ability to apply knowledge to make informed judgments, or even to assess basic biologic processes, is impaired when crucial evidence or data is missing. If physicians do not have access to exactly what medications are administered and each medication's dosage and schedule, they might misinterpret patients' symptoms, laboratory results, and drug–drug interactions. When patients have five or six co-morbidities, as is often the case, and are taking 10 to 14 medications, the information deficit is compounded.

CRITICAL EI&K JUNCTURE 2: ATTENDING Q&A

Again, what are the implications of the rounding scene for information transfer, for finding the most up-to-date evidence, for integration of that evidence, and, ultimately for the ability of the team to gain a synoptic and knowledge-based understanding of the patient and his or her most efficacious treatment?

"Knowledge is shared through informal contact in the context of care delivery."

Positive aspects of large, diverse, technologically-enhanced rounds are the bright, multi-tasking people who are seeking to find either relevant medical literature on illnesses, medications, treatments, and outcomes, or searching laboratory results, radiology reports and talking with the pharmacists. All team members doing real-time information gathering should be able to convey their findings to at least those near them and ideally to the group and the leader, for appropriate dissemination at the organization.

The contemporary hospital rounding team also presents negative aspects, some of which are listed here.

- It is likely that only a few of the team participants, if any, are experts in searching the medical citation and point-of-care databases. Thus, what they find is not as focused or certain as they could be if the results were retrieved by a medical librarian whose primary expertise is literature review and retrieval (McGowan and Sampson 2005).

- The ability to find and integrate different medical reports should be a straightforward function in the electronic medical record, doable by anyone with basic computer skills. However, that is just not the case. And, there are few data standards or agreed-upon terms and acronyms; tests can be labeled as many different things (Kim 2005).

- Clinicians typically search for the most recent data, which may or may not be fully integrated into the patient's records. Knowledge of how the data and information get in to the electronic record (for example, from which lab it will be sent, and sometimes which clerk enters the data on the hour or half hour) alters the awareness of the value and applicability of the information.

- The ability to know what is critical information vs. what is routine may require expert knowledge not yet obtained by some of the participants (Harrison, Koppel and Bar-Lev 2007). Timidity of new doctors, the openness of the attending to irrelevant or unnecessary, but related, information and evidence will largely determine the amount, inclusiveness and speed of information available to the leader and to the group.

Research has shown that humans are not successful multi-taskers, although they believe themselves to be better than they are at carrying out multiple tasks simultaneously (Stephens and Fairbanks 2012). All too often when people try to do a number of tasks simultaneously, information is lost, poorly absorbed or is not integrated. This is not good news for patient care.

Alternative activities could reduce the information transfer gaps in the rounding teams. For example, side conversations could be prohibited, with the proviso that anyone who thinks the team could benefit from additional information and evidence could be allowed to duck out and quickly obtain the information, then come back and communicate it to the team. This approach misses the subtlety, however, that many side questions are as much a testing of understanding, to build knowledge, as they are a seeking of information. Knowledge is shared through informal contact in the context of care delivery. In the chaotic, multi-communication channels rounding team structure, busy participants are able to lose focus for a few seconds and ask for help to re-orient themselves to the task at hand. Also, with ICU background noise as a distraction, many of the "side conversations" are actually requests for repeating information.

Some rounding teams leave patient areas to conduct their discussions in separate rooms. Although this minimizes extraneous noise and distractions, team members are also separated from the patient, the family, and/or the nurse, and are thus unable to draw from the patient's, nurses' and family's knowledge of the condition, experience or current state. Absent team members are also unable to examine the patient to look for suspected but unrecorded symptoms or to see the machines and devices that are providing information or infusing medications.

Finally, the pedagogic process of the rounding team, and how it affects younger physicians, needs to be considered. Rounding is a chance to gather needed information and to convey it to the residents and fellows. It is also a chance for the residents to absorb knowledge on how to present a case, summarize the information and offer an effective synthesis. This process is also used to test and emphasize information and the interpretation of the information. Any enhancement of the routine – for example with large computer screens, additional displays of articles and lab reports – would influence this learning process and would require careful analysis. Information and evidence do not produce knowledge without a lot of thought, work and integration.

CRITICAL EI&K JUNCTURE 3: UNOFFICIAL E&I GATHERING IN RESPONSE TO Q&A

There is an important potential EI&K failure juncture involving use of evidence that affects clinicians' interaction with point-of-care evidence resources to answer their own questions as they make clinical decisions. Clearly, no one clinician can know and remember everything there is to know for every care scenario. Research shows that residents and practicing physicians have many clinical questions each day that go unanswered. In one study, residents were found to generate two new questions for every three new patients, and they only pursued answers to approximately one-third of their questions, primarily due to lack of time and forgetting about the question (Green, Ciampi and Ellis 2000). Another study found that within a group made up of residents and attending physicians, residents generated 1.5 new questions and attending physicians generated 0.8 questions per patient encounter (Ramos, Linscheid and Schafer 2003). This group:

> ... sought immediate answers to 66 percent of questions, found satisfactory answers to 87 percent of these, and later pursued answers to only 6 percent of remaining questions. Most searches (66 percent) took less than 2 minutes (Ramos, Linscheid and Schafer 2003: 257).

"... no one clinician can know and remember everything there is to know for every care scenario." How many of these answered or unanswered questions lead to medical errors is not known, but the importance of the connection is non-trivial. Patients have died in cases where, as part of the chain of events, seemingly authoritative but incomplete resources were consulted (Smetzer 1998) or the best resources to answer the question were overlooked (Steinbrook 2002).

CRITICAL EI&K JUNCTURE 4: NURSE SHARES DATA/LAB VALCUES

At this fourth juncture in rounding, new data, evidence and information are brought to bear, this time via the nurse's participation. The attending is taking notes, writing or typing numbers and information that will become part of the official chart. The nurse is reading off the numbers but must repeat every third one or so at the request of the attending. There is a cacophony of noises that exist at each critical juncture: alarms, tones, announcements (pages), side conversations within the team, other conversations, phone calls, constant but startling tones/alarms. There is no sharing of paper. All of the information transfer is via the nurse's voice. The attending is not writing all of the numbers. The nurse is reading from flow sheets and full attention is not on the discussion. At this juncture information is being shared via one point in the process, the nurse, and the rest of the team members, including the attending physician, are not always receiving the information. Important bits of data and information can be lost at this juncture.

A similar, critical EI&K failure juncture can occur surrounding lab values, pieces of information that are critical supporting data for clinical decision-making. Too often these data are not shared clearly, or with all who need to have them.

CRITICAL EI&K JUNCTURE 5: MD/NURSE EXCHANGE

The final EI&K juncture presented here is launched by the previous juncture, and involves one of the most fundamental aspects of patient safety: communication between nurses and physicians. It is recognized that communication happens at each juncture and that other players participate here, but for the sake of illustration, these two central roles will be discussed. Gaps at this juncture are an important cause of hospital mortality (Knaus et al. 1986; Donchin et al. 1995; Manojlovich 2010). In today's multi-tiered, electronically-supported, team approach to medical care, especially in the ICU, there are many safety nets to prevent inappropriate or dangerous care. Nurses who administer medications offer the final safety net because they are the "last stop" and their experience and training allows them to recognize subtle and unexpected conditions, such as when the physician's well-intentioned order is inappropriate. However, even when doctors and nurses have a similar understanding of the overall plan of care for the patient, and orders are clear and precise, a difference in understanding of physiology, and/or an absence of communication of the reasoning underlying an order between a doctor and a nurse, can create unwarranted delays in the delivery of care.

Human physiology is highly complex, and clinicians often apply heuristics that simplify the decision-making process. These heuristics recommend a typical course of action in the setting of an observed clinical scenario *without* initial regard to the mechanisms contributing to the clinical condition or the specifics of how the interventions work. For example, in the ICU setting, it is not uncommon for a patient's blood pressure to fluctuate between very high and very low values. The heuristic for managing these conditions is to lower blood pressure by administering vasodilators when the pressure is high and to raise blood pressure with vasoconstrictors when the pressure is low. This heuristic is valid much of the time, but not always. The complicated underlying physiology sometimes creates a paradox where the correct decision is to administer vasodilators in the case of low blood pressure. This is because blood pressure is only partially related to the degree of blood vessel dilation or constriction. The other component is cardiac output, such that higher cardiac output raises blood pressure. A clinical scenario exists where the current degree of vasoconstriction is too great and cardiac output is concordantly depressed. In this scenario, the heuristic of administering vasoconstrictors can make the low blood pressure condition worse, and the correct decision is to administer a vasodilator.

In a real instance of this scenario, a physician (author MGW), wrote a seemingly paradoxical order for a vasodilator in the context of a value of low blood pressure. The nurse received the order but was unaware that the underlying physiology warranted the vasodilator; the physician had not conveyed it. As a result, the nurse applied the heuristic that is appropriate most of the time and decided not to administer the medication before contacting the physician. After a clarifying discussion, she administered the medication. The patient's blood pressure improved, and no adverse effect occurred because of the delay.

Although the CPOEs are designed to transmit medication orders unambiguously, they are not designed to convey the *rationale* underlying the order and can impede nurse-physician communication (Harrison, Koppel and Bar-Lev 2007; Pirnejad et al. 2008). A nurse who receives an order is appropriately rewarded for applying heuristics that help avert medication administration in a potentially dangerous situation that the physician did not anticipate. However, as this case illustrates, in the absence of knowledge of the rationale behind an order, this behavior can lead to a delay of appropriate care. The lesson here is that nothing – not EHRs, not CPOEs – can substitute for vigilance, caring professionalism and open lines of communication among care team members. The organizational cultures that foster these critical factors are also those that are necessary for high-quality, safe care.

EI&K Failures at the Intersection of HIT and Point-of-Care Resources: Possible Solutions

The medical or health informatics vision for clinical information needs is to have computerized clinical decision support systems (CDS or CDSS) that contain evidence-based clinical information that is fully integrated into the myriad functions within all EHRs in ways that are tacit, anticipatory and automatic as well as through more interactive, user-initiated mechanisms (Barnett et al. 2008; Osheroff 2009; Osheroff et al. 2007). Within the realm of informatics research and prototypes, when a clinician can look up and find high-quality evidence and information for a definitive answer to any clinical question, all without exiting the EHR, the process is sometimes referred to in shorthand as an "infobuttons" function (Cimino, Elhanan and Zheng 1997; Cimino et al. 2003; Cimino 2006).

Current reality is miles away from this vision. The hospitals and provider practices receiving funds from the HITECH portion of the American Recovery and Reinvestment Act of 2009 must implement integrated electronic health record systems that incorporate CDS (AHIMA 2012; US Centers for Medicare & Medicaid Services 2012; Versel 2012). But the bar is low, and although there are millions of potential drug–drug interaction warnings and hundreds of allergy warnings, the CPOE is required to generate only *one* clinical decision support alert in order to obtain reimbursement and subsidies (US Centers for Medicare & Medicaid 2012). Requirements will become more stringent in the coming years, but the current Meaningful Use phase-one rule is more symbolic than life saving (HIMSS Health Information Exchange Steering Committee

2010). Although it's generally believed that CPOE and EHRs will eventually improve medical practice, the current systems have minimal data standards, a low threshold of functionality, and marginal abilities to work well and operate together to effectively share information across systems (Committee on Patient Safety and Health Information Technology 2011). Healthcare improvement via HIT is proceeding "low and slow."

Increasingly, residents and practicing physicians are using online resources to replace printed pocket guides and textbooks. However, even among hospitals that have annual subscriptions to electronic evidence-based point-of-care resources, use of them is not ubiquitous. Usage is most robust at large academic medical centers with EHR systems developed in-house, where these resources are available directly via the EHR interface (Cimino et al. 2007; Cimino 2008; Oppenheim et al. 2009; Del Fiol et al. 2012). This infobuttons idea circles back to the critical information and evidence sharing juncture. Evidence is mounting that the availability of authoritative electronic point-of-care resources are associated with better care outcomes (Bonis et al. 2008; Isaac, Zheng and Jha 2011). However, availability alone does not ensure that clinicians will use these resources or use them effectively (McKibbon and Fridsma 2006). The questions in Infobox 4.2, then, are key for each clinician to answer. In fact, even when evidence is built into the CPOE itself via clinical decision support systems, provider override rates can be as high as 89 percent (Kuperman et al. 2007).

INFOBOX 4.2: QUESTIONS CLINICIANS MUST ASK ABOUT COMPUTERIZED RESOURCES TO BETTER ENSURE PATIENT SAFETY

- What resources are you using to answer your clinical questions?
- To which resources does your institution subscribe and offer access?
- Are there differences among these online resources? For instance:
  - Which is updated more often?
  - Which has more and broader content?
  - Which is easiest to use for which purposes (Campbell and Ash 2006)?
  - Which is more explicit within the body text about the level of evidence backing the suggested answer?
  - How do you get to them?
  - Is there another, faster, easier way to get to those resources?
  - How did you learn about those resources, how to get to them, and how to use them?
- Need you exit the current patient's electronic record to access the informational database?
- What do your clinical teammates know about any of this and what do they use?

Solutions that ensure effective, consistent use of information are available. For example – the pharmacist, who already plays a critical role in information-transfer – can form a team, with an informationist (Davidoff and Florance 2000) or medical librarian and a designated person from the clinical information systems department. This group can identify key point-of-care resources and optimize online access to those resources, within the CPOE and EHR if possible, or through a least-effort path (with the fewest possible clicks) from an outside source. In addition to obtaining needed resources, this group can serve as a governance group, coordinating frequent updates and communicating changes to departmental leadership, updating and providing access to documentation, and organizing training sessions that make sense for the care setting.

To integrate information sharing and oversight activities into the organizational culture, administrative leadership and patient safety groups must place these activities on their high-priority project lists and communicate their importance in the organization's patient safety work. Only with the support of leadership can information sharing activities be in departmental and unit reporting and feedback mechanisms. Leadership must ensure that sufficient resources are budgeted for information and evidence sharing activities.

The Journey Continues

A recent study by University of Pennsylvania researchers showed that half the residents believed that they could not get to one of their institution's top evidence-consolidation resource subscriptions – UpToDate™ – without exiting their CPOE system, and half believed that they could access the information directly through the CPOE system (Koppel 2012). That is, for half of the residents accessing the tool, UpToDate™ appeared to demand a notable distraction and time allocation issue. This example highlights a path towards resolving these EI&K juncture questions: Don't leave the answers to chance. Take the transfer of knowledge regarding point-of-care resources and access out of the "hidden curriculum," the learning that clinicians are expected to absorb via on-the-job osmosis. Address it explicitly, systematically and systemically. Within clinical settings, departmental policy and practice can be established such that individuals will explicitly state to the rest of the team what resource they are consulting as they provide an answer for the team. During rounds within teaching hospitals, the attending physician can specify which resource residents should access to answer a question.

"Don't leave the answers to chance."

As anyone who has sent an email, memo, or talked with a teenager realizes, *sending* information is *not* the same as knowing it was *received and processed* (Koppel and Gordon 2012). Information and evidence transfer failures are formidable. As part of the complex system of healthcare delivery, IT systems or otherwise, require never-ending vigilance and on-the-floor observation to "get it right" (Koppel et al. 2005; Sinsky 2008).

KEY TAKE-AWAYS

- The process for sharing evidence and information among the diverse set of providers on the frontlines of care is complex with many potential sources of error.
- Health information technology both presents both opportunities and challenges in its contribution to the EI&K sharing process.
- Health informatics expertise is important within hospital teams involved in HIT implementation, optimization/ongoing build-out, and use.
- Bringing informationist and informatics expertise to the bedside can assist in improving the reliability of the complex information and evidence exchange that occurs daily among providers.

Suggested Reading

Committee on Patient Safety and Health Information Technology, Board on Health Care Services, Institute of Medicine. 2011. *Health IT and Patient Safety: Building Safer Systems for Better Care*. Washington, DC: National Academies Press.

Koppel, R. and Gordon, S. 2012. *First, Do Less Harm: Confronting The Inconvenient Problems of Patient Safety*. Ithaca, NY: Cornell University Press.

5

Leadership, EI&K and a Culture of Safety

Della Lin, Margo Farber and Judith Napier

> *Leadership involves finding a parade and getting in front of it (Naisbitt 1982: 162).*

Organizational Culture Sets the Stage

Culture, in the simplest of terms, can be defined as guidelines for living (MacLachlan 2006). British clinical psychologist and human error expert James Reason found the following definition as an effective description of organizational culture, "Shared values (what is important) and beliefs (how things work) that interact with an organization's structures and control systems to produce behavioral norms (the way we do things around here)" (Reason 1997: 192, quoting Uttal). In the context of healthcare, organizational culture might be described as "guidelines for day to day operations."

Reason confirms that culture is more than just "the way we do things around here." Culture is multi-faceted. It is likely to be the result of institutional tradition and current regulatory, quality and financial conditions. It is importantly influenced by leadership. In a recent analysis, Carney and collaborators identified key influences of organizational culture that in turn impact the quality and safety of healthcare delivery. These include:

- excellence in care delivery such as patient safety and quality;

- ethical values;

- strategic involvement (e.g., teamwork and collaboration);

- cost versus quality;

- professionalism and commitment; and

- strategic planning and thinking (Carney 2011).

Leadership within an organization sets the tone for each of these influences. Consequently leadership will impact the ability of the organization to effectively utilize evidence, information and knowledge to problem solve.

This chapter will introduce cultural concepts which healthcare leadership should consider in order to best utilize evidence, information and knowledge (EI&K). Commitment to EI&K can drive transparency, error/incident reporting, communication, teamwork and learning. Challenges in implementing EI&K efforts are mapped to these concepts to underscore the role of administrative leaders and champions in resourcing EI&K programs. It's accepted that through support patterning to EI&K behaviors patient safety can be enhanced. Patterning in this context means establishing a specific design or structure that defines a style or method of leadership that remains transparent for all to know and follow. Leadership needs to "walk the talk" of effective seeking and sharing of evidence, information and knowledge.

SHARP END–BLUNT END

Often in healthcare there is a separation between the institutional structure and policies established by the leadership and administrators (blunt end) of an organization and the realities of the constraints and patient-level practices of the individual healthcare clinician (sharp end). This difference is aptly described as the sharp end–blunt end interaction (see Figure 5.1, derived from Reason 1990). The blunt end of the system creates policies, procedures and regulations that, although well intended, are often contributing factors that facilitate error and subsequent failure. Sharp end knowledge has not been sought or taken into account in the creation of these problematic policies and procedures. Blunt end expectations can be unrealistic, not well defined and not supportive of the needs of the frontline clinician interacting directly with the patients. Errors are more quickly and easily identifiable at the sharp end, yet there is a lack of consideration of or investigation into the potential causes generated at the blunt end.

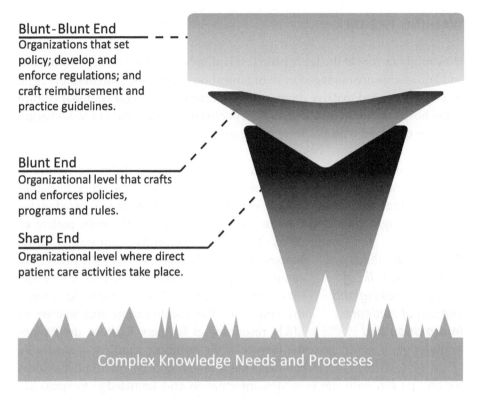

Blunt-Blunt End
Organizations that set policy; develop and enforce regulations; and craft reimbursement and practice guidelines.

Blunt End
Organizational level that crafts and enforces policies, programs and rules.

Sharp End
Organizational level where direct patient care activities take place.

Complex Knowledge Needs and Processes

Figure 5.1   Sharp End, Blunt End, Blunt-Blunt End
Source: Adapted from Reason 1990.

To add complexity to organizational culture, middle managers may alternately find themselves at the sharp end or the blunt end, and have allegiances to both. Even more confounding is when middle managers find themselves caught between a service line and a department structure – with different senior leaders and different frontline teams. To effectively problem solve, the leadership of an organization must be sensitive to both sharp and blunt ends of the system. They must be acutely aware of training, equipment and resources that will enable clinicians to practice in a safe and effective manner. EI&K can be affected by these training, equipment and resources as well. Narrowing the gap between the blunt end and the sharp end in the design of policies and procedures is one way to minimize the difference between these two fields of vision. Explicitly, the design should intentionally promote and reflect strategic multilevel involvement, engagement and collaboration (Carney 2011).

WALKING THE TALK

How might factors at the leadership level influence how evidence, information and knowledge are managed in an organization to promote patient safety? The strategies engaged to drive organizational learning and organizational culture at the hospital should also impact the effectiveness and value of EI&K sharing – and be designed with EI&K explicitly in mind.

Successful use of EI&K can motivate patient safety and shape a culture of safety in organizations. The professionals engaged in EI&K work to gather intellectual resources (i.e., the right evidence, information and knowledge) for use by the right clinician(s), expressed in the context of the right patient or place, at the right time, in the right format. EI&K shapes the application of what is in the brain (that composite of evidence, information and knowledge) into actual behavior. The culture determines the ability for the identification and sharing of EI&K resources to happen. Culture determines the impact of the authority gradient – ideally by reducing the gradient and facilitating behaviours for any person with the evidence, information and knowledge to speak up regardless of hierarchy or rank. For example, evidence might indicate that to prevent hospital-acquired harm, a patient undergoing a central line placement will require a full barrier drape and a 30-second application of chlorhexidine solution. These supplies (drape, chlorhexidine) might technically exist in the organization, but culture can trump whether or not knowledge is surfaced to develop information to support the reliable application of these practices at the bedside. There might be culturally constraining factors (e.g., clinician autonomy or production pressures) trumping these safe practices or, there may be culturally facilitating factors (e.g., transparency of regular performance and information feedback) with the social expectation that these practices be done 100 percent of the time that affect the application of knowledge to procedures. The organization with a culture of safety emphasizes that it is everyone's duty to speak up to share information and knowledge when they see something is not right – it is an ethical imperative to do so. This minimizes the impact of the hierarchy that could exacerbate errors, and enables the ability for individuals at various levels of authority and influence in the organization to speak up. The use of the Joint Commission's Universal Protocol for the time out is one example of this principle (Joint Commission n.d.). Without leadership support and oversight of this practice, staff members with knowledge and an interest

"Leadership needs to 'walk the talk' of effective seeking and sharing of evidence, information and knowledge."

to speak up for effective change may be intimidated and "silenced" by a few clinicians unwilling to practice the safety procedure.

Challenges for Leaders: Connecting EI&K to Safety Improvement

When evaluating complex systems and system failures, Reason (1990) and others frequently refer to the "Swiss Cheese Model" (Figure 5.2). Essentially, a complex systems failure is usually the result of multiple innocuous faults or, as Reason terms them, "latent conditions" (Reason 1997). These latent conditions may be present for years but exist with little fanfare, attention or catastrophe. They can be the result of blunt end decision-making that shapes the distinctive culture that has developed to create error-producing factors within the individual workplaces. Latent conditions combine with local circumstances and active failures to penetrate the organization's defenses – thus creating holes in the "Swiss Cheese" (Reason 1997).

While no single failure or defense may result in or prevent a major event, a series of failures (multiple holes in slices of Swiss cheese) lined up to create a "tunnel" that allows for a major system breakdown or error. This systemic failure typically cannot be linked to an individual; rather, it is the result of faulty design, unclear policies, and overall management. Latent conditions exist in all systems. It is important that leaders be able to understand such

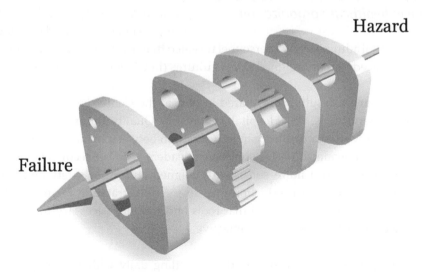

Figure 5.2   Reason's Swiss Cheese Model
Source: Reason 1990.

conditions exist, avoid blaming an individual practice or person when an event occurs, and be responsive to the team when the latent condition is identified. Administrators under pressure to respond may look for the quick fix and target the individual person as the solution to the problem. Instead, a thorough analysis of the system, its complexities and interplay between multiple processes, must be conducted to create an overall safe system. Evidence on the existent latent conditions, information on the interplay of the events, and knowledge of the overall complex system, are critical to effectively problem solve.

Evidence, information and knowledge processes, when seen through the lens of organizational culture, should be characterized as complex. Once gaps and true failures have been noted, addressing them takes commitment and hard work to instill an effective culture to mitigate those failures. There are several important challenges for leaders to recognize in creating more robust linkages between the effectiveness of EI&K and patient safety that address gap recognition, barrier consideration, EI&K element designation and leadership patterning of evidence, information and knowledge-sharing behaviors.

Leadership and Gap Analysis

"... the consequences of cutting off practitioners from reliable sources of information and evidence can be fatal in healthcare organizations."

Having an organizational cultural framework for EI&K effectiveness in patient safety is by no means a given in most hospitals. A survey of approximately 500 mid- and top-level hospital administrative personnel revealed that frontline and management are often faced with misaligned safety cultures (Lin 2006) (see Figure 5.3).

These survey results were shared in part at the Center for Medicare and Medicaid Services (CMS) Hospital Leadership Quality Summit (Lin 2006). The results revealed a distinct gap in perception between management, board members and leadership (i.e., physician leaders, CEOs/Executives). Board members perceived a more consistently aligned culture of safety and clear priorities of safety over production pressure. As illustrated in Figure 5.3, the board and leadership perceived that tools and training necessary for patient safety were highly accessible and effective.

Management, in contrast, reported wrestling daily with an ambiguity of priorities (e.g. safety vs. production) as well as restricted or non-existent access

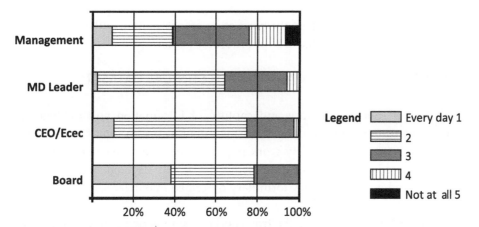

Figure 5.3   Executive Leadership Provides the Tools and Training to be Effective in Patient Safety

Source: Lin 2006.

to tools and training for effective patient safety. This gap in perception can result from inadvertent leadership decisions that limit access to tools. This limitation can delay timely sharing of evidence and the development of new knowledge. As an example, some organizations might limit institutional-wide database and publication subscriptions as an "easy" line item budget cut. But the consequences of cutting off practitioners from reliable sources of information and evidence can be fatal in healthcare organizations. To further illustrate, healthcare organizations have been known to develop mandates that restrict sharing of policies with other hospitals. Collaborative tools such as social media and video sharing are blocked. These limitations potentially constrain frontline teams from accelerated knowledge-creation, and can result in unintentional cost redundancies if personnel must recreate training tools that could have been adopted from collaborators. These barriers violate Carney's organizational culture point supporting strategic involvement as exemplified by teamwork and collaboration (Carney 2011).

Structural Barriers can Limit EIK's Effectiveness

Structural barriers that reinforce cultural constraints can limit the effective use of evidence and information to apply knowledge. Kothari and colleagues' (2011) review of the business sector literature describes several barriers applicable to knowledge management. These barriers – as established in healthcare and discussed below – can impact the harvesting of information and evidence and its application as knowledge in support of safe action.

BARRIER 1: SEEING EI&K AS ONLY A TECHNICAL DATASET

Although a robust inventory and capture of information and evidence is important, true embedding of mechanisms and processes to identify, access and share EI&K into patient safety work requires more than a technical solution. How the data is translated into knowledge can be very different and important, as illustrated in the pharmacy formulary described in Barrier 3.

One technique to bridge the translation of knowledge is to probe further through use of the 5 Whys technique. This technique moves beyond the quick-fix solution or workarounds of "first order problem-solving" and into deeper system-based learning or what is defined as "second order problem-solving."

"... true embedding of mechanisms and processes to identify, access and share EI&K into patient safety work requires more than a technical solution."

The 5 Whys technique, promoted in systems thinking and other disciplines, simply involves asking why enough times to get back to the root causes of a problem (Senge et al. 1994). To illustrate with a scenario, consider a patient who is readmitted within five days of discharge. First order problem-solving reveals that the patient did not follow postop medication instructions. A deeper probe into asking the "why" of medication adherence may reveal that the patient indeed has the prescription and understands the need for medication. However, the patient recalls a previous experience when her primary care doctor did not agree with the medication change after hospital discharge. Rather than filling the prescription with the risk that it may not be what the primary care doctor wants, the patient decides that waiting to fill the prescription until she sees her primary care physician will save her from purchasing costly medications that won't be used.

Without this added second-order problem-solving, a hospital may come up with technical forms and solutions for ensuring that the information reaches the patient, without any improvement on adherence or safety. The solution requires understanding the importance of adaptive challenges – human connections that require a non-siloed structure, one that embraces teams which cross boundaries (Heifetz and Lauirie 1997). Such a boundary spanning solution requires a leadership culture of openness and knowledge creation, a modeling of behavior that includes active questioning and, an environment where staff and patients are respected for the knowledge they have and the way they are putting it to use.

INFOBOX 5.1: FIRST/SECOND-ORDER PROBLEM-SOLVING

Analogous to the concepts of single and double loop learning identified by organizational learning researchers (Argyris and Schon 1978), research on problem-solving makes a distinction between fixing problems (first-order solutions) and diagnosing and altering root causes to prevent recurrence (second-order solutions). First-order problem-solving allows work to continue but does nothing to prevent a similar problem from occurring. Workers exhibit first-order problem-solving when they do not expend any more energy on a problem after obtaining the missing input needed to complete a task. Second-order problem-solving, in contrast, investigates and seeks to change underlying causes of a problem (Tucker, Edmondson and Spear 2001).

Checklists are another example of a strategy used to enhance the translation of evidence and information into knowledge. Checklists have gained extraordinary support throughout healthcare. However, as with many tools and techniques, checklists require adaptive understanding by leaders and can be a double-edged sword. As a positive translation tool, a checklist improves situational awareness – allowing the team to codify the critical elements (evidence and information) relevant to a process or procedure and improve the delivery at the point-of-care (embracing knowledge). However, overzealous focus on checklist compliance and unintentional blindness by leaders in accepting compliance as a default record of performance can actually mask problems. An inadvertent "false sense of safety" (Rydenfalt 2013) emerges as complacency can result when an organization thinks a detractor from safety has been solved (Bosk et al. 2009, Lingard 2012).

BARRIER 2: EMBRACING A TOP DOWN APPROACH

The landmark Institute of Medicine (IOM) series of Quality Chasm Reports and several focused resources provide excellent direction for improving hospital board member engagement in patient safety (Goeschel, Wachter and Pronovost 2010; Conway 2008, Chassin 2013, Chassin and Loeb, 2013; Committee on Identifying and Preventing Medication Errors 2007; Institute of Medicine, Committee on Patient Safety and Health Information Technology, Board on Health Care Services 2011). In an overly top-down approach, "never events," the term in common usage for serious reportable events as defined by the National Quality Forum and others as events that should never occur in hospitals, can and do happen (Lembitz and Clarke 2009). The goal is zero for such events. At the board level this may translate, due to its "murkyiness" as a term and concept, as a blame-ridden event and therefore as punitive if/when serious never events are reported (Lembitz and Clarke 2009).

A single top-down decision to address the accountability of error entirely at the clinician level can create dangerous situations. The unintended consequence the healthcare executive may experience is either the downgrading of the severity of the error before reporting, or worse, not reporting the event altogether. This example of an unintentional blunt end decision – clear articulation of a zero-event goal in the context of a punitive, blame-ridden culture – negatively impacts the sharp end with the result in a reduction in transparency, patient safety and the lack of information and knowledge-sharing at the system level. Such a top-down approach, ultimately puts the patient at greater risk.

Instead, executives and board members should foster the development of leaders throughout the organization. These individuals must serve as a boundary spanner between board level decision makers and the practitioners directly involved in clinical and bed-side care. Everyone must be knowledgeable of the process to achieve safe healthcare. Accurate, consistent reporting and use of knowledge-sharing opportunities will support a climate that is non-punitive.

BARRIER 3: MAKING DECISIONS INDEPENDENTLY TO NEGATIVELY AFFECT PATIENT SAFETY

One example to illustrate how independent decisions by one department can affect patient care is the development of formularies. Formulary decisions, that is, the process by which drugs are selected for use in a given setting such as a hospital, are most often made at the executive level (e.g., chiefs of medical services, pharmacy administrators). A group of healthcare professionals review data regarding the utility of a drug, most often focusing on efficacy, safety and cost, to determine whether it is made available for a practitioner to prescribe (Tyler et al. 2008). While evidence is typically the primary influence, there is a lack of information applied and knowledge sought regarding the realities of the patient needs from the perspective of the clinician directly providing care. For example:

- The patient is prescribed a drug deemed to be the most effective and desirable for a clinical condition, but third party payers may not routinely cover it.

- Without coverage, the patient does not have personal resources to obtain the drug once discharged from the hospital. The patient's health worsens without drug or drug alternate.

- The patient is readmitted with an exacerbation of their condition or, worse, suffers in silence until the condition becomes too grave to manage.

Patient safety is jeopardized. Although the blunt end decisions were based on clinical data and information and perhaps published guidelines (evidence) to support optimal drug selection, provisions were not made at the sharp end to enable clinicians to modify selection of medications as needed to address individual patient scenarios (knowledge).

INFOBOX 5.2: EI&K AS A FRONTLINE SAFETY MECHANISM

A low risk laboring patient begins to show changes during the course of labor suggesting that the fetus is beginning to decompensate (information). The nurse caring for the patient has new evidence relative to reading and interpreting fetal heart tracings as she recently completed the fetal monitor course the hospital required all labor and delivery nursing staff to complete. She also has knowledge due to an experience of a peer where a similar incident happened that heightens her sensitivity to the situation.

She discussed the situation with a more experienced colleague who was busy with another patient and suggested that she should do what she thinks is best. The nurse placed a call to the on-call physician. The fetal heart rate began a significant decrease, the nurse called for an in-house obstetrician and began to prepare the patient for an emergency cesarean delivery.

The newborn was delivered, resuscitated and transferred to the neonatal intensive care unit. No discussion of the near miss takes place.

Infobox 5.2 shares an example of how a well-meaning EI&K sharing tactic at the blunt end (requiring training of the nursing staff) has been used in a top down approach, with separate departments (including the third party payer) enacting policy. The approach was that of first order problem-solving. The immediate issue is resolved but the underlying root cause of potential delay (need to act with approval in an emergent situation due to inconsistent awareness of evidence and knowledge) is not addressed. With this workaround, deeper probes do not take place. Knowledge confined to department silos constrains decision-making to what can be quickly rationalized to seemingly complete the picture. This represents a hole in the "Swiss Cheese" of the EI&K process.

BARRIER 4: LACKING TRUST IN THE EI&K SHARING PROCESS

"Hierarchy should not trump EI&K sharing to support patient safety." Leadership that values and facilitates the dynamic nature of EI&K understands that one event with a bad outcome or one near miss, as in Infobox 5.2, can and should be proactively used to move the sharing of knowledge upstream for prevention of similar events in the future. Infobox 5.2 provides context to both blunt and sharp end elements of effective EI&K sharing that support a culture of safety and build trust in the processes to support learning and continued sharing.

Blunt end elements in this case include:

- During the root cause analysis of the event, with second order problem-solving, it was noted that the nurses did not have the authority to move patients into the operating room before the physician arrived. In past cases, nurses were aware of situations where staff were reprimanded for taking the initiative to begin preparations for patients who were showing signs of fetal compromise without recovery. Nurses would call in the operating team and prepare the operating room and the patient while waiting for the physician to arrive. In some cases, the nurses' approach was welcomed by physicians, but in other cases nurses were reprimanded by both the physicians and the hospital administrators.

- The nurse's quick actions expedited the process and reduced the time frame that the fetus remained in a compromised state. However, without knowing the "rules" or the culture of the department the nurse was taking a risk that could have resulted in a reprimand and jeopardy of her position.

- Hospital administrators had not clearly defined the roles and the expectations. Instead, the myths that evolved from past cases (some from many years ago) lingered and impacted upon nurses decision-making. This inconsistency leads to an environment less conducive for a nurse to ask questions and have the necessary dialog to gather and share knowledge as an equal team member. This is a classic latent condition example such as James Reason describes (Reason

1997). The blunt end chooses to act or not on a known safety issue that may repeat in the future.

Sharp end elements include:

- A safety culture, the expectations are that all staff members, regardless of status or position, have a part to play to keep patients safe. They draw from knowledge to highlight evidence and information that should be shared and take responsibility for participation in activities enabled by it. Hierarchy should not trump EI&K sharing to support patient safety. However, this only works in organizations in which leaders agree with that philosophy. Supporting staff to speak up when something isn't right is one action leadership can promote for patient safety.

Near Misses and Actual Incidents of Harm – Leadership's Subsequent Role

The great enemy of the truth is very often not the lie, deliberate, contrived and dishonest, but the myth, persistent, persuasive and unrealistic (Kennedy 1962).

Transparency is one way that the sharp end staff can gauge the organization's true commitment to the safety agenda. Clarity and demonstration of commitment around questions such as: "where do adverse events get reported in the organization?"; and, "how much EI&K is shared both within and beyond the unit when an event occurs?" are barometers as to executive management's commitment to a true EI&K sharing culture. Visible support from the leadership is required to complete the communication loop to facilitate organizational learning. The story in Infobox 5.2 shares a case example that open recognition in the unit and hospital of the nurse for her quick clinical judgment and decision-making can set the stage for the other staff to act decisively when the time comes, despite hierarchy. In this way true leaders model placing the patient first and improving the systems for better patient care. Over time the myths from the past fade and the new stories that are told around the water cooler are of the support the administration has for nurses acting for patient safety.

In contemplating how to resolve these gaps in understanding, leadership steps into the patient care environment to determine what is needed to gain the staff members' confidence. Tactics such as executive walk arounds, adopt-a-unit structures and other unit-focused "conversation" programs – both in person and virtually – can facilitate these opportunities (Frankel et al. 2003; Pronovost et al. 2004; Luther and Resar 2013; Graham et al. 2009). This emphasis may also include intentional recognizing and mining informal knowledge-sharing opportunities that might take place in lounges and corridors (Waring and Bishop 2010). Despite the lack of structure associated with these informal sources, they are still a viable conduit of otherwise hidden patient safety knowledge that takes into account the culture of sharing that can occur in rich settings of trust. In the end, it is critically important for leadership to use evidence rather than the rumors that surface following an event. But to ignore tacit knowledge may limit proactive responses to problems that, with delay, can become normalized in the culture if not addressed quickly.

EI&K Behaviors Across the Cultural Spectrum

Healthcare organizations providing direct care cannot set fixed targets nor program machines to pump out the parameters the same every time. Practicing surgeon and author Atul Gawande provides a useful metaphor for the discussion – good medicine can't be reduced to a recipe (Gawande 2012). Neither can good food. As Dr. Gawande points out in his description of the Cheesecake Factory restaurants' dishes, every meal that is prepared involves attention to the specifics and individuals make adjustments that require the application of human judgment. In essence, knowledge is applied. In medicine, adjustments for individual clinical nuances are necessary and clinicians make these adjustments every day. Further human factors remain an important component in the delivery of patient care. In healthcare, precision and outcomes are moving targets. The role of leaders is to understand this ambiguity and imprecision by accessing knowledge about the realities of the frontline and then establishing the ground rules or expectations with a focus on recovery and knowledge-sharing thereafter when an adverse event or near miss occurs.

As noted in the discussion of the story above, it was less about the fact that all clinicians were not aware of the evidence that was disseminated in the training. But rather the fact that the nurse on the unit could not sound the alarm and *expect* that the physician would respond. Instead the nurse had a choice to either ignore the information and evidence that was provided or use this opportunity as a teachable moment to share knowledge with a new staff member to garner trust and confidence. The path that this clinician chose is the unacceptable risk that leaders need to acknowledge and be very clear with staff on what will and won't be tolerated. Clinicians look at these signals (what is tolerated by executives and championed by executive "leaders") as the defining moments for the organization in which they work. If the executives accept these behaviors then the staff learns to not trust organizational management and the culture becomes an underground divisive culture.

Leadership Must Respect the Dynamic Nature of EI&K

Healthcare has traditionally put great emphasis on research. Leaders need to value tacit knowledge at least as equally as research. Research can be too slow and can also be limiting without the local contextual knowledge. How tacit knowledge is codified into explicit knowledge in an organization can be a key driver of effective EI&K practice in patient safety.

"... to ignore tacit knowledge may limit proactive responses to problems that, with delay, can become normalized in the culture if not addressed quickly."

EXAMPLE

A large hospital system utilized two unique team members – a knowledge management officer and a librarian – as part of the multi-pronged strategy to change practice patterns in their local hospitals across the region.

The leadership worked directly with management, medical staff and nurses to identify clinical variations from professional standards and best practices in clinical care. Teams were assembled in each of the clinical care specialties with physicians, nurses, quality and risk managers reviewing patient care records from past reported medical liability claims in order to understand the practice patterns that emerged.

Working in conjunction with clinicians, an outside risk management group was charged with identifying guidelines and criteria to monitor and use with local clinical staff in hospitals across the country. The guidelines were designed to focus on key practice issues that were identified as repeating problems in medical liability claim cases in high-risk clinical practices such as obstetrical care. External evidence (i.e. studies) related to the variance and recommended improvements were identified, and discussed amongst the team members. This evidence and information then required a strategy for it to be used to effect knowledge application at the bedside. Although the blunt end leaders in the corporate risk management office were able to define the broad issues that were seen in the medical liability claim cases and published evidence, they were not close enough to the work at the sharp end to understand how best to change or modify practice (translate to knowledge).

This story illustrates a three-pronged approach that incorporated information, evidence and knowledge gathering in consultation with frontline staff to elicit change. The librarian and knowledge officers were two key team members for this translation. The librarian participated in the team focus groups and informal knowledge-sharing opportunities. This engagement allowed the librarian to serve as a key conduit to bring necessary information and evidence to the group for consideration. The librarian functioned as a resource to bridge the literature with the local practices and system claims in order to support the recommended practices, standards and policies that the risk management team was proposing.

The knowledge officer was a key resource in conjunction with the librarian to assist leadership in understanding staff learning through observation to capture tacit knowledge. The officer reviewed national and local educational forums, knowledge-sharing and document delivery methods as potential means of sharing resources to inform modification of the necessary behaviors to enhance the safety of care.

As part of the implementation strategy, tools were established to assist sharp end staff in the local hospitals to collect data and create information based on those numbers to impact behavior before an event occurred. Unit meetings were established as key knowledge-sharing opportunities. In addition, staff came to rely on the knowledge shared from participation in national forums and other avenues to gather outside expertise in addition to a robust interest in using new published evidence as a method to identify areas of emerging risk.

This successful process builds on experience noted by John Kenagy, MD author of *Designed to Adapt*, as being in place at Toyota (Kenagy 2009). He explains that by constantly questioning how things are done, by constantly tweaking and applying knowledge gathered from the frontline, Toyota creates a perpetual competitive advantage (Fishman 2006). Toyota line employees change the way they work dozens of times a year (Kenagy 2009). However, in healthcare, changing a practice or behavior often takes many scientific studies before staff and clinicians are convinced that this is the right thing to do.

In this three-pronged approach, leadership is invested in the implementation of all components of EI&K as separate, yet connected, pieces of a process. Equally important, the implementation included a dynamic feedback loop from which the staff came to expect the incorporation of EI&K into how to best deliver safe care at the bedside.

Leadership Support of EI&K: More than Verbal Blessing is Needed

It is important for leaders to encourage capturing, creating and sharing of EI&K in order to ensure proper adaptation to the complexity and context of patient care. To do so, leaders must invest resources in real time or near real-time feedback to constantly update the body of data, its application and subsequent extrapolation to larger populations. In *The Checklist Manifesto*, Atul Gawande shares an example from the airline industry of rapid update, application and effective extrapolation to all Boeing 777 pilots (Gawande 2010). In the example, (data) from a detailed investigation led to new information (procedures) to recover flight control if icing caused engine failure. Within 30 days, the Boeing team tested and refined a revised checklist by applying knowledge generated by its use and subsequent revision. The checklist was then sent to every owner of a Boeing 777 worldwide with effective and successful knowledge transfer. Similar processes should be resourced and facilitated by leaders in healthcare.

INFOBOX 5.3: LACK OF SHARING=LACK OF SAFETY

Fires in the operating room are rare yet they occur (Hart et al. 2011). If the members of a distinct procedure area experience a surgical fire incident and do not share learnings with the operating room, or, a fire in one hospital in a healthcare system does not result in any shared learnings with the other hospitals in the system, EI&K failures have occurred.

Recent news about six surgical fires that occurred at the Cleveland Clinic over 12 months prompted one patient involved to come forward. The patient's hope is that by sharing her knowledge of the experience she can persuade Ohio lawmakers to make reporting the fires mandatory (Suchetka 2010).

It is tragic when a healthcare sentinel event in one part of the country repeats itself in another (e.g., heparin event in neonates or vincristine misadministration) (ISMP Alert 2010; ISMP Alert 2005). It is equally tragic when an event repeats itself within the same organization, the same unit or even on the same shift on the same unit (see Infobox 5.3). It is critical for leaders to model and create behavior norms for open reporting, active questioning and second order problem-solving to ensure rapid learning turnaround that facilitates patient safety.

"It is important for leaders to encourage capturing, creating, and sharing of EI&K in order to ensure proper adaptation to the complexity and context of patient care."

In comparing healthcare to the example of the Boeing 777 quick hardwiring of procedural change, it is important for healthcare leaders to understand the emerging science around successful spread of EI&K is in its infancy. Currently, very little post-evaluation reflection is performed following large-scale patient safety initiatives. As a result, successful projects reported in the literature typically reflect early pre-post successes and are typically laid out in a linear fashion as an abbreviated bullet form. Recently, the Johns Hopkins Armstrong Institute for Patient Safety reviewed their Michigan Keystone Project work as a collaborative through the lens of social science (Dixon-Woods et al. 2011). They reported that the central line associated blood stream infections (CLABSIs) project success in Michigan was very much about reframing the initiative as a shared social problem capable of being solved. They created a densely networked community – a community of practice – which used rigorous data as a discipline. The community also used multiple interventions with more of an impact in shaping culture than as a technical focus. At the other end of the EI&K spectrum, it was also noted by the Keystone team that social time enabled knowledge to be shared and lent to the success of the program (Dixon-Woods et al. 2011). To lead, executives should value and embrace such collaborations without fear or filter beyond their institutional boundaries for patient safety to continue to improve.

How to Begin to Close the Gap

Leaders need to enable an organizational culture with a commitment that links robust EI&K with patient safety. If there is a chasm between the culture envisioned and the culture that exists, Schein would suggest that organizational leaders create temporary "cultural islands" (Schein 2004). These "islands" are intentionally designed as safe environments for problem-solving without judgment, cynicism and fear. Learner anxiety is reduced, and the team understands that there is a tolerance for failure. Curiosity, questioning, listening, seeking and sharing tacit knowledge are all encouraged to proactively identify and address holes in the Swiss Cheese. In such a culture, leadership detoxifies failure (Edmondson 2011). Managing the learning experience is critical. Since culture is a reflection of a social system's learning experiences, a group will return to the behaviors and problem-solving that resulted in a successful learning experience. When they return to this "way of doing things" frequently enough, it becomes the unspoken "way of doing things" – ergo the culture.

KEY TAKE-AWAYS

- Culture is a primary influence on how evidence, information and knowledge are shared akin to how safety happens in a healthcare organization.
- Leadership is a primary driver in situating EI&K work within the culture of safety construct.
- The context leadership should adopt to generate commitment to EI&K improvements can be enhanced through connecting the work to learning organizational and system safety concepts.
- Leaders at all levels of the organization have a responsibility to "walk the talk" of EI&K sharing through visible commitment, resource and behavioral modeling.

Suggested Reading

Berwick, D.M. 2002. *Escape Fire*. Commonwealth Fund. Available at: http://www. commonwealthfund.org/usr_doc/berwick_escapefire_563.pdf [accessed: 27 March 2013].

Leonard, M., Frankel, A., Federico, F., Frush, K. and Haraden, C. (eds) 2013. *The Essential Guide for Patient Safety Officers, Second Edition*. Oakbrook Terrace, IL: Joint Commission Resources, Institute for Healthcare Improvement.

Nance, J.J. 2008. *Why Hospitals Should Fly: The Ultimate Flight Plan to Patient Safety and Quality Care*. Boseman, MT: Second River Healthcare.

Reason, J. 1990. *Human Error*. Cambridge: Cambridge University Press.

Schein, E.H. 2004. *Organizational Culture and Leadership: The Jossey-Bass Business and Management Series*. Third Edition. San Francisco, CA: John Wiley & Sons Inc.

6

Weakness in the Evidence Base: Latent Problems to Consider and Solutions for Improvement

Amanda Ross-White, Affaud Anaïs Tanon and Sumant Ranji

There is nothing more deceptive than an obvious fact.

Arthur Conan Doyle, The Boscombe Valley Mystery

It's Complicated: The Relationship between Patient Safety and Evidence-Based Medicine

Since the publication of *To Err is Human* (Kohn et al. 2000), many interventions have been developed and implemented to improve patient safety. It has been established that an impressive proportion of these interventions have been implemented without any solid scientific proof of their effectiveness (Auerbach, Landefeld and Shojania 2007; Shekelle et al. 2013). The question of what place should be given to evidence-based medicine in the young field of patient safety has divided the patient safety community since then. For some researchers:

> ... *the paradigm of evidence-based medicine arose from the realization that healthcare interventions, no matter how common sense or physiologically sound, often lack benefit and sometimes even cause harm. Since safety practices also may prove ineffective, wasteful, or*

even harmful, there is no reason to exempt most safety practices from
the scrutiny of an evidence-based approach (Shojania et al. 2002).

That is to say, the research evidence, especially as defined by the evidence-based medicine movement, needs to be considered in every effort to improve patient safety, as Sackett and colleagues have noted (Sackett et al. 2000).

For other researchers like Leape, Berwick and their colleagues, a perspective driven exclusively by research evidence is not appropriate for the patient safety field. They emphasize the fact that the field cannot afford to wait until the kind of evidence required by the evidence-based medicine movement has accumulated to intervene (Leape, Berwick and Bates 2002; Berwick 2008). Other factors they note include the rarity of adverse events that make clinical trials extremely expensive and the fact that patient safety interventions that target the system are not conducive to the kind of experiments favored by the evidence-based medicine movement. They propose to broaden the scope of what should be considered as evidence in the patient safety field and include knowledge produced by learning methods such as "pragmatic science" based on observation methods and reflective practice. Some methods of this pragmatic science include, for example, tracking effects over time, especially with graphs, using the knowledge of local workers, integrating detailed process knowledge into the work of interpretation, using small samples and short experimental cycles to learn quickly, and employing powerful multifactorial designs rather than univariate ones when the better questions for the time are formative, not summative (Berwick 2005).

Since the debate between these two tendencies is not yet solved, what is considered evidence in the patient safety field is very broad and therefore the methods to identify evidence-based information vary widely. Bibliographic databases are established sources, but evidence can also be found in other types of databases, such as those offering cited reference searching, or grey literature, and materials on the open web discovered via search engines like Google or more narrowly through Google Scholar (Haig and Dozier 2003). For clinical practice, the evidence-based medicine movement recommends bibliographic databases like Evidence-based Medicine Reviews (EBMR), as well as evidence-based journals and online services that summarize the evidence contained in traditional journals (Sackett et al. 2000).

But knowing where to look for evidence is not enough. Even the most skilled searchers and users of information, evidence and knowledge can be hampered by latent conditions either in their experience or in the literature itself.

Healthcare executives and clinicians are by now generally familiar with latent problems in healthcare systems, including organizations and equipment (see for example Lowe 2006), problems that may only become apparent when errors or harm occur. There has been less discussion in the patient safety arena of the latent problems inherent in the literature as a factor contributing to failures. These factors – holes in the evidentiary Swiss cheese – can also be devastating, with the Roche case (discussed elsewhere in this text) as a prime example.

Latent conditions in the literature (encompassing evidence and information, if not knowledge) can include:

- Gaps in the evidence base.

- Weaknesses in the primary research process.

- Authors' over-reliance on faulty research tools.

- Slow dissemination uptake.

- Problems of access to primary research.

- Retraction, fraud and bias in primary research and misinformation (Steen 2011a; Steen 20011b), particularly at the patient and primary caregiver level.

This chapter discusses issues with the tools and processes used to gather information and evidence, particularly bibliographic databases, web search engines and point-of-care tools. Also discussed are problems with the evidence base itself, as well as with the information seeker, that could make the resources difficult to use. Some solutions will be proposed to aid those seeking evidence in the patient safety field.

Can't Find the Evidence

All research tools used for gathering evidence are problematic; there is no perfect tool to deliver both all the necessary information as well as compile it in a way that works for every potential user.

Access problems plague all the resources discussed below. While Google and PubMed® are "free" tools (provided, of course, one has Internet access), point-of-care subscription based services can be cost prohibitive for individuals not based in a large healthcare organization that can afford such tools.

Using free tools does not solve factors limiting access to the actual evidence sources, which can cost hundreds of dollars per article, or thousands of dollars for subscriptions. It is important to point out that the costs of medical publications are increasing faster than inflation: one UK study found average price increases of 6.5 percent from 2000–2007 for internationally produced medical titles, with average increases of 12 percent in the social sciences (Creaser and White 2008). Analysis of single journal price increases and other work reflect similar escalations (Day 2010; Eisenberg and Romero 2010).

Access to the medical literature is uneven, as most publishers are UK or US based, leaving other countries subject not just to the vagaries of inflation but also the financial markets that determine the purchasing power of their currencies. As librarians deal with this squeeze on purchasing power, they also are answering to executive decision makers who may lack a full understanding of the publishing market and be under the influence that information is effectively and freely available via the Internet.

In addition to the biases in scope each resource harbors, researchers have their own biases as well. Chapter 14 explores these issues in more detail.

Using Bibliographic Databases

"No database was able to retrieve all the literature on a topic and a search in any single database resulted in only half the literature being retrieved (Lawrence 2008)."

In the landscape of electronic evidence gathering, bibliographic databases are one of the most traditional tools. Bibliographic databases are collections of records or references to published literature, including journal and newspaper articles, conference proceedings, reports, government and legal publications, patents, books, etc. The databases typically include search engines. They are almost always the most abundant source of peer-reviewed scientific evidence. However, finding information using these tools is not always straightforward.

INFOBOX 6.1: QUESTIONS TO ASK OF ANY BIBLIOGRAPHIC* TOOL TO UNCOVER LATENT CONDITIONS

"What biases does the tool introduce?"

    Is it grounded in a particular point of view?

"How can I determine what evidence is missing?"

    What is the scope of the tool?

"How can I find the middle ground between time spent accessing information and time spent processing information?"

    This applies to the whole research process, as well as to particular tools.

* literature, information compilation

INDEXING AND SEARCHING ISSUES

In most bibliographic databases, document surrogates such as abstracts are organized using an index language or thesaurus of keywords. This means that each document in the database is linked with specific terms that describe the document content and the document source (for example, a journal. The terms can be free natural language terms or a controlled vocabulary designed by the database owner, such as MEDLINE®'s MeSH (Medical Subject Headings).

In order to retrieve evidence effectively in databases organized as described above, it is necessary to master the index language and sometimes the Boolean logic function – the manner in which linking operators like "and," "or," "not" broaden or narrow the set of documents retrieved from the search. To ensure the best results possible, database users should be able to make their clinical questions very explicit and to translate them appropriately when searching the database. Some researchers have shown that poor retrieval arises from lack of or inappropriate use of available index terms or from faulty use of Boolean logic operators (Bronander et al. 2004; Herskovic et al. 2007; Markey 2007; Macedo-Rouet et al. 2012).

The fact that bibliographic databases rely on indexing and controlled vocabulary introduces biases as indexers can be inconsistent while coding the documents. Furthermore, due to the length of the indexing process, the most recent articles are not reliably indexed right away nor included in databases. Notable examples such as the Joint Commission's *Sentinel Event Alerts* and flagship patient safety peer-reviewed publication *Journal of Quality and Patient Safety* are typically delayed – the latter routinely a month – before appearing in PubMed®. In addition, papers from less established journals are often included more slowly than those from established journals with which the database company has had a long relationship, which may mean that new fields of research have the potential to be missed. These latent conditions compromise the gathering of evidence. Issues discussed above like poor indexing, lack of coverage of a new discipline, etc., result in a less than complete set of results, but this failure is not always apparent to the researcher: information seeker or librarian.

Further complications in bibliographic databases can introduce additional failures in the gathering of evidence and information. All databases have different designs and embedded search functions. For example, a database can return search results in a variety of list formats – relevance (as determined by the internal structure of the database), year, etc. Search results can often be dauntingly long lists, leaving the researcher unsure of how to extract the relevant evidence.

Indexing language and controlled vocabularies are different from one database to another. Search strategies developed for one database need to be adapted to the indexing structure, limits and special features available to another database. The healthcare professional – clinical or administrative – pressed for time may not be able to effectively transfer search skills from one database to another that is organized very differently.

The language in which a database is placed itself is problematic for access to research. Not only is English the most used language but, when academic texts are written at a high literacy level, even native English speakers struggle with comprehension of the text.

Last but not least, a single database cannot cover the whole health field. To effectively search the literature, a medical professional must know the best and most comprehensive databases to use for answers to the problem at hand.

DATABASE SCOPES AND COSTS: MIND THE GAPS

The perceived notion of completeness of a database can lead to presumptions that when a search has been well-executed, the evidence and information in the literature has been fully explored. This is not the case even with very important databases like PubMed®. Healthcare information is scattered across many disciplines and publications, and therefore throughout a large number of bibliographic resources (Doms and Schroeder 2005). For example, in the area of injury prevention, a very interdisciplinary topic of study, a comparison of four databases found a retrieval rate of between 16.7 and 81.5 percent of research articles on any given topic (Lawrence 2008). No database was able to retrieve all the literature on a topic and a search in any single database resulted in only half the literature being retrieved (Lawrence 2008). Patient safety literature is just as diverse.

Figures are worse in nursing, allied health and other medical-related fields, with only 10.6 percent of articles available through widely accessed tools (Bjork et al. 2010). This leaves at best less than a quarter of research available freely online. The situation may be more limited in developed countries and developing world countries, particularly when other barriers, such as language, are added to the mix.

The Web: Search Engines and Web-Based Bibliographic Tools

Database producers, sometimes in conjunction with librarians and other information professionals, have tried, for the more than 40 years that bibliographic databases have been extant, to find ways to make searching easier but still efficient, without requiring the user to learn arcane indexing languages and the like. The results have been mixed. There remains a learning curve to effectively search most databases.

With the phenomenal possibilities offered by the development of the Internet, new tools have emerged with user-oriented features. Some of these are:

- Natural language queries – the user need not use any particular syntax but can simply enter a statement or a question formulated much as would be done conversationally.

- Query formulation assistance – this encompasses features that help the user reformulate queries from the selection of relevant documents.

- Query by example – where the user can submit a document and ask for "similar" documents to be retrieved from a document database.

However, there is a downside to these easier-to-use search functions that retrieve a broad set of results. The matching process between the user's search query and the documents retrieved is no longer so exact, which means users ultimately have to formulate their searches in very explicit, as well as complete, ways to yield the best set of search results. A typical example of inexactness in databases is the use of "fuzzy" search algorithms, where the system compensates for spelling errors and returns a list of results based on likely relevance even though search words and spellings may not exactly match.

Newer databases with augmented user tools often present the more relevant search results first, using features like ranked retrieval results (systems that list items in order of relevance to the search, based on the database's determination of relevance) and semantic search (systems that try to understand the user intent using various elements like the context of the search, the location from which the search has been made, the user's previous choices, etc.).

GOOGLE: A VAST, BUT LIMITED, SEARCH ENGINE

Google was launched in 1998 and has grown into the most visited search engine in the world. Despite its popularity, Google has been criticized for various reasons, including possible manipulation of search results. Eli Pariser's book *The Filter Bubble* (2011) draws attention to the issue that Google delivers different results to different people, according to signals like the geographic location of the user, the browser used, and the history of the user's searches (Mastrangelo 2010; Noorbakhsh et al. 2012).

"Researchers must be aware of the latent conditions in Google use, and guard against them."

Anecdotal evidence indicates Google is often the first-choice tool for healthcare research, because it is fast, available 24/7 and returns large sets of results. Researchers must be aware of the latent conditions in Google use, and guard against them.

To illustrate a likely Google scenario: a clinician may know how to retrieve a guideline via a Google search based on past experience. If the clinician needs the guideline while in surgery, and asks a unit clerk to grab it, the clerk will likely not have the same experience. The clerk may not have searched for this guideline before, will likely be using a different computer, perhaps even in a different town than where the clinician searched (triggering Google's place-

and person-specific features), and it is likely the involved clinician has not spelled out the exact search terms to use. Thus the clerk's search would likely retrieve different results, which may or may not include the guideline. The surgery process could be delayed while the search for the guideline continues.

Search engines like Google are for-profit businesses and as such they are more interested in serving their advertiser interests than the searcher looking for evidence (Vine 2004; Google Inc 2011). The information accessed through Google has not always been evaluated for its quality. As a result of the diverse experiments on its pages and its users, Google can deliver advertisements to information seekers; this can be another threat to patient safety (McNamera 2008; Google Inc 2011).

While Google easily gives the impression of providing access to all online information, it only reaches what is called the "Surface Web," which represents just a fraction of what is available via the Web. Search engines do not have access to the "Deep Web," which consists of proprietary sites, government and research sites, library catalogs and subscription databases and journals (Bergman 2001). When Google does have access to the Deep Web it only indexes a small portion of it (Grenzeback 2009).

Google Scholar searches more academic, government, literary and non-profit sites, but the complete search algorithm is not known, so one cannot assume a search retrieves all scholarly results, as Scholar does not search all of the Deep Web either. With both Google and Google Scholar, users have no knowledge of what sites, domains or publishers are included in the search and how deep the search goes within the content. While this lack of information of what Google is searching is not typically an issue for the casual user, it illustrates the limitations of Google when accurate information or evidence is required for a complex, high-risk environment such as a hospital.

The global influence of Google and its user-oriented search features have, to many scholars, lead to a preference for unsophisticated searching (Noorbakhsh et al. 2012; Steinbrook 2006; Dogan 2009). The unintended consequence of this has made it more difficult for users to apply more complicated and reliable methods of searching when they are seeking evidence through use of discipline-based databases and search engines which have the potential to retrieve more high-quality evidence and information than a quick Google search (Leiberger and Aldrich 2010).

WEB-BASED PRODUCTS FOR BIBLIOGRAPHIC SEARCHING

Web-based services have also been developed to support user needs when seeking evidence in traditional bibliographic databases. For example, there are now add-on tools that graphically display the results of a search in PubMed® highlighting relationships of genes or proteins (Plake et al. 2006). There are even other search engines or interfaces that access the MEDLINE® database, and present the results of research on genes or proteins in hierarchical clusters (Doms and Schroeder 2005). Indeed, compared to MEDLINE®, PubMed® is itself an interface to MEDLINE® allowing for different sorting and displaying of results (depending on the actual access mechanism), while not always allowing a user to get to all the MEDLINE® content.

Most of these innovative tools are in their infancy and have not yet been fully evaluated in terms of three key bibliographic database standards:

- Precision – the ratio of truly relevant retrieved documents to the number of retrieved documents for a query.

- Recall – the ratio of the number of truly relevant retrieved documents to the total number of relevant documents.

- Response time (Kim and Rebholz-Schuhmann 2008).

These tools are not yet available for the full spectrum of healthcare disciplines.

EVIDENCE-BASED INFORMATION RESOURCES TOOLS

One solution proposed for the problem of computer algorithms delivering tailored search results is to use human filters. Prior to the Internet and easy electronic access, research experts and librarians served as human filters, retrieving and summarizing literature searching results for clinicians and executives, using their knowledge of bibliographic databases and of the clinicians' and administrators' communication styles and information needs. This sort of customized approach is the idea behind point-of-care (POC) tools such as UpToDate™ and others. POC evidence summaries are web-based compendia designed to provide clinicians with comprehensive evidence condensed into easily digestible formats. Physicians are encouraged to

"Clinicians need to be aware of the limitations of point-of-care research products and be cautious when relying on one for evidence-based decision-making."

use the compendia during consultations or as a second opinion in their clinical decision-making (Banzi et al. 2011). These tools promote the use of evidence-based methodologies to develop their content to enhance their credibility for users at the sharp end.

In a recent study, Banzi and colleagues demonstrated that all point-of-care tools are not equal in their updating speed (Banzi et al. 2011). But updating in POC is not only about the surveillance of the literature to detect new publications, it is also about assessing whether the publications offer new information that might change recommendations for clinical practice as well as how that information should be included in the "old" body of knowledge (see discussions by Shekelle et al. 2001; Clark and Horton 2010). Point-of-care tools use different methodologies for updating their content and users should be aware of this.

Some POC tools are not as evidence-based as they claim to be as they provide no explicit methodology for searching, or for what they include and exclude in their results. These two functions, search methodology and refining results, should be the most basic criteria for evaluating evidence-based point-of-care tools, as noted in a 2009 study: "Does the resource provide an explicit statement about the type of evidence on which any statements or recommendations are based? Did the authors adhere to these criteria?" (Straus and Haynes 2009: 944).

In a study using citation analysis, a set of common topics were used to compare the updating speed of five point-of-care tools. The authors found that over 50 percent of references cited by these tools were from pre-2001, or were seven years old or greater, indicating that the most current available evidence was not always used. They also found that the tools vary a great deal in terms of the type of evidence used in their development (Ketchum, Saleh and Jeong 2011). Furthermore, there was little overlap in citations used, suggesting that the authors of the five products examined were not using similar search or inclusion/exclusion criteria. Clinicians need to be aware of the limitations of POC research products and be cautious when relying on one for evidence-based decision-making. Administrators also need to keep this in mind when they allocate the evidence needs of their clinical staff. One stop shopping could open the door to failure.

Despite the importance of currency, illustrated in the information failures in the Roche case, using the most current resources can also be problematic, if critical information is omitted from updates. As the committee investigating the Roche incident discovered, the four most recent editions of Goodman and Gilman's toxicology text, as well as the most recent edition of Fishman's *Pulmonary Medicine*, did not contain information about hexamethonium-related pulmonary toxicity, although previous editions did (Steinbrook 2002).

How much patient safety information can be found within POC tools is also an important question. The patient safety evidence base is not only found in biomedical journals, but also in the legal and engineering literature. How well do point-of-care tools cover these journal areas? This is an area which needs further analysis.

Weaknesses in the Existing Evidence Base

Even if a researcher has executed a perfect search that eliminates as many biases as possible, has searched all available databases, grey literature, newsletters and Internet resources, compiled the results and obtained, either electronically or in print, all the resources, problems can still exist with the results. These problems may not be apparent to the researcher. These include problems with what sort of evidence and information is actually published as well as misinterpretations and misapplications of the results of literature searches.

PROBLEMS WITH THE PUBLISHED LITERATURE

Much has been made of positive publication bias. A 2007 Cochrane review found that only 64 percent of research presented at conferences made it to publication, and that studies that showed positive results were more likely to be published (Scherer, Langenberg and von Elm 2007). While this is more prominent among industry-funded trials, research funded by other sources is also subject to this bias. Authors have many ways to make their studies seem more compelling than they are, such as changing the outcome measure or using an outcome measure that is easier to attain. Trial lengths are shortened or lengthened to better effect outcomes. Note that this doesn't always mean intentional malfeasance on the part of industry-funded researchers alone: a qualitative systematic review on the topic found no significant differences in methodological quality between industry-funded and independent studies (Sismondo 2008). However, industry-funded studies were more likely to be associated with results that favor the sponsor's interests.

Fraud and unintentional errors also happen in medical research. According to Steen and others, some research conditions are more likely to lead to misinformation, unintentional errors and outright fraud, including: small sample and effect sizes; the testing of too many hypotheses at once; wide parameters for the study design and assessment of the study; and highly competitive and/or "hot topic" areas (Steen 2011a).

Steen discusses studies by Ionnadis and colleagues that indicate inaccurate medical studies are further propagated by citations to them (Steen 2011a). Thus the misinformation, error or fraud can be deeply buried, and remain a latent failure even if the original paper is retracted.

The existence of fraud and misinformation provides another argument for a careful search process that encompasses use of multiple databases – ideally by more than one expert. Many database indexing systems provide a means with which retracted studies, corrections and outright fraudulent research can be linked, so that researchers can be alerted to problem studies. However, even in known cases of researcher fraud, it is up to individual journals to review and retract papers, and individual database producers to remove or highlight (e.g., via a watermark on the PDF file) fraudulent or error-filled papers. The International Committee of Medical Journal Editors does provide a recommendation that retracted articles be noted as such in the online table of contents and in the title of the original article, although this practice is not always followed (Wright and McDaid 2011).

The necessity of retractions in the medical literature is in part due to weaknesses in the primary research process. Promotion, tenure and pay increases at universities are often driven by two factors: the ability to produce more research funding and the success of past research, often measured by the h-index (Egghe 2011) or other measures of impact on a profession and its literature. Other issues include lack of application of such impact metrics to primary patient safety journals. For example, the Joint Commission's *Journal on Quality and Patient Safety* is not included in the Thompson-Reuters *Web of Knowledge Science Citation Index*, as of this writing.

Research funding agencies are increasingly requiring applicants to state their h-index measure on applications. This can result in established researchers receiving more funding, and therefore greater opportunity to publish in the future. It also means that less popular areas of research, from rare diseases to diseases that impact the developing world in greater proportion, may receive less funding and less attention because they will in turn have less of an "impact." With an estimated 70 percent of trials reported by major medical journals being funded by pharmaceutical industry money, it is key that the more limited government funding be allocated appropriately (Goldacre 2009).

PROBLEMS WITH INTERPRETING WHAT HAS BEEN FOUND

One problem with being unable to use the evidence is that clinicians are often not explicitly taught how to read a paper (Roberts and Klamen 2010). It is often assumed by professors and administrators at post-secondary schools, and medical schools in particular, that students are capable of reading critically and efficiently. Even when students are taught such analytical skills, the skills are often not reinforced. If physicians are unable to adequately read a paper, what about healthcare administrators? When executive directors of healthcare organizations were asked if they ever read research articles, they said the articles were often inaccessible and took too much time to read (Bigelow and Arndt 2003). Nursing students have also demonstrated, in some instances, low literacy skills, which can result in poor use of evidence which has which has the potential to contribute to patient safety issues (Hardy, Segatore and Edge 1993).

While all the tools discussed have their problems, latent or more obvious, how often do clinicians take the time to verify their results in a second, or third, source? Once an answer has been found, how often is it taken at face value, with full trust placed in the source, however reliable it may be? From a systems perspective, the lack of skill individuals have in using search tools, evaluating the information and evidence found, and providing access to resources is often not recognized or built into the evidence-gathering process. Searches are not always done by librarians, or people with current training in literature searching, and when they are, they are rarely reviewed by a second person, a recommended practice which would provide a check to ensure that evidence has not been missed (McGowen and Sampson 2008).

Both clinicians and researchers often depend on abstracts to determine the relevancy of an article, a practice that can be problematic. Clinicians rely on abstracts due both to time pressures and to the lack of availability of full text of some articles (almost all abstracts are free; many articles are not). Clinicians can also experience difficulties in comprehending and analyzing the content of a paper.

"When executive directors of healthcare organizations were asked if they ever read research articles, they said the articles were often inaccessible and took too much time to read (Bigelow and Arndt 2003)."

In the case of primary researchers, systematic review protocol requires a screening of articles at the title/abstracts level to determine which papers to include or exclude from the review (Joanna Briggs Institute 2011). However, numerous studies have demonstrated problems with abstracts as they are currently written. Some of the most frequent errors in abstracts being:

- Inaccuracies of data presented (Pitkin, Branagan and Burmeister 1999).

- Omissions of key information that is in the full paper (Ward, Kendrach and Price 2004).

- Failure to report harms (Berwanger et al. 2009; Bernal-Delgado and Fisher 2008).

A patient safety-related example of difficulties in using the evidence is the development of rapid response teams, or medical emergency teams. While initial studies showed largely positive effects of teams in reducing mortality, these were often small studies with poor methodological rigor. Subsequent review has found that while rapid response teams reduce cardiac arrests outside of intensive care units, and may be beneficial in some specific populations (for example, pediatrics), they do not significantly reduce overall mortality (Chan et al. 2010). Despite this, only three years after many of the initial studies were done, many more hospitals have implemented rapid response teams.

Some Solutions, and, What All This Means for Patient Safety

It is very important for those seeking evidence in the patient safety field to be aware of the abundance of bibliographic tools (databases, search engines, and more) available to them and to understand the strengths and the weaknesses of these tools in order to use them appropriately.

Depending upon the kind of question being researched, some tools may be more appropriate than others. A distinction can be made between "Background" questions asked to acquire general knowledge about a condition or a thing and "Foreground" questions asked for specific knowledge to inform decision-making (Sackett et al. 2000).

To answer background questions, sources like online textbooks and bibliographic databases (especially topic searches) are typically useful.

However, search engines like Google can be used as a first step if the following conditions are fulfilled:

- The information seeker knows exactly what to look for and is confident that the evidence is available free on the Web;

- The quick, simple and most popular answer is good enough; and

- The searcher does not have access to a research library but can use Google Scholar or Google Books (Leibiger and Aldrich 2010).

Some point-of-care tools (not all of them) offer information for background questions like UpToDate™ (Weinfeld and Finkelstein 2005).

To answer foreground questions, bibliographic databases, especially evidence-based ones, and point-of-care tools, are the preferred resources. The Web-based tools to search the bibliographic databases can assist the information seeker in more sophisticated activities. For example, GoPubMed can be used to browse an area of potential interest and select document clusters that seem more interesting, and the PubMed® feature of displaying queries history with results numbers can be used to identify less studied topics for new discovery (Kim and Rebholz-Schuhmann 2008).

When searching bibliographic databases, clinical hedges or search filters can compensate for the user's lack of skills (Haynes et al. 1994; Greenhalgh 1997). Some filters have been developed for the patient safety field (for further discussion, see Golder and Loke 2009; Tanon et al. 2010).

INFOBOX 6.2: BACKGROUND AND FOREGROUND

Sackett et al. (2000) suggest that there are a variety of types of questions that affect evidence and information seeking in medicine. Those related to physiology, pathophysiology, epidemiology and disease/condition progression are "background" questions, and are associated within underpinning knowledge. For example, what are the changes to the cardiovascular system during pregnancy? Care questions constitute the majority of EBM questions and are "foreground questions."

Source: Cluett (2006: 38).

Another important point is for those seeking information and evidence to take any opportunity to be more informed and to be able to critically appraise the evidence they retrieve, or at least find people who can help them do so. In this way, the knowledge of their colleagues can be applied to improve the reliability of the process.

Information and Knowledge: Prerequisites for Effective Literature Searching

Evidence-based practice is one of the cornerstones of patient safety. Activities from the blunt end to the sharp end need to be designed, implemented and carried out to ensure evidence is reliably applied to patient care.

For healthcare executives, this means recognizing that the process of reading and applying research evidence to practice takes time. It involves ensuring that all employees (not just physicians) have access to effective information retrieval tools. It means staff know not to blindly rely on any single source. It is important to ensure that all employees are appropriately trained in the use of these tools and that seeking out additional evidence is encouraged. These must be leadership and cultural priorities to support safe care.

Healthcare executives can start to lead by embracing these behaviors. They should take the time to access the best available evidence, from the medical, patient safety and management literature. When executives make the best use of the resources available to them, ensure their staff are adequately trained to use evidence and information access tools, apply the evidence found, and continually evaluate their own EI&K use processes they encourage clinicians to do the same. Healthcare educators also must take into account the importance of teaching and modeling appropriate information and evidence seeking and usage behavior.

For clinicians, successful use and safe application of the published evidence means learning to read and analyze a paper from the methods section, not just the abstract. Clinicians must take advantage of all the resources at their disposal, both point-of-care tools and databases, and commit to being trained in the usage of these resources, or have staff who have competence that is demonstrable. Furthermore, awareness of the strengths and weaknesses of all of these resources is required. Clinicians must use the other pillars of evidence-based medicine – clinical competence and patient circumstances – to judiciously use the evidence in decision-making. Lastly, clinicians must be prepared to advocate for the use of these tools from healthcare executives who may not be aware of the role these tools play in their daily work.

Patients have an expectation, and indeed a right, to the best available treatment. They expect clinicians to base their decisions on sound research and to provide care accordingly. In order to improve the safety of patients, clinicians must ensure that patients are not receiving harmful, ineffective or delayed treatments. Leadership and management must resource systems to provide access to this evidence. Thus calling for clinicians to be familiar with evidence and being able to find it, access it, read it, understand it and apply it.

KEY TAKE-AWAYS

- The evidence and information base is rife with latent conditions that could affect its reliability if accessed blindly.
- This weakness represents a systemic failure that could be a contributor to poor clinical decision-making and potentially patient harm.
- Robust processes including search and resource experts should be designed and enabled to ensure the EI&K identification and acquisition mechanisms that help to inform care take the weaknesses of the resources and the tools used to find them into account.

Selected Readings

Jacsó, P. 2008. Google scholar revisited. *Online Information Review*, 32(1), 102–14. Available at: http://www.cs.unibo.it/~cianca/wwwpages/dd/08Jacso.pdf [accessed: 20 March 2013].

McGowan, J., Sampson, M. and Lefbvre, C. 2010. An evidence-based checklist for the peer review of electronic search strategies (PRESS EBC). *Evidence Based Library and Information Practice*. Available at: http://ejournals.library. ualberta.ca/index.php/EBLIP/article/view/7402 [accessed: 28 March 2013].

Pariser, E. 2011. *The Filter Bubble: What the Internet is Hiding From You.* New York, NY: Penguin Press.

Steen, R.G. 2011b. Retractions in the medical literature: How many patients are put at risk by flawed research? *Journal of Medical Ethics* [Online]. Available at: http://dx.doi.org/10.1136/jme.2011.043133 [accessed 28 April 2012].

Zorzela. L. et al. 2014. Quality of reporting in systematic reviews of adverse events: systematic review. *British Medical Journal*, January 8, 348:f7668.

PART 3

Building Blocks of Safety that Affect Information, Evidence and Knowledge-sharing

Chapter 7 Synopsis – Systems Thinking, Complexity and EI&K for Safe Care

The author introduces attributes of the systems thinking framework, with the idea of viewing healthcare as a complex system. The chapter covers major concepts of systems thinking and presents selected techniques that stem from systems thinking in order to demonstrate how evidence, information and knowledge are central resources to organizational learning. The chapter places the evidence, information and knowledge-sharing continuum within the messy context of complex systems to foster a dialog on the different ways that EI&K processes can contribute to patient safety.

Chapter 8 Synopsis – Aviation Contexts and EI&K Innovation: Reliability, Teamwork and Sensemaking

This chapter introduces select concepts core to aviation safety as frameworks through which to enhance the recognition of evidence, information and knowledge processes as contributors to safe healthcare delivery. The authors discuss communication, teamwork and sensemaking as vehicles for transferring EI&K. Exploration of high reliability as an organizational construct, crew resource management as a unit-level application, and checklists at the individual level are presented as contexts through which to view EI&K to encourage innovation.

7

Systems Thinking, Complexity and EI&K for Safe Care

Howard Fuller

> *Only with networks to connect the fragmented knowledge base and the capacity to use feedback loops will it be possible to meet the goals of a learning health system: to get information when and where it is needed to make better decisions (Diamond 2011: 166).*

Application of Concepts to Generate EI&K Improvements

Systems thinking is a "conceptual framework, a body of knowledge and tools ... to make the full patterns (information and behavior) clearer, and helps us see how to change them effectively" (Senge 1990: 7). Systems thinking builds a link between four main underlying concepts: personal mastery; mental models; building shared vision; and team learning. The practice of systems thinking is in "seeing" the environment in a particular way which impacts approaches to situations, issues and problems – it allows individuals and organizations to see both the forest and the trees. It facilitates interpretation of actions in an organization as being influenced by culture, work and tasks, and the education and learning of its people.

To Err is Human provided legitimacy to the emerging discipline of patient safety (Kohn et al. 2000). The report declared that the healthcare system was not only in need of repair; the system itself was sick. This new concept of a sick system turned the conversation from blaming individuals to conversations that questioned what, why and how the system failed. It is surmised but not conclusively documented, that often healthcare failures include problems associated with the incorrect communication of evidence, information and knowledge. The *Crossing the Quality Chasm* report discusses the improvement of quality and safety in the US by suggesting systems thinking and complex system (CS) frameworks as effective approaches to aid in making sense of issues or situations and building in processes to enable a system to learn as a whole (Chasm 2001).

Ten years after the publication of *To Err is Human*, prominent patient safety advocate and author Robert Wachter stated "Stronger [research] methods are emerging ... field still debating fundamental questions regarding evidence standards for safety studies" (Wachter 2010: 166). An example of a safety issue in one area, medication, illustrates the ongoing challenges in the complex field of patient safety – Ross Koppel, professor of sociology at the University of Pennsylvania, stated, "The whole idea that we have a good measure of medication errors is stunningly optimistic but entirely unrealistic ... I estimate we capture about 4 percent of all such errors – so we don't know about 96 percent of the errors" (Mitka 2009: 587). The reality of not knowing about the problems indicates a communication failure at a system level.

Accessible evidence, information and knowledge (EI&K) is growing in many fields. This change suggests that healthcare entities could shift how they approach and apply the management and flow of EI&K through prisms like systems thinking in order to improve patient safety. A deeper dive into the networks required to support high-quality EI&K sharing for all healthcare stakeholders suggests EI&K transfer is a broken element in a broken system. A recent IOM report lists some of the breaks in the healthcare systems that are related to EI&K:

1.   A lack of a controlled environment for assessing therapeutic options.

2.   The heterogeneity of patient characteristics.

3.   The distributed nature of both the requirements for and the sources of information (Institute of Medicine 2011: 166).

This report suggests that the more important (and messy) issue is how to truly improve the decision-making that supports safe care and that information, evidence and knowledge are critical in this decision-making process.

This chapter places the evidence, information and knowledge-sharing continuum within the messy context of complex systems (CSs) and promotes the use of systems thinking in EI&K contexts to improve learning and patient safety improvement. To this end, the chapter introduces major concepts of the systems thinking framework and explains how healthcare is a complex system. Also discussed is the transitory nature of information and how knowledge shifts from a static to a dynamic state. Selected techniques used in systems thinking oriented explorations are presented to highlight how evidence, information and knowledge can be used to embed systems thinking philosophies into programs to align with the organization's efforts to learn from the experiences of its staff, leadership and patients.

This chapter also presents two models that demonstrate how evidence, information, and knowledge have flow. An examination of the flow aspect of the sequence adds validity to describing EI&K as a complex element of patient safety. This concept of flow takes information from the realm of something tangible – a commodity transferred from one location to another – to a look at its content, character and behavior (Gleick 1987). Information and evidence are dynamic, changing variables (Bohmer 2009).

Systems Thinking: Concepts, Connections and Healthcare Examples

SYSTEMS THINKING FRAMEWORK: CORE CONCEPTS

Systems thinking, widely disseminated as a business strategy with the publication of *The Fifth Discipline* (Senge 1990), is a set of problem-solving principles rooted in several disciplines, most notably systems dynamics. Systems dynamics, developed by Jay Forrester and others at Massachusetts Institute of Technology (MIT), is a model that seeks to understand complex systems through causal loop diagramming. The model is also used to examine organizational changes and how they affect work (Ackoff 1981). Ackoff described the conceptualization of complex problems as "messy" (Ackoff 1974; Zimmerman, Lindberg and Plsek 2001), a concept which is relevant to the complex issue of patient safety.

This systems approach is different from the concept of continuity of care (moving the patient through the system in a linear fashion). The systems approach focuses on the relationships

"System thinking offers a holistic approach to how EI&K impact safe patient care."

between people and groups of people, and the underlying structure of the system, as will be further illustrated below.

A systems approach often uses continuous improvement techniques and methods to assist an organization to evolve into a *learning* organization. The core attributes of systems thinkers are: personal mastery, mental models, team learning and shared vision.

- Personal Mastery "goes beyond competence and skills ... it means approaching one's life as a creative work" (Senge 1990: 141). Senge and colleagues see personal mastery as continually clarifying what is important and continually learning. Individuals oriented to personal mastery are motivated to continuously learn by achieving clarity around what is important to them. If patient care is of the utmost importance to an individual, viewing workplace interactions through that lens is part of personal mastery. The struggle to seek vision yet remain realistic drives the individual to master new, information and knowledge in order to attain goals in an applicable, actionable way.

- Mental Models "are deeply ingrained assumptions, generalizations, or images that influence how we understand the world and how we take action. Very often, we are not consciously aware of our mental models or the effects they have on our behavior" (Senge 1990: 8). People who are consciously aware of their mental models "expose their own thinking effectively and make that thinking open to the influence of others" (Senge 1990: 9). For example, a cardiologist who has performed one method of catheterization for years, and is aware of this habit, may say aloud to a younger colleague, "I typically do X, but I understand you do Y in this instance, and I would like to understand a new and possibly more effective technique." Infobox 7.1 provides another example of a mental model that could have effects on the safe care of patients.

- Team Learning is a discipline that starts with a "dialog," a technique that requires members of a team to suspend personal assumptions and enter into a mindset of thinking together as a group (Senge, 1990). Team learning implies some kind of positive change whether in understanding, knowledge, ability/skill, processes or routines, or system coordination. (Edmondson, Deillon and Roloff 2007). Teams differ considerably in the extent to which they engage in team learning, and there is a positive correlation between learning and team performance (Edmondson 1999; Gibson and Vermeulen 2003).

- Shared Vision refers to the capacity of all members of an organization to "hold a shared picture of the future of what they seek to create" (Senge 1990: 9). Evidence, information and knowledge – such as sharing stories which serves the dual function of helping individuals attain personal mastery and raising awareness of patient safety – influences mental models and enables the development of shared vision. Sharing stories is a systems thinking technique that has been heralded as an effective method to improve safety (NHS Wales 2010; ISMP 2011).

INFOBOX 7.1: IMPACT OF MENTAL MODELS – AN EXAMPLE

A recurring issue that continually challenges one's mental model is how a geriatric patient is defined and conceptualized. Chronological age is a poor indicator of what makes someone a geriatric patient, but it is often the defining metric. This use of age as a sole metric of a geriatric patient has broader implications when one considers a patient's safety.

For example, if the evidence or information sought is limited by age, this puts into question the completeness of the resources discovered to guide decision-making given that other, less concrete variables may be omitted. If the right questions aren't asked due to false assumptions the results may be flawed.

Reductionism, an aspect of the scientific approach, breaks events into manageable and measurable tasks. It fixes or accounts for several variables to enhance measurement of just one task and demonstrates a cause-and-effect or correlational relationship between two events. A syllogism can illustrate reductionism, for example: if all dogs are animals and this is a dog, then this is an animal. Logical reductive thinking has provided the world great breakthroughs, but the scientific method of approaching problems is only one approach, and is not a means particularly suited to solving social issues involving subjective and emotional factors.

People who work in healthcare often turn to reductionist thinking, rather than systems thinking, to solve problems (Van Beurden et al. 2011) because this approach is more tested, easier and how most healthcare professionals are trained. However, the safe care of patients requires navigating a complex healthcare system that involves multiple events and players that at first glance may seem unrelated. It can benefit a hospital to look at problems holistically to consider a variety of views and perspectives to design effective improvements. In particular, problem solvers must seek to uncover how system feedback loops occur throughout the system from the perspective of the person moving through the system and how processes and work is interconnected. In this way, the two ends of the spectrum – the sharp end and the blunt end – don't inadvertently set their changes up for failure through unintended consequences of a change that didn't fully take impacts across the system into account. This would include decisions made that effect how evidence, information and knowledge moves throughout the system.

SYSTEMS THINKING FRAMEWORK: RELATIONSHIPS AND EI&K

A systems thinker embraces tools and techniques to help understand and resolve complex situations involving people and EI&K in a blame-free fashion. This approach underscores the importance of a focus on the relationship between the people and EI&K as a piece of the structure and contributor to a particular situation. It recognizes that relationships are influenced by feedback loops, mental models and organizational structure. When a medical mishap occurs, a systems thinker does not place blame on any one individual but rather recognizes that human mistakes are expected – as often the systems individuals interact with are not particularly well designed (Agency for Healthcare Research and Quality 2012). Systems thinkers see that a primary focus on reprimand, chastisement and condemation is not the most effective approach to deaing with individual failure and won't help correct the conditions that enabled it. Instead a broader, more tolerant view is taken – an approach that encourages both sharp end and blunt end healthcare workers to pauce to think through the gaps in thesystem, situations of system use, and features of the sytesm that open to door to error.

SYSTEMS THINKING FRAMEWORK: VISUALIZING CONNECTIONS

Loop diagrams are key tools for understanding systems and can help teams surface complex issues, relationships and latent interconnections. Diagramming unearths relationships and boundaries that define the system and environment. Feedback loops, also known as causal loops, are tools that are used to solve problems, while keeping the ebb and flow of the system in mind. Like all diagrams, a feedback loop tells a story.

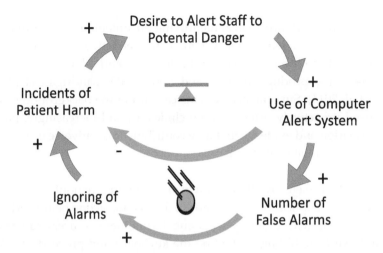

Figure 7.1   Simple Causal Feedback Loop for an Alert Fatigue Situation
Source: Molloy, J. (2012), used with permission.

Table 7.1   Symbols in a Systems Thinking Causal Loop Diagram

Symbol	Name	Represents	Description
Text	Boxes	Links	Descriptions of specific activities that contribute to the loop.
➡	Arrows	Loops	Circles of causality among links where every element is both cause and effect.
☄	Snowball	Reinforcing loops	Loops that grow or shrink at an ever-increasing rate: virtuous or vicious spirals.
⚖	See-Saw	Balancing loops	Loops that grow or shrink within limits, maintaining stability and achieving equilibrium.
+/-	Plus and Minus signs	Effects	Positive or negative effects of a given link: effects change depending on what part of the story is represented.

Source: Moore, M. (2014), based on the work of Peter Senge. Reproduced with permission.

For example, an existing problem in identifying risks and hazards that negatively impact patient safety is alert fatigue. Alerts from various computerized systems can bring to the surface potential care problems dealing with the process of care rather than underlying physiological conditions (Singh et al. 2010; Singh and Sittig 2009). The mass adoption of electronic health record (EHR) systems and integrated surveillance systems can produce many alerts, in fact too many. EHRs are good at identifying documented harm. Surveillance systems, sometimes called trigger systems, can be effective for alerting patients and clinicians to indicators of known harm or potential harm, despite some limitations in the products (Griffin and Resar 2009; Landrigan et al. 2010; Classen et al. 2011). Surveillance systems can run in the background of EHRs and be used proactively. Alerts supply clinicians, and increasingly, patients, with information and evidence that may contribute to an adverse event (Yackel and Embi 2010; Singh et al. 2012).

If alerts are too sensitive they result in an abundance of notifications. Given the lack of direct application of the alerts to the distinct action being performed, to clinicians – as with other systems and technologies – users can fall into ignoring them (e.g., hitting "enter" on the keyboard and proceeding without reading a text pop up). Full stops are not built into any known EHR systems, to keep busy clinicians from clicking through surveillance alerts or other evidence that is shared to minimize patient harm.

Patient safety researcher, physician and champion, Lucian Leape, suggests a number of systemic changes that have the potential to reduce failure at the sharp end (Leape 2009). "Designers [of environment and equipment] should provide feedback through instruments that provide monitoring functions and should build in buffers and redundancy" (Joint Commission International 2008: 75). Current practices have emerged incorporating these techniques.

BUFFERS

Drug information resources are buffers that alert clinicians to potential drug–drug, drug–food, or allergic interactions. A number of medical and some public libraries now offer patients and consumers access to drug/medical informatics tools – from inside the library or from their homes – where they can get information on similar interaction and other hazard warnings. Some tools also flag computer practitioner order entries which are contraindicated and available to multiple agents within the healthcare system. Studies have shown that computer physician/practitioner order entry can reduce serious medication errors by 60–80 percent (Bates et al. 1998, 1999).

REDUNDANCY

"Redundancy is a system design principle that introduces duplicate components to provide fault tolerance. When a component fails, a backup takes over to ensure the system still performs as designed" (Ong and Coriea 2010: e32). The concept, built into aviation and other complex systems, is being considered more broadly in healthcare, although the rigor to make it successful hasn't been collectively embraced (Stahel et al. 2009; Ong and Coriea 2010). Redundancy in tools and validation procedures has been encouraged, for example, in surgical units as a safety mechanism. To illustrate, The Joint Commission's Universal Protocol requires that hospitals mark the joint or limb to be operated upon, and/or that a physician "check in" with a patient to verify the operation and body part prior to going into surgery (Joint Commission n.d.).

STANDARDIZATION

Standardizing how visual information and data are made available through consistent displays is helpful. Layouts used in computerized systems can minimize error by increasing types of pattern recognition that are performed well by all human beings (Bordeaux 2008). Standard procedures and mechanisms for capturing information can bolster evidence-based medicine approaches.

Standardization in Daily Work: The Checklist

Standardization bears a bit more discussion, as checklists are an increasingly important and useful method for standardization in healthcare. (Soong 2013, Thomassen 2014) Checklists were brought prominently into public discourse by Pronovost's "Keystone ICU" project (Provonost et al. 2006), which was promoted globally in the 2008 WHO Surgical Safety Checklist and its accompanying manual (World Alliance for Patient Safety 2008). Atul Gawande's book *The Checklist Manifesto* also raised public awareness of the use of checklists in healthcare (Gawande 2009).

Properly used, a checklist is not a static "to do" list. Rather, a checklist is a mechanism that provides structure for informing learning, embedding new routines and facilitating continuous improvement. The most effective checklists are viewed as living documents. Because they reflect systemic organizational learning, checklists are central to a systems approach to improving patient safety. The ideal checklist is embedded in work processes in which all members of the care team have the power, authority and obligation to question the processes and content at any point in time. The checklist is a regenerative, ever-evolving tool that reflects process learning as it incorporates new research and discoveries in medicine alongside the local knowledge of what works. Communities of practice – groups of practicing individuals who gather to work together to explore and devise practice improvements (Wenger

2006) – have been suggested as one way to create shared knowledge that can be used to develop checklists that will improve patient safety (Lashoher and Pronovost 2010).

Transitioning EI&K from a Static to Dynamic State

Poor communication is often noted as a root cause of a host of organizational problems (O'Daniel and Rosenstein 2008; Joint Commission 2012). Poor communication in healthcare ranges from a person's inability to read handwritten medical orders to cultural barriers to simple misunderstandings of what was stated.

Clinicians tend to "use the first information that comes to mind" (Leape 1994: 1853). Human beings have a tendency to look for evidence that confirms what they have already determined is a course of action, disregarding information that tells them otherwise (Groopman 2007; Leape 1994). And, though individual clinicians may gain knowledge from their mistakes, the changes in practice that result from experience are typically not shared, thus remaining in a silo or vacuum. In other words, external, objective evaluation of what went wrong (and what was learned from the error) often does not occur (Leape 1994).

Information is a changing and dynamic element. "Information is unique as a resource because it can generate itself … with every new interpretation" (Wheatley 2006: 97). In other words, information can contribute to multiple types of knowledge. Because of information's unique ability and because of the heavy workloads of staff at the sharp end: "the information [and knowledge] needs of frontline staff may be latent, and may not recognize their potential knowledge gaps related to patient safety, which can contribute to the erosion of procedures and routines" (MacIntosh-Murray and Choo 2005: 1332).

An informationist or medical librarian has an important role in filling these knowledge gaps and spanning boundaries related to patient safety as a change agent for improvement. For example, informationists can function as a knowledge "bridge" between:

- The nurses' focus on patients and intersections with the system, process and management level activities; and

- The nurses within individual units and resources external to the unit (MacIntosh-Murray and Choo 2005).

Informationists are good at "recognizing patient safety issues and acting as an information seeker... and using the information (research, policies, procedures, standards) as a knowledge translator to explain to the nurses how it applies to their practice" (MacIntosh-Murray and Choo 2005: 1335).

The fundamental mistake often made when trying to address communication and information issues is the misperception of knowledge: what constitutes "knowledge", how knowledge *behaves* and how to *work* with knowledge once it's been *identified*. Knowledge has long been misunderstood as a tangible commodity that bestows power to an individual or a group. Thinking of knowledge as a commodity diverts what may be the more important dimensions of knowledge: its substance, i.e. content, behavior and character (Gleick 1987).

An awareness of information and knowledge issues is becoming even more crucial as strategies are designed, accuracy of tools is tested and reports are relied upon to motivate healthcare decision-making. For example, exploring realities around how and who will keep tools such as databases current and whether or not the changing evidence and information can be validated will reveal complexities on the changing nature of EI&K, if only the right questions are asked (see Infoboxes 4.2 and 6.1).

If EI&K is to function as a source of healthcare system reliability, hospital administration must recognize that all EI&K cannot be controlled and, in fact, must encourage and model its free movement throughout the organization. For example, leadership unit conversations are designed to not only collect information, but as an opportunity for leaders to share information and their knowledge with unit level staff to gather insights on what improvements should take place (Luther and Resar 2013). When an organization adopts this open approach, all users of the EI&K system notice new information, embrace new evidence, and seek new knowledge as it materializes during their work within the EI&K system and the organization (Wheatley 2006).

Key Concepts of a Complex System

> *Systems thinking is especially useful when problems are complex (vs. simple or complicated) (Tompson and Zipperer 2011).*

Wilson and colleagues (2001) define complex systems as a "collection of individual agents with freedom to act in ways that are not always totally predictable, and whose actions are interconnected so that the action of one part changes the context for other agents" (Wilson et al. 2001: 685). Complex systems are defined by four characteristics shared by the individuals who work in them: diversity, connection, interdependence and adaptation. These characteristics interface with learning to generate complexity in a way that highlights how each individual's actions influence the actions of many people (Page 2009).

Because healthcare delivery organizations are complex systems, they are increasingly turning to systems frameworks to solve problems and improve organizational effectiveness. The key concepts of complex system models, derived from an annotated literature review (Bordeaux 2008) are:

- Agents: Agents are the actors within the system. They perceive their surroundings, develop a schema (mental model or paradigm) to interpret what they perceive and then make decisions based on their own criteria.

- Adaptive: Complex systems are adaptive in that the Agents will modify their behaviors based on the circumstances in which they find themselves. The specific adaptation may not be knowable in advance.

- Emergent Behavior: Emergent behaviors are unanticipated patterns of action demonstrated by the agents in the system. They represent adaptations to the environment. What occurs on the macro level may differ from what is seen in the parts of a system.

- Self-Organization: Actors within a complex system self-organize, that is, they form new structures and connections, networks, and systems to carry out a task should their existing structure prove cumbersome or ineffective.

- Equilibrium/Non-equilibrium: In many cases, complex systems never achieve equilibrium. There is no steady, resting state. Complex systems are in flux constantly, and no manner of influence can drive them to a state of no change.

- Diversity: Complexity theory recognizes that the agents of a system are themselves diverse, both in terms of their behaviors and their perceptions of their situation. This diversity of viewpoints and behavior interact and modify each other.

- Schema: Schema are the mental models (or paradigms) that an agent holds regarding a situation. Schemas are how agents interpret their environment and form the basis for future decision-making.

- Network and Cohesiveness: A complex system is any network that exhibits cohesiveness that holds together.

Systems include processes and methods to organize and perform EI&K work. These processes exist regardless of the field of endeavor. These processes take place whether that environment is simple, complicated, complex, chaotic or in disorder.

Models and Frameworks for EI&K Flow Clarity

Knowledge is paradoxically both a thing and a flow (Snowden 2002: 102).

FLOW

During the past two decades, models or frameworks have been developed in order to study how knowledge flows for problem-solving, decision-making and knowledge transfer. Some of these are discussed below:

- Von Hippel (1994) discusses the levels of "stickiness" in solving problems and decision-making. Information stickiness is associated with the flow of explicit and tacit knowledge and the effort required to share it with others. Those issues with higher levels of stickiness, or complexity (and cost), often require higher levels of subject matter expertise and/or more EI&K from agents in the system.

- Nissen and colleagues incorporate a staged knowledge flow approach into several life cycle models (Nissen, Kamel and Sengupta 2000). Nissen has also developed a four-dimensional model that "can be used to classify and visualize a diversity of knowledge-flow patterns through the enterprise" (Nissen 2002: 264). Patterns, in turn, can lead to the discovery of relationships and may show emerging behaviors within the organization.

- Nonaka proposes a mental model for "managing the dynamic aspects of organizational knowledge creating process" (Nonaka 1994: 14). He proposes a "spiral model of knowledge creation [that] illustrates the creation of a ... continual dialogue between tacit and explicit knowledge. As the concept resonates around an expanding community of individuals, it is developed and clarified" (Nonaka 1994: 14). He furthers the notion of knowledge flow by assuming four modes or processes: internalization, combination, socialization, and externalization, that enable individual knowledge to be "enlarged" or "amplified" (Nonaka 1994: 21).

A DEEPER LOOK AT ONE MODEL: CYNEFIN

One knowledge flow framework that is of particular interest is "Cynefin." Cynefin is Welsh and means something like "place" or "habitat," and was developed by knowledge management and complexity science expert David Snowden and other scholars of organizations (Snowden 2000). The Cynefin framework allows all members of an organization, including managers and leaders, to visualize their systems from a fresh vantage point in order to integrate complex concepts into decision-making processes to address their specific daily challenges as well as to see opportunities for improvement.

> The [Cynefin] framework sorts the issues facing leaders into five contexts defined by the nature of the relationship between cause and effect. Four of these – simple, complicated, complex, and chaotic – require leaders (agents) to diagnose situations and to act in contextually appropriate ways. The fifth – disorder – applies when it is unclear which of the other four contexts is predominant (Snowden and Boone 2007: 70).

The framework helps people make sense of "which context they are in so they can not only make better decisions but also avoid the problems that arise when their preferred management style causes them to make mistakes" (Snowden and Boone 2007: 70).

Cynefin is not a category-making framework, but rather a structure where the data precedes the sensemaking and pattern recognition. The framework emphasizes identifying environmental signals through analysis, sensing and probing that leads to the formation of narratives and knowledge transfer. In this framework, narratives are the enablers of knowledge flow throughout an organization, and are also the means by which teams collectively hold knowledge.

COMMONALITIES ON DISCUSSIONS OF KNOWLEDGE FLOW

There is a common theme in all models and frameworks of knowledge flow: the flow of knowledge falls on a continuum from ordered (meaning simple or close in location) to complex or complicated. Three heuristics or "rules of thumb" derived from Snowden illustrate the requirements for managing knowledge:

1.   Knowledge cannot be conscripted; it must be offered freely.

2.   The nature of knowledge is such that humans always know, or are capable of knowing more than they have the physical time or the conceptual ability to say.

3.   Knowledge is deeply contextual; it is triggered by circumstance. Humans know what they know when they need to know it. In understanding what people know an understanding of the context of their knowing is valuable if meaningful questions or actions are being planned to enable knowledge use (Snowden 2002).

A Further Exploration of EI&K Processes

Table 7.2, on the next page, emphasizes the dynamic nature of team learning functions at different levels along the simple to chaotic continuum. Due to the rapid pace of discovery in healthcare, agents draw from multiple domains at different times, and each domain uses diverse strategies to generate knowledge and solve problems.

The following table suggests interdependent relationships as highlighted through the flow aspect of knowledge. Information and knowledge are constantly being discovered and produced leading to a false sense of best evidence or end product, at best a temporary mental model. As more information and knowledge emerge, current facts or evidence become obsolete or replaced with new knowledge. This brings into question what is the paramount evidence, knowledge or level of information to determine best practice. Best practices today are often perceived as static practices which lead to a false sense of knowing in which practitioners see or sense only part of the system. A rigid model of EI&K often lacks the required flexibility for patients and medical professionals to make the best and safest decisions.

Table 7.2   Team EI&K Use from Simple to Chaotic

Continuum level	Simple: Following a recipe	Complicated: Launching a rocket	Complex/Emergent Practice: Raising a child	Chaotic/Novel Practice: Taking action to create craziness then trying to stop the response
How Team Learns	• Cause and effect. • Rules and predictability. • Best practices. • System constrains agents.	• Cause and effect discovery through investigation or rigorous expert knowledge-sharing. • Formal analysis.	• Pattern/behaviors emerge retrospectively. • Cause and effect may not be replicable.	• Dominant pattern when group changes. • Lack of perceivable causal relationships. • Stability-focused interventions and crisis management. • Navigation of temporary state.
EI&K Examples	• Packaged information to direct practice (i.e., Implement unit dosing (Leape 1994). • Use of textbook/database resources.	• Communities of practice. • Checklists. • Practice guidelines. • Clinical queries as an evidence-based info tools.	• Human factors exploration of EI&K use. • Decision-making over time due to misdiagnosis. • Social networks.	• Emergency medicine decision-making. • Trial and error real-time experimentation.

Source: Headings derived from Westley, Patton, and Zimmerman 2006.

Seeing EI&K in a Systems Light

Medical decisions are often fuzzy. Sharing information and talking through the decisions with colleagues and the patient are key to patient safety. Sharing information is different from team learning. Sharing information is critical on a person-to-person level, but, simple information sharing does not always translate into optimal colleague, patient or organizational knowledge. For example, patient-centered care and health literacy are new concepts that are evolving and stand in stark contrast to the model of the physician as the disseminator of all information and chief decision maker. As the healthcare hierarchy flattens, non-physician clinicians and patients and families will become partners in all aspects of patient care (including EI&K sharing). As patients and families and their advocates play a more significant role in decisions regarding their health and safety, there is hope the transfer of EI&K will improve (Beresford 2010).

But sharing information is not enough to improve patient safety. The transfer of knowledge, from clinician to patient at key leverage points in the healthcare system, such as patient transition, is crucial.

The rapidly growing patient safety evidence base suggests the current state of EI&K discovery leads to uncertainty contributing to complexity. Real improvement requires genuine change and new mental models if the healthcare professions want to reach the safety levels of other industries. This change will require systemic thinking and a context-driven approach to patient care models. Evidence-based medicine and other established practices have limitations. If the profession is to do more than make simple improvements in patient safety it will require more than tinkering around the edges of what is often a hierarchical and stratified environment. Systemic and interdisciplinary approaches using multi-modal techniques, such as Cynefin, causal loop diagramming, and complexity orientations are more likely to lead to the improvements sought and desired in care models described in *To Err is Human* (Kohn et al. 2000).

"... simple information sharing does not always translate into optimal colleague, patient or organizational knowledge."

How organizations incorporate EI&K into patient care and safety processes needs to take into account the evolving and disparate needs of clinicians, consumers, managers and leaders. Each member of the system needs to better understand what evidence and information is uploaded into the tools they increasingly rely upon and how that content can be used to support decision-making. If the approach adopted is too rigid and fails to account for the complexity of the process and the environment within which it is employed EI&K will not achieve its optimal contribution.

KEY TAKE-AWAYS

- Effective and reliable evidence, information, and knowledge processes require alignments with systems thinking to be successful.
- Complexity theory and knowledge flow are two avenues for exploration to ensure EI&K processes are designed and implemented to be highly reliable in the healthcare environment.

Suggested Reading

British Medical Journal four-part series on complexity:

Fraser, S.W. and Greenhalgh, T. 2001. Coping with complexity: Educating for capability. *British Medical Journal*, 323(7316), 799–803. Available at: http://www.ncbi.nlm.nih.gov/pmc/articles/PMC1121342/ [accessed: March 28, 2013]

Plsek, P.E. and Greenhalgh, T. 2001. Complexity science: The challenge of complexity in healthcare. *British Medical Journal*, 323(7313), 625–28. Available at: http://www.ncbi.nlm.nih.gov/pmc/articles/PMC1121189/ [accessed: March 28, 2013]

Plsek, P.E. and Wilson, T. 2001. Complexity, leadership, and management in healthcare organisations. *British Medical Journal*, 323(7315), 746–9. Available at: http://www.ncbi.nlm.nih.gov/pmc/articles/PMC1121291/ [accessed: March 28, 2013]

Wilson, T., Holt, T. and Greenhalgh, T. 2001. Complexity science: Complexity and clinical care. *British Medical Journal*, 22; 323(7314), 685–8 [Erratum in *British Medical Journal*, October 2001, 323(7319), 993]. Available at: http://www.ncbi.nlm.nih.gov/pmc/articles/PMC1121241/ [accessed: March 28, 2013]

Leape, L.L. 1994. Error in medicine. *Journal of the American Medical Association*, 272(23), 1851–7.

Lindberg, C., Nash, S. and Lindberg, C. 2008. *On the Edge: Nursing in the Age of Complexity*. Bordentown, NJ: PlexusPress.

Senge, P. 1990. *The Fifth Discipline: The Art and Practice of the Learning Organization.* New York, NY: Doubleday.

Sturmberg, J.P., Martin, C.M. and Katerndahl, D.A. 2014. Systems and complexity thinking in the general practice literature: An integrative, historical narrative review. *Annals of Family Medicine,* 12(1), 66–74.

Zimmerman, B., Lindberg, C. and Plsek, P. 2001. *Edgeware: Insights from Complexity Science for Health Care Leaders.* Irving, TX: VHA, Inc.

8

Aviation Contexts and EI&K Innovation: Reliability, Teamwork and Sensemaking

Jeff Brown, Sara Tompson and Lorri Zipperer

> *... the health care community ... stands to benefit by learning how other complex, high-risk enterprises such as aviation ... have confronted considerable technical and political challenges in the pursuit of safe operations and public confidence (Cook, Woods, and Miller 1998: i).*

Making Sense of Individuals vs. Teams in Complex Systems

This is not the first and certainly not the last text to elucidate a crosswalk between aviation and healthcare with the goal of improving patient safety. For several examples, see Infobox 8.1 on the next page.

Beneath their differences, organizations that engage in flight operations and organizations that provide healthcare can both be accurately defined as socially and technologically complex systems. Within each, the reliable and safe achievement of intended outcomes was seen, historically, as dependent upon the performance of human problem solvers who must work effectively as individuals.

INFOBOX 8.1: SAMPLING OF AVIATION MODELS APPLIED TO HEALTHCARE

Billings 1998: Incident reporting systems in medicine and experience with the aviation safety reporting systems. *A Tale of Two Stories.*

Gaba 2000: Structural and organizational issues in patient safety. *California Management Review.*

Helmreich and Merritt 1998: *Culture at Work in Aviation and Medicine: National, Organizational, and Professional Influences.*

Leape 1994: Error in medicine. *JAMA.*

Lewis et al. 2011: Counterheroism, common knowledge, and ergonomics. *Milbank Quarterly.*

Wilf-Miron et al. 2003: *From Aviation to Medicine.*

As the social and technological complexity of both domains advanced in the twentieth century, this perspective evolved to recognize that aviation and healthcare are "complex sociotechnical systems" (as defined by Woods and Hollnagel 2006) where safety, risk mitigation and outcome reliability hinge not only on the knowledge and skill of *individuals*, but upon the knowledge, reasoning, problem-solving and coordinated actions of *teams* using information and evidence to support their work in effective fashion. Figure 8.1 illustrates the interrelationships in such systems.

In parallel with the identification of team processes as critical to safety and risk mitigation at the delivery end of complex sociotechnical systems, awareness has increased about the pivotal role communication plays in such organizations. Decisions made not only at the sharp end, but also elsewhere in the organization, have the potential to undermine safety where the actual service or product is delivered if changes are not communicated with an eye toward systems improvement and organizational learning. These unintended decision effects may be characterized as decision side-effects (Rasmussen 2000).

THEMES FOR EXPLORATION

Several overarching themes that could crosswalk from aviation to EI&K delivery are explored in the following pages. Teamwork, the sharing of what is known, sensemaking, and error.

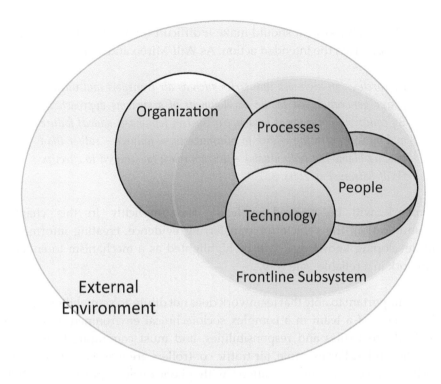

Figure 8.1   Complex Sociotechnical System
Source: Brown 2012.

Teamwork

One of the overarching themes in the many   *"It is important to note*
comparisons between aviation and healthcare   *that teamwork does not*
is that *teamwork* is further developed and   *dilute accountability."*
more routinely encouraged in aviation than in
healthcare (see Brown 2005; McFadden, Henagan and Gowen 2009; Lewis et
al. 2011). In healthcare, surgeons and others on the sharp end are arguably
conceptualized and trained as being on the top of a hierarchy more so than
are pilots (the primary sharp end role in aviation), notwithstanding the
regulatory designation of the "pilot-in-command" as the final authority for the
operation and safety of an aircraft (US Federal Aviation Administration 2014).
Air carriers operating under "Federal Aviation regulation, Part 121, Operating
Requirements: Domestic Flag, and Supplemental Operations" are required
to train aircrews in crew resource management methods, to enhance crew
decision-making and coordination (US Federal Aviation Administration 2004).
However, historically there have been strong commonalities between surgeons
and pilots, a comparison that continues to ring true (Helmreich 1998).

A safe, reliable system should make it difficult for an *individual* human to err, or deviate from the intended action. As Wilf-Miron and colleagues note:

> Research ... in high-risk industries such as air transport and nuclear power generation led to the development of a systems approach ... By conceiving of error as evidence of system [emphasis added] failure and by concentrating efforts to minimize these failures – rather than placing blame [on individuals] – this approach has proved to effective (Wilf-Miron et al. 2003: 35).

Teamwork will be covered explicitly and implicitly in this chapter. Communication, the vehicle for transferring evidence, creating information and developing knowledge, will be highlighted as a mechanism to enhance teamwork in a reliable, safe way.

It is important to note that teamwork does not dilute accountability. Instead, all members of a team in a complex sociotechnical environment must have clearly defined roles and responsibilities, and must communicate precisely from their roles. For example, air traffic controllers are mandated to use very specific phrases in communications with pilots during ground and flight operations. The phrases are changed if and when evidence from accidents and near misses indicates misunderstandings have occurred.

The Sharing of What is Known

Evidence, information, knowledge and understanding are critical components in high-risk, sociotechnically complex systems, and must be taken into consideration in order to make useful comparisons between the two such systems under discussion, aviation and healthcare. Systems thinker Russell Ackoff effectively describes a knowledge pyramid (see Figure 8.2) though he himself never drew the hierarchy as a pyramid (Wallace 2007):

> Wisdom is located at the top of a hierarchy of ... types of content of the human mind. Descending from wisdom ... are understanding, knowledge, information, and at the bottom, data. Each of these includes the categories that fall below it – for example, there can be no wisdom without understanding and no understanding without knowledge (Ackoff 1989: 3).

The portion of the hierarchy that frames the discussion here is *understanding*, which is achieved through evidence application due to knowledge. Data

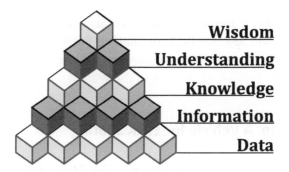

Figure 8.2   Ackoff's Hierarchy
Source: Ackoff 1989.

is compiled to create information, and fleshed out with communication, including sensemaking, to arrive at knowledge that is critical for those in high-consequence (or high-risk) organizations to do what they do reliably.

Sensemaking

Individual and team sensemaking as an EI&K application may be easier to first define in an aviation context, though it is an aspect of communication and of high reliability in any setting (Weick, Sutcliffe, and Obstfeld 2005; Klein, Wiggins, and Dominguez 2010). In aviation, sensemaking is integral to making the progression from scattered bits of data (for example, the reading on an aircraft heading indicator) into information and then into the knowledge that results in understanding (Ans and Tricot 2009). Even in today's modern aircraft, a pilot needs to pull together many data (from instruments, some of which may "disagree" with each other, from air traffic control, from looking out the window, and so on) to quickly create information about the flight at that very point in time. Further, this data-into-information process is iterative during a flight. Post flight, the various pieces of information (in the pilot's electronic tablet, lapboard notes, memory, and so on) are compiled to inform the pilot's aviation knowledge base drawn from the actual experience of flight.

Error

There is a difference between error and failure. The use of the word "error" is used in the context of how people do what they do with possible missteps. This is not the same as "failure." An exploration from the latter perspective is more about how systems do not achieve goals or actions for which they are designed.

In hospitals, there is intense peer pressure on clinicians to perform as error-free individuals, and less emphasis on making the system as a whole safer. In essence, there is an embedded emphasis on dealing with error rather than mitigating failure.

Communication: A Vehicle for EI&K Sharing

Communication is critical for individuals and particularly teams in high-risk domains, and has been suggested as the most workable concept to port from aviation to healthcare to improve safety (Nemeth 2008). In general, the contribution of poor communication to accidental patient injury and death is well established (Reader et al. 2007). Crew Resource Management (CRM) methods have been adapted from aviation and applied extensively in healthcare to address this problem (Salas, Rhodenizer and Bowers 2000; Department of Defense and the Agency for Healthcare Research and Quality n.d.). CRM is fundamentally aimed at improving team management of not only routine operations, but sensemaking, decision-making, coordination of activity, and effective adaptation of routines to address problems and anomalies (Mudge 1997; Brown 2004; Brown, Tonkel and Classen 2013). These benefits are pursued through communication processes such as briefing, debriefing, cross-checking and call-outs, which have been identified as beneficial for risk mitigation and safety management through extensive research (Leva et al. 2010; Brown 2008), and have yielded significant reduction in morbidity and mortality when applied in healthcare settings (Uhlig et al. 2002).

INFOBOX 8.2: PRIMARY TERMS – AN AVIATION CONTEXT

Crew Resource Management (CRM) emphasizes using all resources, human and machine, to safely operate a flight.

High Reliability Organizations (HROs) manage high-risk, high-consequence processes with low rates of failure and harm.

Resilience is the ability to quickly recover from unexpected changes or adverse conditions. Systems and machines, as well as people, can be described as resilient.

Sensemaking is an ongoing effort to analyze data and information from all sectors and build these inputs into knowledge.

Situation Awareness requires that clinicians can *perceive* the information they need, *comprehend* the importance of this information, and *forecast* the implications of this information (i.e., adverse consequences that might happen) (Koch et al. 2012).

Christopher Nemeth is an expert on human performance in high hazard environments. His five points on effective crew communication will serve here as a core set of elements upon which to build evidence, information and knowledge illustrations. The points can be summarized as:

Point 1   Create and share situation models;

Point 2   Address plans and decision alternatives to cope with emergent problems;

Point 3   Establish a positive crew climate through briefings to support open communication;

Point 4   Monitor and manage problems and errors; and

Point 5   Use explicit, efficient communication (Nemeth 2008).

Point 1, a shared situation model, is especially important. Very often in aviation and in healthcare informed and knowledgeable professionals work in teams. For example:

- Pilot/Copilot/Air Traffic Controller/Flight Attendant.

- Surgeon/Anesthesiologist/Nurse/Scientist/Research Coordinator/ Librarian.

To illustrate the value in looking at communication through the EI&K lens, point 2 has been augmented in Table 8.1, with the addition of an EI&K structure to delineate team problem-solving in aviation (A) and in healthcare (H).

Table 8.1   EI&K in Two Contexts

Nemeth's point 2	Evidence	Information	Knowledge
Address plans and decision alternatives to cope with emergent problems.	A: First officer points out intense rain on weather radar to captain. H: Nurse anesthetist tells surgeon that the patient's blood pressure is dropping.	A: Flight plan must be changed; quickly discuss alternatives with crew. H: Surgical team must alter management of the patient to recover blood pressure.	A: Alternative flight plans should always be ready or close to ready to go. A: Mental rehearsal of alternate route should take place. H. Surgical team should identify unique knowledge in the group to address potential problems.

Nemeth's points 3 and 4 are fairly self-explanatory, but both team/unit culture and error monitoring do continue to present problems for healthcare organizations. Edmondson (2003) is one of several researchers writing on interpersonal climates in teams and documents their impact on how care can be derided by poor team culture.

Point 5 on the importance of effective communication can be augmented with the concept of "common ground." Common ground refers to:

> ... the pertinent mutual knowledge, mutual beliefs and mutual assumptions that support interdependent actions in some joint activity. Common ground permits people to use abbreviated forms of communication and still be reasonably confident that potentially ambiguous messages and signals will be understood (Klein, Feltovich and Woods 2004: 8).

This quote is rich in concepts. Shared knowledge is highlighted. Abbreviated forms of communication can be a hallmark of complex sociotechnical systems like aviation and healthcare. Time is often of the essence in safely landing aircraft, safely performing surgery, and so on, hence the need for coded conversations. But sensemaking is critical here, everyone on the team (implied by the concept "joint activity") must be able to fill in the gaps of each abbreviated message or piece of information communicated, so mutual understanding is achieved and thus errors are avoided as much as possible. Granted, short cuts in language can create opportunities for misunderstanding.

A unique vehicle for communication in the aviation sector is the cockpit voice recorder (CVR) and how the data and information it records can enhance safety in the future. CVR analysis has enabled accident investigators to uncover team process factors that contributed to accidents and incidents, such as one crewmember's failure to "hear" another crewmember's concerns, the failure to harness the knowledge of team members in problem-solving, and the failure to effectively allocate roles and responsibilities when managing anomalies.

Despite well-documented need, adoption of team-based practice models has been inconsistent in healthcare (Weaver et al. 2010). Medical and nursing education still emphasizes *individual* knowledge, skill and performance over *team*-based practice. It is entirely likely that blunt end training (for example, of risk managers, librarians or administrators) has also emphasized the individual over the team approach. Many curricula could benefit from increased usage of aviation and other successful models of team-based practices to prevent and mitigate errors in high-risk environments (Manser 2009; Salas et al. 2013).

EI&K and Aviation Safety: Synergies for Healthcare Consideration

Table 8.2 dissects selected safe practices in aviation and healthcare with an eye toward evidence, information and knowledge use. While less detailed than some other treatments (for example, that of Lewis et al. 2011), it does add a new element to the discussion by bringing in evidence, information and knowledge as separate factors to consider.

Table 8.2   **Selected Aviation Safety Strategies Applied to Healthcare EI&K Processes**

Key aviation concepts	Evidence element	Information element	Knowledge element
Organizational Level			
High Reliability Organization	• Ensuring evidence compiled is unbiased both in its selection and its development. • Doing literature reviews twice to ensure complete results.	• Making available credible organizational information on a timely basis (LaPorte 2002).	• Recognizing failure given tacit understanding of what should be. • Identifying and recognizing gaps (Dervin 2003). • Understanding connections (Klein et al. 2004).
Unit Level			
Crew Resource Management/ Teamwork	• Using research-based instructional design (Helmreich, Merritt 1998; Salas et al. 2000). • Reviewing of appropriate studies and best practices to enhance safety. • Building psychological safety and trust through the experience of work together.	• Recognizing data and its application to the task at hand as communicated to the team. • Knowing who is on the team, their roles and immediate tasks and goals.	• Recognizing tacit knowledge as a valued and shared asset for an interdisciplinary team. • Interacting as based on the experience of working together or on previous tasks.
Individual Level			
Checklist Use	• Reviewing of the evidence to identify credibility of the specificity of the actions.	• Translating evidence into actionable, relevant and specific process points.	• Applying points in real time draws from knowledge to enable the generic checklist to work in the specific instance/unit/hospital given local norms.

Detailed Discussions

The concepts in the table above are further explicated and discussed below in terms of aviation and healthcare from an EI&K viewpoint: High Reliability

Organizations; Crew Resource Management; and, Checklists. The concepts progress from the broad to the specific.

HIGH RELIABILITY ORGANIZATIONS (HROS)

Todd LaPorte, one of the "fathers" of the High Reliability Organization (HRO) movement in aviation, concurs that high reliability is required in risky settings. Further, in an HRO: "...operations are beneficial but hazardous in their design, that is, the work is intrinsically dangerous" (LaPorte 1996: 67).

"... high-risk is the driver for high reliability."

Traits of HROs are salient for their emphasis on information and knowledge. The traits LaPorte and colleagues (2002) have discussed in detail can be succinctly represented in the briefer points taken from Weick and Sutcliff – see Infobox 8.3.

HROs manage high-risk, high-consequence processes with low rates of failure. *Military Standard 721C* defines reliability in several related ways and many authors have based their definitions on those in the standard. The main definition of reliability in the standard is useful for consideration here: "... the duration or probability of failure-free performance under stated conditions" (Department of Defense 1981: 8). This definition is applicable in both healthcare and aviation because both strive to avoid failures, as the consequences of failures in both settings can mean loss of life. In other words, high-risk is the driver for high reliability.

INFOBOX 8.3: HIGH RELIABILITY ORGANIZATIONS

- Track small failures.
- Resist oversimplification.
- Remain sensitive to operations.
- Maintain capabilities for resilience.
- Take advantage of shifting locations of expertise.

(Weick and Sutcliffe 2007: 2)

Aviation is an HRO industry. Healthcare is striving to become an HRO industry. As McFadden and her collaborators have noted:

> HRO's implement safety initiatives that have resulted in remarkable safety outcomes ... The most important outcome for HROs is high

operational reliability ... and these hazardous organizations have achieved a high level of safety over long periods of time ... Previous healthcare research, on the other hand, has found considerable differences between perceived level of importance of PSIs [patient safety initiatives] and the actual level of implementation of these initiatives within hospitals (McFadden, Henagan and Gowen 2009: 394).

SYSTEMS

High-risk, high-consequence organizations are by their very nature complex sociotechnical systems. They are comprised of a large number of components – human, machine, process, structure, infrastructure, and so on. Complex organizations are largely a result of the industrial revolution. It is important to note that complex organizations are systems, wherein a change in one component may well affect another. These interrelationships are not always apparent, which is all the more reason to identify them and call them out when enhancing frontline operations to support high reliability practices. Information problems are crucial to understanding why disaster or crisis signals are often ignored (Westrum 2004).

As Chun Wei Choo, professor in Information Studies, has stated, an organization without a systems view can run into situations where signals are simply not seen. The use of evidence, information and knowledge to document one or more of the following indicators – product glitches, management of money or reduction in sales – could help uncover a problem. Such problems and problem indicators can be missed if an orientation and sensitivity to the value of EI&K is not part of the culture or belief system (Choo 2005). They can also be missed when groups only have partial information and no one has a view of the situation as a whole (Choo 2005). These malfunctions remain latent until they manifest themselves in a failure and are surfaced during the subsequent investigation.

In the patient safety reporting realm, mechanisms to collect data such as trigger tools and standard core measures present problems as well – particularly if the context associated with the numbers is removed from the data collection and the vision is misaligned to identify *absence* of harm rather than identifying *harm itself* (Landrigan et al. 2010; Classen et al. 2011). The solution is a vigilant information and knowledge-sharing culture that reliably enables conversations and reflections in a multimodal strategy to support learning from failure.

RESILIENCY AND SENSEMAKING

Two important traits of HROs are resilience and sensemaking. Resilience – agility and the ability to bounce back – is a fundamental requirement in complex organizations where risk is involved. Individuals and teams must be able to move quickly and recover when conditions change, all the while maintaining a safe environment: "Safety is achieved by ... personnel solving problems, noting differences and adapting in changing conditions" (Brown 2004: 15).

Sensemaking is an evidence-information-knowledge process. Sensemaking is what happens when participants in a communication attempt to make sense of the inherent gaps. Professor of Communications Brenda Dervin has expanded, nuanced and applied the concept of sensemaking as a systematic construct to describe communication, particularly in organizations: "The core construct of Sense-Making is the ideas of the gap – how people define and bridge gaps in their everyday lives" (Dervin 2003: 223). If evidence and information are needed to apply the knowledge bases of the people involved to make sense in high reliability organizations, practices and structures must support the clarification (that is, sensemaking) of any gaps in communication (Battles et al. 1996).

HOW CAN EI&K BE MADE HIGHLY RELIABLE?

The identification, sharing and application of evidence, information and knowledge should be addressed within the construct of HROs to effectively contribute to safety and prevent failures. Information failures can contribute to disaster in a wide range of industries (Choo 2005). The Roche case illustrates that the result of unreliable, incomplete evidence retrieval can contribute to catastrophic failure: the death of an individual. The librarian profession has not yet fully explored the application of HRO principles to patient safety improvement work, although the need to view failures of evidence, information and knowledge through the complexity lens has been raised (Macintosh-Murray and Choo 2002, 2005; Zipperer 2006).

Aviation is ahead of healthcare in determining system weaknesses, but that sector also has not advanced in the application of HRO and safety principles in terms of pilots' use of information and failures that could result from incomplete or unclear information (Ans and Tricot 2009). Other potential types of failures and factors that enable them are discussed in Chapters 5 and 13.

CREW RESOURCE MANAGEMENT (CRM): A TEAMWORK APPROACH

The aviation concept crew resource management (CRM) serves as an example of interdisciplinary knowledge-sharing – it is a sensemaking, meaning-making, adaptive action. CRM emphasizes "The importance of considering the interfacing of human factors with the vareity of organizational cultures and management styles on team interaction in high consequense settings (Shojania, Wachter and Hartman n.d). Aviation accidents where human "error" was identified as a root cause were a driver for the airline transport industry to develop CRM. The overall intent of CRM is not only to effectively navigate routine processes, but also to detect (data), make sense of (information) and recover from (understanding) potentially catastrophic situations through the application of EI&K.

"The identification, sharing and application of evidence, information and knowledge should be addressed within the construct of CRM to effectively contribute to safety."

To the extent that a CRM methodology evokes and invokes knowledge-sharing in decision-making processes, it may enhance the social system as an adaptive control, sensitive to anomalies and capable of restoring operations following disruption – in other words, knowledge-sharing supports system resilience. CRM is one method for matching the technical complexity of the *whole* system through a *social* system like a team capable of sensitive detection and adaptive response to emergent threat and hazard.

Research conducted since the early days of CRM reveals that the notion of error as a cause of accident is insufficient (Helmreich and Wilhelm 1999). To simply identify erroneous action or inaction as the cause of an accident fails to illuminate the situational or endemic environmental, technological and cultural constraints that might drive deviation from practices established by policy and procedure. "Error-provoking" conditions arise, sometimes rapidly, and often stem from decisions made at a great distance from the frontlines or sharp ends of aviation and healthcare (Cook and Woods 1994; Dekker 2002).

In the healthcare domain, interprofessional *teams*, with their inherent variety of experience, expertise, and perspective can apply a CRM approach by scanning:

1. A patient's situation;

2. The care processes serving that patient; and

3.   The environment of care much more thoroughly than an *individual*.

Harnessing knowledge of the situation for problem detection, sensemaking and action is what team development efforts should be about. But these efforts should also be about documenting problems for risk review, wherein failure may be averted through understanding; that is, the proactive application of imagination based upon past evidence, information and knowledge.

How Can EI&K Be Improved Using CRM Concepts?

The identification, sharing and application of evidence, information and knowledge should be addressed within the construct of CRM to effectively contribute to safety. One interesting opportunity for the healthcare and information and knowledge management sectors to explore is that of the communication exchange process that precedes evidence identification. Would a structured communication tool to enable discussion around the evidence query set enhance the retrieval of *reliable* evidence? Is there peer review in place to help ensure reliable, complete and effective EI&K delivery to enable the use of such a tool? Given the discussion here of team communication, awareness of the application of the evidence and its value in real time, such a tool may be useful. Assessment tools for individual search skills that are available for blunt end applications may provide insights and a foundation from which to initiate the design of such a tool for the sharp end (Rana et al. 2011; McGowan, Sampson and Lefebvre 2010).

CHECKLISTS TRANSFER EVIDENCE INTO INFORMATION

Checklists are a "murky" (as described in Chapter 2) concept despite the successes their use has had in both in aviation and in healthcare. The application of checklists as tools to enhance the reliability of distinct evidence, information and knowledge processes as described for this text is limited.

Aviation

Checklists have been used in aviation from early on, during preflight and in flight (Degani and Weiner 1993). In the early days of airline aviation, each captain had his own checklists and procedures, and co-pilots kept notebooks to keep track of their preferences. This variability contributed to coordination challenges on the flight deck when copilots inadvertently followed the procedures of another captain. Ultimately, the exponential rise in flight activity during World War II led to standardized checklists and procedures to improve crew coordination and fleet performance.

Pilots and aviation organizations learned that following set checklists consistently, in both routine and emergency operations, can help prevent or mitigate the risk of an oversight or improper action during a critical process or task, such as setting of wing flaps as part pre-takeoff procedures.

Checklists have demonstrably prevented erroneous and potentially harmful actions or inactions, such as overheating a power plant during start-up procedure, or failing to ensure that people and debris were clear of jet engine inlets on start-up. Furthermore, checklists are cognitive aids that help pilots make sense of a situation, for example by providing a diagnostic sequence to understand and resolve a guidance system failure in flight. Often a pilot will read aloud a checklist and a copilot or other crewmember will check the instrument in question and reply with the data; in other words, clear communication is part of implementing a checklist.

The components of an aviation checklist are focused on checking and correlating various data to build up information. For example, what does the oil pressure gauge read when the propeller's pitch control is cycled (moved) through its full range of movement prior to take off? Reviewing all the available data gives the pilot information about the airworthiness and likely performance of the aircraft. In other words, leads the pilot to a sensemaking analysis regarding the safety of the planned, or in-progress, flight.

Healthcare

The application of checklists in healthcare delivery has resulted in notable safety achievements (Pronovost et al. 2010; Lin et al. 2012; Neily et al. 2010; Weiser et al. 2010). The chief champions of checklist usage are "rock stars" in the patient safety field (Gawande 2009; Pronovost and Vohr 2010). Checklists have been used in initiatives based at local, state, country and international levels to reduce:

- Variations in quality of care;

- Costs associated with hospital infections and errors in surgery; and

- Disconnects amongst the care team.

Limitations

Despite their documented value, the routinization of checklist use can harbor dangers as well (Rydenfält, Ek and Larsson 2013). Checklists are *not* the answer to every process and safety problem. Cockpit voice recorders have illustrated that the following of checklists does not necessarily resolve the potential for omissions (National Transportation Safety Board 1988; Veillette 2011). Even the best checklist program will stumble if not implemented with the appropriate attention to the social, cultural, and human factors and evidentiary requirements (Bosk et al. 2009). Context has been found to be a "highly consequential" influence on the success of an checklist-grounded improvement program (Dixon-Woods et al. 2013: e1).

There has been pushback on the use of checklists as an information/ knowledge-sharing tool at the sharp end of healthcare. The case has been made that strict adherence to a checklist can minimize the opportunities for dialog and engender too standardized a communication process that steers handoffs, rounding and bedside change of shifts away from rich knowledge exchanges, focusing instead upon constrained information and data exchanges (Cohen, Hilligoss and Kajdacsy-Balla 2012). Minimal exploration of this concept as a frontline *in situ* EI&K process has been identified (McGowan, Sampson and Lefebvre 2010).

Passengers and Patients

Passengers on commercial aircraft flights are typically considered customers; there is little or no challenging of this concept, as a passenger pays money for the service of being transported, and has some choice in the airlines, routes and seats for the trip. The job of the aviation team – pilot, copilot, flight attendants, air traffic controllers, ground crew and service staff – is to get the passengers safely and efficiently to their destinations. Commercial airline passengers are *not* typically part of the aviation team; their role is by design fairly passive once they are on board. More often than not, passengers do not possess the knowledge and skills to run the flight.

In contrast, patients and their family members *do* have salient knowledge to contribute to the safety of their care and to improve the reliability and effectiveness of processes. They actively experience the care they receive and can share knowledge of that experience in a deeper way than can passengers on a plane. However, there has been controversy in the healthcare literature in the US and in Europe on the concept of patients as "customers" since at least the 1990s. The notion seems to be gaining traction, with more in healthcare moving towards, for example, John Deffenbaugh's 1997 definition:

> *It would be more beneficial for enhancing patient care to think of a patient as a customer, instead of a consumer. This assertion is based on experience of dealing with people, rather than splitting hairs over definitions. The word 'customer' is commonly accepted, such as in the axioms 'the customer is always right' or 'the customer is king.' The phrase, 'the customer is always right,' could be taken as a glib statement, but behind it lies a way of thinking … a culture that says 'think marketing, think customer.' To survive and prosper, businesses must adopt a customer service culture (Deffenbaugh 1997).*

Recent activities support an expanded view of the patient's role and take the notion of healthcare patients a step further: patients can become part of their own healthcare teams, if the team is conceptualized in a distributed notion, as some authors have recommended (Balik et al. 2011). There is increasing data that the fairly radical notion of including patients in the definition of the healthcare team increases patient safety. The notion is radical because of the typical hierarchy in healthcare with surgeons at the top and patients at the bottom. As Martin and Finn note:

> *… the concept of the multidisciplinary team is being expanded to include patients and care-givers as well, as user involvement comes to involve not just consultation, but partnership, with shared decision-making, shared responsibility and some degree of equality of influence between professionals and users (Martin and Finn 2011: 1053).*

Understanding what patients/customers need and can readily use is a complex undertaking. Issues associated with their general literacy, health literacy, information literacy, cultural differences, privacy, costs, and so on, can influence the customers':

- methods of requesting information;

- understanding of the evidence at hand; and

- their respect for and sharing of knowledge in an effective way.

Patient education and patient-centeredness initiatives are addressing some of these issues. A full understanding of how patients/customers can utilize safety information and evidence and share their knowledge to enhance reliability has yet to be studied.

Closing the Gap: Accountability, Collaboration and EI&K

Being held to account for *individual* fulfillment of tasks, rather than the performance of tasks in close coordination with *other* care providers, remains a powerful source of fragmentation and patient harm (Brown 2005; Patterson et al. 2002). Although the extent to which individual versus team accountability varies with the social dynamics of any given organization; for example, the fulfillment of clinical tasks in contemporary hospital-based care is more of an individual than a truly team-based activity (Dominguez et al. 2005; Lawrence 2002).

"Group performance may often exceed individual performance–reason enough to promote collaboration to enhance safety (Nunamaker, Romano and Briggs 2001)."

The social and technological complexity of contemporary healthcare is overwhelming the century-old model of hospital organization and management that was conceived to support the independent practices of individual physicians (Merry and Crago 2001; Merry 2005; Sharpe and Faden 1998; Starr 1982). Although the current picture may seem bleak, the good news is that clinical environments are rich in diverse knowledge, which, if harnessed, accessed and shared through team processes, may yield unprecedented positive results.

Collaboration, especially in the context of clinical care, may be defined as a communication process that is verbal and non-verbal, explicit and implicit. Collaboration is a practice integral to the problem detection, analysis, and resolution that is woven into interactions among team members (Hollnagel, Woods and Leveson 2006; Mudge 1998; Manoj and Taylor 1999). Different members of any team observe different data, to some degree. What the pilot sees aloft differs from what the controller sees on the scope. What the surgeon sees differs from what the nurse anesthetist sees. All team members need to communicate information, translate evidence and respect each other's knowledge, to see the whole complex system, and increase the system's reliability and thus safety. Group performance may often exceed individual performance–reason enough to promote collaboration to enhance safety (Nunamaker, Romano and Briggs 2001).

Moving Forward–Sharpening the Blunt End

As valuable and provocative as the oft-utilized comparisons between patient safety and aviation have been to illustrate similarities between the two complex domains with an eye toward highlighting opportunities for patient safety improvement, these comparisons should not be considered the only way to improve patient safety. The presentation of these comparisons in this chapter has been intended to increase understanding in the use of aviation models to particularly enhance evidence, information and knowledge delivery in healthcare.

The concepts bridged in the aviation/healthcare analogy and lessons related to safety improvement are most notably applied to explorations specific to the sharp end of high-risk enterprises. Further exploration of EI&K applications to training and situation awareness of *blunt* end workers is needed. Social processes and individual awareness are in place at the sharp end to allow for the knowledge that failure is real and its impact potentially catastrophic. This connection with the blunt end has not yet been demonstrably established beyond that related to direct experience with failure and its consequence.

The potential of evidence, information and knowledge failures throughout the sharp end/blunt end continuum should be analyzed further to generate the study, commitment, resources and change needed to best extract the lessons learned for safety improvement. Indeed, it is the collective intellectual resources – team and organizational knowledge – that ultimately will enable the application of information and evidence to improve patient safety and care reliability.

KEY TAKE-AWAYS

- Methods of improving safety in aviation have application to evidence, information and knowledge-sharing in the healthcare environment.
- Elements of high reliability show promise for improving the effectiveness of EI&K in the care environment.
- Team sensemaking, crew resource management and checklists are intriguing examples of aviation concepts that illustrate the viability of cross-walking lessons and actions from aviation to inform EI&K application, use and delivery strategies and initiatives.

Suggested Reading

Clancy, C.M. and Reinertsen, J.L., (eds) 2006. Keeping our promises: Research, practice, and policy issues in health care reliability. *Health Services Research,* 41, 535–1720.

Dervin, B. 2003. Audience as listener and learner, in *Sense-Making Methodology Reader: Selected Writings of Brenda Dervin,* edited by B. Dervin, L. Foreman-Wernet and E. Lauterbach. Cresskill, NJ: Hampton Press.

Helmreich, R.L. and Merritt, A.C. 1998. *Culture at Work in Aviation and Medicine: National, Organizational, and Professional Influences.* Aldershot: Ashgate Publishing.

Weick, K.E. 1993. The collapse of sensemaking in organizations: The Mann Gulch disaster. *Administrative Science Quarterly,* 1993(38), 628–52.

PART 4

Practical Applications to Drive EI&K Progress in the Acute Care Environment

Chapter 9 Synopsis – EI&K Sharing Mechanisms in Support of Patient Safety

The authors discuss the role of various tools to reliably disseminate information, evidence and knowledge to facilitate improvement in patient safety. Tactics highlighted to award success, enable dialog and expedite learning from failure include stories, medical literature, communities of practice and social media.

Chapter 10 Synopsis – Health Information Technology in Hospitals: Towards a Culture of EI&K Sharing

A central premise of this chapter is that evidence-based medicine and health information technology solutions that share data are not sufficient in and of themselves to improve patient safety. The authors introduce three components that are essential to improving patient safety: evidence, information and knowledge, particularly evidence; health information technology in the form of a well-developed electronic health record (EHR); and a safety culture facilitated by a culture of sharing. The case is made that it is the strength of the safety culture within the organization that promotes or inhibits EI&K sharing through these components.

Chapter 11 Synopsis – Critical Intersections in Patient Safety: Evidence and Knowledge Transfer at the Sharp and Blunt Ends

This chapter discusses practical tactics to enable EI&K sharing to be reliable at both the point of delivery (sharp end) and administrative side (blunt end) of acute care activity. The authors highlight formal and informal roles and tools that enable effective EI&K.

Chapter 12 Synopsis – Patient and Families as Vital EI&K Conduits

This chapter describes the various ways that patients and family members can act as channels for information, evidence, and knowledge within the acute care setting in order to have a positive impact on safety. The authors take an in-depth look at these different roles, offer specific language to describe them, and employ stories that illustrate how a patient's knowledge-sharing contributes to the learning of the clinical team and the organization.

Chapter 13 Synopsis – Humans and EI&K Seeking: Factors Influencing Reliability

This chapter explores the contribution of human factors engineering to EI&K transfer and safety improvement. The authors discuss the value added by EI&K to safety improvement work. Strategies to enable EI&K programs and initiatives are presented – in the context of the hierarchy of actions and set the stage for identifying factors that contribute to EI&K failure.

EI&K Sharing Mechanisms in Support of Patient Safety

Susan Carr, Barbara Olson and Lorri Zipperer

> *The computer is the most remarkable tool that we've ever come up with. It's the equivalent of a bicycle for our minds.*
>
> Steve Jobs, interview for the documentary
> Memory and Imagination, 1990.

The Promise of Effective EI&K Sharing

Patient safety is improved when evidence, information and knowledge as a continuum are shared in ways that support clinicians in their work, contribute to a culture of patient safety and promote change that improves care. Evidence that is inaccessible, information that stays locked up in databases, and knowledge that is siloed in units cannot lead to meaningful improvement.

To establish effective sharing of EI&K, organizations need a diverse portfolio of reliable mechanisms to disseminate high-quality EI&K from a wide array of sources. Equally important, organizational learning and sharing strategies must include a commitment by administrators to measure and re-evaluate the effectiveness of chosen EI&K strategies. Over-reliance on any one tool or process will increase the risk that EI&K – intended to inform the clinical treatment of patients or the clinical practice of professionals – is not current or not shared effectively. Using only a limited range of sources or narrowing the focus of EI&K to single-discipline approaches may stifle effective sharing and possibly cause harm. To sustain patient safety improvement, organizations should seek to integrate a variety of mechanisms for sharing EI&K into models that acknowledge the complexity of the acute care environment. As many stakeholders as possible should be involved in EI&K distribution – clinicians at the sharp end, executives who contribute to the blunt end, support staff and patients and their families. This comprehensive approach allows a healthcare organization to quickly adapt to ever-evolving circumstances.

Learning from Traditional EI&K Exchanges: A Seminal Story

Lucian Leape, MD, the recognized father of the modern patient safety movement, had an exchange with a librarian at Harvard Medical School that provides an example of the power, subtlety, and even serendipity of effective evidence, information and knowledge-sharing mechanisms. This interaction helped spur the patient safety movement. Leape tells the story in an exchange with patient safety expert and author Robert M. Wachter, MD, published as an Agency for Healthcare Research and Quality online interview.

> RW: *As you were in the middle of that study [Leape, Brennan, Laird et al. 1991. Harvard Medical Practice Study], what was your sense of its potential?*
>
> LL: *We always were convinced it was an important study, if nothing else, because of its magnitude. Looking at 30,000 patients gives you some clout. None of us had really thought much about the preventability issue, and nobody knew anything about systems, of course. We weren't completely surprised by our results, because earlier work had shown similar findings. But we were, shall we say, dismayed to find that four percent of patients had adverse events. The surprise for me was that two thirds of them were caused by errors. I'll never forget – I went to the library one day and did a literature search on what was known about preventing errors, and I didn't find anything. And I went to the librarian and said, "I'm interested in how you prevent medical errors, and I've found papers about complications, but nothing much about errors." And I asked her to look over my search strategy because I was not finding anything. She looked at it and she said, "Well, your strategy looks all right. Have you looked in the humanities literature?" And I sort of looked at her and said, "The what?" I know what humanities are, mind you. But it really never occurred to me. So she tried the same*

*search strategy in the humanities literature, and boom, out came 200
papers. I started to read them and discovered James Reason and Jens
Rasmussen and all those people. A year later, I came up for air and
realized that we in health care could use this. If I didn't know how
errors happen, most other people wouldn't know it either. So I decided
to write a paper.*

RW: *So, a medical school librarian set off the modern patient safety
movement?*

LL: *Ergo, there we go.*[1]

In this example, Leape shared information with the librarian about his area
of study and the questions he wanted to research. The librarian used her
broader knowledge of tools to enable him to find evidence from disciplines
outside of his experience, which he most likely would otherwise have missed
(Leape 1994). Leape, in turn, created information that distilled and presented
the evidence that continues to inform and inspire further research and spur
knowledge-sharing, dialog and commitment in patient safety 20 years later.

Mechanisms for Sharing EI&K

Tools for sharing EI&K have different strengths and weaknesses in various
circumstances. A librarian's or informationist's skill and experience with a
variety of tools improves the reliability of a healthcare team by broadening
the search for resources to help fill gaps in EI&K (Sollenberger and Holloway
Jr, 2013). To increase patient safety, clinicians should also improve their
"literacy" with different sharing mechanisms and should be encouraged
to consult with librarians and others who have professional skills in this
area. All members of a healthcare team can increase their efficacy by using
collaborative or social approaches to sharing and building expertise and
interest networks.

The effectiveness of sharing mechanisms improves as an individual's
communication skills progress in all media: writing, live presentation, and
video and audio recording. Technical skill with computers, cameras, recording

---

1   Reprinted with permission of *AHRQ WebM&M*. In conversation with Lucian Leape, MD
    [interview]. *AHRQ WebM&M* [serial online], August 2006. Available at: http://www.webmm.
    ahrq.gov/perspective.aspx?perspectiveID=28

devices, and web-based tools also contributes to the quality of EI&K. Many computer programs and tools make it easy and entertaining to produce and publish information, but the goal of improving patient safety should ground all efforts to share EI&K regardless of the tools and mechanisms used.

The range of mechanisms available to organizations, teams, and individuals interested in disseminating EI&K is expanding rapidly. Especially in the area of information and knowledge-sharing, online tools provide nimble and interactive options to support and augment monitoring of topics via traditional, paper-based publications. Through direct access to experts and the opportunity for discussion and follow-up, social media offer new ways to create and share knowledge. In the area of evidence, publishers now rely on digital formats and social media such as Twitter and blogs to create awareness or gather insights and reactions to the research and analysis they publish in print and their authors present at conferences.

Social Media – Opportunities and Potential Hazards

> *Through interactions mediated by digital technologies people may be able to perform new social acts not previously possible (Davis as quoted by Greenhow and Gleason 2012: 467).*

A large and growing number of hospitals have established online resources for communication, education, promotion, and social networking. The Mayo Clinic-supported social media tracking site "Social Media Health Network" reported in December 2013 that 1,544 hospitals in the United States were collectively responsible for 6,500 social networking tools. As illustrated in the figure below, these tools include: 716 YouTube channels, 1,292 Facebook pages, 998 Twitter accounts, 651 LinkedIn accounts, 1,090 FourSquare accounts and 205 blogs (Mayo Clinic 2013).

Social media tools enable powerful opportunities for sharing information about patient safety and potentially developing diverse, multidisciplinary communities for distributing knowledge. The primary focus of social media to date has been marketing, but these tools hold great potential to create readily accessible EI&K portals that welcome and benefit from the perspective of many stakeholders, including patients (Hamm et al. 2013a; Hamm et al. 2013b; Heyworth et al. 2014).

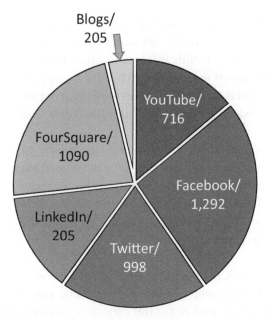

Figure 9.1   US Hospitals that Use Social Networking Tools – Updated on December 2013 (n=1544)

Source: Mayo Clinic 2013.

Understandably, both staff and executives in hospitals may be concerned about a number of issues related to social media:

- Patient privacy violations.

- Liability arising from inappropriate use of social media by employees and clinical staff.

- Loss of consumers' trust arising from open discussion of safety problems.

- Increased staffing and funding necessary to create, monitor and sustain social media efforts.

In addition to these concerns, organizations may not know how to begin incorporating social media into their communications and educational strategies (Cheston, Flickinger and Chisolm 2013). As mentioned above, the number of healthcare organizations active in social media is growing, but hospitals may not have staff or partners with experience in using social media for professional purposes. In the webinar "Can healthcare providers afford to ignore social media?" health information technology expert John Glaser encouraged organizations to look beyond healthcare for expertise and guidance when developing social media: "What can we learn from others, not just within healthcare, but across other industries?" (HealthWorks Collective 2012).

As Glaser suggests, there is a growing community of professionals and organizations outside of healthcare that have developed expertise in the use of these tools. Within healthcare, some organizations that have instituted policies to guide the use of social media have published those policies on their websites. In his blog "Found in Cache" Ed Bennett has aggregated links to sites where those policies are available.[2]

In July 2010, Mayo Clinic established a Center for Social Media[3] to promote training and communication among its clinicians, patients and healthcare patients and families, as well as to offer consulting services to help healthcare organizations develop social media strategies.

VERIFICATION OF SOURCES

While, in theory, readers have always been responsible for verifying the sources they trust, the world of social media and user-generated content poses new challenges and calls into question previous assumptions about the reliability of resources. In the past, most professional readers trusted peer-reviewed journals implicitly to supply objective, scientifically valid evidence. Recent reports of bias and improprieties remind us that no profession or enterprise deserves unquestioning trust (Singer 2009; Curfman, Morrissey and Drazen 2006; Smith 2006).

"... the world of social media and user-generated content poses new challenges and calls into question previous assumptions about the reliability of resources."

The most effective strategy is to take nothing for granted and continually evaluate sources for their reliability, relevance and usefulness. Print and online publications are not the only resources that deserve careful evaluation. While an environment of trust is important for patient safety and EI&K sharing, it does not mean that the advice of co-workers or managers

---

2   See http://ebennett.org/hsnl/hsmp
3   See http://socialmedia.mayoclinic.org

should always be taken at face value. In all circumstances, acceptance must be balanced with a healthy sense of curiosity and skepticism.

INFOBOX 9.1: VERIFICATION OF RESOURCES

Evaluating the trustworthiness and reliability of sources is a discipline of its own. The following is a brief list of resources to help develop an inquisitive, informed approach to evaluating sources of EI&K:

- Critically Analyzing Information Sources (Cornell University Library). Available at: http://olinuris.library.cornell.edu/ref/research/skill26.htm
- Understanding Risk: What Do Those Headlines Really Mean? (US National Institutes of Health). Available at: http://www.nia.nih.gov/health/publication/understanding-risk-what-do-those-headlines-really-mean
- Health News Review: Independent Reviews of News Stories. Available at: http://www.healthnewsreview.org/
- *How to Read a Paper: The Basics of Evidence-Based Medicine* (Greenhalgh, T., 2014, 5th edition, BMJ Books).
- Retraction Watch: Tracking retractions as a window into the scientific process. Available at: http://retractionwatch.wordpress.com/

Multipurpose Mechanisms

Table 9.1 (see Appendix 2 for an expanded listing) shows a selection of different sharing mechanisms organized under evidence, information and knowledge with characteristics that heighten or detract from their value with some primary examples. For clarity, general types of mechanisms are described under the elements to which they most naturally apply – for example, journals and databases are listed under evidence – but they should not be viewed as limited by these categories. All forms of social media – from microblogs (such as Twitter), to integrated sites (such as LinkedIn and Facebook) to traditional email discussion lists – provide tools for exchanging information, and they can enable connections among individuals that may lead to knowledge-sharing.

In some circumstances, a combination of tools is most effective. Suzette Woodward is a leader in patient safety in the National Health Service (NHS) of the United Kingdom, first as director of patient safety at the National Patient Safety Agency and currently as director of safety, learning and people at the

Table 9.1   Selected EI&K Tools and Mechanisms by Primary Function

Tool/Mechanism	Characteristics	Examples
Evidence		
Peer-reviewed journals	• Rigor of review • Reported results supported with data • Transparency of content development process	• *Journal of Patient Safety* • *BMJ Quality & Safety* • *Joint Commission Journal on Quality and Patient Safety*
Information		
Newspapers, magazines and newsletters	• Not evidence-based, may be highly influential via investigation, reporting and storytelling • Not listed in PubMed® or other medical databases (see below)	• *New York Times* • *Wall Street Journal* • *Patient Safety and Quality Healthcare* • *Trustee Magazine* • ISMP medication safety alerts • Local newspapers and hospital newsletters
Knowledge		
Collaboratives	• Facilitate sharing of frontline team-based experience • Focus on a pre-defined project with a distinct goal in mind keeps sharing on-point	• Institute for Healthcare 100,000 and 5-million Lives Campaigns • Keystone Project • MCIC Emergency Department Patient Safety Collaborative

NHS Litigation Authority. Woodward is an active user of social media and used a blog post to describe participating in a journal club on Twitter:

Last Sunday I joined the twitter journal club (@twitjournalclub) and sat with iPad on knee furiously tapping away as we debated the NEJM *[New England Journal of Medicine] article on the use of the WHO Surgical Checklist [Haynes et al., 2009]. As I did so I wondered about the medium of twitter and its ability to support the patient safety movement in healthcare. There are a lot of social media tools for reaching out and connecting with others or for finding out information and it is hard to know which one will work best. My advice is to concentrate on just the one and for me that is Twitter.*

Well, let's return to my Sunday night. During the twit journal club we had the opportunity to learn from others about the benefits of using the checklist, the challenges they face and tips for progressing with its implementation. It was fabulous when Atul Gawande [co-author of the

NEJM article] joined in. Hopefully the next day those doctors, nurses, managers and others felt energised to keep going with the checklist knowing it saves lives and knowing there are others out there who are with them every step of the way (Woodward 2011).

Although Woodward chose to concentrate on Twitter as a primary social media method, her story involves sharing information through Twitter and a blog, sharing evidence through links to a peer-reviewed journal, and potentially sharing knowledge in the interactive discussion with content experts and others in the journal club. This use of interactive social media extended the perceived impact of evidence published in *New England Journal of Medicine* beyond the community of journal readers to the world at large, which was able to join freely in the discussion on Twitter. Woodward's story also illustrates the way that social media tools enable direct connections among people who may not otherwise have had the opportunity to connect. Not only was the journal club on Twitter international, it allowed the author and readers to share information and knowledge directly, informally, and in real time.

Storytelling

History matters. It matters not just because we can learn from the past, but because the present and the future are connected to the past by the continuity of a society's institutions (North 1990: vii).

Storytelling deserves special mention as a knowledge-sharing mechanism in patient safety. A well-told story is a unique way to engage listeners and, therefore, drive understanding and, potentially, improvement. It has been suggested that through storytelling and dialog, leaders can shape organizational evolution (Boal and Schultz 2007). Social psychology research suggests that: "… narratives, where compared with reporting statistical evidence alone, can have uniquely persuasive effects in overcoming preconceived beliefs and cognitive biases … stories are an essential part of how individuals understand and use evidence" (Meisel and Karlawish 2011: 2023).

Because stories seem informal and subjective, they may be discounted as vehicles for sharing serious EI&K, but increasing numbers of organizations and individuals are using stories to promote advances in patient safety. Social media have helped spread these stories far and wide, broadening their impact on patient safety efforts. Several examples follow:

- "Escape Fire" is an essay written by Don Berwick, MD when he was president and chief executive officer (CEO) of the Institute for Healthcare Improvement (IHI). Berwick first presented "Escape Fire" as a keynote address to IHI's National Forum in 1999. In it, Berwick tells the story of a forest fire in Mann Gulch, near Helena, Montana, which took the lives of 13 men in August 1949. After recounting a concise and moving version of the story, Berwick applies lessons from the fire (as analyzed by Norman Maclean in 1992's *Young Men and Fire*) to problems in healthcare using characters and imagery from the Man Gulch story to create vivid and compelling recommendations to improve the safety and quality of healthcare (Berwick 2004). In the same essay, Berwick tells a family story that further personalizes and illustrates his message. In addition to being an expert in healthcare improvement, Berwick is an accomplished story teller who has made that gift an important aspect of his teaching and advocacy.

- A multidisciplinary committee at Newton-Wellesley Hospital in Massachusetts uses narratives to describe patient safety incidents that they review and discuss during weekly meetings of the Service Operations Committee (SOC). The SOC consists of approximately 40 people representing executive management, department chairs, directors and managers of all service lines. The CEO of the hospital chairs the committee. At each meeting, safety reports are presented by the clinical leaders of the areas where the incidents occurred. The SOC discusses the reports and identifies "opportunities for multi-department shared learning" (Lightizer and Thurlo-Walsh 2012: 35).

- Hospital Corporation of America Inc. (HCA) found that the lessons learned from inpatient falls reported in its adverse event reporting system were different when the *narrative* descriptions in the reports were analyzed in addition to data, compared with lessons learned from the *data alone*:

  > The study revealed that the use of voluntarily reported data might be misleading if viewed solely from a quantitative perspective. Classification coding and trending based on event type alone do not reveal the complexity behind fall events. Narrative data provided by first responders and

direct care clinicians contain rich insights that can help focus prevention efforts along a more sustainable path for preventing falls, especially those that result in patient harm (Jones et al. 2011: 34).

PATIENT AND FAMILY STORIES MOTIVATE

Individuals who experience medical harm, either as patients, friends or family members, also share their stories to educate healthcare professionals and consumers, inspire change and protect others from similar events. Some of these individuals' stories have become touchstones for the patient safety movement. Among them are:

- Helen Haskell, whose son, Lewis Blackman[4] died following elective surgery in 2000 (Johnson, Haskell, and Barach 2012). Subsequently, Helen founded Mothers Against Medical Error, an advocacy and support group for parents and families of medical error victims. She was also instrumental in passing a state law in South Carolina to require hospital personnel to wear badges clearly indicating their professional role as a lack of clarity around clinician roles and responsibilities was a factor in her son's death.

- Sorrel King, whose daughter, Josie, died following medical errors in 2001 (King 2009). Her advocacy of improving patient safety and the value of listening to the family has resulted in the forming of a Foundation – The Josie King Foundation – and motivated leaders to drive improvement in their organizations to serve as a model to other hospitals worldwide (Pronovost and Vohr 2010).

- Sue Sheridan, whose son, Cal, suffered severe brain damage in 1995 after a failure to diagnose, and whose husband died in 2002 from a cancer that went undiagnosed when his pathology report was filed away apparently unread and effectively lost (Sheridan 2011). As the lead for the World Health Organization's Patients for Patient Safety initiative from 2004–2011, Sheridan helped other patients and family members who have experienced harm to develop their stories and to act as Patient Safety Champions in their own countries (World Health Organization 2012).

---

4   See http://www.lewisblackman.net/

- In July 2012, *The New York Times* published a story by reporter Jim
  Dwyer about Rory Staunton, the 12-year-old son of a family friend
  (Dwyer 2012). Staunton had died earlier in the year from sepsis,
  having been treated in a physician's office and hospital emergency
  room for what doctors believed was a stomach virus. Despite
  symptoms that in hindsight seem obvious and lab testing that was
  positive for serious bacterial infection but was not transmitted to
  the family or physicians, Staunton's illness was not recognized
  and treated until it was too late to save him. Staunton's story, as
  told in the *Times* and by his father, Ciaran Staunton, has prompted
  hospitals to examine their processes for prompt diagnosis of
  sepsis and communication of critical test results. In January 2013,
  New York State Governor Andrew Cuomo announced a series of
  reforms, referred to as "Rory's Regulations," that were designed to
  assure that patients receive accurate and timely diagnosis of sepsis
  (Governor's Press Office 2013).

Published stories about incidents that happened to public figures have had
considerable impact on patient safety. When actor Dennis Quaid went public
with the story of his infant twins' serious medication errors in 2007, the story was
covered by national media outlets and gained more notoriety and press coverage
than previous patient safety stories (CBS News 2008). Betsy Lehman was a health
reporter for the *Boston Globe* when she died from a chemotherapy overdose in
1994 (Knox 2012). Her story, as reported initially in the *Globe*, also received
national coverage and struck a nerve with the medical community because she
was harmed at one of the country's premier cancer centers (Kenney 2008).

SHARING STORIES WIDELY CREATES IMPACT

Countless other patients and families in the United States and across the world
have shared their stories in ways that have had profound impacts on healthcare
providers and consumers. Social media and the openness such mechanisms
allow facilitate the sharing of patient safety stories in a way unparalleled by
traditional publishing, information and evidence dissemination modalities.

Less frequently, clinicians have described their feelings and experiences
following adverse events through stories that illustrate the emotional toll that
those events may have on professionals who were directly or indirectly involved
(Hilficker 1984; Ring, Herndon and Meyer 2010). Sharing those experiences
through stories improves patient safety by promoting a healthier emotional
environment for clinicians, recognizing that emotional stress increases risk for

error, and helping to improve clinicians' performance (Scott, Hirschinger and Cox 2008; Kenney 2011).

Video is an effective mechanism for capturing and sharing stories and has been used to encourage clinicians tell their stories. "Healing the Healer" presents four case studies in which clinicians describe what happened as well as their feelings about particular adverse outcomes and their need for the support of colleagues and organizations, which in each case was lacking. The film seeks to assist clinicians involved in medical error – sometimes referred to as "Second Victims" (Wu 2000) – with their own recovery so they are able to continue delivering effective care to their patients (CRICO 2009).

Although stories may seem casual compared to most published evidence, they must be crafted purposefully to achieve intended goals (Denning 2004). The same may be said for all tools used to improve patient safety, but personal stories and stories about patients pose special challenges. The Institute for Safe Medication Practices (ISMP) describes elements of power derived from storytelling and of challenge, including legal and public disclosure issues. ISMP also has practical advice for ways to collect, craft, and share stories so as to "fully break the code of silence surrounding medical errors and make substantial headway on our journey to safer healthcare" (Institute for Safe Medication Practices 2011: n.p.).

Collaborative Networks

Collaborative networks, including communities of practice and collaboratives are another mechanism for sharing EI&K about patient safety. Collaborative networks often operate in part online, but the concept is rooted in a natural human tendency to come together to share information, swap stories and solve problems collectively. This robust sharing of tacit knowledge builds community.

COMMUNITIES OF PRACTICE

> *Communities of practice are groups of people who share a concern or a passion for something they do and learn how to do it better as they interact regularly (Wenger 2006: n.p.).*

Communities of practice (CoP) are an established strategy in knowledge management work (White et al. 2008). Though not common in healthcare in general nor in patient safety circles, the communities of practice model suggests this mechanism is particularly well-suited for sharing EI&K to advance work in this sector (Hara and Hew 2007; Li et al. 2009).

Wenger and colleagues use metaphors from everyday life to describe communities of practice: "Just as a good park has varied spaces for neighborhood baseball games, quiet chats, or solitary contemplation, a well-designed community of practice allows for participating in group discussion, having one-on-one conversations, reading about new ideas, or watching experts duel over cutting-edge issues" (Wenger, McDermott and Snyder 2002: n.p.). Wenger's communities of practice rely on elements that also describe a culture of safety: trust, open communication and willingness to work outside traditional hierarchies. Specifically, he recommends that communities seek information and expertise from "outsiders" in part so that community members – those who are "inside" – may "benefit from new thinking and the expansion of what they see could be possible effectively motivate and serve as agents of change" (Wenger, McDermott and Snyder 2002).

Communities of practice may well be a prescription written for developing and sharing EI&K about patient safety, fostering the learning environment requisite for high reliability. Among other benefits, active communities of practice would offer promise as a place for evidence-based and best practice tools and tactics (such as checklists) to evolve from stand-alone expectations to a hub of focused activity. The absence of defined, accessible, iterative forums which allow highly specialized, end-user clinicians, process coaches, and engaged patients to refine valued tools has been a barrier to promoting and sustaining safety-sensitive change in complex environments.

Early examples of communities of practice with a patient safety focus are emerging among member hospitals of the United States Centers for Medicare and Medicaid (CMS) Partnership for Patients (PfP),[5] a public-private partnership which began in 2011. PfP articulated a clear three-year goal to the 26 Hospital Engagement Networks (HENs) that were awarded contracts: reduce nine healthcare-associated conditions by 40 percent while simultaneously improving transitions of care such that hospital readmissions decline by 20 percent. More than 3,600 US hospitals are enrolled in HENs. While PfP supports HENs through contracted content developers, data analysis, and engagement resources, strategies for goal attainment are articulated and executed by each HEN.

---

5   See http://partnershipforpatients.cms.gov/

INFOBOX 9.2: THE MICHIGAN KEYSTONE PROJECT – DRIVING IMPROVEMENT THROUGH COLLABORATIVES ON A GRAND SCALE

The landmark Keystone Project is an example of using a collaborative to advance EI&K processes (Lashoher and Pronovost 2010) and support safety improvement.

"An intervention to decrease catheter-related bloodstream infections in the ICU."

Pronovost, P.J. et al. 2006. *New England Journal of Medicine*, 355(26), 2725–32.

More than 100 intensive care units (ICUs) in Michigan hospitals participated in a collaborative patient safety initiative designed to reduce the incidence of catheter-related bloodstream infections (CRBSI). CRBSI are common in ICUs and, although they are preventable, often cause serious, sometimes fatal harm to patients. Units that participated in the initiative, known as the "Keystone ICU" project, implemented five evidence-based strategies recommended by the Centers for Disease Control and Prevention (CDC) for CRBSI prevention. In addition, the units used a collaborative process to support provider behavior change and multidisciplinary education that included infection control staff and was considered an important part of the initiative. The project resulted in near elimination of CRBSI in participating units over an 18-month period.

"Improving patient safety in intensive care units in Michigan."

Pronovost, P.J. et al. 2008. *Journal of Critical Care*, 23(2), 207–21.

In addition to CRBSI reduction, the Keystone ICU project studied the effects of implementing a patient safety collaborative on "teamwork climate" among providers. Researchers from Johns Hopkins University and Michigan Health and Hospital Association used the comprehensive unit-based safety program (Timmel et al. 2010) to improve teamwork and safety culture and the Teamwork Climate Scale of the Safety Attitudes Questionnaire to measure results. In addition to improving adherence with evidence-based patient care interventions, the project improved safety culture significantly in participating units.

"Explaining Michigan: Developing an ex post theory of a quality improvement program."

Dixon-Woods, M., Bosk, C.L., Aveling, E.L., Goeschel, C.A. and Pronovost, P.J. 2011. *Milbank Quarterly*, 89(2), 167–205.

Why was the Michigan Keystone ICU project such a success? Authors of this study used an "ethnographic" approach to evaluate sociological elements of this improvement program. While the evidence-based interventions, presented as a checklist, were important, the authors found that the collaborative program was supportive and provides learning that can inform other quality improvement efforts. Elements of the social context among providers that contributed to the project's success were intensive networking, framing the incidence of infections as a "social problem," encouraging a "culture of commitment" to improvement, and using data to support change.

The absence of a prescriptive roadmap in the context of a rigorous timeline, the availability of data to drive priorities, and engaged champions appear to have created favorable conditions for patient safety-focused communities of practice to take hold. Over the past two years, eight virtual communities, termed Affinity Groups, emerged and now contribute to rapid improvement of vexing problems. Covering topics ranging from rural health to medication safety, these groups bring individuals charged with reducing harm associated with defined populations or specific aspects of care in close proximity for purposes of learning and spreading relevant evidence, information, and knowledge.

Members-only portals exist within a larger web-based platform to make standard educational and performance-shaping tools (like checklists; videos, and slide decks) available on-demand. The site also makes visible data that reflect commitments and levels of engagement. Affinity Group members also have the opportunity for real-time engagement using a wide array of technologies and platforms. Scheduled webinars, often beginning with a patient or family story and featuring gains shared by individuals in peer organizations, provide opportunity for structured learning. Audience reactions and virtual debriefings are facilitated using online polling technologies as well as through informal post-conferencing. Equally important, individuals have the opportunity to build relationships with peers and mentors. The ability to pick up the phone or email a virtual colleague – who would likely have remained unknown and whose knowledge would have been unexplored – brings the promise of more intimate ways of EI&K exchange to members.

Wenger highlights a barrier to establishing communities of practice that is relevant for many healthcare organizations: "… the very characteristics that make communities of practice a good fit for stewarding knowledge – autonomy, practitioner-orientation, informality, crossing boundaries – are also characteristics that make them a challenge for traditional hierarchical organizations" (Wenger 2006: n.p.). A community of practice works best if it is not too bound by an organization's formal hierarchy, but it takes a great deal of effort to create and sustain a group to support individual and organizational boundary spanning. It's possible the CMS Affinity Groups involve structure and accountabilities that may differentiate them from communities of practice formed more organically using Wenger's description. The foundational infrastructure for these communities of practice was in place, with potential beneficiaries invited to use and further develop. The website, however, does not yet support an optimal end-user experience for a full complement of activities.

Wenger's observation that a fully mature community of practice supports divergent interests and activities much the same as a park serves people may be useful in considering the current state of safety-focused communities of practice. Healthcare's early examples are, perhaps, best thought of as green spaces in development rather than fully mature parks. The extent to which the community partakes and invests in further development remains to be proven. Affinity Groups – and other, intentionally-formed quality improvement communities – may represent healthcare's welcome adaptation of solutions proven elsewhere.

COLLABORATIVES

Collaboratives are purposefully formed, voluntary networks comprised of similar care units that share a common improvement goal. They made the transfer to healthcare in the 1990s through their adoption for quality improvement efforts spearheaded by the IHI (Institute for Healthcare Improvement 2002; Sorensen and Bernard 2012). In collaborations, interdisciplinary clinical leaders in disparate facilities are joined with peers – through telephone calls, webinars and Internet-enabled team rooms – to learn about and implement evidenced-based or other promising best practice strategies, often under the guidance of a subject matter expert coach. Provisions for executive and local subject matter experts are typically secured as a condition of participation. EI&K sharing within the collaborative infrastructure extends beyond dissemination of clinical information to include activation of executive attention and practical tools for improving team communication.

The emergency department of MCIC Vermont, Inc. (MCIC) has facilitated a patient safety collaborative for its 13 insured organizations since 2009. The collaborative focused initially on processes that occur within the "four walls" of emergency departments (ED) in order to decrease the incidence of adverse events, promote best practices, optimize patient safety staff education and improve patient satisfaction scores. The MCIC collaborative emphasizes the role of leadership and multidisciplinary discussion of problems drawing from their experiences in working with Johns Hopkins as related below (Goldfarb, Scheulen and Patch 2012).

Three hospitals in the Johns Hopkins system used the collaborative in 2010–2011 to reduce the time patients spend waiting to be seen in the ED, driven by the awareness that patients with conditions of moderate urgency often wait the longest to be seen by an emergency department physician. An administrator involved in the initiative reflected that ED physicians worry most about patients in the waiting room. Prior to full evaluation, physicians cannot be certain how sick or injured patients are; once they are evaluated, problems can be addressed.

To improve emergency department wait times, the Hopkins teams spent a number of days with colleagues from two hospitals in the collaborative to learn from their experiences – to share knowledge. Rather than learning "one program that we had to make fit wherever we took it," the Hopkins teams learned strategies they could tailor to their own EDs. The program has resulted in process improvement that should lead to decreased risk: length of stay for 20 percent of patients has decreased an average of three hours (Goldfarb, Scheulen and Patch 2012).

The collaborative planned to address communication failures, diagnosis-related errors, and – expanding beyond the walls of the ED – issues related to radiology, especially interpretation discrepancies, documentation and responsibility (Goldfarb, Scheulen and Patch 2012).

Overall, since MCIC started the ED Patient Safety Collaborative, claim frequency has decreased approximately 33 percent, close to $7 million has been saved per year through 2011, and safety climate survey results have improved (Goldfarb, Scheulen and Patch 2012). Collaboratives of this sort, that involve sharing EI&K in the course of working on a defined, measurable goal, offer opportunities to *quantify* patient safety improvement. In most other collaborative networks, especially when social media tools are used to enhance communication and teamwork, demonstrating progress with quantitative reporting is a challenge.

EI&K Sharing: Measuring Effectiveness

There are now more ways to share evidence, information and knowledge than ever before, especially online. While this book was in development, new social networks were launched, smartphones with new capabilities came to market, and innovative news sites were introduced. As with any new technology, however, there is no guarantee that these new tools will further the mission to improve patient safety. Email, a transformative tool in

"It is still true that improvement is driven by the quality of interactions and real progress on culture change – not by use of the tools themselves."

the 1980s, comes with the risk that it creates the *illusion* of communication. Email can be efficient and effective *if* the receiving correspondent actually receives and reads the message and takes action. Sending email messages and tweets, commenting on email discussion groups, reading journal articles and attending conferences creates activity but doesn't guarantee change. It is still true that improvement is driven by the quality of interactions and real progress on culture change – not by use of the tools themselves.

A study by Nembhard and colleagues illustrates the challenge of measuring and understanding the effect of using social media to share EI&K (Nembhard et al. 2011).

An online community was created as part of a quality improvement campaign called the D2B (Door to Balloon) Alliance, which sought measurable clinical improvement for certain cardiac patients. More than 1,000 hospitals in the United States joined the campaign, and designated contacts and their colleagues at each hospital were invited to participate in an online community. Enrollment was considered to be successful; more than half of the hospitals were represented by individuals who joined the community, and 52 percent of those hospitals had individuals who participated by posting messages to the community. On average, each message that started a new topic in the community received 6.5 replies. Study authors found that "hospitals are highly collaborative and responsive in this context … the online community created an opportunity for organizations to learn and share knowledge not only about reducing door-to-balloon times but also about other quality improvement goals, a positive spillover of community formation" (Nembhard et al. 2011: 74).

Users of the online community reported that participation was helpful. The authors, however, did not find a correlation between use of the online community and the desired clinical improvement: "Thus, it appears that the use of the online community had a positive impact for users, but not with respect to our objective measure of performance" (Nembhard et al. 2012: 74). They acknowledge the study's limitations: follow-on discussions (prompted by the online community but occurring elsewhere) were not measured; "silent users" who were signed on but never posted a message could not be confirmed as actual "users," and the study looked only at this one online community, which may not be representative of others.

The study authors do not doubt the reports of members who found participation in the online community to have value. The only objective measure of improvement was a specific clinical intervention, so the authors and others can only speculate about what other benefits accrued to the participants and the characteristics and size of the "spillover" effect on other improvement efforts.

Seeing EI&K Sharing Through the HRO Prism

One approach to realizing the most from evidence, information and knowledge dissemination mechanisms is to apply principles of high-reliability to their use. These principles shore up high reliability organizations (HROs) where conditions change constantly, professionals and staff members with different training and experience must work together effectively, and opportunities abound for errors to cause serious harm. In fact, reliability comes in large part from the unsettling awareness that it is impossible to eradicate error and risk (Weick and Sutcliffe 2007: 3).

Healthcare has learned from industries that have achieved high-reliability – aviation and nuclear power, for example – that certain values, beliefs and behaviors promote a culture of safety and reliability even when working in environments of high-risk and complexity (ISMP 2005).

Considerable work has been done to apply HRO principles such as resisting oversimplification and maintaining the capacity for resilience to improving the reliability and safety of clinical processes and the policies and administrative structures that enable them (Nolan et al. 2004). It can be hoped that healthcare organizations are beginning to apply these same principles to ensure that mechanisms for sharing patient safety evidence, information and knowledge are equally effective. A full discussion of the application of HRO principles to any element of the EI&K continuum is lacking, to date. This book attempts to address that gap in a modest way.

> "One approach to realizing the most from evidence, information and knowledge dissemination mechanisms is to apply principles of high-reliability to their use."

Opportunities and Impacts

The story of Leape's exchange with the librarian illustrates EI&K challenges that individuals and organizations face when they aspire to improve patient safety:

- How does any organization, team or individual know what it doesn't know?

- Is there a process that will insure that gaps in evidence, information, and knowledge are minimized?

- Has the EI&K process been designed to address potential biases – both in the sources and in the people utilizing them?

- How can the effectiveness of EI&K sharing as individual components as well as a collective transformative process be measured?

Effective sharing involves choosing a mechanism for transmitting the information that is timely, engaging, and appropriate for the audience; that supports the workflow; and that improves the culture and reliability of the organization. These goals are served best by a multi-modal approach to sharing EI&K that includes everyone on the team, clinicians, administrators, librarians, patients and their advocates. In all healthcare settings, patients and their families are important participants in the safety culture and in the give-and-take of evidence, information, and knowledge. Patients and families typically have a wide range of levels of experience, styles of learning and communication, and cultural backgrounds, which does increase the challenge of designing methods for sharing EI&K in a way that works. Nevertheless, an effective process needs to take these individuals into account as participants in EI&K exchange. It is their involvement with the tools and technologies touched on in this chapter that improves sharing EI&K, while offering opportunities to develop and support the culture of patient safety within an organization.

"Simply using the tools does not guarantee success."

Internet-enabled social media and networking tools can be used to counteract hierarchies and reach across boundaries that separate people. They enable access across silos to sources of evidence and information that can help change culture and improve the sharing of what is known. Although patient safety is a different kind of social movement, than, for example, the 2011 "Arab Spring" uprisings facilitated by communication technologies, patient safety does involve changes for which social media are well-suited (Lim 2012). Simply using the tools does not guarantee success. Leape's incomplete use of databases described earlier is an example. To engage with information, evidence and knowledge mechanisms effectively requires sensitivity to how they affect what EI&K is at hand, sought out and applied toward the achievement of clear goals to enable system safety. Only through this prism can the pure value of evidence, information and knowledge be capitalized upon to drive and generate sustainable impact as an important feature of a strategy for patient safety improvement.

KEY TAKE-AWAYS

- There is a wide array of tools to share stories and lessons learned in patient safety, which all have pros and cons.
- Strategies are required to make the best use of the tools that are available to access evidence, information and knowledge.
- A single channel for seeking and distributing EI&K is apt to not be comprehensive and may contribute to latent failures if not considered from a systemic improvement perspective.

Suggested Reading

Hamm, M.P. et al. 2013a. Social media use among patients and caregivers: A scoping review. *British Medical Journal Open*, 3(5), e002819.

Hamm, M.P. et al. 2013b. Social media use by health care professionals and trainees: A scoping review. *Academic Medicine*, 88(9), 1376–83.

Li, L.C., Grimshaw, J.M., Nielsen, C., Judd, M., Coyte, P.C. and Graham, I.D. 2009. Use of communities of practice in business and health care sectors: A systematic review. *Implementation Science*, 4, 27. Available at: http://www.implementationscience.com/content/4/1/27 [accessed: April 7, 2013].

10

Health Information Technology in Hospitals: Towards a Culture of EI&K Sharing

Prudence Dalrymple and Debora Simmons

> *It is clear that much greater use of information technology is needed if healthcare is ever going to attain even reasonable standards of reliability and safety (Vincent 2010: 265).*

Essential Challenges and HIT

A fundamental assumption in healthcare is that evidence, information and knowledge (EI&K) are essential to providing safe patient care. To understand this assumption it is necessary, however, to look beyond the development and promulgation of guidelines and sharing of patient data. Instead, the ways that people and organizations can fully implement what they know to be effective need to be examined. That is, identifying scientific evidence is but an initial step in the creation of a culture based on evidence; the next step is developing practice guidelines that are then disseminated.

Typically in today's healthcare environment, evidence dissemination involves the use of health information technology (HIT) through mechanisms such as clinical decision support. The combination of highly developed methods of bringing evidence to the practice of healthcare and the evolution of HIT would seem to be sufficient to ensure that patients remain safe, errors are avoided and best outcomes are achieved. However, this three-fold goal remains elusive. HIT is not a panacea for effective evidence delivery in the daily practice of healthcare.

A central premise of this chapter is that evidence-based medicine and health information technology solutions are not sufficient in and of themselves to improve patient safety. Rather, it is the culture within the organization that determines the use of such strategies and whether patients are cared for in a safe manner. It will be argued that three types of intellectual resources are essential to improving patient safety: evidence, information and knowledge. This chapter pays particular attention to evidence and its distribution via health information technology in the form of a well-developed electronic health record (EHR) against the backdrop of a safety culture that facilitates openness and sharing. Insights from high reliability organizations (HROs) will be described along with their potential application to healthcare organizations. It is important to note that while data is not a primary focus for this book, it is a core piece of what is shared by health information technology and is thus essential to this chapter.

INFOBOX 10.1: PRIMARY TERMS – CULTURAL MURKINESS

Blame Culture:

… a blame culture is reactive. There is a distinct focus on identifying specific individuals when things go wrong (Patankar et al. 2012).

Just Culture:

… a just culture recognizes that competent professionals make mistakes and acknowledges that even competent professionals will develop unhealthy norms (shortcuts) but has zero tolerance for reckless behavior (AHRQ n.d.; Marx 2001).

Organizational Culture:

A pattern of shared basic assumptions that the group learned as it solved its problems that has worked well enough to be considered valid and is passed on to new members as the correct way to perceive, think, and feel in relation to those problems (Schein 1992: 12).

Safety Culture:

The safety culture of an organization is the product of individual and group values, attitudes, perceptions, competencies, and patterns of behavior that determine the commitment to, and the style and proficiency of, an organization's health and safety management (ACSNI 1993). It's why organizations do what they do (Patankar et al. 2012).

Application of Evidence to Healthcare Practice

Since the 1990s when Sackett and other introduced and advocated evidence-based medicine (EBM) the movement has made great strides in assessing what is known about a clinical topic based on comprehensive literature searches and careful appraisal of the research (Sackett 2000; Sackett et al. 1996). Evidence denotes the results of scientific investigation, which at its most credible level have been identified through comprehensive, systematic reviews of the literature, appraised for their validity, then summarized and disseminated through resources such as the Cochrane Collaboration.[1] EBM refers to the use of clinical practice guidelines supported by scientific evidence rather than consensus alone.

INFOBOX 10.2: EBM AND PATIENT SAFETY PRACTICES – AN EVIDENCE REVIEW

The seminal AHRQ *Making Health Care Safer* report, issued in 2001, used evidence-based medicine principles to identify key patient safety practices (PSPs). (Shojania et al. 2001) Although its recommendations were somewhat controversial, the report galvanized patient safety efforts at hospitals nationwide and provided a stimulus for further rigorous research on PSPs. In doing so, the report laid the foundation for the most prominent successes of the safety field. This newly issued follow-up report combines traditional systematic review methodology with the judgments of key stakeholders and technical experts in the field (Shekelle, Wachter and Pronovost 2013). The authors critically examine the evidence supporting 41 separate PSPs and ultimately arrive at a list of 10 strongly encouraged practices. These practices, if implemented, should result in reduced harm from a wide range of safety threats, including healthcare-associated infections, medication errors, and pressure ulcers. The report also examines how cost, implementation, and contextual considerations may affect the real-world effectiveness of PSPs, details how foundational concepts such as human factors engineering should be incorporated into safety efforts, and provides a blueprint for future research in patient safety (AHRQ 2013).

Source: Reprinted with permission of AHRQ PSNet. Shekelle, P.G., Wachter, R.M. and Pronovost, P.J. (eds) 2013. *Making Health Care Safer II: An Updated Critical Analysis of the Evidence for Patient Safety Practices*. Rockville, MD: Agency for Healthcare Research and Quality; March 2013. AHRQ Publication No. 13-E001-EF. Available at: http://psnet.ahrq.gov/resource.aspx?resourceID=25758.

Where possible, meta-analysis is used to produce a statistically sound body of evidence that forms the foundation for EBM. Although objections to evidence-

---

1   See http://www.cochrane.org/

based medicine are still raised, such as critiquing it as "cook book medicine" or arguing that it overly privileges the double-blind randomized controlled trial over other research designs, EBM is still regarded as a more scientifically sound approach to promoting effective clinical practices, and therefore plays a central role in decreasing medical errors – of both omission and commission – and increasing patient safety through application of strategies that are known to work. Indeed, the evidence-based approach has been taken up throughout the healthcare enterprise, having been adopted not only by physicians but also by nurses and other health professionals, where it is referred to as evidence-based practice or EBP. The use of evidence upon which to base practice decisions is now viewed as essential to achieving the goals of improving patient safety as well as managing more professionally satisfying and financially sound practice. The application of the latter has been referred to as evidence-based management (Shortell, Rundell and Hsu 2007).

Despite these benefits, progress toward applying evidence to practice has been notoriously slow and its impact has been modest (Cabana et al. 1999; Wallace Nwosu and Clarke 2012). At first, this may seem counter-intuitive; after all, if providing patients with the "best care possible" doesn't keep patients safe, what will?

Lack of Compliance

Understanding the reasons for apparent non-compliance is essential if health outcomes and patient safety are to improve. Numerous initiatives have been advanced to increase the application of evidence to practice, often described as "compliance with" guidelines (Carthey et al. 2011). Gurses and colleagues have identified four main categories of factors affecting compliance:

- clinician characteristics;

- guideline characteristics;

- system characteristics; and

- implementation characteristics (Gurses et al. 2010).

They developed a conceptual framework that specifies the relationships among these factors that can be used to design more effective ways to improve patient safety (Gurses et al. 2010). Reducing the complexity of guidelines, making them easily accessible and providing decision support and reminders are all thought to increase guideline compliance, under the assumption that if a clinician knows what's right, s/he will opt to do it. However, it is also true that if following the guideline is not seen to be immediately advantageous in terms of time or effort, the incentive to comply with the guideline diminishes (Dalrymple et al. 2010).

Qualitative research, because of its ability to "look beneath the surface" is often used to take a deeper look at the reasons for non-compliance with guidelines. Greenhalgh has advocated a "narrative approach" when considering research in quality improvement research; she notes that stories can vividly illustrate how organizations and individuals behave in particular situations (Greenhalgh, Russell and Swinglehurst 2005). These illustrative stories create knowledge that can inform future decisions. Similar narrative approaches can be used to examine how the actions of individuals and organizations affect patient safety and are particularly useful in understanding the organizational factors that may impede the individual's propensity to "do the right thing."

Health Information Technology

Adoption of evidence in practice can also be facilitated through information, especially health information technology, primarily in the form of electronic health records (EHR) enhanced by decision support. Built-in alerts to inform clinicians of possible adverse effects when combining certain medications or to remind them of the probable consequence of an action, can protect patients are examples that can bring the evidence to bear in daily work. However, over-use of alerts can lead to alert fatigue causing the clinician to ignore or override the alerts (Isaac et al. 2009). Other examples of unintended consequences of HIT may be found in Chapter 3 of this text and the broader literature (Harrison,

---

INFOBOX 10.3: VARIOUS HIT COMPONENTS

Health IT is not a specific product but is composed of several component, such as:

- electronic health records;
- clinical decision support;
- computerized provider order entry;
- bar-coding;
- health information exchange;
- patient engagement technologies; and
- other health information technology used in clinical care (Hayrinen et al. 2008; Institute of Medicine 2011).

Koppel and Bar-Lev 2007; Yackel and Embi 2010; Palmieri, Peterson and Corazo 2011; Institute of Medicine 2011). Sensitivity to unintended consequences characterizes both a systems approach to HIT implementation as well as application of high reliability principles associated with a keen interest in failure identification.

One way to look at the holistic impact of effective EI&K sharing in healthcare is to explore how the sharing continually affects improvement of care. The effective point-of-care exchange contributes to population health. Initiatives focusing exclusively on the *physician's* actions in prescribing fall short; from a systems thinking approach it is the larger whole of the organization or healthcare system at large that influences overall health of relationships, organizations and populations. Figure 10.1 illustrates how the

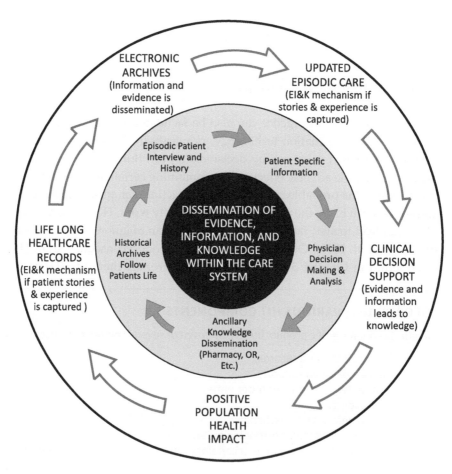

Figure 10.1   Electronic EI&K Management in the Healthcare System

various components of an HIT system contribute to this improvement. By viewing individual elements (clinical decision support or electronic healthcare records) of the HIT system as feeding into the next source of EI&K, the figure shows how shared information contributes to the need for individuals and organizations to improve through embracing electronic means of managing evidence information and knowledge-sharing in the clinical environment.

HIT Implementation Barriers

The continued adoption of electronic health records and ancillary clinical information systems have the potential to access and analyze data across space and time feeding into improvements through the creation and application of EI&K. But actual examples of HIT bringing organizations – that have traditionally

"... it is the use of these [HIT] systems by people that contributes to the failure to realize the promise of health information technology to improve patient safety (Institute of Medicine 2011)."

been siloed – into a cohesive whole are not common. Barriers to successful implementation of health information technologies can be found at and between multiple levels of organizations – from the sharp to the blunt end. Furthermore, decisions regarding the selection, implementation and use of HIT are affected by cultural norms, regulatory mandates and local practices. The Committee on Patient Safety and Health Information Technology of the Institute of Medicine (IOM) has cited the followed barriers to successful HIT implementation:

- Failure to employ incremental implementation and thereby eliminating the opportunity to build upon knowledge gained throughout the change process.

- Failure to consider workflow when configuring systems.

- Failure to build in sufficient flexibility to adapt to changing patterns of care.

- Failure to consider the natural patterns and preferences in human performance, both in training and in clinical workflow.

- Failure to design tools to optimize the capture of quality data (Institute of Medicine 2011).

While it is clear that HIT can provide support through reminders, over-reliance on technology to improve patient safety has its own inherent dangers. Indeed, some may argue that the ability of HIT to improve patient safety has been over-promised particularly as the unintended consequences of HIT have become more apparent (Institute of Medicine 2011).

While some of these unintended consequences are endemic to the systems themselves, it is also recognized that it is the use of these systems *by people* that contributes to the failure to realize the promise of health information technology to improve patient safety (Institute of Medicine 2011). Ironically, EBM – with its emphasis on objective scientific evidence – also fails to address what is increasingly recognized as a critical factor in patient safety: creating an organizational culture that does not focus on individual compliance with guidelines, but rather examines the systemic changes that are necessary to create a culture that shares effective practice through dissemination of evidence, information and knowledge.

Role of the Organization

The importance of the organization's role in supporting clinicians in their work to comply with evidence-based guidelines can hardly be overstated. Efforts at patient safety that focus solely on compliance with guidelines can be detrimental in that they can create an environment that is perceived as disrespecting clinical judgment and disallowing clinicians to put the interests of the patient first.

Particularly when guidelines are enforced with alerts and other clinical decision support mechanisms within the EHR, deviating from the prescribed approach may be flagged and a culture of blame can develop. When that occurs, the individual resists taking responsibility fearing retribution or censure. In a blame-oriented environment, individuals are unlikely to share their experiences or their insights for fear of personal reprisal. Such a "blame and shame" approach constrains any natural desire to share experience or to work together.

The role of organizational culture on improving healthcare performance has generated great interest, as the field has sought to more effectively adapt to these changes while maintaining a commitment to the basic tenet "first, do no harm." Yet this endeavor has been shown to be much more difficult than anticipated and progress has been slow. Indeed, a 2011 Cochrane review concluded that while the management of organizational culture is increasingly viewed as a necessary part of health reform, until recently there has been little evidence to support a link between organizational culture and health performance, nor is there any rigorous evidence of effective strategies to change organizational culture on healthcare performance (Parmelli, Peterson and Corazzo 2011). An Agency for Healthcare Quality and Research-funded review in 2013 came to a similar conclusion (Weaver et al. 2013).

Technology Can Support a Sharing and Just Culture

A third component in achieving an environment supportive of patient safety is a safety culture. A culture of safety has been described as consisting of a just culture, characterized by an engaged leadership and strong programs of team training and effective communication (Frankel, Leonard and Denham 2006). A just culture is one that examines its own failings and weaknesses with as much openness as it shares its areas of excellence (Marx 2001; Shojania, Wachter and Hartman n.d.). Individuals within a just culture are not fearful of reprisals should they speak out, admit weakness, or seek assistance and therefore they are comfortable working as a team. They are not isolated from others, and accept that they are accountable to one another, to their peer group and to their organization for their actions.

In organizations that encourage a just culture blame is not placed on the individual, but on the organizational entity of which the individual is a part. The individual who experiences the problem can choose to share her knowledge and experience with the failure, pointing out the structural flaws that contributed to the errors. Thus the individual shame initially associated with the error becomes an opportunity to advocate for change (Frankel, Leonard and Denham 2006).

In a just culture, sharing experiences is rewarded with peer respect. A just culture is often found in high reliability organizations (HROs) where freedom from blame enables team members to speak up when they see a dangerous situation without fear of reprisal (McFadden, Henagan and Gowen 2009). Team members are empowered to make suggestions that will improve processes that will affect safety. Increasingly, healthcare organizations are working toward achieving high reliability (Chassen and Loeb 2011).

"The will to create … information and then to share it is a concern not of technology but rather of culture."

Highly Reliable Use of EI&K

In contrast to what has happened in healthcare, the relationship between organizational culture, safety and performance has been more fully acknowledged in high reliability organizations. In HROs, a safety culture is well established. In healthcare, safety culture is the third – and often missing – relational component lacking in healthcare's question to achieve a delivery system that is as reliable and as safe as other HROs.

Awareness about evidence does not reliably result in its application to patient care: "Health care clinicians successfully apply proven medical evidence in common acute, chronic, or preventive care processes less than 80 percent of the time" (Resar 2006: 1677). Evidence-based medicine (or more generally EBP) applied in a systems-oriented, HRO fashion can provide the strong scientific EI&K for practice. Effective HIT process design can support highly reliable EI&K use. In this situation, standardized procedures are in place, based on the best evidence available. Exceptions are tolerated, but only when expert knowledge, based on experience, is available. In fact, in a high reliability organization, individuals are encouraged to share the knowledge gained from practice, thereby leading to the creation of a body of experiential knowledge that can be used by the whole organization. The creation and aggregation of this experiential knowledge is what Greenhalgh and colleagues refer to in proposing meta-narrative analysis as an approach to knowledge creation that allows for contextual nuance and sensible adaptation (Greenhalgh, Russell and Swinglehurst 2005). High reliability organizations support a culture that enables and ensures that information and experiential knowledge are shared throughout the system to enrich subsequent analysis and application, further strengthening the evidence the supports frontline decision-making.

High reliability organizations are also data and information intensive. Thus, the technologies engaged to enable EI&K identification, packaging and sharing processes would benefit from being seen through the HRO prism as well. The management of data and information is facilitated through information technologies such as the electronic health record or EHR (the more encompassing term for electronic medical record). The advent of sophisticated EHRs has created volumes of data to the point that clinicians are drowning in it. Only when those data are managed, presented, analyzed and discussed does the information become accessible throughout the hospital system. That is, the capability and the opportunity to create information from data have never been as abundant as they are currently, but the *will* to create that information and then to share it is a concern not of technology but rather of culture. Understanding the ways in which data is transformed into information and how that information is shared is the concern of the organizational culture. In an extensive case study of a tertiary care unit, Macintosh-Murray and Choo described the ways in which clinicians failed to harness the data that were available in order to engage in full scale problem-solving and critical thinking (Macintosh-Murray and Choo 2005). These authors observed that in the organization being analyzed, the culture of individual accountability superficially appeared to be contributing to improved patient safety, but in fact, prevented it from realizing its goals.

In organizations that adopt the principles of HROs, adverse events are viewed as opportunities to analyze root causes, to learn from experiences, and to improve care. In one qualitative study reported by Curry and colleagues, individuals working in a culture that valued learning and team participation as well as data-based decision-making and accountability reported incorporating data feedback into their decisions (Curry et al. 2011). This organization's culture also instituted a non-punitive approach to problem-solving that focused on learning rather than blaming. The Chief Executive Officer of one high-performing hospital reported: "There are four stages in dealing with adverse events: The data are wrong; the data are correct but it's not a problem; the data are correct and it's a problem, but it's not my problem; the data are correct and I own the responsibility to fix the problem" (Curry et al. 2011: 388).

It is this sense of individual accountability for addressing problems that characterizes the high reliability organization, and, in this example, a high-performing hospital. This approach has been advocated by the IOM as a key component in creating a culture of safety (Institute of Medicine 2011).

The Systems Approach: Moving from the Individual to the Organization

Upon first opening a chapter on health information technology, readers who think only in terms of bits, bytes, ontologies and hardware may fail to appreciate that a different approach to designing systems is needed in order to see improvement. *To Err is Human* and *Crossing the Quality Chasm* repeatedly called for viewing medical errors as a function not of the *individual* but as an artifact of the *organization* in which individuals work (Kohn, Corrigan and Donaldson 2000; Committee on Quality of Health Care in America 2001). That is,

" ... a systems approach to HIT reinforces a culture of sharing within an organization."

errors may occur because of a failure to examine the error within the context of process and workflow. As a result, the occurrence of an error is associated with an individual who is held responsible and is blamed. Performing a root cause analysis (RCA) can identify multiple factors that contributed to the error and move the focus to the broader system – the hospital – rather than taking the easy and incorrect approach of putting all the responsibility for an error on one individual.

INFOBOX 10.4: PRIMARY TERMS – SYSTEM MURKINESS

Terms building off the root of "system" occur frequently, and although they have properties in common, they carry distinctive meanings:

- A system is a whole entity comprised of many parts. A health information technology "system" is comprised of several different technologies such as lab reporting, radiology imaging, admissions and billing data, patient data, and so on.
- Systematic is a descriptive term indicating that an activity follows a prescribed method. Evidence reviews are systematic reviews because the method of review is stated explicitly and can be replicated.
- Systemic refers to something that is spread throughout an entity, affecting a group or system. Many medical errors are systemic in that they are embedded is healthcare processes and activities.
- Systems thinking regards individual problems as parts of a much larger system. It assumes that the different parts of a system can best be understood by looking at them in relation to each other and to other systems, rather than in isolation.

This perspective has also been noted as being of value in the implementation of health information technologies. In a 2011 report on HIT and patient safety, the IOM called for the creation of mechanisms to ensure the "voluntary, confidential and non-punitive" reporting of HIT-related patient safety issues and incidents (Institute of Medicine 2011: 9). In addition, the IOM noted that simply reporting of these incidents is not enough; it is also essential to learn from and share this information and knowledge.

This recommendation parallels those aimed at developing a clinical evidence base to support evidence-based practice. Indeed, the aforementioned IOM reports address the need to move from looking at patient safety and quality outcomes not as individual achievements but as the products of shared evidence, information and knowledge (Kohn, Corrigan and Donaldson 2000;

Committee on Quality of Health Care in America 2001). That is, without data regarding errors it is not possible to create any information about patterns that affect patient safety. Without encouragement and ability to share that information, there is no opportunity to generate knowledge to support learning from mistakes and improve performance. This integrative, holistic systems approach characterizes a healthcare environment in which patients are safe from medical errors and receive the best care with the most positive outcomes.

Currently available HIT enables clinicians to make better decisions by seeing beyond the individual patient in the moment to recognizing patterns and trends both across time and across patients. The application of systems thinking to patient safety enables a view of individuals as parts of a larger whole, each influencing and being influenced by others. Current efforts to encourage adoption of electronic health records have the goal and promise of moving from the individual level to systems thinking by linking the individual practitioner and patient to a wider network of information sharing across the healthcare system. Through systems thinking, the organization sees itself as part of the overall environment, and recognizes how it influences and is influenced by external forces.

Ideally, a systems approach to HIT reinforces a culture of sharing within an organization. This perspective can also help manage the unintended consequences that are increasingly a concern when implementing a new HIT system. The introduction of HIT interventions – when approached with the organizational "system" in mind – makes explicit the inter-relationships and patterns of data that make the technology work. This "systems approach" should facilitate an organization's adoption of an open, sharing culture by creating a unified view of the larger effort of patient care. The data and information now accessible through health information technology allow for analysis of the success or failure of the organization to reach its goals, particularly those related to improved quality and patient safety.

A Culture of Sharing Enables HIT to Support Patient Safety

The preceding discussion examines how an environment in which HIT has become pervasive can support healthcare's transition to an organizational culture that resembles high reliability organizations. A culture in which sharing information, evidence and knowledge, as well as responsibility and accountability, is essential to creating an environment in which patient safety

"The twin accomplishments of evidence-based practice and health information technologies take on new power when they are embedded within an organization that embraces a culture of sharing." is an achievable goal. Through current and evolving HIT, the technological ability to support EI&K sharing are at hand. The insights gained from examining high reliability organizations can be brought to bear in healthcare by recognizing the influence of organizational norms that encourage a culture of sharing and a culture of safety. Responsibility for creating this culture lies with engaged leaders who are willing to commit resources to building the capacity for change and innovation within their organizations. A culture of sharing starts with institutional values that are instilled through investment in team learning and communications skills, both of which are intrinsically connected to EI&K. The twin accomplishments of evidence-based practice and health information technologies take on new power when they are embedded within an organization that embraces a culture of sharing. Together, the goal of patient safety comes within reach.

KEY TAKE-AWAYS

- Health information systems can enable the sharing of EI&K in healthcare.
- HIT as an evidence delivery mechanism presents a unique opportunity for improvement if the systems and the cultures that support their use are aligned.
- Progress and systems can fall short if not enabled through a systems thinking high reliability view.
- Accountabilities for the use of HIT reliably – from the entering of data through the sharing of stories – can contribute to sustainable improvements.

Suggested Reading

Committee for Data Standards for Patient Safety and Aspden, P. et al. (eds) 2004. *Patient Safety: Achieving a New Standard of Care.* Washington, DC: The National Academies Press.

Institute of Medicine 2011. *Health IT and Patient Safety: Building Safer Systems for Better Care.* Washington, DC: Institute of Medicine.

Jones, S.S., Koppel, R., Ridgely, M.S., Palen, T.E., Wu, S. and Harrison, M.I. 2011. *Guide to Reducing Unintended Consequences of Electronic Health Records.* Available at: http://www.ucguide.org.

11

Critical Intersections in Patient Safety: Evidence and Knowledge Transfer at the Sharp and Blunt Ends

Julia M. Esparza, Melissa Cole and Gunjan Kahlon

> *Knowledge has to be improved, challenged, and increased constantly, or it vanishes (Drucker and Wartzman 2010: xv).*

Gaps of Concern for Healthcare Workers

An October 1996 fatal incident in Denver illuminates the critical intersection of patient safety and reliable EI&K transfer. In this case, three nurses were indicted for criminally negligent homicide and faced possible jail terms for their role in the death of a newborn who received IV penicillin G benzathine (Smetzer and Cohen 1998). A retrospective review uncovered 50 points of failure in the medication use system, including failures of information, evidence and knowledge transfer (Smetzer and Cohen 1998). An intervention at any one of these points of failure would have prevented the infant's death (Committee on Identifying and Preventing Medication Errors et al. 2007). Points of failure included: faulty information interpreted from an outdated drug reference book, misreading of the dose by a pharmacist, incorrect route of administration, miscommunication with the child's mother, and lack of institutional knowledge regarding treating of the condition. These failures were all sharp end challenges for this clinical team that placed the infant at risk.

The Denver case also highlights how the five rights of medication checking (the right patient, the right drug, the right dose, the right route, at the right time) exponentially expands safety measures when used in parallel with the five rights of evidence, information and knowledge (EI&K) delivery: the *right resource*, to the *right person*, for the *right patient or purpose*, through the *right modality*, at the *right time*.

INFOBOX 11.1: THE FIVE RIGHTS OF EI&K DELIVERY

- The *right resource* (whether evidence, information or knowledge);
- To the *right person*;
- For the *right patient or purpose*;
- Through the *right modality*;
- At the *right time*.

As the Denver case illustrates, having the right information, evidence and knowledge at the point-of-care is crucial for patient safety. It's important that not only are the right questions asked, but that the resources referred to answer the questions are accurate – which means more than having them close at hand. Diagnostic error leader Mark Graber and colleagues found that most clinical staff did not find answers for their questions via electronic resources at the point-of-care (Graber et al. 2008). Interruptions, distractions, lack of time or the possibly mistaken belief that the answer did not exist were the reasons literature was not searched 28 percent of the time (Graber et al. 2008). This situation perpetuates itself amongst many groups in healthcare and is often latent in its character. In an age when evidence, information and knowledge are accessible via a collection of technologies and processes, how is it that having the right information, evidence and knowledge in the right place at the right time, is not reliably achieved?

LACK OF EXPLICIT INTEREST ON THE BLUNT END

In 1955 business consultant and educator Peter Drucker set out to define "Management Science" for the manager. In his description, managers benefit by using knowledge in order to make the best decisions relevant to their individual organizations (Drucker 1955). Drucker moved the concept of management away from specific tools toward defining the elements essential for a manager to conduct management science.

Fast forward to 2010. *Health Care Administration: Planning, Implementing, and Managing Organized Delivery Systems,* a widely used textbook for healthcare and health service administration programs, has little discussion of evidence, information and knowledge (Wolper 2010). While specific sections briefly discuss information technology systems and provide background on information required for compliance, administrators and managers reading the book will be provided only a limited view of the role EI&K plays in healthcare at the bedside. In order to plan, implement and manage complex delivery systems, administrators at the blunt end of organizations can execute patient safety initiatives and deliver knowledge by harnessing EI&K at the bedside.

As mentioned in Chapter 2, EI&K lacks a cohesive definition across the spectrum of its use. In a 2007 *JAMA* commentary, Shortell and colleagues discuss the importance of evidence-based medicine (EBM) and the need to translate the clinical evidence to make it usable at the bedside (Shortell, Rundall and Hsu 2007). In building on what is known through the EBM initiatives, institutions and clinicians would benefit by understanding how EI&K plays a pivotal role in patient safety, ensuring the right EI&K is available to the right clinician at the right time to enable the safest practice decision to be made for that patient at the point-of-care.

Capitalizing Use of EI&K Through Existing Processes

The healthcare delivery process is replete with EI&K sharing exchanges. Several illustrations are presented in Table 11.1.

Table 11.1   EI&K Sharing in Healthcare: Select Examples

Strategy	Sharp End Examples	Blunt End Examples
Rounding:	Patient Rounds: Driving EI&K to the patient bedside, patient-centric care, including patient knowledge seeking and input.	Administrative Rounds: Leadership collecting EI&K for improved decision-making and safe support.
Embedded Information Expertise Strategies:	Medical Librarian Reviews: crafting standard search strategies and delivery mechanisms to share information; Providing critical answers to clinical questions directly to clinical staff; gathering awareness of how care is delivered to apply that knowledge to frontline evidence delivery strategies.	Proactive Problem Identification: EI&K sharing from administration to staff and collection of external failures to proactively inform action and identify improvement opportunities (Conway 2008).
Teamwork:	Multidisciplinary Teamwork: Collecting experts to review cases at the point-of-care for immediate answers to clinical questions and care delivery.	Shared Governance: Collection of experts to form an informed (EI&K) direction of leadership.

Rounding and teamwork as EI&K sharing opportunities are explored further below.

ROUNDING INITIATIVES

"Management by Walking Around" (MBWA) was advocated by Peters and Waterman as a mechanism for the executive and administrators to be in touch with what is happening at their frontline (Peters and Waterman 1982). Healthcare has adopted this concept on the blunt end as a safety improvement strategy (Morello et al. 2013). MBWA has materialized in healthcare as a strategy that patient safety officers, librarians and others have embraced to discover information needs and facilitate knowledge and evidence sharing, as illustrated below.

- As CEO of The Studer Group, Quint Studer devised a version of rounding that encouraged administrators at all levels to round on employees to ensure staff have the needed resources to be successful and see if patients and physicians are treated well by staff (Studer 2003).

- At Johns Hopkins, senior administrators adopted units to support organizational learning and demonstrate commitment to a culture of safety. The program was successful in reducing patient risks in the selected units (Pronovost et al. 2004). Other applications of this idea are shown to have had impact on improving safety culture (Morello et al. 2012).

- With Transforming Patient Care at the Bedside, younger nurses were encouraged to find solutions to common issues with rapid deployment of the solutions (Robert Wood Johnson Foundation 2008).

In each process, administrators involved themselves at the bedside or empowered those at the bedside to make rapid improvements. These examples stimulated EI&K to utilize an existing process in a unique and different way.

Opportunities for clinical exchange of information during the course of providing care are typically what come to mind when rounding is discussed. Proactive rounding on patients hourly during the day and every two hours at night has been shown to significantly decrease falls, medication errors and patient use of call lights, nursing overtime while increasing patient satisfaction (Meade, Bursell and Ketelsen 2006). Transforming Patient Care at the Bedside (TCAB) initiatives took this proactive approach one step further. The TCAB approach of empowering less-senior nurses to develop creative solutions (such as "red/yellow/green" labels on a locator board or tagging staff with the most patients and the highest acuity) allows for the resources to flow and support those in need; in other words, for knowledge to move to where it is needed. This process has senior mentor oversight providing ongoing support and knowledge. It is a strong intersection of the sharp end and the blunt end EI&K (see Table 11.1).

TEAMWORK

The provision of high-quality, safe healthcare is increasingly a team sport (Wachter 2012: 157).

Evidence supports the use of multidisciplinary teams as a means of improving quality indicators, better patient experience and preventing errors (de Mestral et al. 2011; Dy et al. 2011; Heintz, Halilovic and Christensen 2011; Kim et al. 2010). The Joint Commission standards under the Provision of Care section states: "care, treatment, and services are provided to the patient in an interdisciplinary, collaborative manner" (The Joint Commission 2012: PC-18.). Multidisciplinary teams and activities can break down silos created by specialization and departmentalization to enable cross-professional knowledge and information exchange. Building teams over time or quickly in response to immediate care concerns have been noted to be effective in establishing safe, effective care (Bohmer 2009; Wachter 2012; Edmondson 2012).

Reports in the literature describe adding pharmacists, case managers and other allied health professionals to teams to improve patient care. Adding disparate members to teams also enhances overall access to EI&K.

- Pharmacists on teams use their knowledge to mitigate or catch errors and improve the process of medication reconciliation (Gillespie et al. 2009; Mueller et al. 2012; Schnipper et al. 2006). Pharmacists on teams can also reduce the amount of time the patient may wait to have a specific drug started if the drug considered for care is not on the formulary. A pharmacist's knowledge can prevent a medication delay (Heintz, Halilovic and Christensen 2011; Leape et al. 1999). Pharmacists in close proximity to the care delivery activities can proactively enable the physician to tap into their knowledge to change the drug or start to initiate the non-formulary process.

- Case managers can assist the care team when dealing with patients by smoothing transfers of patients to other facilities. By applying their process knowledge, they are able to quickly identify information to detmerine in the patient meets medical necessity and has the abilty to pay, can be placed in a facility near social support and whether that facility has space (Kelly and Penney 2011).

- Physical therapists provide the information that can be used with their knowledge of working directly with the patient to transfer the patient safely from the hospital. If a report from the physical therapist is needed for transfer, having a physical therapist on the team allows these evaluations to be made expeditiously.

The roles and improvements noted above rely upon the physician seeing the other healthcare professionals on the team as partners. Providing the safest care through a multidisciplinary team enables EI&K to flow properly. Efficient EI&K flow means potential additional transitions and handoffs are avoided, which can reduce opportunities for harm, miscommunication and hospital-acquired infections.

Librarians on the Frontline: Finding and Filling EI&K Gaps

Evidence is developing regarding the use of medical librarians (embedded or as in a distinct library space) in assisting clinicians, in teams or on their own, with information needs. The involvement of clinical librarians that participate in bedside rounds has been noted to improve information and evidence seeking behaviors to enhance the effectiveness of decision-making (Aitken et al. 2011; Dhaliwal 2013).

Multiple studies document that healthcare professionals fail to pursue answers to their clinical questions, primarily due to lack of time (Ely et al. 2002; Ely et al. 2007; Graber et al. 2007; Tod et al. 2007). Some healthcare professionals may assume an answer does not exist. Or, when they do pursue answers, they may fail to find the evidence they need for patient care. When in need of EI&K, those healthcare professionals often turn

"If the professional doesn't have the time or can't find relevant information, patient safety may be in question."

to colleagues to find information even with technology, databases, decision support and the Internet at close proximity. Such clinicians rely not on evidence but on the memory and knowledge of colleagues. Does the healthcare professional confirm the knowledge is current and correct? Incorporating new, current evidence can be a problem for established clinicians.

INFOBOX 11.2: LESSONS FROM THE FIELD

A hospital librarian utilized the required rounding not on her staff which was only 1.25 (Full-time Equivalent) and rounded on nursing units one a month. By rounding on nurse managers, the librarian is able to push policy development (a goal of hospital administration) by actively searching on policy topics nurses find challenging on their units. Nurses, as a result, are able to receive information for their policies from a trusted resource. The qualified medical librarian, searching appropriate database(s), provides the structure for a successful process that helps reduce the time for policy creation and updating policies. This also ensures their policies are evidence-based which helped with Joint Commission accreditation and then later the pursuit of the MAGNET accreditation process (Esparza 2010).

Physician training is scant on the EI&K sharing process. In many curricula, there is little focus on how evidence is transferred from electronic databases into the hands of the healthcare professional. Many healthcare professionals rely on one or two electronic resources. Yet recent reports in the literature are creating a cause for concern on the currency of those resources. Several author groups have shown that further research and discernment is indicated when choosing electronic information (Ketchum, Saleh and Jeong 2011; Banzi et al. 2011). The speed with which the literature is being identified can surpass the time in which it is updated into the electronic system. When the intersection of evidence, information and knowledge come together at the point-of-care, the result is better patient care quality and better outcomes performance, plus shorter lengths of stay (Banks et al. 2007).

Other barriers occur even when healthcare professionals search standard resources that are updated regularly such as the National Library of Medicine's PubMed®. Many hospitals do not have librarians, and fail to purchase journal literature in accessible formats available to the whole institution. Individual articles from PubMed® and other sources can range between $15 to $100 each, while library-purchased journal subscription packages cost less overall (see further discussions in Chapter 6). Studies still show that healthcare professionals fail to incorporate vetted evidence into practice even when barriers like those listed above are minimal or non-existent (Banzi 2011; Cabana 1999; Salinas et al. 2011). If the professional doesn't have the time or can't find relevant information, patient safety may be in question. An evolving innovation at this critical intersection of the patient and the care team is integrating librarians into care or project teams (Davidoff and Miglus 2011; Aitken et al. 2011). Called an "Informationist" in an editorial by then editor of *Annals of Internal Medicine* physician Frank Davidoff and Valerie Florance PhD, the informationist was submitted as a new approach to bring the expertise of the librarian to the sharp end (Davidoff and Florance 2000).

Organizations that use informationists are engaging in practice change that can potentially minimize clinician distraction due to evidence gaps and uncertainty while they practice. It is a truism in healthcare that the trajectory of evidence generated in controlled trials and reflected in practice guidelines takes 17 years to emerge in the daily care behaviors of clinicians (Goldstein et al. 2004; Committee on Quality of Health Care in America 2001). The informationist can assist in a knowledge translator role to liberate clinicians from the burden of holding all information and evidence in their head and instead may attend to the task of being present with the team and the patient and process the EI&K presenting before them (MacIntosh-Murray and Choo 2005). It is posited here that patient safety is therefore improved through the infusion of evidence gathering expertise into the clinician decision-making process which would result in the potential for few gaps and distractions.

INFOBOX 11.3: CLINICAL LIBRARIANS – ILLUSTRATIONS OF IMPACT

While participating in morbidity and mortality rounds and at the request of a physician in the critical care units, a librarian helped reduce the use of total parental nutrition (TPN) by providing evidence showing the possible harm done to patients with this method of feeding (Brandes 2007). A change from a possible harmful practice to other methods of feeding was a based on the evidence the librarian team member retrieved for the team (Brandes 2007). Without the librarian this question might not have been pursued, and knowledge of the evidence showing the harms would not have been incorporated as quickly.

McGowan conducted a randomized controlled trial evaluating changes in cognitive impact from using a "Just-in-time Information" approach (McGowan et al. 2008). Information provided by a librarian changed "cognitive impact of the provided information on participants' decision-making" 63 percent of the time in the intervention group but only 15 percent when physicians in the control group did their own searches (McGowan et al. 2008: e3785). This study showed that physicians do not pursue answers to their questions 59.5 percent of the time.

Reviews of the literature concerning librarians' interaction with healthcare professionals show a positive influence in patient care, though better numbers are needed to fully understand the impact of librarians' role (Brettle et al. 2011). Data to show that clinicians have used information provided by librarians to change their practice (Marshall 1992; Marshall et al. 2013; Klein et al. 1994; Schwing and Coldsmith 2005; Brandes 2007; Banks 2007; McGowan et al. 2008). Two studies documenting this impact are summarized in Infobox 11.3.

Holes in the Swiss Cheese of EI&K Delivery

Clinical practice is not the only places where EI&K may break down. An example of a critical intersection of knowledge transfer between the blunt and sharp ends is in the case of venous thromboembolism (VTE), a common preventable cause of hospital death, increased morbidity and length of stay (Heit et al. 2002).

In an Agency for Healthcare Research and Quality (AHRQ) evidence review report, *Making Healthcare Safer*, the provision of appropriate VTE prophylaxis is listed as the paramount effective strategy to improve patient safety (Shojania et al. 2001). In addition, there are hundreds of good quality studies that document the impact of preventive measures in reducing the incidence of VTE and protect the safety of the patient. Unfortunately, despite these studies and more than 20 clinical practice guidelines recommending the use of thromboprophylaxis, the adherence to these guidelines or practice of this essential patient safety issue was at that time less than 50 percent (Shojania et al. 2001). In the 2013 update of this evidence report, the practice was still found to be underused (Shekelle, Wachter and Pronovost 2013).

In 2003 the American Public Health Association stated that the "disconnect between evidence and execution as it relates to deep vein thrombosis (DVT) prevention amounts to a public health crisis" (American Public Health Association 2003: 5). Several other authors have designated breakdowns in the process of incorporating evidence into patient care (Cabana et al. 1999; Goldstein et al. 2004; Salinas et al. 2011). For Cabana, awareness and familiarity are two major reasons for physicians not utilizing the best evidence to treat their patients. How does one bridge this gap? VTE – resulting from DVT and pulmonary embolism – is a situation where evidence and information on the subject are so abundant as to almost be "common knowledge." Yet, practice lags far behind the evidence and the recommendations of healthcare organizations.

The American College of Chest Physicians developed an exhaustive document on the condition, and their number one recommendation is that every hospital develops a formal written policy on VTE (Geerts et al. 2008). AHRQ has formulated a guide – an informational resource – to help hospitals establish a VTE prevention policy (Maynard and Stein 2008).

Once again the medical librarian can assist in this enhancing use of safe evidence-based practice to reduce VTE. On rounds or in committee meetings the librarian can provide information on treatment in a format that would be accurate yet useful in practice. In addition, deeper investigation would incur looking for guidelines, meta-analyses and systematic reviews which are considered higher levels of evidence, in addition to literature indicating updates in those resources are needed (Greenhalgh 2010). Given work with clinicians or administrators could help design the processes for these updates to be repackaged and delivered effectively in a way that makes sense given daily work demands. This nuance – gathered by knowledge of seeing the organizational processes *in situ* – would allow the important information to be shared effectively to enhance its use at the bedside where the safety of the patient is priority. This example illustrates how knowledge feeds into evidence and information to enhance its use among clinical staff, to improve patient safety and outcomes.

Another innovation enhanced by a frontline medical librarian with experience as an informationist could be to raise the thinking of the reporting of near misses (or "good catch") and evidence use. For example, if these good catch dialogs included examination literature reviews not completed or poorly done, clinical questions that went unanswered and knowledge that wasn't surfaced and applied to the task at hand. In addition, if it was seen that clinical care teams weren't addressing the five rights of EI&K, did not have the information and evidence at the right place at the right time – at the point-of-care – if caught by the librarian or another individual on the team, could also be noted as near misses. Through this type of reporting, a stronger idea of the prevalence and impact of weaknesses in the processes would be more visible.

EI&K Juncture: Handoffs

One juncture of EI&K that affects patient safety is when care is handed off from one team or clinician to another. The fact that errors occur during handoffs is not a new problem in healthcare or in human interaction in general. It is commonly recognized that information gets diluted and distorted as it is transmitted from one source to another. This is best exemplified, though over simplified, in the common children's game "Telephone."

According to a Joint Commission evaluation of root cause analyses submitted to their office between 2004 and June 2013, communication problems were named as a factor in 532 of the 901 sentinel events submitted (Joint Commission 2013). It has been estimated that 80 percent of serious medical missteps take place during patient handoff activity (Seifert 2012; Nagpal 2010).

These studies indicate the healthcare industry is now realizing the importance of effective handoffs in patient safety. But even now very few hospitals have a uniform process of handoffs for physicians (Kripalani et al. 2007). This is despite the fact that there is a long standing tradition of standardized nursing handoffs in most hospitals (Riesenberg, Leisch, Cunningham 2010). To understand the handoff as a critical point in the transfer of information, a hypothetical example is provided.

Mrs. A complains to her nurse that she feels faint. The nurse records Mrs. A's vitals and informs the physician that the patient looks comfortable but her heart rate is low at 45, her blood pressure is normal, but she is on blood pressure medications. The physician informs the nurse that he is finishing up an ICU admission but will pass on the information to the receiving physician who comes on duty in fifteen minutes.

This seemingly innocuous process of "passing on the information" is full of opportunities for EI&K failures, as demonstrated in the Figure 11.1 on the following page. It shows factors contributing to the breakdown in the sharing of information, evidence and knowledge on a single patient with a single care activity. Fatigue, cognitive overload and production pressures are overarching concerns that affect the spinning of the cogs of EI&K sharing during handoffs. Consider the fact that most physicians carry patient loads of at least 10–20 patients and each patient that is admitted to a hospital has between four to five care concerns to be addressed (Lindenauer et al. 1999). Each factor represents a hole in the Swiss Cheese. The potential that some critical information will be withheld or not acted upon is therefore exponential and could contribute to the system failure Reason's metaphor illustrates (Reason 2000). Now what if a hospital committed to patient safety chose to make a difference? How would they go about changing this process and closing the holes in the Swiss Cheese to keep those factors from combining to contribute to patient harm? Failure analysis techniques, such as the 5 Whys and others rooted in engineering and systems thinking would provide teams with an effective place to start the exploration toward improvement.

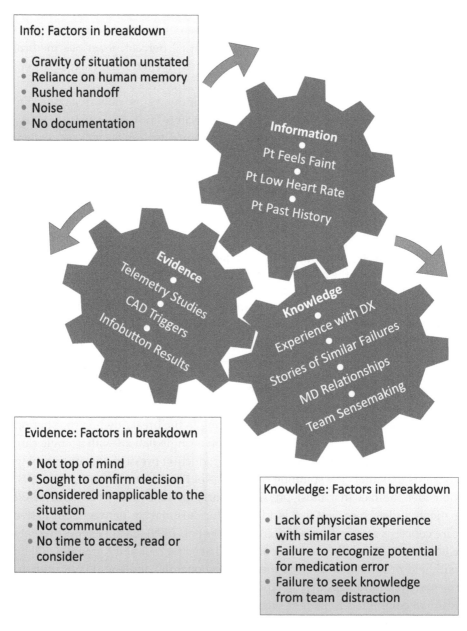

Info: Factors in breakdown

- Gravity of situation unstated
- Reliance on human memory
- Rushed handoff
- Noise
- No documentation

Information
- Pt Feels Faint
- Pt Low Heart Rate
- Pt Past History

Evidence
- Telemetry Studies
- CAD Triggers
- Infobutton Results

Knowledge
- Experience with DX
- Stories of Similar Failures
- MD Relationships
- Team Sensemaking

Evidence: Factors in breakdown

- Not top of mind
- Sought to confirm decision
- Considered inapplicable to the situation
- Not communicated
- No time to access, read or consider

Knowledge: Factors in breakdown

- Lack of physician experience with similar cases
- Failure to recognize potential for medication error
- Failure to seek knowledge from team distraction

Figure 11.1   Critical EI&K Intersections EI&K: Misaligned Handoff

EI&K Sharing Process: A Key to Improvement

Looking at where EI&K failure factors intersect can reveal insights to apply to the design of improvements to enhance the reliability of handoffs. For example, enhancements could start with information:

- Quantitative information could be developed based on how many sign offs occur daily at the hospital.

- Documentation could be developed to explore the processes used to determine if they are consistent across the organization/unit.

- Sentinel event reports and external information could be analyzed to raise awareness of potential inadequate handoffs in distinct situations.

The next step would be to gather evidence:

- Techniques currently in use in the field that make a difference in the reliability of the handoff process could be brought to the table for discussion.

- Protocols and science to understand how to best test and implement handoff improvement could be considered for application.

- Case studies on installing policies or procedures that have demonstrated effect could be reviewed to assist in the implementation of the improved handoff process to ensure changes are in place and sustainable.

Knowledge could then be captured to illustrate how the evidence and information is being applied and used to support effective handoffs:

- Nurses and physicians should be asked and encouraged to talk about near misses that may not have been reported.

- Rapid tests of change would be employed to capture learning from the application of the new process in real time. In this way feedback and open dialog about the new process could be routinely converted into tools that work given the local culture of the unit (Pronovost and Vohr 2010).

ARTIFACTS DON'T ALWAYS RESULT IN SUCCESS

Just creating a tool or policy however does not necessarily generate success. For example, The Universal Protocol by the Joint Commission aimed to address the reoccurring problem of wrong site surgeries through an EI&K approach (Joint Commission n.d.). While the true incidence of wrong site surgeries is hard to estimate, it is considered a never event; that is, given they are largely preventable and the effects on the patient are so catastrophic that a single episode is seen as unacceptable (National Quality Forum 2011). Evidence that the problem was persistent and occurred rarely yet regularly, information through translating in a concrete way what site should be operated on through the site marking and, through use in the field, the knowledge that to ensure the protocol was applied in a local, team oriented, yet standardized way. Site-signing, coupled with a standardized checklist that identifies the correct patient and correct site has been promoted in the US and worldwide (Joint Commission 2011; Wachter 2012). However, the incidence of wrong site surgeries has not declined as expected. A more holistic approach is needed for success (Wachter 2012). The sharing of EI&K can help establish the system and learnings-based orientation to help generate improvement.

Fatigue: A Contributor to EI&K Missteps

> If anything comes up … I want to call you. If there is a problem at four in the morning call at four in the morning. Most likely, I'll listen to what you tell me and fall right back to sleep. I may even forget that you called. But call (Bosk 2003: 51–2).

Why is healthcare unsuccessful in improving patient safety despite establishing evidence-based sharp end interventions? There is more work to be done on the sharp end, the individuals that are directly taking care of patients. A whole range of human factors that influence cognition, skill and knowledge must be considered when studying clinicians and care delivery. Considering that it is likely most individuals go into healthcare with an altruistic thought of helping others, what would cause these individuals to fail to comply with processes that improve or support safe care? One key cause seems to be forgetfulness, especially brought on by fatigue. Cognitive overload refers to the impaired problem-solving skills due to increased load on the working memory of an individual with conflicting responsibilities. A beeper going off can interrupt a physician's flow of thought, especially if he or she is close to cognitive overload and/or tired.

The topic of fatigue in the healthcare workplace has been discussed and researched for some time. The highly visible aftermath of the death of Libby Zion brought it to the fore in the 1980s (Robins 1995). The subsequent struggles to understand and manage the problem with work-hour requirements for residents and house staff are still being studied and debated (Wachter 2012).

The report *AHRQ Research Relevant to Understanding the Impact of Working Conditions on Patient Safety* built on a taskforce developed in 1999 to study medical errors and how they can be addressed (AHRQ 2002). The Institute of Medicine explored the impact of fatigue and the correlation between nurses' working conditions and their effects on medication safety (Page et al. 2004) and again their report highlight the problem of fatigue in residents (Ulmer et al. 2008).

More recently The Joint Commission published a *Sentinel Event Alert* (SEA) to convey with urgency the link between healthcare worker fatigue and adverse events (Joint Commission 2011). This alert outlines the impact of fatigue on an individual clinician and the safety of care they deliver. Handoffs are identified as particularly risky times, if the staff providing the report to the next shift member is tired. The factors in Figure 11.1 are more apt to occur. Studies have shown that residents working 24-hour shifts have twice as many on-the-job attention failures at night and reported making 300 percent more fatigue-related preventable adverse events that led to a patient's death (Lockley et al. 2007). Nurse staffing and mandatory overtime have also been noted as issues that can affect patient safety due to increased workload and fatigue (Page et al. 2004). Mandatory overtime – a practice of working regularly beyond a predetermined schedule – has long been used during staff shortages yet can contribute to unsafe patient care and nursing burnout. This practice is currently not universally legislated as being unsafe perhaps due to the fact that nurse staffing level regulation has received mixed results on quality of care (Page et al. 2004; Mark et al. 2013; American Nurses Association 2011). The Joint Commission has reported that staff that are fatigued, lack concentration, have impaired problem-solving skills and lack empathy (Joint Commission 2011). Each of the factors listed in the Commission's *Sentinel Event Alert* have an impact on a healthcare professional's ability to effectively seek, assimilate, disseminate and communicate EI&K.

Further Improvements in EI&K for Patient Safety

> *Arriving at meaningful solutions is an inevitably slow and difficult*
> *process. Nonetheless, what I saw was: better is possible. It does not*
> *take genius. It takes diligence ... it takes a willingness to try (Gawande*
> *2007: 246).*

There are many factors that impact patient safety in a complex organization. James Reason has written: "Just as medicine understands more about disease than health, so the safety sciences know more about what causes adverse events than about how they can best be avoided" (Reason 2000: 375). As healthcare organizations develop a pervasive culture of safety they should look towards other high-risk, high reliability organizations (HROs) like aviation for models. HROs are discussed in Chapter 8, but here it is important to highlight that perhaps the most important distinguishing feature of high reliability organizations is their collective preoccupation with the possibility of failure. HROs expect to make errors and train their workforces to recognize and recover from if not prevent them. HROs continually rehearse familiar scenarios of failure and strive hard to imagine novel ones. Instead of isolating failures, they generalize them. Instead of making local repairs, they look for system reforms. Instead of blindly simplifying they seek knowledge drawn from context and multidisciplinary insights (Weick and Sutcliff 2007). Such reforms can be affected by improving the five rights of EI&K discussed above: the *right resource*, to the *right person*, for the *right patient or purpose*, through the *right modality*, at the *right time*.

Healthcare is continually adding to its body of evidence. In patient safety this evidence is growing rapidly. The culture of safety now needs to incorporate elements supporting the seeking and application of information and evidence to enhance knowledge-sharing in order to increase the reliability of care to improve patient safety. Events demonstrating the impact of failures in the EI&K chain, such as the Ellen Roche case discussed throughout this book or the Denver case outlined above, even if rare, should be embraced to provide lessons toward preventing similar tragedies (March et al. 2003). The process of EI&K use by healthcare professionals at both the sharp and blunt ends should be designed to minimize opportunities for similar incidents. Healthcare must take the time needed to understand how to best fold learning from these incidents into their spectrum for safety improvement. Innovators, leaders and experts from a variety of professions must take part in that work so healthcare can learn from mistakes so as to not make them again, for the patient's sake.

KEY TAKE-AWAYS

- The "Five Rights" for EI&K delivery should guide standards for processes in hospitals that affect how evidence, information and knowledge are used in healthcare: the *right resource*, to the *right person*, for the *right patient or purpose*, through the *right modality*, at the *right time*.
- EI&K failures have the potential for contributing to failure across the spectrum of both sharp end and blunt end decision-making.
- Medical librarians represent a unique opportunity to enhance the reliability of EI&K processes in the healthcare environment. Direct engagement in the frontline of care improves the possibility for that involvement to be rich and proactive.

Suggested Reading

Burt, H. *Selected Articles on Patient Safety and Libraries and Librarians.* [Bibliography] Patient Safety Resource Seminar: Librarians on the Front Lines. National Networks of Libraries of Medicine. Available at: http://nnlm.gov/training/patientsafety/psrs_bibliography.doc [accessed: March 31, 2013].

MacIntosh-Murray, A. and Choo, C.W. 2005. Information behavior in the context of improving patient safety. *Journal of the American Society of Information Science Technology*, 56(12), 1332–45.

Salas, E. and Frush, K. (eds) 2013. *Improving Patient Safety Through Teamwork and Team Training.* Oxford: Oxford University Press.

12

Patient and Families as Vital EI&K Conduits

Amy Donahue, Linda Kenney and Kathryn K. Leonhardt

> *If health is on the table, the patient must be at the table, every table (Leape et al. 2009: 426).*

Giving and Receiving EI&K

As the dialog around patient safety continues to gain momentum, a growing number of discussions center on roles that patients and their families can play – the ways they can impact their own care as well as contribute to organizational patient safety (Ford 2006; Scobie and Persaud 2010; National Patient Safety Foundation 2008). Given that everyone will be either a patient or the family member of a patient at some point in their lives, these contributions will be significant. Understanding how patients and family members can act as channels for information, evidence and knowledge (EI&K) in the acute care setting will help develop these roles into an effective strategy for improving safety. This chapter takes an in-depth look at the distinctive roles that come under the umbrella of channeling EI&K, offers specific language to describe these functions, and uses stories to demonstrate how patients and family members can influence safe care by being active conduits of information, evidence, and knowledge.

Because patients and family members often play very similar roles as EI&K conduits in healthcare settings, the compound term "patient(s)/family

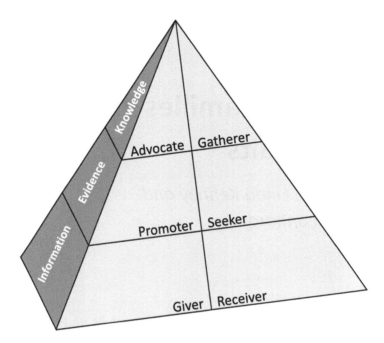

Figure 12.1   Parallel Roles in the EI&K Pyramid

member(s)" is used in this chapter unless a difference between the two is being discussed. Figure 12.1 illustrates the roles the patient/family can play in EI&K exchange.

These roles can be separated into two parallel behaviors: roles that center on *giving* information, evidence, and knowledge and those that are based on *receiving* it (Ford 2006; Ong et al. 1995). The division between these two functions may be more or less academic in view of the complicated interactions that happen in any healthcare encounter, but this pyramid serves as a starting point for looking at how patients/family members can become conduits for the exchange of EI&K that contribute to patient safety. The reciprocal roles of giving and receiving cannot be one-sided; healthcare providers (doctors, nurses, etc.) must also participate. When healthcare providers support these roles – and patients/family members become more comfortable in them – the level of exchange can mature from a basic information transfer to a true partnership based on knowledge-sharing.

The three levels of exchange – information, evidence, and knowledge – divided between the parallel giving and receiving functions (as illustrated in Figure 12.1), create a platform for exploring patient/family roles and the structures that foster them. The reciprocal roles of the patient/family and the provider will be exemplified using actual experiences in the form of stories that describe both positive and negative outcomes. These roles typically play out at the patient/provider level, but EI&K can be exchanged at the organizational or hospital level as well, and this chapter explores the various ways that the patient/family can contribute to patient safety at all levels. Unfortunately, barriers exist that hinder the ideal EI&K exchange between patients/family members, providers, and organizations, especially related to patient safety events; these challenges are also reviewed.

Structure and Roles

In Table 12.1, the roles diagrammed in Figure 12.1 are expanded by providing titles and actions that illustrate each role.

Table 12.1   Patient/Family EI&K Roles and Actions

EI&K Level	Role	Action
Information	Giver	The patient/family member is a Giver of information when he/she provides an answer to a question asked by a provider.
	Receiver	A patient/family member is a Receiver of information when he/she hears about the diagnosis, gets the name of a medication, listens to a treatment plan, etc.
Evidence	Promoter	Patients/family members act as Promoters by sharing with providers the evidence they deem critical to understanding their own care. The evidence can come from both personal experience and outside sources. The patient/family member directs the provider's attention to self-identified needs.
	Seeker	As Seekers, patients/family members may use multiple sources to get an answer. The patient/family member draws on this gathered evidence to seek awareness and understanding of the condition.
Knowledge	Advocate	As Advocates, patients/families combine information they possess on their current situation with evidence obtained through active seeking. Advocates work hard to understand not only how that information may help improve their own condition but share their experience to make the information more broadly contributive to efforts to ensure safer care for other patients. They share these insights with a broad array of audiences.
	Gatherer	As Gatherers, patients/family members consciously and proactively build knowledge by dynamically and purposefully organizing information and evidence then synthesizing the disparate pieces through the benefit of their experience in ways that contribute to safer care for themselves and others, through partnerships with their providers and their healthcare organizations.

INFORMATION LEVEL: GIVER/RECEIVER

Patients/family members have been conduits of information since patients began seeking help from healthcare professionals. When a provider asks a simple question and the patient *gives* an answer, the patient is acting as an information conduit (when the patient is unable to provide needed information, a family member can fill this role). In this way, the patient's medical history

"When the provided information is correctly given and received, a basic level of safety is achieved. However, it is the moment an incorrect statement is made that safety may be at risk."

develops and the provider can then in turn *give* information through diagnosis, prescriptions, and treatment regimens. *Giving* information (whether provider or patient) is a basic aspect of clinical care, influencing patients' clinical outcomes, satisfaction, compliance, and even preventing harm (Kinnersley et al. 2008).

Receiving information (whether provider or patient) is the other side of the same coin. The provider *receives* information when the patient answers a question or states a fact, while a patient/family member *receives* information when he/she hears about the diagnosis, gets the name of a medication, or listens to the treatment plan.

INFOBOX 12.1: TONI'S STORY

Thirty years ago, Toni visited her gynaecologist for a problem she was having. Her doctor told her that it was an "easy repair." (She would later find out that she had a prolapsed uterus.) She scheduled the surgery and signed the consent forms. Toni had undergone other procedures and knew her signature was needed in order to do the "easy repair." The surgery was successful, but, at her six-week checkup, Toni found out from the nurse that she has undergone a hysterectomy. It was the first time she had even heard the word. She was totally embarrassed and felt very stupid.

Toni had graduated from high school reading at only a 5th grade level. Because of her difficulty with reading and understanding, she had been signing whatever was put in front of her for years. When Toni looks back, she wishes that they would have given her the consent forms in advance to bring home so that she could have gone over them at her own pace and discussed them with her husband (Cordell 2007).

What if ... Toni and her doctor had sat down and discussed the consent form line by line, and she was encouraged to ask questions?

This level of information exchange is the most common role for patients today and is ubiquitous within the traditional model of the patient/provider relationship, where the provider could be considered almost paternalistic, controlling the level of communication. When the provided information is correctly given and received, a basic level of safety is achieved. However, it is the moment an incorrect statement is made (in whatever form that takes – incomplete, unintelligible, misspoken, misheard, etc.), that safety may be at risk. The story of Toni Cordell (summarized in Infobox 12.1) demonstrates how basic information exchange can have devastating effects when communication breaks down (Cordell 2007).

At this first level of information exchange, basic communication skills and a good relationship between patient/family and provider are necessary. In fact, poor communication has been cited as a top contributor to medical errors (Agency for Healthcare Research and Quality 2003). As good communication is a major determinant of trust, it is difficult to separate these two essential components (DeLemos et al. 2010). Through effective communication, a trusting relationship can develop where the patient/family feels empathy and understanding from the provider (Ong et al. 1995). For information to be given or received correctly, the content must be clearly transferred – and communication involves more than just the words used. Only 7 percent of communication is conveyed through the words spoken; tone of voice (38 percent) and body language (55 percent) powerfully influence how a message is perceived (Mehrabian and Ferris 1967; Mehrabian and Wiener 1967). Both the patients/family members and providers need to use effective methods of communication (verbal, non-verbal, written, others) to successfully convey information.

The work environment can also facilitate or impede this basic level of information exchange. Several environmental factors in a hospital setting that affect patient/family information giving and receiving include:

- Time with the provider: Patients/family members need to feel that a sufficient amount of time is spent with the provider in order to be comfortable with exchanging information (Beisecker and Beisecker 1990; Mehrabian and Ferris 1967).

- Non-verbal attributes: Non-verbals, such as the provider sitting while talking with the patient, appropriate touch, eye contact, and physical proximity, all influence the patient/family understanding of the message (Ong et al. 1995). These gestures are attributes of active listening; research has shown that these active listening techniques impact clinical and non-clinical outcomes (Denham et al. 2008).

- Privacy: Confidence in the adequacy of the privacy of the conversation can influence the ability of the patient/family to give or receive information.

- Tools and aides: The availability of basic tools facilitates information exchange between patient/family and provider. Simple writing materials, for example, allow patients/families to convey information to providers, record information received during a hospital stay, and play a role in reducing adverse events. In one study conducted in a Wisconsin community, medication lists documented by patients/family were shown to be effective in improving medication safety (Leonhardt et al. 2008). Many hospitals are incorporating logs and paper pads to facilitate communication among patients/families and providers (Siebens and Randall 2005; Rhiner 2004).

EVIDENCE LEVEL: PROMOTER/SEEKER

"The patient/family member draws on their own assembled evidence, such as experiential observations collected from the hospital surroundings, from his/her own medical condition, or from other sources such as healthcare providers, medical librarians and publications."

Building on the basic roles of giver and receiver, the Promoter/Seeker level moves beyond information into the realm of evidence. As a *promoter*, the patient/family member directs the provider's attention to self-identified needs. Patients/family members *promote* themselves by giving providers evidence that they deem critical to understanding their case, evidence that may come from both personal experience and outside sources. Providers fulfill the role of *promoter* when they encourage patients/family members to become more active participants in their own care, incorporating the patient perspective into the plan of care.

The role of *seeking* evidence is more proactive than the basic giving and receiving information exchange. As *seekers*, patients/family members may use multiple sources of evidence to get answers. The patient/family member draws on his/her own assembled evidence, such as experiential observations collected from the hospital surroundings, from their own medical condition, or from other sources such as alternative healthcare providers, medical librarians and publications (in print or online). Patients/family may *seek* supporting evidence for a diagnosis or treatment, as well as quality/safety data on their own healthcare provider or the hospital. When the provider takes on the role of *seeker*, they may also collect evidence from different available sources beyond the standard information received to include evidence provided by the patient/family members. When the provider does not seek (or accept) evidence from the patient/family member, safety may be at risk.

A heartbreaking example of a failed attempt by a family member to be embraced as a *promoter* (and the providers' failure to accept the role of *seeker*) is that of Josie King. Sorrel King, the mother of a small child who was admitted to a hospital for treatment of burns, noticed that her child was not responding normally. But the healthcare system did not accept Sorrel's opinion as evidence, thus leading to a preventable death of the child from dehydration and narcotic overdose (King 2009).

At this intermediate level of exchanging information and evidence, the communication and relationship between the patient/family and the providers is more mature. This approach is consistent with a patient/family-centric model of care, where the roles of the patient and the provider are more egalitarian and evidence provided by the patient/family is incorporated into the decision-making process. Patients/family members as promoters may share a more comprehensive description of their condition than can be gleaned from the basic information provided through responses to specific questions. This personal evidence may assist providers to effectively manage their care- and avoid mistakes or errors. To be effective promoters, patients/family members may need to be educated, prepared and supported before they are willing and able to share. As seekers, patients may probe their doctor, nurse or other provider with questions or move beyond the clinical team to other resources, such as friends, the library, or the Internet. These more proactive patients gather additional evidence (published and/or experiential) to reduce their anxiety, identify additional questions to ask, or reduce their risk of adverse events (Zipperer, Gillaspy and Goeltz 2005; Weingart et al. 2005).

There are tools and training that can help facilitate the promoter/seeker roles for patients/families and providers. Providing written materials and coaching to patients prior to consultations with providers can help empower them to be more self-promoting (Kinnersley et al. 2009). Medical librarians who provide consumer health classes on topics such as evaluating and understanding health information are effective resources that support patients/family members in applying this evidence-seeking role. Provider skills at this intermediate level of communication can also be enhanced through education and training (Levinson 2010; Kinnersley et al. 2009). Tactics such as speaking in plain language, incorporating visual aids and the utilization of "teach-back" have been shown to improve patient understanding and clinical outcomes (DeWalt 2007; Schillinger et al. 2003). Teach-back is defined as having the patient repeat, in his/her "... own words, key information about the proposed treatments or procedures for which he or she is being asked to provide informed consent" (National Quality Forum 2009: viii). In fact, the National Quality Forum recommends teach-back as a top patient safety practice (National Quality Forum 2009).

KNOWLEDGE LEVEL: ADVOCATE/GATHER

At the most advanced level of EI&K exchange, patients/family members give and receive not only information and evidence, but also knowledge. Though less conventional, examples of these roles in healthcare can be found. Infobox 12.2 tells one real life story experienced by one of the chapter authors who was working as a hospital librarian.

INFOBOX 12.2: JAMIE'S STORY

A hospitalized patient, Jamie, wished to gather personalized information on a new diagnosis/treatment program. She had the knowledge to recognize a gap in her experience, and advocated for herself in a conversation with her physician in order to learn more about how to recognize a gastrointestinal bleed and when to call a health professional or go to the emergency room.

During the conversation, the physician acknowledged his limitations in providing the broad-spectrum and appropriate level of information that Jamie was seeking (these limits included a lack of time and of expertise in consumer health resources). He did not brush Jamie's concerns aside and instead addressed her request by bringing the hospital librarian to the bedside. The outcome of the advocacy was an information packet tailored to Jamie's needs.

Throughout this interaction, all three of the individuals involved – Jamie, the physician, and the librarian – gained knowledge regarding the information gathering processes which could be replicated to support future patient information requests.

Building on the previous roles and adding the requirement of a knowledge component, the ultimate role patients/ family members can play is that of *advocate*. The advocate role is similar in some respects to the promoter role, but at this level the patient/family member is (in addition

"... at this level the patient/ family member ... is contributing knowledge that comes from a deeper understanding of the larger picture."

to offering basic information and evidence from individual experiences) contributing knowledge that comes from a deeper understanding of the larger picture. In other words, patients/family members become *advocates* when they combine their own information of the current situation with evidence obtained through active seeking, and apply this information and evidence not only towards improving their own condition, but towards contributing to safer care for other patients by advocating for broader changes.

The other role at the knowledge level moves beyond seeking additional information and experiential evidence – the patient/family member becomes a *gatherer*. This is a proactive role in which the patient/family member consciously gathers knowledge by dynamically and purposefully organizing information and evidence then synthesizing the disparate pieces in ways that contribute to safer care. At this point, the two roles of advocate and gatherer are inextricably intertwined. Through the process of gathering knowledge based on experience, the patient/family member becomes an advocate as he/she learns to interject themselves into the process through active involvement, education, or voicing concerns.

Although the roles may seem difficult to achieve, there is evidence to suggest that some patients/families are willing and equipped to be effective advocates and gatherers for patient safety. For example, hospitalized patients may be better able to identify adverse events affecting their care than the hospital staff (Weissman et al. 2008; Weingart et al. 2005). Once the patient/family identifies and expresses a concern, they may then contribute not only to their own personal safety and care, but to others' as well, by advocating based on the gathered materials and the context their knowledge brings to improvement opportunities. In one study, hospitalized patients who participated in their own care had reduced rates of adverse events (Weingart et al. 2011).

Like the other roles, the advocate/gatherer role applies to providers as well as patients. Providers participate in knowledge-sharing at the advocate level by combining patient information, evidence learned from medical literature, knowledge provided by patients/family members from a specific instance of care, and experiential lessons learned from similar cases they have seen previously. A collaborative approach with patients allows the patient/family to contribute and be valued in the decision-making process. At this level, both the patient and the provider are considered experts in their interdependent roles. As Ong states: "the patient leads in areas where he is the expert (symptoms, preferences, concerns) ... ideally, the doctor leads in his domain of expertise (details of disease, treatment)" (Ong 1995: 904). The provider supports and encourages the advocate/gatherer role, by partnering with the patient/family, sharing equally in exchanging their respective knowledge, as well as in the decision-making process. An example of this collaborative relationship between patient/family and provider is demonstrated by a situation one of the authors experienced (see Linda's story Infobox 12.3).

To achieve the knowledge level of exchange, patient/family-centered communication needs to be fully integrated into the patient/provider relationship. This advanced type of communication builds on the basic and intermediate skills described at the information and evidence levels with the addition of the emotional engagement of the patient and provider. The National Cancer Institute recognizes six functions of patient/family-centered care that support the knowledge stage: fostering healing relationships, exchanging information, responding to patients' emotions, managing uncertainty, making informed decisions and enabling patient self-management (Epstein and Street 2007). For patients/family members to participate in this level of communication, a trusting relationship must exist. (Trust can also facilitate information giving, as described earlier, but it is a necessity at the knowledge level.) The patient/family must be comfortable enough in the relationship with the provider to ask questions, participate in decision-making, share experiences and voice needs and concerns. The provider needs to support this level of communication through encouragement, accessibility, and participation. This support is particularly crucial when patients/family members need to communicate about adverse events, where additional skills may be necessary. Patients/family members need to be aware of and understand patient safety terminology and risk-related events (Hibbard et al. 2005). In order for the patient/family to participate in dialogue concerning their safety, they must first have an understanding of the risks of treatment and feel a level of self-efficacy in their ability to help prevent adverse events (Hibbard et al. 2005). With this level of knowledge, patients may be able to recognize potential adverse events and participate in decision-making that could reduce their risk (Zhu et al. 2011).

The advent of health information technology has allowed patients/family members to become more engaged in their own care (The President's Council of Advisors on Science and Technology 2010). Eighty percent of Internet users (59 percent of all American adults) go online for health information (Fox 2011). One specific tool that may lead to enhanced communication between the patient/family and their clinical team is through personal health records or access to the electronic health record (EHR). This electronic communication may even improve the accuracy of the health information in the patient's medical record, ultimately with positive implications for patient safety (Zulman et al. 2011). A specific example of the benefits of a patient accessing their electronic medical record was told by Saul Weingart and his associates.

> As the result of a series of system failures, such as lack of clinician use of standard processes for communicating test results and insufficient results tracking systems, a patient was not alerted that his meningioma diagnosis was extremely urgent. But when he saw the diagnosis on his electronic personal health record and linked it with worsening headaches and new onset nausea and vomiting, he contacted the on-call physician who immediately got the patient to the emergency room and ultimately a successful outcome (Weingart et al. 2011).

EI&K Exchange at the Hospital/Organizational Level

A role for the patient/family member at the organizational level is strongly promoted in healthcare as recognition grows that patients/families can contribute information and knowledge on ways to improve organizational outcomes. Through knowledge-sharing based on their experiences, patient/family member contributions at the organization level not only have the potential to prevent personal harm but also to contribute to the organizational learning of system failures. Proactively or after an adverse event, the patient/family and the provider working together can help identify improvement opportunities for patient safety. When patients/family members become valued partners within the organization, learning from a harmful experience may provide the personal and organizational lessons that will help improve the operational issues, such as processes and practices, as well as aid in the emotional recovery that is so important after the traumatic experience of a preventable adverse event.

"As advocates for themselves and for other patients/families, they can share their knowledge to influence operational programs, policies and procedures."

As in their roles with a provider, patients/family members can exchange information, evidence and knowledge at the hospital level through education, advocacy, and eventual culture change. Patients/family members as educators can have a powerful impact on an audience, whether that audience is made up of other patients or providers. As advocates for themselves and for other patients/families, they can share their knowledge to influence operational programs, policies and procedures. A cultural shift begins when patients/families are at the table influencing an organization's willingness to embrace and embed safety principles of patient-centered care.

There are a variety of roles patients/ families can fulfill as part of the healthcare team to improve safety, including:

- Observer: The patient/family member can be encouraged to provide observations and report safety concerns or anything that does not seem correct. When they have knowledge of important policies and processes, patients/family members can serve as advocates, encouraging providers with appropriate reminders (such as hand washing or checking patient identification).

- Initiator of care: Patients/family members can initiate rapid response teams if they feel that urgent clinical care is warranted to keep themselves or their loved one safe (Robert Woods Johnson Foundation 2008).

- Advisor on a team: Patients/family members can share their knowledge by serving on patient advisory teams. Hospitals and health systems are utilizing this format to engage patient/family representatives at the organizational level in order to improve quality and safety. For example, by involving a diverse group of patients, family members, healthcare providers, and community leaders, the Aurora Health Care Patient Safety Advisory Council improved medication safety in the outpatient setting (Leonhardt et al. 2008). The Institute for Patient and Family Centered Care (IPFCC) and others have promoted councils which have achieved a variety of outcomes (IPFCC 2012; Ponte et al. 2003; Weingart et al. 2011).

- Event analyst: The patient/family can participate in Root Cause Analyses (RCAs) after adverse events (Institute for Safe Medication Practices 2008).

- Survey respondent: The patient/family perception of service quality as conveyed on patient satisfaction surveys may shed insight into the level of clinical quality and safety within a hospital. For example, poor service quality (as measured by poor communication, poor care coordination, and inappropriate professional behaviors) has been shown to be associated with adverse events (Isaac et al. 2010; Taylor et al. 2008; Wennberg et al. 2009).

Regardless of how the patient/family member is involved – through direct observations, as members of a process improvement team, or through survey results – hospitals can and should use the valuable knowledge provided by patients and families in developing their safety programs.

Barriers

The following section highlights barriers that challenge the free flow of EI&K exchange among patients/families, providers, and the healthcare organization.

PATIENT/FAMILY CHALLENGES

Skills and knowledge: Patients/family members may not have the communications skills or ability to convey EI&K because of language or cultural differences, their medical condition, or anxiety. Patients/family members may not understand patient safety terminology and definitions and may not be getting all the information they want (Kinnersley et al. 2008). Educational materials used to engage patients/family may not be clearly defined or may not plainly delineate behaviors (e.g., the ambiguous "speak up"). Even when interventions are applied to encourage patients to ask more questions, the results have not been successful (Kinnersley et al. 2008). Low health literacy, which affects more than a third of American adults, is a known factor that contributes to poor clinical outcomes as well as patient safety events (Weiss 2007). See Toni Cordell's story, summarized in Infobox 12.1.

Resistance to change: Patients/family members often feel intimidated by the provider in the traditional patient:provider relationship (Maguire and Pitceathly 2002; Kinnersley et al. 2009). Overcoming this lack of confidence to change this relationship can be extremely difficult. However, even as patients/family members are encouraged to become more empowered, the ultimate responsibility of keeping the patient safe should not shift from the provider to the patient (Entwistle, Mello and Brennan 2005).

"Providers may resist change because of concerns around altering the traditional patient/provider relationship, the cost of training in communication skills, and the belief that in-depth communication will take more time."

Resources: For patients/families, the amount of information on the Internet can be overwhelming, confusing, and inaccurate (Cooper and Feder 2004; Meadows-Oliver and Banasiak 2010; Eysenbach et al. 2002; Chung et al. 2012). In addition, access to the Internet (and other sources of EI&K) is not always readily available. Not having access to a medical librarian at the hospital or community level to support patient/family EI&K is a related barrier, and one that is getting worse as hospital libraries continue to close or lose staff. It has been estimated that between 1989 and 2006, the percentage of hospitals with on-site library services dropped from 44 percent to between 29.1–33.6 percent and this trend may be continuing (Thibodeau and Funk 2009). There are a number of examples of the ways librarians contribute to the patient safety movement (Zipperer, Gillaspy and Goeltz 2009), and medical librarians are directly involved with patients/family members and consumer health outreach (Donahue et al. 2012).

PROVIDER CHALLENGES

Skills and knowledge: Physicians and nurses may not have the communication skills necessary for effective information giving (Maguire and Pitceathly 2002). In fact, a higher risk of malpractice among physicians is associated with patients' dissatisfaction with their relationships with their physicians and specifically with their physicians' communication skills (Hickson et al. 2002; Vincent, Young and Phillips 1994). Information giving by physicians may be poor because of their limited or ineffective training in communication skills, misperception of patient/family desire for information, and/or use of medical jargon instead of plain language.

Resistance to change: Providers may resist change because of concerns around altering the traditional patient/provider relationship, the cost of training in communication skills, and the belief that in-depth communication will take more time. With the pressure to see large volumes of patients in limited time periods, providers may not feel able to devote sufficient time to listening to the patient's/family's full story to glean their knowledge from their experience. The average office visit lasts 12 minutes and patients are often interrupted by the physician in 23 seconds or less (Zipperer, Gillaspy and Goeltz 2005). Patients perceive these physician behaviors as disrespectful and they are barriers to developing a trusting relationship (Wofford et al. 2004). In actuality, effective communication between the patients and their provider may result in subsequent shorter, more efficient visits (Levinson, Lesser and Epstein 2010; Kinnersley et al. 2009). Even when providers seem amenable to receiving EI&K from a patient/family regarding safety issues, this communication may be difficult to accept. Examples include providers' reactions when patients/family members ask them to wash their hands. Resistance to taking patient EI&K seriously is demonstrated by Linda's story (Infobox 12.3).

Access to resources: A lack of libraries and trained librarians may be a barrier to the growth of providers' acceptance of the librarians roles (and recognizing their patient/family roles) in EI&K exchange. Supporting evidence-based medicine (e.g., through literature searching and education) and providing knowledge management expertise are just two examples of ways librarians can partner with providers to support patient safety (Zipperer, Gillaspy and Goeltz 2004).

INFOBOX 12.3: LINDA'S STORY

It was November of 2003, and Linda was at her surgical pretesting appointment at the hospital. She was having surgery on her right ankle to realign the foot in preparation for an ankle replacement. This surgery would be number 21, so this process was very familiar to her. She had her blood drawn, met with the nurse, and was now meeting with the anesthesiologist to discuss the plan for surgery. The anesthesiologist recommended that Linda have a popliteal fossa block (an injection behind the knee that numbs from the knee down and is usually used for this type of surgery).

Linda told the doctor that she did not want a block and that she preferred general anesthesia. He then told her that the medications for blocks had come a long way and were very effective. He added that blocks were great for post-operative pain management. Once again, Linda told him that she wanted general anesthesia. He then asked her why she was so opposed to having a block.

Linda knew something that the physician did not. Four years prior, at the same hospital, she had a popliteal fossa block for a right ankle replacement. Unfortunately, the medication used in the block was delivered intravascularly which led to Linda's having a grand mal seizure followed by a full cardiac arrest. The only way they could save her life was to take her to a cardiac suite where they opened her chest and hooked her up to a cardiopulmonary bypass machine. At her follow-up appointment with the cardiac surgeon, Linda was told that it would be a good idea if she never had any kind of block in the future.

Linda asked the doctor if he had heard about a case a few years back: "The Block." When he told her that he had, she said, "Well, meet the patient!" His jaw dropped, and he said, "Oh my God, we use that case for teaching!

HEALTHCARE ENVIRONMENT BARRIERS

Use of technology: Though technology has the potential to improve the exchange of knowledge, information systems bring other problems (Institute of Medicine 2011). A comprehensive description of the impact of technology on patient safety is discussed in Chapters 4 and 10. Hospitals' own safety data, even that which is publicly available, can be difficult to find on websites designed to market their services. During individual encounters between patients and their provider, the computer use interferes with communication and the ability to develop a trusting relationship. Policies and procedures for communicating effectively through patient portals in the electronic health records have not been standardized to assure efficiency and effectiveness. To date, few studies have been done on the impact of patient portals on outcomes. The results are mixed, with some patients and families who used the patient portal becoming more dissatisfied with their relationships with their providers (Emont 2011).

Ability to establish collaborative partnerships: For health systems to effectively partner with patients/family members at the organizational level, knowledge about the strategies and principles of collaboration is required. Yet most patients/family members and hospitals have not been taught nor experienced the process of creating patient/family advisory councils. Barriers include the patients/family members' own fears, resistance to a change in the traditional relationship, a lack of confidence in the efficacy of councils, and unfamiliarity with this format of collaboration. Both patients/ families and organizations worry about sharing sensitive information that is not usually transparent at the organizational level. Patients worry about how it will affect their relationship with their provider; organizations worry about the risk implications of sharing negative information in the community. Effective collaboration requires a common language; patients/ families may not be familiar with terminology used in healthcare, including medical jargon and patient safety definitions. Misunderstandings based on miscommunication can undermine confidence in the collaborative process as well as their confidence in the quality of care provided by the healthcare system. Clarifying the differences (as well as the relationships) between safety and service issues is also important, as some studies have shown that the patient/family perception of errors or unsafe incidents are actually service issues, not true clinical errors (Solberg et al. 2008; Weingart et al. 2007). Yet safety may be an important mediator of their perception of service quality (Rathert, May and Williams 2011).

Conclusion

This exploration of the range of roles patients/families can play along the information, evidence, and knowledge spectrum encapsulates the ways they can be important conduits in the hospital setting, working with healthcare providers and organizations. The roles of giver and receiver, separated into three levels based on what is being exchanged (information, evidence or knowledge), are played by both the patient/family member and by providers. This collaborative relationship can generate change in our healthcare system that can improve patient safety. In reality, the roles may not be as clear-cut as described here, but this framework is useful to understand and build on the important role patients/families play as conduits of EI&K in preventing adverse events in hospitals and tragedies in people's lives.

KEY TAKE-AWAYS

- Patients/families participate as EI&K conduits at three levels of interaction: giver/receiver, promoter/seeker, and advocate/gather.
- Examples from the field share this experience and demonstrate value on both the patient/provider interaction and organizational level.
- Establishing and maintaining a transparent and open relationship between patient/family member and provider enables EI&K to be communicated effectively.
- Barriers to an effective EI&K communicative relationship exist but are not insurmountable.

Suggested Reading

Agency for Healthcare Research and Quality. 2013. *Guide to Patient and Family Engagement in Hospital Quality and Safety.* Rockville, MD: Agency for Healthcare Research and Quality. Available at: http://www.ahrq.gov/professionals/systems/hospital/engagingfamilies/patfamilyengageguide/index.html [accessed: 24 January 2014].

Gerteis, M., Edgman-Levitan, S., Daley, J. and Delbanco, T.L., (eds) 1993. *Through the Patient's Eyes: Understanding and Promoting Patient-Centered Care.* San Francisco, CA: Jossey-Bass.

Johnson, B., Abraham, M. and Conway, J., et al. 2008. *Partnering with Patients and Families to Design a Patient- and Family-Centered Health Care System: Recommendations and Promising Practices.* Bethesda, MD: Institute for Family-Centered Care.

Sanders, L. 2009. *Every Patient Tells A Story: Medical Mysteries and the Art of Diagnosis*. New York, NY: Broadway Books.

Spath, P. (ed.) 2008. *Engaging Patients as Safety Partners*. Chicago, IL: AHA Press.

Wen, L. and Kosowsky, J. 2013. *When Doctors Don't Listen*. New York, NY: St. Martin's Press.

Humans and EI&K Seeking: Factors Influencing Reliability

Linda Williams and James P. Bagian

Insufficient facts always invite danger.

Spock, "Space Seed," Star Trek: The Original Series

Recognizing Human Impact on EI&K Processes

Investigating the interaction of humans with the processes and elements of systems of healthcare allows envisioning and designing a future for safety improvement. Evidence, information and knowledge (EI&K) processes will also benefit from this approach. However, this dialog has yet to become a part of patient safety improvement discourse from the perspective of a distinct group of experts engaging in daily EI&K work: the information professional. To lay the foundation, this chapter will provide examples of human factors engineering (HFE) methods that can aid the identification, acquisition, application and transfer of EI&K, and ultimately influence patient safety improvement. In addition, this chapter will focus on the systems characteristics that make clear the value added by medical librarians and informationists (referred to under the general term "librarian") to the work of patient safety problem-solving.

THE LIBRARIAN AS EI&K BOUNDARY SPANNER

Librarians add value to the interdisciplinary healthcare team (Banks et al. 2007). The librarian involved in improving patient safety is a "boundary spanner" without whom making changes to the complex system of EI&K transfer within healthcare is frustratingly difficult and error prone (MacIntosh-Murray and Choo 2005). Other people can of course do this boundary-spanning work. However, for the purposes of this chapter the librarian as the actor and the EI&K process have been considered as one element to illustrate the importance of the combination of the expert and process, as a powerful dyad to span boundaries. In this boundary spanning role the librarian is a strong contributor to patient safety progress, but also vulnerable as are all humans, to cognitive biases, latent system weakness and other system stressors that reduce reliability.

There are three characteristics of healthcare that reveal the significant importance of the role of EI&K and librarians:

- the tendency for healthcare services to exist in silos of professional disciplines;

- the expanding volume of evidence that is produced in medical science and related fields; and

- the urgent need for improving patient safety.

Silos may develop as a result of a variety of causes, including:

- professional boundaries that develop during education and credentialing;

- the publishing of literature in specialty journals;

- the layout of physical space; and

- development of dedicated computing systems.

Spanning the boundaries of silos requires recognition that they present an impediment to attaining common goals. It also requires recognition that effective boundary spanning takes effort, energy and specific education. While specialized expertise may reinforce silos, it also necessitates reliance on others who have broader, more generalized knowledge.

Research and development in healthcare occur at a pace that makes being prepared for every patient encounter a difficult if not impossible goal for the individual clinician. It is estimated that it would take a primary care physician 627.5 hours/month to keep up with relevant published literature; with potentially even more time required for those in general practices such as internal medicine and pediatrics (Alper et al. 2004; Hersch et al. 2002; Shaughnessy 2009; Wallace et al. 2012). The healthcare encounter occurs within a complex system, and the literature of the system is extensive and complicated (Carayon 2007; Kohn, Corrigan and Donaldson 2000). Thus evidence, information and knowledge, often identified, communicated and leveraged by librarians is a critical component of healthcare delivery.

Information and evidence seeking by clinicians is more likely to be focused on clinical aspects (diagnosis and treatment) of care than on system improvement (MacIntosh-Murray and Choo 2005). When patient safety problem-solving teams form for the purpose of doing a root cause analysis (RCA) clinicians may not be aware of the relevant evidence published outside of medicine (Wallace et al. 2012). This is an information silo that the librarian can bridge – as notably illustrated by Leape (AHRQ 2006). This expertise, when engaged, enables development of services and crossing of silos to affectively apply EI&K to patient safety work. Just as it is difficult or impossible for a clinician to consistently deliver the best healthcare without relying on team members, so it is difficult for the librarian to be highly reliable as a sole resource provider for clinical or patient safety teams. EI&K processes should be examined for latent vulnerabilities and to optimize them with human performance, teamwork and communication in mind to avoid failure. The hierarchy of actions, discussed at the end of this chapter, can help verify the strength of tactics selected to enhance the reliability of EI&K process performance.

Essential Considerations: Human Factors and Ergonomics

How humans interact with systems and with each other is extensively studied in the fields of human factors engineering and ergonomics (considered together as HFE). Human factors engineers and ergonomists have long been employed in nuclear industry, transportation, aerospace and computer science (Bagian et al. 2012; Gurses, Ozok and Pronovost 2012). The murky terms "human error" and "human factors" are often used as if interchangeable. However, an error is clearly a negative, a mistake, something unintended. A factor is simply descriptive, whether a strength, vulnerability or a mix of both.

"EI&K processes should be examined for latent vulnerabilities and to optimize them with human performance, teamwork and communication in mind to avoid failure."

The goal of HFE is to engineer systems to optimize human performance and make it reliably possible to achieve the desired result. Knowing the anatomical, physiologic, and cognitive characteristics of humans allows process and equipment design to support what humans do well, while compensating for those they don't do well. Error represents an opportunity to discover how and why an error is provoked; and how to improve the system through redesign given the knowledge gained through that experience (Williams 2012). The cause of an error is diagnostic for system weaknesses. A newspaper headline declaring that a disaster was a result of human error reveals nothing of the real cause except to say that the underlying system design is flawed in some yet undiscovered way; and worse still, implies that the only available solution is to instruct the humans involved to be more careful in the future. As noted in the hierarchy of actions (Table 13.1/Appendix 3); instructional approaches (training, blaming and shaming, safety signage, etc.) are not effective for permanent improvement.

As a field of research, HFE is concerned with physical and cognitive human characteristics and their consideration in device design and the system within which humans function. The ideal design of the system will fit the needs, abilities, limitations and vulnerabilities of the people expected to successfully and safely use it (Carayon 2007).

Much is known about human cognition, anatomy and physiology – how humans function under stressful conditions, and when fatigued or ill. Research in HFE continues, as does the development of new designs in healthcare (Williams 2012). Unfortunately, there is no guarantee that design in healthcare is grounded in HFE rather than driven by the market. The US Food and Drug Administration's guidance for applying human factors and usability engineering to medical device development is an encouraging move in that direction (US Food and Drug Administration 2011).

In HFE, researchers have often specialized in particular areas. Cognitive science research may focus on perception (visual, tactile, aural, and so on), the processing of information received through perception, and the varying methods of communicating information that is perceived and processed (Wickens and Hollands 2000; Miller 1956). Applied HFE research may consider the effects of fatigue, noise, and distraction or interruption on task performance with or within a specific system (Trafton and Monk 2008; Pape et al. 2005; Hillel and Vicente 2003).

BEING NORMAL

The effects of being a normal (vulnerable to erring) human working in and with flawed healthcare systems are well documented (Bogner 1994; Carayon 2007). However, to diagnose the cause of an adverse event as *human error* offers no more insight than does diagnosing cause of death as trauma. The more important question is: how did a traumatic injury lead to death? Without knowing the underlying cause of death from trauma it is not possible to formulate a countermeasure that will mitigate future risk of death due to trauma.

Similarly, from a HFE perspective, the root question is what leads the human to err? There is known variance in human capabilities, and yet HFE research documents that a range of normal that exceeds typical design specifications. When one is asked to work in a flawed environment with faulty tools, it is as if one has been asked to make the hand fit the glove rather than designing the glove to fit the hand while performing skillful and safe work.

Just as human clinicians are at risk of making mistakes, so are human librarians and other information seekers vulnerable to cognitive biases (Crosskerry 2000), inattentional blindness (Maruenda 2004; Cook 2003; Chabris and Simons 2010; Most et al. 2001), fixation, and over confidence (Berner and Graber 2008). To become highly reliable, the librarian must also employ effective teamwork and communication strategies to compensate for systems that are not entirely supportive of the work of completely normal but naturally flawed humans.

"... to diagnose the cause of an adverse event as human error offers no more insight than does diagnosing cause of death as trauma."

EI&K Encompasses HFE Analyses

In consideration of the potential impact of EI&K on patient safety, the EI&K process itself needs to seek high reliability. A successful HFE method to evaluate a system or procedure for vulnerabilities is Failure Mode and Effect Analysis (FMEA). The Veterans Administration (VA) has developed a variant, Healthcare Failure Mode and Effect Analysis (HFMEA) (DeRosier et al. 2002). Concepts key to FMEA analyses are listed in Infobox 13.1.

INFOBOX 13.1: PRIMARY TERMS – FAILURE ANALYSIS

Failure Mode and Effect Analysis (FMEA): 1) A prospective assessment that identifies steps in a process with the goal of reducing the risk of failure; 2) A systematic approach to identify and prevent process problems before they occur.

Detectable hazard: A circumstance that can be discovered before it interferes with completion of the task or activity.

Failure mode: The state of being out of the expected process path; ways that the process could go wrong; what could go wrong?

Failure mode cause: Why things could go wrong – root causes and contributing factors that will send the process into failure mode.

Hazard analysis: The work of the FMEA team – gathering information about the process and the hazards associated with it. The goal is to develop a prioritized list of hazards that are significant in potential cause for effecting delivery of safe patient care.

Single point weakness: A place in the process so critical that its failure will result in failure of the process.

Note, any part of the process that is identified as a single point weakness, particularly if it is found not to be a detectable hazard, is the one most urgently in need of correction (DeRosier et al. 2002).

An effective HFE method that retrospectively investigates an adverse event or near miss is root cause analysis (RCA). The sections that follow will look at these two slightly different methods:

1.   A Failure Mode and Effect Analysis (FMEA) team assigned to prospectively evaluate the EI&K process for healthcare.

2.   A root cause analysis (RCA) team assigned to retrospectively evaluate an adverse event and make recommendations in order to prevent similar future bad outcomes.

FMEA Analyses of Healthcare EI&K

EI&K is potentially an *essential* contributor to safe patient care (Zipperer 2004; Shekelle et al. 2011; Saimbert et al. 2010). Processes supporting EI &K work are worth considering for the impact of failure.

To effectively analyze the EI&K process, perspectives from clinicians, librarians and other information seekers will lend knowledge to the examination. Technical experts from other disciplines can also bring a useful perspective to EI&K issues in the healthcare arena. An ideal FMEA team will be comprised of people with a variety of experience and responsibilities within the EI&K process.

This team of experts will define the scope of the evaluation. Graphical representation of the FMEA process and selection of a sub-process for evaluation are illustrated in Figures 13.1 and 13.2. The first figure illustrates

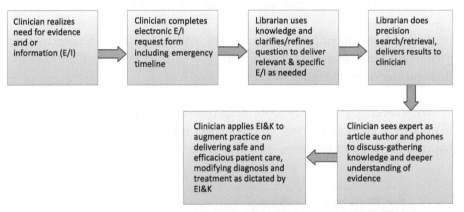

Figure 13.1   EI&K Transfer to Improve Patient Care: Expected Process

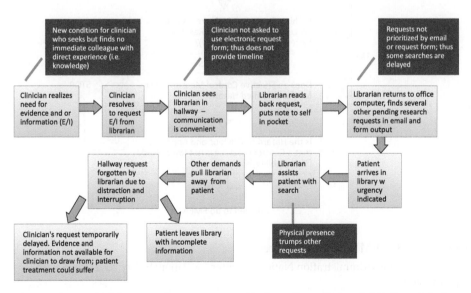

Figure 13.2   EI&K Transfer to Improve Patient Care: Potential Failure Modes

the ideal process. In the second, experience guides the depiction to illustrate potential failure modes and effects. The FMEA team will necessarily work at a more specific level than illustrated in these figures. This simplified version is presented to clarify the process. An example of the more granular and at the same time, larger, process can be seen in the work of the Canadian Institute for Safe Medication Practices (Institute for Safe Medication Practice 2005).

The multidiscplinary FMEA team will select some part of the process being analyzed to evaluate for risk of failure. Scoring systems may be used to prioritize the identified vulnerabilities. The first step in scoring is to estimate the severity and probability of failure (DeRosier et al. 2002).

Each of the identified vulnerabilities with an estimated severity and probability score that reaches a certain level is then processed through the decision algorithm in Figure 13.3 below.

If the severity-probability score is high enough, the answer to the first point in the tree is likely to be "yes." If the answer is determined to be "no," is the hazard a single point weakness – if this process fails (e.g. the forgotten reminder

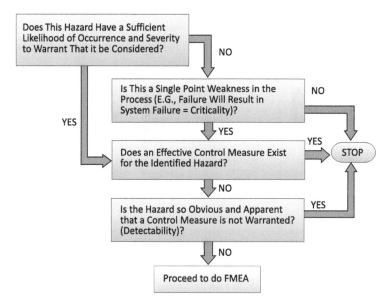

Figure 13.3   FMEA Decision Tree

Source: Veterans Administration National Center for Patient Safety 2001. Used with permission.

in the librarian's pocket) does the entire process fail? The next question would be, if it is a single point weakness, is there an effective control measure in place to compensate (e.g. an electronic reminder to check pocket for notes; request that physician use the electronic request system as a backup)?

The use of the FMEA algorithm allows prioritization of issues to be addressed through an anticipatory problem-solving method. An FMEA team will want to consider first those sub-processes with a high severity-probability score and criticality; especially when failure or impending failure is not obvious, that is, not detectible as defined (or described) in Infobox 13.1.

Root Cause Analysis

Root cause analysis (RCA) is a process used to diagnose and treat system problems by finding their source. Healthcare has identified and fixed serious systems issues as a result of this type of investigation (Bagian et al. 2002). Part of the RCA process requires a search to identify best practices to develop an evidence base for patient safety problem-solving.

The initial phase of an RCA is to consider the adverse event that has occurred – writing or drawing a chronology in order to provoke questions about why and how things went awry. During this phase, EI&K and librarians can play an important role in understanding any departures from established, evidence-based healthcare and/or system dysfunctions (Saimbert et al. 2010). If the RCA team is comprised only of clinicians, insight from other disciplines may not be available. The boundary spanning capabilities of the librarian can be especially invaluable in an RCA team, as an obvious source to bring in other perspectives and from the searchable literature of many disciplines (Saimbert et al. 2010; MacIntosh-Murray and Choo 2005).

The team may employ cause-and-effect diagramming and rules of causation to improve the analysis (Woodcock et al. 2005). The Institute for Safe Medication Practice, Canada has published an RCA using such tools in their *Hydomorphone/Morphine Event* report (ISMP Canada 2004).

If the librarian is not an integral part of the RCA team, the second phase of RCA may require a consultation with a librarian as the team considers what actions will best prevent the recurrence of the adverse event and span discipline boundaries to discover solutions (Gurses, Ozok and Pronovost 2012;

Saimbert et al. 2010; Harrison et al. 2007). EI&K will provide remedial actions from the evidence base in non-clinical areas of research (Williams and Bagian 2010; Saimbert et al. 2010; Holden et al. 2008; Agency for Healthcare Research and Quality 2006).

In addition a librarian may be needed as the RCA team works to gain acceptance and then implementation of suggested changes by hospital leadership and clinicians (Tamuz and Harrison 2006). Publications in the fields of organizational, social and cultural studies may aid in supporting such change (Shojania et al. 2001). Recommendations for change may be ignored or short-lived if not bolstered by supporting, evidence, information and knowledge.

Both FMEA and RCA problem-solving teams will benefit if the librarian is a consistent team member rather than being drawn in intermittently throughout in the process. Just as having an librarian present in morning patient rounds allows the librarian to understand and refine the search query on the spot with a contextual understanding of the activities playing out in daily work, so having an librarian involved in problem-solving can allow for immediate research into problem-solving literature in a way that makes sense in the particular environment and situation (Banks et al. 2007).

The Hierarchy of Actions and its Application to EI&K Improvements

> *We are now recognizing that strategies to promote a change in workers' behaviors that were once thought of as most effective are the least successful in bringing about change (Foley 2004: n.p.).*

Healthcare – as in many industries today – has resource challenges to be considered when planning for improvement and innovation. The prioritization of activities needs to go beyond the bottom line to consider the sustainable effectiveness of the initiative. Implementing solutions that do not effectively address deeper problems leads to difficult and time consuming redesign in the near future. The VA National Center for Patient Safety (NCPS) encourages patient safety teams to look for corrective actions that are permanent rather than temporary and that rely on changes to system design rather than relying on training or on affixing warning labels (National Center for Patient Safety 2011). The evidence for this approach is from the National Institute for Occupational

Table 13.1   Selected Hierarchy of Actions: Information Seeker Examples

	Type	Suggested Information Seeker Example	Clinical Example
Stronger Actions	Architectural/ physical plant changes	Situate information expertise at the point of need; Librarian is present for patient rounds.	Suicide-resistant door set for mental health patient room; acuity-adaptive patient rooms; shock absorbing flooring to reduce harm from patient falls (Hignett and Lu 2007; Rashid 2006; Henriksen et al. 2007; Hendrich et al. 2004; Joseph and Rashid 2007).
	Engineering control/forcing function	On-line information request form includes date-filled to be completed before submit button is clicked.	IV tubing auto-clamp when pump door opens; drive bar on portable x-ray machine (Grout 2007; Carayon 2007).
Intermediate Actions	Redundancy	Formulary listings for high-alert medications are researched independently by more than one person with differing expertise.	Abnormal X-ray follow up to both general medicine and subspecialty physicians; and separately to technician, with confirmation that report was received (Choksi et al. 2006; Gosbee and Gosbee 2010).
	Eliminate look and sound-alikes	Eliminate out of date hard copy drug information materials – or boldly mark previous editions.	Losec and Lasix not stored near each other; that is, store medications by category of use rather than alphabetically (ISMP 2011).
Weaker Actions	Procedure, memorandum, or policy	New policy: After three lab tests and no substantial diagnostic results, call librarian.	Policy/procedure directing nurses to check IV sites every 2 hours; policy instructing placement of green adapters only on compressed gas oxygen wall outlets (Wiklund 2011; Hildebrand et al. 2011; Wieringa et al. 1999).
	Training	EBM training for physicians and/or librarians.	In-service on hard-to-use defibrillator with hidden door; training is necessary for complex endoscope cleaning process, and also requires support of cognitive aids. Training efficacy is improved with usability testing of device to precisely target training to problematic steps (Anderson et al. 2010; Hildebrand et al. 2011).

Source: Adapted from Alligood, E., Jones, B., Williams, L. and Zipperer L. *Hierarchy of Actions – Librarian/Information-centric Examples*. [Presentation handouts]. Diagnostic Error: Team Up and Tackle It. Medical Library Association Annual Conference, Minneapolis, May 13, 2011.

Safety and Health (NIOSH). NIOSH has used a hierarchy of actions as a way to determine the most effective controls for known hazards. This approach borrows from engineering and is focused on devices and materials, but has been successfully extrapolated to healthcare. From most effective to least, the controls are:

1.   Eliminate the hazard.

2.   Substitute a safer method (or device or procedure).

3.   Engineer and test new safety controls.

4.   Use administrative methods.

5.   Provide workers with personal protective equipment and clothing.[1]

Table 13.1 and Appendix 3 builds upon the VA's approach to a hierarchy of actions, and provides examples in both the information/library domain and the healthcare domain, to illustrate the functionality of this hierarchical approach to implementing EI&K strategies that could address failure points to affect patient safety.

Meeting the Future Challenges of EI&K Delivery Through Human Factors Awareness

Available knowledge is too rarely applied to improve the care experience and information generated by the care experience is too rarely gathered to improve the knowledge available (Smith et al. 2012: S1).

The connection of system vulnerability to human errors is well documented and work is underway in the field of HFE to redesign healthcare systems (Bogner 1994; Carayon 2007; Gosbee and Gosbee 2010). EI&K and the L/I should also be able to identify and fix (or compensate for) system vulnerabilities in the EI&K process. Just as the futuristic librarian Ravna Bergsndot faced difficult decisions about which resources, strategies and libraries to bring on the spaceship *Out of Band II* (Vinge 1992), so each literature search necessarily represents a human information seeker making decisions like those faced by physicians making diagnostic decisions. The application of librarian expertise to identify and address root causes and contributing factors for the lack of appropriate EI&K in healthcare is an innovation that can shape the future. However, EI&K deliverables rely on databases and search strategies designed by humans and therefore at risk of failure. Search and retrieval errors may not be as obvious as patient care errors, and so may not be as obviously in need of improvement. The drive for highly reliable healthcare systems must include

---

1   National Institute for Occupational Safety and Health 2010.

highly reliable evidence, information and knowledge and the communication thereof.

> *Ravna realized this was not just a favor. She was the best person for this job. She knew humans, and she knew archive management ... They would need an effective onboard database and strategy program. It was up to Ravna to decide what library materials to move to the ship, to balance the ease of local availability against the greater resources that would be accessible over the ultrawave from Relay (Vinge 1992: 182).*

Both FMEA and RCA problem-solving methods benefit from the work of a boundary spanner equipped to guide the analysis towards effective diagnosis and treatment of EI&K systems ills. Recognizing and fixing faulty systems builds expertise in systems safety. Doing this using the proactive problem-solving method of FMEA builds skills that will be equally effective during RCA, as well as for developing the role of a librarian toward improving patient safety.

Other HFE methods to bring high reliability to the EI&K process itself are less time intensive than the two discussed here, but may also be less systemically effective. Observation of EI&K and the work of the librarian will reveal workarounds that indicate system vulnerabilities. For example, sticky notes or warning labels added to equipment are flags inviting redesign of a system that is, in its present form, likely to provoke human error (Anderson et al. 2012).

As patient safety research continues and the evidence base for patient safety problem-solving grows, the EI&K contribution will be even more essential – at both individual and professional levels. The work to bring high reliability to the EI&K process will result in better preparation for involvement in problem-solving contributions for patient safety.

KEY TAKE-AWAYS
- Evidence, information and knowledge processes are vulnerable to failure given their design by humans.
- HFE principles and methods are readily applicable to EI&K systems improvement in order to support optimal human performance.
- Boundary spanning EI&K professionals are uniquely positioned to contribute to the work of designing patient safety improvement strategies.

Suggested Reading

Bogner, M.S.E. 1994. *Human Error in Medicine*. Mahwah, NJ: Lawrence Erlbaum Associates.

Chabris, C. and Simons, D. 2010. *The Invisible Gorilla: and Other Ways Our Intuitions Deceive Us*. New York, NY: Crown Publishing Group.

Dekker, S. 2002. *The Field Guide to Human Error Investigations*. Aldershot: Ashgate Publishing.

Lau, A.Y. and Coiera, E.W. 2007. Do people experience cognitive biases while searching for information? *Journal of the American Medical Informatics Association*, 14(5), 599–608.

PART 5
Future States

This chapter examines breakdowns in the EI&K pathway, and the negative consequences that can ensue. Analyzing these breakdowns is essential to understanding what went wrong and why, and is the first step in re-designing systems and processes to prevent similar breakdowns in the future. A case of evidence access failure provides context for the discussion to explore the value of analysis mechanisms and their ability to reveal areas for improvement. A root cause analysis of the EI&K failures related to Ellen Roche's death illustrates how this process can help identify the various factors that contributed to the tragic outcome.

The authors posit, through a discussion of a rare, yet persistent type of sentinel event, how effective EI&K could impact patient safety improvement. The chapter shares the EI&K elements supporting one organization's response to such an incident, and draws from that experience to explore how EI&K could improve the safety of healthcare. This chapter closes with questions to motivate, investigate and innovate EI&K improvement as a key mechanism to drive and sustain advances in patient safety. It explores the past to envision the future.

14

Analyzing Breakdowns in the EIK Pathway

Barbara Jones, Mark Graber and Elaine Alligood

> *Confidence is what you have before you understand the problem.*
>
> *Woody Allen (as quoted in Gerry 2007: 9)*

EI&K Breakdowns

Delivering safe medical care is critically dependent upon the clinician's ability to obtain and synthesize information to make appropriate clinical decisions. The preceding chapters have introduced several foundational concepts that shed light on designing this complicated process to work reliabilty and the potential it has for positive impact on clinical care when it works well. This chapter more specifically explores – breakdowns in the evidence, information and knowledge (EI&K) pathway, and the potential for disastrous consequences that can ensue. Analyzing these breakdowns is essential to understanding what went wrong and why, and is the first step in re-designing systems and processes to prevent similar breakdowns in the future.

Accident investigation needs to proceed in a highly organized fashion to avoid missing important contributing factors. The goal of this chapter is to review the breakdown in the EI&K pathway using the root cause analysis (RCA) paradigm, and to present different options for performing the RCA. Root cause analysis is a tool for retrospective investigation that excels at dissecting where and why processes fail, and identifying the steps that need attention and repair.

Normal Accidents

Sociologist Charles Perrow's "normal accident" paradigm provides instructive context for discussing EI&K breakdowns and error analysis in healthcare (Perrow 1999). Perrow's framework emphasizes the complexity of the whole, the importance of how the different parts interact with each other, and how these interacting failures can result in disaster. Healthcare meets all of Perrow's criteria, as the Ellen Roche case discussed later in this chapter will illustrate.

Breakdowns in the flow and interpretation of information and evidence are hardly unique to healthcare. Virtually every known man-made disaster includes examples of how failure to know, appreciate, and act on critical information at the right time played a role in causing the subsequent accident. The most critical nuclear power accident in the United States involved the Three Mile Island plant in 1979, resulting in a partial meltdown of the nuclear reactor core and release of radiation into the atmosphere. As described by Perrow in his book *Normal Accidents* this accident was triggered by an inconsequential leak in the reactor's cooling system, but the catastrophic outcome was more the result of subsequent breakdowns in finding and analyzing information that would have allowed the operators to respond more appropriately to the original problem (Perrow 1999). A key pressure gauge was located on the back of a cabinet, not in direct sight; an indicator light, which would have alerted the operators to a stuck valve, was hidden by a paper repair tag; and a balky temperature gauge failed to convey that actual temperatures were reaching critical level. These simple impediments to the flow of data were judged to be critical failures in the accident's causation.

Perrow's point is that disasters like the Three Mile Island accident are inevitable when the systems involved are so complex their true state cannot be known with certainty, and when breakdowns are "tightly coupled" to consequences, meaning that there is not enough time to intervene and avoid harm.

Root Cause Analysis

Errors like straws upon the surface flow: Who would search for pearls must dive below (John Dryden, All for Love, 1678).

Accident and failure investigations require an orderly process that identifies all of the contributing factors. If done well, this process uncovers a detailed and rich understanding of what went right, what went wrong, and why. Root cause analysis is based on the 5 Whys analysis described by Sakichi Toyoda that served as the foundation of the Toyota Production System. RCA has been embraced by the UK's National Health Service, and the US Department of Veteran's affairs as well as by systemsthinkers like Peter Senge as a productive approach to retrospective risk assessment (Ohno 1988; Senge et al. 1994; National Patient Safety Agency 2004; US Department of Veteran's Affairs National Center for Patient Safety, n.d.). Because the true root causes often differ dramatically from the superficial ones that jump out during the initial stages of an accident review, digging ever deeper into the factors contributing to a process failure, and repeatedly asking "why?", "why?", "why?', provides the insight needed to identify remediable elements.

RCA is best undertaken by a team with diverse perspectives and expertise. The members should be chosen to include those with the content knowledge relevant to the breakdown being analyzed, as well as frontline staff who understand work flows and realities. Ideally, the RCA team should include individuals with expertise in human factors, patient safety, and EI&K processes, such as trained medical librarians (Zipperer and Sykes 2009; Tompson and Zipperer 2011). RCA teams should also include staff members involved in the accident; no one is more motivated to understand what went wrong and why than someone involved.

Instruction manuals with step-by-step directions for conducting a RCA are available from both the United Kingdom's National Patient Safety Agency[1] and from the US Department of Veteran's Affairs National Center for Patient Safety.[2]

Team members performing a root cause analysis need to be given the time and support necessary to perform a thoughtful and comprehensive analysis, and "just in time" training on the process itself. The team should also keep in mind the intrinsic limitations of root cause analysis:

1.   Some root causes may be missed because the team didn't dig deep enough, or lacks the knowledge to identify them.

2.   The process tends to identify concrete, discrete causes, and tends to overlook the more complicated interactions amongst them, as well as intangible factors such as culture, resiliency and resourcefulness.

---

1   See www.npsa.nhs.uk/rcatoolkit
2   See www.patientsafety.gov/rca.html

3.   The process is not reproducible – a different team will likely identify different root causes; and most critically.

4.   Identifying root causes does not mean they are fixed – the work has just begun.

Every RCA should produce a finite number of recommendations and action items for preventing similar problems in the future.

A key factor to remember at the conclusion of each RCA is to share the knowledge gained through the process as widely as possible, to enable learning at both the team and the organizational levels.

A challenge with every root cause analysis is to examine the entire spectrum of factors that might have influenced the outcome. Several different approaches have been described that can help ensure that the analysis was comprehensive in scope. An introduction to three of these approaches follows:

1.   Perrow described using the DEPOSE method for RCA investigation. Although DEPOSE was suggested in the context of industrial accidents, the elements are easily remembered, and could be considered just as appropriate for investigating healthcare-related incidents.

      Design
      Equipment
      Procedures
      Operators
      Supplies and materials
      Environment

2.   Another simple-to-remember framework for root cause analysis is the SHEL approach depicted in Figure 14.1. SHEL encompasses:

      Software: Policies, procedures, guidelines, etc.
      Hardware: Equipment, informatics infrastructure, etc.
      Environment: Stress, distractions, culture, etc.
      Liveware: Training, experience, supervision; doctors, nurses, clinical staff, librarians, patient/family and caregivers.

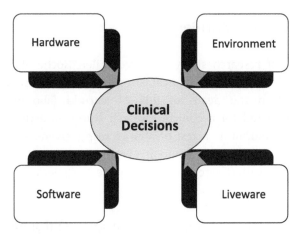

Figure 14.1   The SHEL Approach
Source: Adapted from: Molloy and O'Boyle 2005.

3.   Although either the DEPOSE or the SHEL approach could be used
to analyze EI&K failures, the use of an approach specifically tailored
for the major elements that need consideration in these cases should
be employed. A framework that includes these elements is presented
in Figure 14.2, which illustrates how clinical decisions and actions
evolve from finding and integrating a diverse array of information
and evidence, then using appropriate clinical knowledge and skills
to apply the evidence and information to the problem at hand.

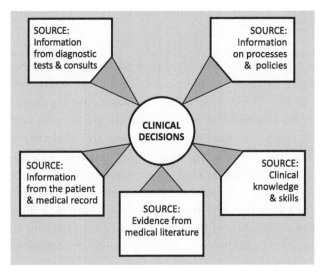

Figure 14.2   A Specific Framework for Analyzing EI&K Breakdowns

Analyzing the Roche Accident

The tragic case of research study volunteer Ellen Roche at Johns Hopkins University in 2001 has been noted as catastrophic example of EI&K breakdowns that culminated in the death of this 24-year-old laboratory technician. Ellen had volunteered for a clinical research study on asthma, which used inhaled hexamethonium as a test of airway responsiveness. In Ellen's case, she experienced an unexpected and irreversible reaction to this agent that culminated in her death (Keiger and De Pasquale 2002; Becker 2001; Steinbrook 2002).

The post-hoc analysis of Roche's death discovered that toxic reactions to hexamethonium had been previously described, but neither the investigators, the funders, nor the local Institutional Review Board were aware of these findings; in other words, there was an evidence identification failure (Zucker 2001).

The root causes of the Roche tragedy can be identified using the EI&K framework in a fishbone diagram as illustrated in Figure 14.3. The areas examined are in the boxes and the issues discovered are listed as offshoots from those "bones." Many separate identifiable elements can be described that contributed to the ultimate administration of the hexamethonium. Once the compound was administered, the toxicity was apparently immediate, as Roche's symptoms developed overnight. By the end of the first week, she had critical acute lung injury leading to her death (Keiger and DePasquale 2002). This is an example of the tight coupling between a failure and its consequences as discussed by Perrow.

Figure 14.3 hints at the complexity of the error causation in the Roche case, but doesn't do justice to the concept of 'system visibility' that Perrow emphasizes. In the Three Mile Island accident, the accident causation in part reflected the fact that the true state of the system was not known. The same problem applies in the Ellen Roche case, and probably in most cases of EI&K breakdown. Knowledge simply isn't "visible" and it is difficult or impossible to know in real time whether adequate EI&K exists or not; it is only in retrospect that this question can this be examined. EI&K processes by their nature are distributed amongst multiple parties in the system, none of whom takes ownership of the responsibility for ensuring that all of the needed information is available and incorporated appropriately into clinical decisions.

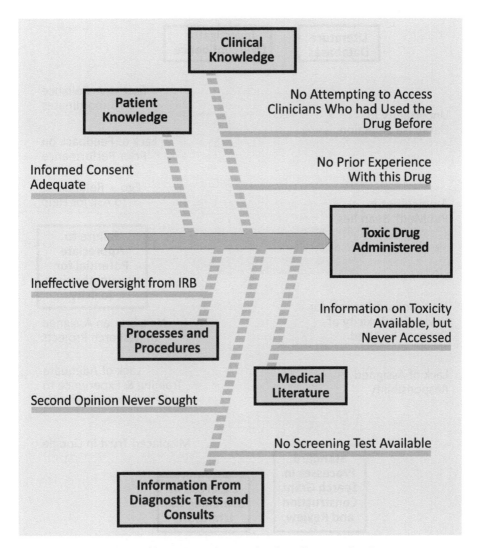

Figure 14.3   EI&K Failure Root Causes in the Ellen Roche Case

It should also be emphasized that Figure 14.3 illustrates just the beginning of an appropriate root cause analysis. In an actual investigation, much more detail would be desirable.

Each of the individual branches on this overview could be further studied by a similar process of analysis. Figure 14.4 illustrates this kind of secondary analysis by examining just one limb of the primary diagram, the breakdowns in searching the medical literature.

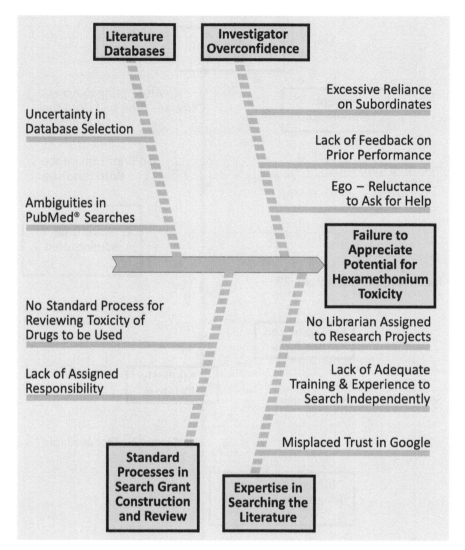

Figure 14.4   Possible EIK Breakdowns in a Medical Literature Search

Even this secondary analysis is incomplete, but it identifies some of the problems that may occur when searching for information or evidence. As illustrated by the progressive refinement of systematic reviews over the past decade, searching the medical literature has become a highly refined and complex skill, requiring specialized expertise and experience. What databases should be searched and what is known about their limitations? What are the right key words, terms, and subject headings to search? What about searching the "grey" literature? These concepts, and their relevance to their clinical or research questions, may not be apparent to many clinicians or medical trainees, some of whom rely on Google as their primary information source or Google Scholar an access point for evidence (Duran-Nelson et al. 2013).

Lack of competency using search tools and databases is a common failure mode in EI&K breakdowns. Medical librarians and informationists are well suited to address this EI&K gap, given their skills in finding appropriate evidence relevant to the questions at hand, combined with an appreciation for the importance of information and knowledge management and experience

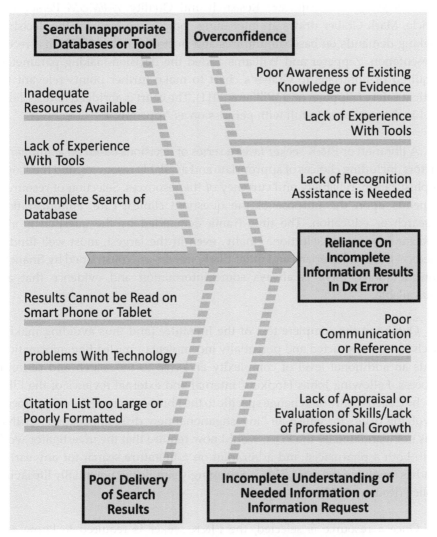

Figure 14.5   Potential Failures in the Information Seeking Process

in implementing systems to assure their effective use. Many of the same concepts appear in Figure 14.4 and 14.5. Figure 14.5 is expands the diagram to translate the discussion of information failure in the Roche case (Figure 14.4) into the broader, messier world of EI&K failure. These types of failures noted here can easily occur in any search for information and evidence and demonstrate the need to include appropriate identification and retrieval skills in any search process.

FAST AND FURIOUS DECISION-MAKING: LEARNING FROM BASEBALL

In an Agency for Healthcare Research and Quality *WebM&M* Perspective article, Mark Graber draws an interesting comparison between the decision-making demands on baseball umpires and doctors (Graber 2007). In a recent presentation, Zipperer and Williams added the decision-making parameters required of librarians to Graber's chart to make further points relevant for patient safety (Zipperer and Williams 2011). The chart is abridged here as Table 14.1 and reproduced in full with permission as Appendix 4.

A librarian or EI&K seeker faces a series of decisions based on a number of factors, including choices of appropriate and available resources, and the scope, sophistication, reliability and currency of the resources. Selection of resources depends upon the purpose of the question: clinical care, administration, research or education. The time frame demanded by the question is also a factor in resource selection. Finally, even in the largest, most well-funded medical centers, librarians and other EI&K seekers are constrained by financial considerations; there is always some information and evidence that are unavailable.

Obtaining the complete text of the literature (and thus avoiding making decisions on abstracted and potentially incomplete or misleading information) adds an additional level of complexity and cost to the search and retrieval process. Following Johns Hopkins' internal and external reviews of the Ellen Roche tragedy, only one change specific to the library emerged: future protocols involving drugs for which an "investigational new drug application" or IND was not mandated by the FDA, would now require that the investigator work with both a pharmacist and a librarian on a literature search for any earlier studies involving the drug. This is a seemingly simple but potentially lifesaving policy (Roderer 2012).

Once a resource is selected, the EI&K seeker is required to know and understand the structure and capabilities of the resource. Understanding the

Table 14.1   Doctors, Umpires, and EI&K Seekers – An Abridged Exploration (Zipperer and Williams 2011; Adapted from Graber 2007)

Issue	Umpires	Doctors	EI&K Seekers
What is the complexity of the decision?	Binary – It's a strike or a ball.	There are thousands of diseases and syndromes, but typically the number of reasonable choices is less than 10.	Multiple choices of terms, resources, cost and timing considerations, scope and applicability of identified resources. Librarians also need to diagnose the MDs thinking.
What are the consequences of error?	Typically, no impact. Rarely, errors lead to lost games, a losing series, or career changes.	Typically, no impact – the error is inconsequential or is not discovered. Rarely, the error may cause injury or death.	Unknown, unexplored. Lack of organizational concern for its importance and lack of overall personnel commitment to the exploring and defining the reliability of the research process.
What types of cognitive processes are used to make the decision?	The umpire integrates his perception of the ball's path in the context of his knowledge of the strike zone, all interpreted automatically (subconsciously).	Most patient problems are very familiar to clinicians. Physicians integrate their perception of the facts in the context of their medical knowledge base. This occurs automatically (subconsciously) and involves recognizing patterns (schema) they have seen before.	Heuristics, self-satisfaction bias. Premature closure and reliance on colleagues can block awareness of the need to seek information to confirm decision-making.

Source: Adapted with permission of *AHRQ WebM&M*. Graber, M.L. Diagnostic Errors in Medicine: What Do Doctors and Umpires Have in Common [Perspective]? *AHRQ WebM&M* [serial online]. February 2007. Available at: http://www.webmm.ahrq.gov/perspective.aspx?perspectiveID=36.

capacity of the search engine and construction of the database are both critical factors for achieving a thorough literature search result. If the subject headings and indexing have not kept up with developments or issues in the clinical arena, literature searching requires additional knowledge and creativity. For example, the term "patient safety" was only added as a Medical Subject Heading (MeSH term) in 2012 (National Library of Medicine 2012). Prior to 2012, evidence seekers had to be creative in order to effectively retrieve potentially relevant publications on patient safety, using synonyms for the concept, or "free text" words, as well as MeSH terms indicating medical error such as "wrong side surgery," "iatrogenic," etc.

The knowledge of the seeker needs to be applied to translate the original question into language and concepts that are actionable in the particular resources. When the seeker and the searcher are different, for example, a clinician and a librarian, the seeker's knowledge must be effectively and correctly communicated to the searcher. Insightful and articulate communication skills are critical to this element of the search process. Often an initial search question is unclear or poorly defined. Librarians as searchers must be able to probe the seeker and the request in ways that elicit information clarity while eliminating bias and the temptation of premature decision-making. Furthermore, evidence and information seekers must remain vigilant in recognizing their biases (Lau and Coiera 2007), in their awareness of what they don't know, and in their awareness of what they need to know. Plus they must know where they need to look. Good questions can help surface those factors that could potentially result in an incomplete or delayed search result.

It is imperative to address the "elephant in the room" here: the need for the crucial absence of hierarchy in the EI&K research and communication processes. Ego or pride can potentially inhibit the necessary free exchange of ideas in service to a patient's wellbeing. The librarian or informationist in pursuit of clarity queries the requestor (clinician, leader, administrator etc.) for additional detail to fine-tune the terms and methods used to identify information and evidence to inform action. This process is in essence a search strategy. The strategy must be accepted by the requestor without ego interference. A conversation around the search request can spark an idea, additional terms, or a new approach to a tough query. Effective searches emerge from this iterative communication of ideas, questions, and concepts. In essence the knowledge of the intermediary helps the evidence and information identification process run smoothly.

Accuracy and error rates for the three professions of umpire, doctor and librarian vary. Major League Baseball umpires' accuracy rates are between 92–94 percent, while for physicians the accuracy rate is probably close to 90 percent (Berner and Graber 2008). Thus umpires' error rates are between 6–8 percent and physicians' about 10 percent. For librarians, accuracy and error rates are unknown and virtually unexplored. If the medical librarianship community does not explore librarians' success rates, as well as their potential for overrating the ability of their colleagues and peers at the sharp end to search the literature, and how these issues affect healthcare decision-making, who will?

Fortunately, most errors do not cause major consequences for either umpires or physicians. But the potential for harm is there, and as the Roche case illustrates, catastrophic outcomes are possible. This should be sufficient motivation to improve the EI&K process at every opportunity, especially in cases leading to harm. A quotation from Vernon Law captures this perfectly: "Experience is a hard teacher, because she gives the test first … the lesson afterward" (Credo Reference 2003).

EI&K Improvement: Error as a Learning Mechanism

> *Not only do … people reach erroneous conclusions and make unfortunate*
> *choices, but their incompetence robs them of the metacognitive ability*
> *to realize it (Kruger and Dunning 1999).*

Healthcare organizations don't have evidence access skill requirements in place to make this piece of daily medical practice reliable and standardized. Standards for accessing evidence do exist in the context of systematic reviews and have proved valuable in establishing quality reviews, but the standards have not been uniformly adopted in the frontline practice of healthcare (Sampson et al. 2009; McGowan, Sampson, Lefebvre 2010). It would behoove healthcare to take what has been applied to enhance information and evidence quality in the context of systemic review and seek to understand how it should be applied to improve the daily practice of medicine (Eden et al. 2011).

The librarian community and evidence- or information-seekers are slow to adopt a standard review or evaluation process for effective searching, either qualitative or metric-based. For instance, in a multi-librarian facility such as an academic medical center, librarians informally or formally look to each other for assistance, clarification, and peer review, a standard practice in the systematic review and Cochrane librarians' arenas (Hausner et al. 2012). However, in the instance of a community hospital, a solo librarian must rely on her/his own skills and commitment to excellence in order to create data metrics to measure effectiveness. However, unless there is a follow-up conversation between the healthcare provider and the librarian about the quality of the search and the information and evidence provided, the librarian has no real idea of the quality or impact of the search.

Librarians and healthcare professionals both need to develop metrics and/ or new approaches to complete the information and evidence provision cycle, looking for both positive and negative aspects in order to locate the errors or places in the cycle where errors might occur. Those using librarians' services must be part of a more evaluative approach as well. It is not helpful for the librarian to hear: "That was great!" from a requestor (physician, etc.), nice as the verbal pat on the back may be. Specific feedback, such as how the information retrieved was used in a treatment regimen; concepts missed in the first search that emerged from use of the first search results and point to a possible need for follow-up; concepts that rewarded the requestor's need for evidence; and, what could have improved the communication exchange regarding the search is important for improvement and increased quality. Librarians need to proactively seek knowledge from those for whom they provide resources in order to gather feedback to apply to their practice to inform future activities to improve the reliability of the evidence and information search processes.

As a part of the improvement effort advocated here, librarians and other EI&K seekers need to explore and recognize the role of cognitive biases in the search and retrieval process (Lau and Coiera 2007). The ability to scrutinize the cognitive processes used in searching the literature and evaluating search results for the clinician should be nurtured in the skill set of the librarians as experts doing the work (Ross 2009; Zipperer et al. 2010). By applying knowledge on how individual seekers think about the evidence and information search, the potential for error in incomplete searching (due to bias, consideration of free vs. cost information, inappropriate resource selection, poor searching skills, poor communication, etc.) can be reduced.

Exploring and Recognizing Knowledge Access Failure

As has been discussed here and elsewhere, librarians are well suited to address information and evidence needs in clinical care. Given that, several questions emerge about the factors leading to the omission of librarian consultation in the drug trial design process that resulted in Roche's death.

"... the knowledge of the intermediary helps the evidence and information identification process run smoothly." The lack of librarian involvement opened the door for the knowledge breakdown in this particular case (the librarian was unable to contribute knowledge to the situation because s/he was not consulted) (Perkins 2001). Using the root cause analysis technique of 5 Whys, some of the initial questions that could be asked are:

1. Why didn't the Hopkins researcher use the services of the librarian?

2. Why didn't the researcher know about the library?

3.   Why didn't the researcher know about the earlier *Index Medicus* for literature prior to PubMed®?

4.   Why wasn't the librarian involved with the Institutional Review Board (IRB) on a routine basis?

Starting the analysis process with any of these questions and uncovering the first answer will typically lead to more questions (see InfoBox 14.1). The questions and subsequent answers will build on each other until the actual root causes of the problem are identified. Traditionally, it will take at least five rounds of questions and answers to get to the root of a complex issue, hence the name of the analysis. See the explication of just one of the numbered questions in the Infobox to illustrate the depth to which a 5 Whys analysis can go.

INFOBOX 14.1: A 5 WHYS SUBSET ANALYSIS – THE ROCHE CASE

Why 1. Why wasn't the librarian involved with the Institutional Review Board on a routine basis?

Because the VP to whom the librarian reported had almost no contact with the IRB; it was not "on her radar."

Why 2. Why didn't the VP have contact with the IRB?

Because the VP was not a researcher and was not brought in on any research design discussions for the trial.

Why 3. Why wasn't the VP brought in on research meetings or discussions?

Because research and administration were very siloed in the organization.

Why 4: Why were research and administration siloed?

Because hospital leadership hadn't built multidisciplinary work into their strategic plan and cut it from their departmental budgets.

Why 5: Why was funding for multidisciplinary work cut from the budget?

Staff had no mechanism in place to document the ROI for the efforts and their activity costs.

This method of investigating failure should point to a part of the process that is not working, and not an individual. Because the process is identified as the failure, the organization and the individuals involved can learn without blame from the analysis and institute changes that will prevent reoccurrence.

The other challenge here is the latent nature of knowledge failure in that knowledge is a characteristic that is in many ways intangible. Tracking knowledge failures (whether cognitive, process or systemic in nature) is apt to require unique approaches. These approaches have yet to be employed in the spectrum of analysis currently in place in patient safety circles. The recognition and understanding of EI&K failure as a factor in medical error is nascent: future efforts are required to fully address this problem.

Vigilance Required

The processes that underlie clinical diagnosis and management critically depend on the ability to access and synthesize information, evidence and knowledge. Highly reliable healthcare demands constant vigilance to the potential for error or failure in this EI&K domain from all areas within the hospital environment from clinical care through administration. The cognitive biases resulting in hyperbole of attributes and effectiveness is a human condition (Cook and Woods 1994). Individuals perceive themselves to be more successful than results indicate, and an awareness of this self-satisfaction bias should force the recognition of the need to constantly examine the information seeking process for errors. This reality should be explored in the EI&K seeking arena through the use of failure analysis tools to learn from near misses and errors.

Everyone involved in seeking information and evidence ought to be aware of his or her skill level, and should not hesitate to seek the knowledge of those with higher expertise as needed. Leadership should enable that seeking by providing easy access to those with greater expertise and by sharing the evidence identified through the subsequently better-informed actions. In the Ellen Roche case, the lack of this awareness and function resulted in error and gaps that contributed to a fatality. In most cases, the consequences of EI&K breakdown will be less severe. However, given the possible stakes involved, complacence is unacceptable.

"Highly reliable healthcare demands constant vigilance to the potential for error or failure in this EI&K domain from all areas within the hospital environment from clinical care through administration."

KEY TAKE-AWAYS

- Evidence, information and knowledge failures can contribute to tragedy, so this reality needs to be established to generate investigation to design improvement.
- Processes to improve EI&K identification and distribution can be realized through highlighting breakdown potentials through system-failure analysis techniques.
- Clinical, administrative and librarian experts need to be engaged in identifying weaknesses and designing solutions.

Suggested Reading

Bagian, J.P. et al. 2002. The Veterans Affairs root cause analysis system in action. *Joint Commission Journal of Quality Improvement*, 28(10), 531–45.

McLellan, F. 2001. 1966 and all that-when is a literature search done? *Lancet*, 358(9282), 646.

Perrow, C. 1999. *Normal Accidents: Living with High-Risk Technologies*. Princeton, NJ: Princeton University Press.

Sampson, M. et al. 2008. *PRESS: Peer Review of Electronic Search Strategies*. Ottawa: Canadian Agency for Drugs and Technologies in Health.

Tavris, C. and Aronson, E. 2008. *Mistakes Were Made (But Not by Me): Why We Justify Foolish Beliefs, Bad Decisions, and Hurtful Acts*. Boston, MA: Houghton Mifflin Harcourt.

15

A Case to Illustrate the Opportunity for Healthcare in EI&K Enhancement

Grena Porto, Suzanne Graham and Lorri Zipperer

He who tells all that he knows, tells more than he knows.

George Harrison, quoted by Fine 2002: 10.

In July of 2005, a 21-year-old patient was admitted to a Kaiser Permanente Medical Center for treatment of lymphoma. The patient was started on an intrathecal chemotherapy regimen and was responding well to it. Several weeks after admission, the patient was to receive the fourth chemotherapy treatment. Instead of getting the prescribed drug, the patient received vincristine, a medication that should only be given intravenously and that was intended for another patient. This medication error led to the patient's death three days later (Graham et al. 2008).

Setting the Stage for Learning

Evidence regarding the hazards of inadvertent intrathecal vincristine administration errors was available at the time of this event (Noble and Donaldson 2010). Within days of the tragedy described above, The Joint Commission – then called the Joint Commission on Accreditation of Healthcare Organizations, or JCAHO – released information in an alert to warn the industry about errors involving administration of vincristine into the spine (Joint Commission 2005).

INFOBOX 15:1: ACCIDENTAL INTRATHECAL VINCRISTINE ADMINISTRATION INCIDENTS – SELECTED TIMELINE

1968: Young leukemia patient resulting in death three days later.

1978: USA: Five-year-old leukemia patient resulting in death.

1980: Accidental intrathecal vincristine administration resulting in death.

1991: New York: 59-year-old woman who later died (ISMP 1998).

1995: USA: Six-year-old boy who survives with neurological impairment.

1997: UK: 10-year-old girl who survives with paraplegia.

2001: UK: 18-year-old man, resulting in death. (ISMP 2005).

2003: 49-year-old man, resulting in death (ISMP 2005).

2004: 69-year-old woman who later died (ISMP 2005).

2005: California: 21-year-old man who died three days later (ISMP 2005).

2007: Hong Kong: a 21-year-old female died (World Health Organization 2007).

2011: 63-year-old man with diffuse large B-cell lymphoma dies 12 days after administration (Pongudom, S. and Chinthammitr 2011).

Source: Nobel and Donaldson 2011 – unless otherwise noted.

In 2006, the Institute for Safe Medication Practices (ISMP) published the results of a survey on intravenous (IV) vincristine safety practices (ISMP 2006). The results showed that pediatric, outpatient and specialized oncology facilities had implemented specific error-reduction strategies more frequently than adult, inpatient and general acute care facilities. Other highlights of the survey results include:

- Only 23 percent of respondents had implemented the seemingly most effective strategy – diluting vincristine in minibags prior to use, although 53 percent did report diluting the drug in syringes. (Diluted IV vincristine is less likely to be administered intrathecally due to the volume of solution.)

- About 55 percent of respondents packaged vincristine in a distinctive manner with use of unique overwraps and/or labeling to help distinguish it from IV medications. Again, pediatric and outpatient facilities reported using this information delivery-based error-reduction strategy more often than adult and inpatient facilities.

- Despite a 1991 US Food and Drug Administration (FDA) and United States Pharmacopeia (USP) requirement for distinctive labeling, 7 percent of all respondents reported an information failure in that they did not use the special warning labels on extemporaneously prepared IV vincristine, and 24 percent did not use the manufacturer-supplied overwraps as required.

- Approximately 94 percent of respondents reported that two health professionals independently check IV vincristine doses before administration (ISMP 2006).

Since The Joint Commission's alert was published in July 2005, ISMP has published two subsequent articles regarding this issue, and the World Health Organization has also released an added warning (ISMP 2005; ISMP 2006; WHO 2007). Each new notice was prompted by additional fatal vincristine errors (Nobel and Donaldson 2011). A series of recommendations – well-evidenced and developed by consensus – were available, and still are, yet this error still occurs. How do these failures to implement effective solutions perpetuate given the available evidence, information and knowledge (EI&K) to apply to the problem? Could a lack of understanding of how EI&K can strategically contribute to improvement be weakening efforts toward enhanced patient safety?

This chapter seeks to raise awareness of a vision for a future in which EI&K plays a strategic role in patient safety improvement. It is submitted that even rare occurrences – such as vincristine misadministration – should provide opportunities to motivate and encourage innovation in EI&K practice for individual practitioners, hospital leadership and the patient safety community to more reliably share knowledge to reduce errors. This chapter will use the context of vincristine administration error to explore how the *ineffective* use of EI&K could be construed as system failure contributing to patient harm. The discussion will illustrate the value of effective organizational application of EI&K to learn from error experience in order that the healthcare community at large may generate improvement through motivation, investigation and innovation.

The Past Must Serve as a Resource

> ... *if we are looking back upon a decision which has been taken, as most decisions, in the absence of complete information, it is important that we should not assess the actions of decision-makers too harshly in the light of the knowledge which hindsight gives us (Turner and Pidgeon 1997: 135).*

British psychologist and human error expert James Reason's discussion of a high profile and well-documented 2001 vincristine administration error that took place in the United Kingdom provides a thoughtful systemic failure analysis drawn from the widely disseminated government report on the incident (Reason 2004; Toft 2001). The supposition here builds on that analysis to generate a sense of urgency on the importance of learning from failure.

Table 15.1   Selected EI&K Categorization's of Reason's (2004) Analysis of Toft-reported Failures (2001)

Reason's noted failures/Definitions from Zipperer (2011: 302). *Italicized statements not noted by Reason, but contributed by the authors.*	Evidence: "Evidence refers to the scientifically sound, fully researched and validated information and data collected during the pursuit of the understanding and validation of a hypothesis."	Information: "Data that is processed and repurposed and printed for distinct use."	Knowledge: "What an individual knows. [...] It is dynamic in nature and embedded in the actions of experts."
Individual – level	• *Practitioners lack of seeking existing evidence to be aware of vincristine errors elsewhere.* • *Evidence was available broadly but was it sought or available at the institution?*	• Warning on the syringe was not detected. • Assumptions that the information on the vials would be read by others.	• Inflated assumptions of colleagues' know-how. • Opportunity to gain knowledge via shadowing didn't occur.
Organizational – level	• Two versions of code/protocol (i.e. evidence resource) were available; the one used was incomplete). • Protocol had no mention of highly problematic consequences of misadministration of vincristine.	• Supervisors unaware of available code of practice. • Training of new clinical staff didn't include information on the safety issues specific to the ward involved.	• Knowledge of specific issues in the distinct unit were not transferred into information sources reliably. • *Organizational strategy to address barriers to uptake of evidence not in existence (Wallace et al. 2012).*

Learning from failure is not only required to address medical errors, but is a platform to commit to needed change in EI&K processes to assure learning and sustainability of improvements.

Reason's dissection of the UK incident highlights failures that fall into several EI&K buckets at both the system and individual level. The value here is in articulating a set of noted and potential holes in the EI&K "Swiss Cheese." These elements have not been uniformly noted within the patient safety community as being latent conditions that weaken EI&K use and contribute to failures and near misses.

Table 15.1 illustrates that failures influencing the delivery, use and availability of EI&K need specific attention at national, organizational and individual practice levels. Granted, these themes are represented in discussions around communication errors, handoff errors, etc. However, an explicit declaration on the value of identifying EI&K process failures that can contribute to incidents is a tactic that would enable more learning about these factors. The resulting transparency and increased understanding generated through this work would support a safer future for patients.

To Engage in the Future, Learn from Current Realities

The error that took place within the Kaiser Permanente system in 2005 still resonates with leaders, medical center staff, and physicians who were at the organization at that time. They can still recall exactly where they were and what they were doing when

"... differences in education represented evidence and knowledge transfer gaps that lessened the reliability of the [educational] effort."

they were notified of the harm caused to the young man and his subsequent death three days after the error occurred.

The published account enables analysis drawn from a health system's experience in dealing with that vincristine error. It illustrates how EI&K can be used to generate improvement, both sharp and blunt end buy-in, and organizational commitment to progress (Graham et al. 2008).

Other stories emphasizing the successful use of EI&K in response to a sentinel event to generate support and resources to facilitate its application in

Table 15.2 EI&K Categorizations of Selected Kaiser Permanete Tactics Responding to the 2005 Vincristine Incident

Graham and colleagues' noted successes @ Kaiser Permanente/ Definitions from Zipperer (2011: 302). *Italicized statements not noted by authors, but contributed by the authors.*	Evidence: "Evidence refers to the scientifically sound, fully researched and validated information and data collected during the pursuit of the understanding and validation of a hypothesis."	Information: "Data that is processed and repurposed and printed for distinct use."	Knowledge: "What an individual knows. [...] It is dynamic in nature and embedded in the actions of experts."
Individual – level	• Individuals in the program were empowered to get the evidence they needed.	• Use of the high-alert medication list. • Reportable-event forms provide data and information on potential problems. • "Non-interruption wear" provided information to all to not interrupt nurses preparing medications.	• Observational work helped to surface compliance issues with newly developed protocols.
Organizational – level	• Funds are available to acquire what is needed to inform improvements. • Policies and procedures were updated and standardized. • Improved access to the published evidence through a robust training and educational program.	• Development of the high-alert medication list. • Communication plan to share news and updates on improvement program development. • Toolkit was designed and disseminated to package materials for broad distribution. • Patient Safety University designed to transmit information in a uniform consistent way to staff.	• Use of consensus to develop a list and process to implement the list that worked on the sharp end. • Tapped into experience of individuals at sharp and blunt ends (i.e. Quality Liaisons program of boundary spanners) (Graham et al. 2008). • Stories of error were shared to transfer knowledge and engage individuals in improvement work.

a reliable fashion are needed. Table 15.2 provides an analysis similar to that in Table 15.1 to translate the Kaiser Permanente experience into an EI&K context.

The analysis of the error provided information to the organization's leadership that illuminated factors that permitted human error to align and contribute to a patient's death. The deeper analysis revealed multiple systemic issues that weakened the existing processes for high-alert medication delivery at Kaiser Permanente. A sense of urgency motivated the organization to address the problems as it was seen that they had led up to the failure and, that, if not corrected, could lead to similar errors in the future. A broader assessment at all of the medical centers in Kaiser Permanente Northern California (KPNC) revealed information indicating that variation in how high-alert medications (drugs in which errors in administration can cause catastrophic clinical outcomes) were handled. A review of KPNC medical centers' high-alert medication lists surfaced substantial variation in the drugs included on the list. The policies and procedures related to the handling and administration of high-alert medications also varied. These in essence were information failures to be addressed, in other words, holes in the Swiss Cheese. Medication handling education was in place but the depth and breadth of this education also varied between locations. These differences in education represented evidence and knowledge transfer gaps that lessened the reliability of the effort. All medical centers monitored for mediation errors through their incident reporting process, but other monitoring programs were scarce.

Based on the findings, a multidisciplinary team (High Risk Medication Safety Task Force) was established by senior leadership to address the health system's medication delivery processes. The importance of having all involved departments work together to share their knowledge rather than concentrating on what was known in silos was recognized when developing this team. The task force was built with representatives from leadership, frontline and administrative managers, active clinical staff, and physicians. The overall goals of the resulting High Alert Medication Program (HAMP) was to put in place safe medication practices and to reduce medication errors that cause harm to patients (Graham et al. 2008). These goals were to be achieved through the work of HAMP by:

- Standardizing medication handling practices.

- Enhancing education programs related to medication practices, to embed standard practices into annual core competencies of all staff who handle medications.

- Developing monitoring functions at both the regional and local levels to sustain the new processes and generate on-going systems improvements.

DATA AS A FOUNDATIONAL STEP

A traditional focus on data collection to track improvements was implemented. Despite this tracking being outside the focus of this text, it is worth mentioning briefly to illustrate synergies with the EI&K prongs of the response at Kaiser Permanente. Several data mechanisms employed included the following:

Success measures: One of the first questions addressed by the high-alert medication safety team related to measurements of success of the improvement program. The first measurement related to compliance of medical centers with the implementation process. The implementation threshold was set at 90 percent. The overall compliance threshold was quickly exceeded. Compliance with work processes is now measured on an ongoing basis by the medical centers and at least annually by an internal survey team.

Observational audit monitoring: These audits were designed to measure whether or not all medications on the high-alert medication list were handled in accordance with policy requirements. Audits were done on a quarterly basis for two years. The average compliance rate during the second year of these audits reached 98 percent. Facilities were surveyed and it was found in general that the audits had been effective in monitoring the initial implementation of the program but it was time to explore more actionable metrics that would support continued performance improvement. Auditing was reduced to an annual schedule with the stipulation that if there are any life-threatening injuries or death from a high-alert medication error that observational audits continue monthly for a minimum of three months or until a 95 percent compliance level has been achieved, whichever is greater.

Sustainability monitoring: As the HAMP program matured, trigger tools were employed to monitor the sustainability of the improvements explored (IHI 2007). Triggers, or clues (i.e. data), to identify adverse drug events can help track the overall level of harm from medical care in a healthcare organization. Trigger audits provided information, identified several opportunities for improvement, and action plans were developed and implemented. Subsequent evaluation revealed that the trigger tool process was time-consuming and not granular enough to identify patients who had received high-alert medication.

Thus a strategy to perform audits using the in-house automated medical record is now in development.

In-house reporting effort: The HAMP captured data related to medication events – near misses and adverse drug events. The reports are analyzed using control chart methodology to determine whether variations from the mean are caused by "special cause," in this case or to track improvement by watching days between major injury and death from medication events.

EI&K AS A LAUNCH POINT FOR INNOVATION

KPNC's goals were supported through attention to EI&K transfer. They also analyzed how EI&K drawing from the experience would be used to sustain improvements and assist in spreading what was learned. Some of these examples are listed in Table 15.2 above. Tactics that were particularly successful in utilizing EI&K strategically and effectively in the post-incident learning and improvement process are described in detail below:

Evidence: There was a lack of a standardized approach to education regarding medication safety – particularly in the area of high-alert medications. To that end, an education plan for the Northern California region was established and implemented. The initial educational program was aimed at training of all pharmacy, nursing and medical staff in a short time frame. Standardized educational tools were developed and provided across the region. The initial training was accomplished in less than two months' time. The education program content is continually updated based on new information and evidence (internal and external) and is part of training for new employees who will be involved in drug handling, as well as part of education and ongoing annual competency programs. Members of the task force acquired the evidence and purchased what was needed that wasn't already available via organizational subscriptions or texts.

Information: Using the current literature, recent medication-related events in KPNC, and the expertise of the participants, the High-Risk Medication Safety Task Force broke into working groups to develop an information tool already discussed above: the high-alert medications list. Each group had content and experience experts and was charged to bring forth the listing of drugs, methods of administration and patient-specific requirements that the large group would evaluate to formalize the final list. The high-alert medication list and management requirements were developed by

consensus. The task force then determined that the HAMP would have the
following responsibilities:

- To standardize the high-alert medication list, drug concentrations,
  and management requirements at all facilities throughout the
  region.

- To require approval of any change to the list via the appropriate
  Regional Medication Safety Committee (composed of staff,
  physician and management from each of the medical center and
  regional leadership).

- To apply the HAMP tools across the continuum of care, including
  specialty areas.

- To make available the appropriate resources to design, implement
  and equip units to meet the requirements of high-alert medication
  list (Graham et al. 2008). This list has increased in length since
  development based on new information and evidence obtained
  through the literature and knowledge based on the organization's
  experience with it.

Knowledge: Medical centers within the Kaiser Permanente system utilized the
story of the vincristine misadministration death as well as their own stories
about medication errors in order to capture both the hearts and the minds of
all medical center employees and physicians. Wrapping the organizational
error data in stories is a strategy that has been incorporated into all system
safety programs at Kaiser Permanente. The latest tactic to enhance storytelling
has been the adoption of videoethnography and its use to capture stories
directly from patients and staff. The organization found that leaders, staff and
physicians responded favorably to actual stories about the impact of error on
patients and their families. Many KP medical centers now begin meetings by
sharing knowledge of error through stories prior to presentations of evidence
and data. At some sessions, pictures of the patients harmed are shown along
with the story to personalize the impact. The use of videoethnography has
been successful. The Kaiser Permanente Care Management Institute now
provides a two-day training program that incorporates films of patient and/
or staff members telling their stories of both positive and negative experiences.
Individuals who participate in the training now have the ability to record
additional stories in an effort to share knowledge organization-wide.

Taking Steps Toward a Dream State: The Leadership Angle

As with other culture and safety change initiatives, the EI&K improvement ball should start and stop at the foot of leadership. The change in EI&K behaviors and how they intersect, support and scuttle safe care will require: motivation for the change; investigation to identify what should be changed; and, innovation to determine the most effective and efficient ways to make change to support improvement. Lessons from Kaiser Permanente demonstrate that robust utilization of information, the experiences of organizations, evidence and staff knowledge can be applied to adapt internal systems to improve safety.

"As with other culture and safety change initiatives, the EI&K improvement ball should start and stop at the foot of leadership."

Effectively translating the Kaiser Permanente experience to impact the healthcare system at large, however, will take motivation, investigation and innovation. Suggested avenues to achieve movement in these directions follow below.

Motivate: How can healthcare drive change in EI&K processes and relationships as both safety and failure enablers? As with other safety issues, leaders must engage staff, physicians, management and patients to:

- Seek evidence and knowledge even though they feel informed or think their staff members are informed.

- Identify and apply information and evidence in a highly-reliable fashion and track it as other care processes are.

- Determine the appropriate funding in a challenging economic environment for healthcare providers and health insurers.

- See and design improvements in EI&K identification and sharing processes from a systems thinking perspective to identify what works, highlight potential failure modes and explore these elements when failures occur from a learning perspective.

- Modify work processes to support effective EI&K behaviors to enable individuals, teams and organizations to learn through sharing knowledge supported by evidence.

- Invite staff from different silos with EI&K expertise (librarians, drug information specialists (Brand and Kraus 2006), clinical informaticists and knowledge managers) to participate in their work.

- Treat EI&K workarounds as action signifying the need to generate investigation and innovation.

- Create momentum for thinking outside of mental models that limit improvement by connecting EI&K work as a core safety element.

Investigate: What does healthcare need to know to substantiate what parts of EI&K processes and philosophies should be changed to support safe care? To improve processes, leaders must ensure that staff, physicians, management and patients are enabled to:

- Use evidence identification and access processes in reliable fashion.

- Report decision making on non-complete results (as what described earlier in the Roche case) so incidence and impact can be measured.

- Make efforts to understand the reasons why EI&K is not reliably applied and create synergies aligned with quality and safety improvement to enhance those efforts (Smith et al. 2012; Glasziou, Ogrinc and Goodman 2011).

- Operationalize the reporting of EI&K failures to help gain awareness of broad-based problems to be addressed at an organizational, specialty or industry level.

- Minimize the murkiness of EI&K elements in their organization to reduce miscommunciation and inertia in driving innovations, to support improvments in its use and resources supporting EI&K enhancements.

- Explore forcing functions and human factors elements to enhance EI&K sharing, identification and application as a safety condition to minimize workarounds that bury the problem.

- Define a standard and skill set specific to EI&K reliability to inform hiring and training decisions to enhance the process and support it with resources.

- Make institutional knowledge available through effective capture of what leaving experts instill in processes prior to their exiting the system (DeLong 2004).

Innovate: How can healthcare use EI&K failures, near misses and successes to drive learning and contribute new tools to patient safety improvement? EI&K practice must be transformed so staff, physicians, mnanage and patients can:

- Establish effective measures to demonstrate the value and impact of the EI&K continuum on patient safety.

- Bring new thinking to EI&K processes to translate successes from other industries into healthcare.

- Enhance knowledge exchange to design EI&K distribution mechanisms to enable effective spread of lessons learned and sustainably of resulting improvements.

- Capitalize on new technologies (video, simulation, social media) and forms of practice and personal behavior to enhance the use of what is known.

- Enable a process to confirm that information and evidence is received and acted upon to enhance the sustainability of the improvements and subsequent learning from experience with them over time.

Taking Steps Toward Realizing the Vision

THE CLINICIAN/EI&K USER ANGLE

Once leadership sets the stage for improvement, the sharp end is what "makes the engine run." Accountability, while seen as being an organizational responsibility, is being shifted to the sharp end (Wachter 2013). Therefore, a sense of accountability toward EI&K use must be established and infused into the sharp end to ensure success, safety and sustainability of improvements. To generate this engagement, clinicians and EI&K users should:

- Not be comfortable with the status quo and do without EI&K because the organization hasn't enabled robust EI&K functionality.

- Report problems with evidence access as near misses or failures in the event reporting system at their organization.

- See information and evidence access workarounds as problems waiting to happen.

- Participate in EI&K sharing initiatives; to fail to do so creates weaknesses in the processes and systems in place.

- Emphasize thorough and effective literature searches done by trained and appropriate personnel to identify existing evidence and information for clinical care, process improvement and organizational improvement work.

- Minimize the hierarchy that squashes knowledge seeking through storytelling, water cooler interaction and face-to-face conversation.

- Build awareness amongst their colleagues, patients and those involved in safety and clinical quality improvement on the importance of EI&K.

- Seek to be trained on how to use tools and build multidisciplinary, non-hierarchical networks to seek and share appropriate evidence, information and knowledge.

- Engage workers across the sharp end–blunt end continuum in the design of processes to enhance their use of EI&K.

THE LIBRARIAN/INFORMATIONIST ANGLE

> *It is time to build a medical information delivery system worthy of the medical profession (Davidoff and Miglus 2011).*

A premise of this text is that a gap in expertise exists too often in EI&K work in hospitals that serves to open the door to failure: trained information professionals' lack of active involvement in the work of safety improvement of the systems they touch. Exploratory surveys have supported this reality (Zipperer and Sykes 2009). Yet the responsibility for ameliorating this situation lies with leadership, staff clinicians and the professionals whose impact has yet to be fully operationalized in safety work (Zipperer 2004; Bandy, Stemmer-Frumento and Langman 2009). To support this needed change of information professionals' role, healthcare should:

- Set implementable, measureable standards for what constitutes "thorough and effective" EI&K seeking that are useful from the sharp end to the blunt end. These should apply for where the searching takes place and make sense in the process of daily work.

- Hold management and leadership accountable for resourcing EI&K effectiveness.

- Design EI&K management systems to track developing bodies of evidence and information on safety issues – just as with the New York MRI incident, all vincristine administration errors that have occurred since 1991 have occurred against a backdrop of official recommendations for processes to prevent such errors (Gilk and Latino 2010). This includes a system for monitoring the literature of emerging safety recommendations, and for consulting the evidence when developing programs, processes and safety recommendations internally. It also would build out into knowledge maps to enable healthcare at large to build on what is known by individuals yet not available in the evidence or information (Zipperer, Gluck and Anderson 2002; Davenport and Prusak 1998).

- Build awareness in the librarian/informationist profession that EI&K failures are a systems issue and go beyond the traditional skills of organization, identification and dissemination of materials.

- Provide reliable access to EI&K expertise and resources – ideally through bundled internal EI&K resources such as librarian/informationists, information button programs, decision support infused within EHR programs, maintained and designed electronic libraries (Davidoff and Miglus 2011). If the expertise and resources cannot all be in-house, enable external access reliably through consortium agreements, contractors or partnerships.

- Involve librarians/informationists in background research for improvement ideas.

Employing EI&K for Patient Safety: Sharing Accountability for Success

> *The issue has very little to do with the will or capability of human beings, who almost never intend errors to happen. It has a lot to do with whether leaders, board members, and managers employ the best available knowledge about safe designs for tasks, equipment, rules, and environments instead of relying on outmoded traditions and impoverished theories about motivation and "trying harder" (Berwick 2002: 49–50).*

Errors in healthcare resulting in catastrophe are difficult. More problematic still would be awareness after the fact the EI&K that may have altered the chain of events was available to be applied to fill a hole in the Swiss Cheese, yet was not. As a part of the fast pace of care delivery – whether on the sharp end or blunt end – stopping a process due to lack of EI&K isn't always an option. If clinicians stopped to do a literature search, hold a focus group or call a librarian to inform every decision they made, care would cease to be delivered in a reasonable fashion. However, knowing when to "stop the line" due to omission of application of EI&K at certain defined points of the process could shed light on what priorities should be addressed and how.

EI&K missteps, gaps and errors aren't typically a part of the discussion of safety improvement. They are "under the radar" and represent a latent condition of failure. A change in the discourse is required so missteps, gaps and errors are explicit, and individuals and organization can learn from them. Distinct types of EI&K failures should be tracked and successes shared. New partnerships should be built, with publishers, librarians/informationists, clinicians, risk managers, database designers, patients, volunteers and leadership etc. to scrutinize the status quo and challenge it, including decipher the problems and challenge EI&K access barriers as safety problems (Wallace 2012).

As illustrated by several stories, such as the exchange between Lucian Leape and the Harvard librarian (AHRQ 2006), the evidence omission of the Hopkins team affecting the care of Ellen Roche (Perkins 2001), and the lack of clinician acceptance of patient/family provided evidence (Barnett and Barnett n.d.), it is evident that the EI&K sharing continuum can affect the safety of care. EI&K sharing has the potential to stop bias at both the sharp and blunt ends, reduce omissions and alter decision-making (Marshall et al. 2013), package knowledge and evidence into information tools that work (i.e., checklists, per Pronovost and Vohr 2010), and engage patients in their own care and in identifying and shaping effective sustainable safety solutions.

This is the age of increased access to unprecedented information, evidence and knowledge. Yet, "available knowledge is too rarely applied to improve the care experience, and information generated by the care experience is too rarely gathered to improve the knowledge available" (Smith et al. 2012: Summary 1). Healthcare has been challenged to use these resources to enable its own learning (Smith et al. 2012). The complexity of the process, the rapidly changing landscape and the increased demands only accentuate the incredible challenges for healthcare EI&K use and its application to assure safety.

Can healthcare professionals allow the industry to be a laggard in understanding this issue? Can they wait for more known errors to happen and wonder if EI&K resources could prevent failure? It remains to be seen.

KEY TAKE-AWAYS

- Sentinel cases can serve as a platform to explore where and how things might have gone wrong and how poor EI&K processes can contribute to system failure.
- Learning from response to sentinel cases is improved through effective use of EIK at an individual and organizational level.
- Discussions of EI&K failure and successes at this level of specificity have yet to become infused in how healthcare explores system failure. This view can generate new approaches if embraced and the appropriate experts are involved.

Suggested Reading

Graham, S. et al. 2012. Medication safety: Reducing error through improvement programs, in *The Nurses Role in Medication Safety*, edited by L. Cima and S. Clark. Oakbrook Terrace, IL: Joint Commission Resources.

March, J.G., Sproull, L.S. and Tamuz, M. 2003. Learning from samples of one or fewer. *Quality & Safety in Health Care*, 12(6), 465–71.

Wachter, R. and Shojania, K. 2004. *Internal Bleeding: The Truth Behind America's Terrifying Epidemic of Medical Mistakes*. New York, NY: Rugged Land.

References

Association of Academic Health Sciences Libraries (AAHSL). 2013. *2011–2012 Annual Statistics of Medical School Libraries in the United States and Canada*, 35th edition. Seattle, WA: AAHS.

Abbas, J., Schwartz, D.G. and Krause, R. 2010. Emergency medical residents' use of Google for answering clinical questions in the emergency room. *Proceedings of the American Society of Information Science and Technology*, 47, 1–4.

Ackoff, R.L. 1974. *Redesigning the Future: A Systems Approach to Societal Problems*. New York: John Wiley and Sons.

Ackoff, R.L. 1981. *Creating the Corporate Future: Plan or Be Planned For*. New York, NY: Wiley.

Ackoff, R.L. 2006. *Idealized Design*. Philadelphia, PA: Wharton Business School Press.

Agency for Healthcare Research and Quality. 2002. *AHRQ Research Relevant to Understanding the Impact of Working Conditions on Patient Safety*. Rockville, MD: AHRQ. [Online]. Available at: http://www.ahrq.gov/research/findings/factsheets/errors-safety/workfact/working-conditions-and-patient-safety.pdf [accessed: March 25, 2014].

Agency for Healthcare Research and Quality. 2003. *AHRQ's Patient Safety Initiative: Building Foundations, Reducing Risk*. [Online]. Available at: http://www.ahrq.gov/qual/pscongrpt/ [accessed: March 25, 2013].

Agency for Healthcare Research and Quality. 2006. In conversation with ... Lucian Leape, MD. *AHRQ WebM&M*. [Online]. Available at: http://webmm.ahrq.gov/perspective.aspx?perspectiveID=28 [accessed: March 15, 2013].

Agency for Healthcare Research and Quality. 2012. *Patient Safety Primers: Medication Reconciliation*. [Online]. Available at: http://www.psnet.ahrq.gov/primer.aspx?primerID=1 [accessed: March 29, 2013].

Agency for Healthcare Research and Quality. 2013. *FY 2013 Congressional Justification Overview of AHRQ Budget Request By Portfolio*. [Online]. Available at http://www.ahrq.gov/about/mission/budget/2013/web13over.pdf [accessed: March 20, 2013].

Agency for Healthcare Research and Quality, Patient Safety Network. *Patient Safety Primers: Systems Approach*. [Online]. Available at: http://psnet.ahrq.gov/primer.aspx?primerID=21 [accessed: September 24, 2012].

Agency for Healthcare Research and Quality. 2013. *Guide to Patient and Family Engagement in Hospital Quality and Safety*. Rockville, MD: Agency for Healthcare Research and Quality. Available at: http://www.ahrq.gov/professionals/systems/hospital/engagingfamilies/patfamilyengageguide/index.html [accessed: January 24, 2014].

Aitken, E.M., et al. 2011. Involving clinical librarians at the point of care: Results of a controlled intervention. *Academic Medicine*, 86(12), 1508–12.

Alligood, E., Jones, B., Williams, L. and Zipperer, L. *Hierarchy of Actions – Librarian/Information-centric Examples*. [Presentation handouts]. Diagnostic Error: Team Up and Tackle it. Medical Library Association Annual Conference, Minneapolis, MN, May 13, 2011.

Alper, B.S. et al. 2004. How much effort is needed to keep up with the literature relevant for primary care? *Journal of the Medical Library Association*, 92(4), 429–37.

Amalberti, R. et al. 2005. Five system barriers to achieving ultrasafe health care. *Annals of Internal Medicine*, 142(9), 756–64.

American Health Information Management Association (AHIMA). 2012. What is the difference between ARRA and HITECH? [Online]. Available at: http://www.ahima.org/advocacy/arrahitech.aspx#difference [accessed: September 1, 2012].

American Broadcasting Service (ABC). 1982. The deep sleep: 6,000 will die or suffer brain damage. *20/20*. New York, NY: ABC.

American Nurses Association. 2011. *Mandatory Overtime: Summary of State Approaches*. Available at: http://nursingworld.org/MainMenuCategories/Policy-Advocacy/State/Legislative-Agenda-Reports/MandatoryOvertime/Mandatory-Overtime-Summary-of-State-Approaches.html [accessed: April 1, 2013].

American Public Health Association. 2003. *Deep-Vein Thrombosis: Advancing Awareness to Protect Patient Lives*. [White Paper]. Public Health Leadership Conference on Deep-Vein Thrombosis Washington, DC, February 26, 2003. Available at: http://www.apha.org/NR/rdonlyres/A209F84A-7C0E-4761-9ECF-61D22E1E11F7/0/DVT_White_Paper.pdf [accessed: April 1, 2013].

American Society of Hospital Pharmacists. 1993. ASSP guidelines on preventing medication errors in hospitals. *American Journal of Hospital Pharmacists*, 50, 302–14.

Anderson, J., Wagner, J., Bessesen, M. and Williams, L.C. 2012. Usability testing in the hospital. *Human Factors and Ergonomics in Manufacturing and Service Industries*, 22(1), 52–63.

Ans, M. and Tricot, A. 2009. Information seeking in documents by pilots: Assessment of the reliability problems caused by the transition from paper to electronic. *Safety Science*, 47(9), 1241–7.

Arbous, M.S. et al. 2005. Impact of anesthesia management characteristics on M&M. *Anesthesiology*, 102(2), 257–68.

Argyris, C. and Schon, D. 1978. *Organizational Learning*. Reading, MA: Addison-Wesley.

Auerbach, A.D., Landefeld, C.S. and Shojania, K.G. 2007. The tension between needing to improve care and knowing how to do it. *New England Journal of Medicine*, 357(6), 608–13.

Bagian, J.P. 2012. Health care and patient safety: The failure of traditional approaches – how human factors and ergonomics can and MUST help. *Human Factors and Ergonomics in Manufacturing and Service Industry*, 22(1), 1–6.

Bagian, J.P. et al. 2002. VA's root cause analysis system in action. *The Joint Commission Journal on Quality Improvement*, 28(10), 531–45.

Baker, D.P., Gustafson, S., Beaubien, J., Salas, E. and Barach, P. 2005. *Medical Teamwork and Patient Safety: The Evidence-based Relation*. Rockville, MD: Agency for Healthcare Research and Quality. Available at: http://www.ahrq.gov/research/findings/final-reports/medteam/index.html

Banja, J. 2010. The normalization of deviance in healthcare delivery. *Business Horizons*, 53(2), 139–48.

Balik, B. et al. 2011. *Achieving an Exceptional Patient and Family Experience of Inpatient Hospital Care*. Cambridge, MA: Institute for Healthcare Improvement.

Bandy M., Stemmer-Frumento, K.R. and Langman, M.M. 2009. *Patient Safety – Roles for Librarians*. [Online]. Chicago, IL: Medical Library Association. Available at: http://www.mlanet.org/government/positions/patient-safety.html [accessed: November 17, 2012].

Bandy, M., Condon, J. and Graves, E. 2008. Participating in communities of practice. *Medical Reference Service Quarterly*, 27(4), 441–9.

Banks, D.E. et al. 2007. Decreased hospital length of stay associated with presentation of cases at morning report with librarian support. *Journal of the Medical Library Association*, 95(4), 381–7.

Banzi, R., et al. 2010. A review of online evidence-based practice point-of-care information summary providers. *Journal of Medical Internet Research*, 12(3), e26.

Banzi, R., et al. 2011. Speed of updating online evidence based point of care summaries: Prospective cohort analysis. *British Medical Journal*, 343(22), d5856.

Barach, P. and Moss, F. 2001. QHC to become QSHC …. *Quality in Health Care.* [Online]. 10(4), 199–200. Available at: doi: 10.1136/qhc.0100199 [accessed: June 24, 2012].

Barnard, P., Napier, J. and Zipperer, L. 2014. What is knowledge anyway?, in *Knowledge Management in Healthcare,* edited by L. Zipperer. London: Gower.

Barnett, G.O., et al. 2008. Senior member presentation proposal. DXplain – 20 years later – what have we learned? *American Medical Informatics Association Annual Symposium Proceedings,* 1201–2.

Barnett, T. and Barnett, P. Do No Harm, Jess' Story. [Online]. Available at: http://www.projectjessica.ca/ [accessed: November 17, 2012].

Barr, D.P. 1955. Hazards of modern diagnosis and therapy – the price we pay. *The Journal of the American Medical Association,* 159, 1452–56.

Baseball Almanac [Reproduced]. Available at: http://www.baseball-almanac.com/humor4.shtml

Bates, D.W. et al. 1998. Effect of computerized physician order entry and a team intervention on prevention of serious medication errors. *Journal of the American Medical Association,* 280(15), 1311–16.

Bates, D.W. et al. 1999. The impact of computerized physician order entry on medication error prevention. *Journal of the American Medical Informatics Association,* 6(4), 313–21.

Battles, J.B. et al. 2006. Sensemaking of patient safety risks and hazards. *Health Services Research,* 41(4), 1555–75.

Bauder, L. April 13, 2012. *LinkedIn Group KM Practitioner's Group.*

Beach, C. 2006. *Lost in Transition.* [Online]. Available at: http://webmm.ahrq.gov/case.aspx?caseID=116 [accessed: July 5, 2012].

Becker, L. 2001. *Report of Internal Investigation into the Death of a Volunteer Research Subject.* [Online]. Baltimore, MD: Johns Hopkins University. Available at: http://www.hopkinsmedicine.org/press/2001/JULY/report_of_internal_investigation.htm [accessed: October 7, 2012].

Beisecker, A.E. and Beisecker, T.D. 1990. Patient information-seeking behaviors when communicating with doctors. *Medical Care,* 28, 19–28.

Bennet, N.L. et al. 2004. Physicians' Internet information-seeking behaviors. *Journal of Continuing Education of Health Professions,* 24(1), 31–8.

Bennett, N.L., et al. 2005. Family physicians' information seeking behaviors: A survey compared with other specialists. *BMC Medical Informatics and Decision Making,* 22(5), 9. Available at: http://www.biomedcentral.com/1472-6947/5/9 [accessed: April 6, 2013].

Beresford, L. 2010. Change you should believe in: Care transitions challenge hospitalists to improve systems, communications. *The Hospitalist,* 14(7). Available at: http://www.the-hospitalist.org/details/article/747213/Change_You_Should_Believe_In.html [accessed: September 24, 2012].

Bergman, M.K. 2001. The Deep Web: Surfacing hidden value. *The Journal of Electronic Publishing* [Online], 7(1). Available at: http://dx.doi.org/10.3998/3336451.0007.104 [accessed: April 28, 2012].

Bernal-Delgado, E. and Fisher, E.S. 2008. Abstracts in high profile journals often fail to report harm. *BMC Medical Research Methodology* [Online], (8)1. Available at: http://www.biomedcentral.com/1471-2288/8/14 [accessed: April 28, 2012].

Berner, E.S. and Graber, M.L. 2008. Overconfidence as a cause of diagnostic error in medicine. *American Journal of Medicine*, 1(5 Suppl.), S2–S23.

Berwanger, O. et al. 2009. The quality of reporting of trial abstracts is suboptimal: Survey of major general medical journals. *Journal of Clinical Epidemiology*, 62(4), 387–92.

Berwick, D.M. 1989. Continuous improvement as an ideal in health care. *New England Journal of Medicine*, 320(1), 53–6.

Berwick, D.M. 2002. Escape Fire [Online]. Commonwealth Fund. Available at: http://www.commonwealthfund.org/usr_doc/berwick_escapefire_563.pdf [accessed: November 17, 2012].

Berwick, D.M. 2004. *Escape Fire: Designs for the Future of Health Care*. San Francisco, CA: Jossey-Bass.

Berwick, D.M. 2005. Broadening the view of evidence-based medicine. *Quality and Safety in Healthcare*, 14(5), 315–16.

Berwick, D.M. 2008. The science of improvement. *Journal of the American Medical Association*, 299(10), 1182–4.

Bigelow, B. and Arndt, M. 2003. Teaching evidence-based management: Where do we go from here? *Journal of Health Administration Education*, 20(4), 305–12.

Billings, C. 1998. Incident reporting systems in medicine and experience with the aviation safety reporting systems, in *A Tale of Two Stories: Contrasting Views of Patient Safety*, edited by R.I. Cook, D.D. Woods, and C. Miller. Chicago, IL: National Patient Safety Foundation.

Berwick, D.M. and Leape, L.L. (eds). 2000. Reducing error, improving safety. *British Medical Journal*, Theme Issue (March 18), 320(7237).

Bix, L. 2002. The elements of text and message design and their impact on message legibility: A literature review. *Journal of Design Communication* [Online], 4. Available at: http://scholar.lib.vt.edu/ejournals/JDC/Spring-2002/bix.html.

Bjork, B.C., et al. 2010. Open access to the scientific journal literature: Situation 2009. *PLoS ONE* [Online], 5(6), e11273. Available at: http://www.plosone.org/article/info:doi/10.1371/journal.pone.0011273 [accessed: April 28, 2012].

Boal, K.B. and Schultz, P.L. 2007. Storytelling, time and evolution: The role of strategic leadership in complex adaptive systems. *Leadership Quarterly*, 18, 411–28.

Bogner, M.S. (ed.) 1994. *Human Error in Medicine*. Hillsdale, NJ: Lawrence Erlbaum Associates.

Bohmner, R.M.J. (ed.) 2009. *Designing Care*. Boston, MA: Harvard Business Press.

Bonis, P.A., et al. 2008. Association of a clinical knowledge support system with improved patient safety, reduced complications and shorter length of stay among Medicare beneficiaries in acute care hospitals in the United States. *International Journal of Medical Informatics*, 77(11), 745–53.

Bordeaux, J. for the Knowledge Management Working Group. 2008. *Complexity Annotated Bibliography Prepared for the Center for the Study of the Presidency, Project on National Security Reform*. Available at: http://0183896.netsolhost.com/site/wp-content/uploads/2011/11/complexity-annotated-bibliography.pdf [accessed: February 13, 2013].

Bosk, C. 1979. *Forgive and Remember: Managing Medical Failure*. Chicago, IL: University of Chicago Press.

Bosk, C.L. et al. 2009. Reality check for checklists. *The Lancet* [Online], 374(9688), 444–5.

Boyd, C.M. et al. 2005. Clinical practice guidelines and quality of care for older patients with multiple comorbid diseases: Implications for pay for performance. *Journal of the American Medical Association*, 294(6), 716–24.

Brandes, S. 2007. Experience and outcomes of medical librarian rounding. *Medical Reference Services Quarterly*, 26(4), 85–92.

Brennan, T.A. et al. 1991. Incidence of adverse events and negligence in hospitalized patients. Results of the Harvard Medical Practice Study I. *New England Journal of Medicine*, 324(6), 370–76.

Brettle, A., et al. 2011. Evaluating clinical librarian services: A systematic review. *Health Information and Libraries Journal*, 28(1), 3–22.

Bronander, K.P. et al. 2004. Boolean search experience and abilities of medical students and practicing physicians. *Teaching and Learning in Medicine*, 16(3), 284–9.

Brown, J. 2004. Achieving high reliability: Other industries can help health care's safety transformation. *ASHRM Journal*, 24(2), 15–25.

Brown, J. P. 2004. Structuring communication for team-based error management. *Journal of Healthcare Risk Management*, 24(4), 13–20.

Brown, J.P. 2005. Key themes in healthcare safety dilemmas, in *Safety Ethics: Cases from Aviation, Healthcare and Occupational Environmental Health*, edited by M. Patankar, J.P. Brown and M.D. Treadwell. Aldershot: Ashgate.

Brown, J., Tonkel, J. and Classen, D. 2013. Using technology to enhance safety, in *The Essential Guide for Patient Safety Officers, Second Edition*, edited by A. Frankel, M. Leonard, F. Federico, K. Frush and C. Haraden. Oakbrook Terrace, IL: The Joint Commission.

Brown, J.P. 2008. Collaborative cross-checking, in *Improving Health Care Team Communication: Building on Lessons from Aviation and Aerospace*, edited by C.P. Nemeth. Chicago, IL: Ashgate, 155–78.

Burt, H. *Selected Articles on Patient Safety and Libraries and Librarians*. [Bibliography] Patient Safety Resource Seminar: Librarians on the Front Lines. National Networks of Libraries of Medicine. Available at: http://nnlm. gov/training/patientsafety/cama-bibliography.pdf [accessed: January 24, 2014].

Butler, K. April 18, 2012. *LinkedIn Group Patient Safety Professionals*.

Byrd, G.D. and Shedlock, J. 2003. The Association of Academic Health Sciences Libraries annual statistics: An exploratory twenty-five-year trend analysis. *Journal of the Medical Library Association*, 91(2), 186–202.

Cabana, M.D. et al. 1999. Why don't physicians follow clinical practice guidelines? A framework for improvement. *Journal of the American Medical Association*, 282(15), 1458–65.

Campbell, R. and Ash, J. 2006. An evaluation of five bedside information products using a user-centered, task-oriented approach. *Journal of the Medical Library Association*, 94(4), 435–41, e206–7.

Carayon, P. 2007. *Handbook of Human Factors and Ergonomics in Health Care and Patient Safety*. Hillsdale, NJ: Lawrence Erlbaum Associates, 3–19.

Cardiff, K. 2008. Is quality safety? Is safety quality? MS Thesis, Lund University, Ljungbyhed, Sweden. [Online: Lund University]. Available at: http://www. leonardo.lth.se/uploads/media/thesis-2007-Cardiff-Is_Quality_Safety_Is_ Safety_Quality.pdf [accessed: June 24, 2012].

Cardiff, K. et al. 2008. Is safety quality? Is quality safety? 3rd International Symposium on Resilience Engineering, Juan-les-Pins, France, 28–30 October 2008. Available at: http://www.resilience-engineering.org/RE3/papers/Cardiff _Sheps_Nyce_Dekker_text.pdf [accessed: 24 June 2012].

Carthey, J. et al. 2011. Breaking the rules: Understanding non-compliance with policies and guidelines. *British Medical Journal (Clinical Research Edition)*, 343, d5283.

Carney, M. 2011. Influence of organizational culture on quality healthcare delivery. *International Journal of Health Care Quality Assurance*, 24(7), 523–39.

CBS News. 2008. Dennis Quaid recounts twins' drug ordeal. *60 Minutes* [Online]. Available at: http://www.cbsnews.com/2100-18560_162-3936412. html [accessed: April 4, 2012].

Chabris, C. and Simons, D. 2010. *The Invisible Gorilla: and Other Ways Our Intuitions Deceive Us*. New York, NY: Crown Publishing Group.

Chan, P.S. et al. 2010. Rapid response teams: A systematic review and meta-analysis. *Archives of Internal Medicine*, 170(1), 18–26.

Chang, A. et al. 2005. The JCAHO patient safety event taxonomy: A standardized terminology and classification schema for near misses and adverse events. *International Journal for Quality in Health Care*, 17, 95–105.

Chassin, M.R. 2013. The quality of health care: What's taking so long? *Health Affairs (Millwood)*, 32 (10), 1761–5

Chassin, M.R. and Loeb, J.M. 2011. The ongoing quality improvement journey: Next stop, high reliability. *Health Affairs (Millwood)*, 30, 559–68.

Chassin, M.R. and Loeb, J. 2013. High-reliability health care: Getting there from here. *The Milbank Quarterly*, 91 (3), 459–90.

Cheston, C.C., Flickinger, T.E., Chisolm, M.S. 2013. Social media use in medical education: A systematic review. *Academic Medicine*. 88(6), 893–901.

Choo, C.W. 2005. Information failures and organizational disasters. *MIT Sloan Management Review*, 46(3), 8–10.

Chung, M. et al. 2012. Safe infant sleep recommendations on the internet: Let's Google it. *Journal of Pediatrics*, 161(6), 1080–84.

Churchman, C.W. 1979. *The Systems Approach and its Enemies*. New York, NY: Basic Books.

Cimino, J.J. 2006. Use, usability, usefulness, and impact of an infobutton manager. *American Medical Informatics Association Annual Symposium Proceedings 2006*, 151–5.

Cimino, J.J. 2008. Infobuttons: Anticipatory passive decision support. *American Medical Informatics Association Annual Symposium Proceedings 2008*, 1203–4.

Cimino, J.J., Elhanan, G. and Zeng, Q. 1997. Supporting infobuttons with terminological knowledge. *American Medical Informatics Association Annual Symposium Proceedings 1997*, 528–32.

Cimino, J.J. et al. 2003. Use of online resources while using a clinical information system. *American Medical Informatics Association Annual Symposium Proceedings 2003*, 175–9.

Cimino, J.J. et al. 2007. Redesign of the Columbia University infobutton manager. *American Medical Informatics Association Annual Symposium Proceedings 2007*, 135–9.

Citrome, L. 2007. Impact factor? Shmimpact factor! The journal impact factor, modern day literature searching, and the publication process. *Psychiatry*, 4(5), 54–7.

Clark, S. and Horton, R. 2010. Putting research into context – revisited. *The Lancet*, 376(9734), 10–11.

Clancy, C.M. and Reinertsen, J.L. (eds). 2006. Keeping our promises: Research, practice, and policy issues in health care reliability. *Health Services Research* [Special Issue], 41, 535–1720.

Classen, D.C. et al. 2011. 'Global Trigger Tool' shows that adverse events in hospitals may be ten times greater than previously measured. *Health Affairs*, 30, 581–9.

Cohen, M.D., Hilligoss, B. and Kajdacsy-Balla, A.C. 2012. A handoff is not a telegram: An understanding of the patient is co-constructed. *Critical Care*, 16, 303.

Collins, M.F. and Peel, D.C. 2012. Big issues (A special report) – should every patient have a unique ID number for all medical records? *Wall Street Journal*, January 23, 4-R.4

Committee for Data Standards for Patient Safety, Institute of Medicine and Aspden, P., Corrigan, J.M., Wolcott, J. and Erickson, S.M. (eds). 2004. *Patient Safety: Achieving a New Standard of Care*. Washington, DC: The National Academies Press.

Committee on Identifying and Preventing Medication Errors and Aspden, P., Corrigan, J.M., Wolcott, J. and Erickson, S.M. (eds). 2007. *Preventing Medication Errors*. Washington, DC: The National Academies Press.

Committee on Quality of Health Care in America, Institute of Medicine. 2001. *Crossing the Quality Chasm: A New Health System for the 21st Century*. Washington, DC: National Academies Press.

Committee on Standards for Systematic Reviews of Comparative Effectiveness Research, Institute of Medicine. 2011. *Finding What Works in Health Care: Standards for Systematic Reviews* [Online], edited by J. Eden, et al. Washington, DC: Institute of Medicine.

Committee on Patient Safety and Health Information Technology, Board on Health Care Services, Institute of Medicine. 2011. *Health IT and Patient Safety: Building Safer Systems for Better Care*. Washington, DC: National Academies Press.

Conway, J. 2008. Could it happen here? Learning from other organizations' safety errors. *Healthcare Executive*, 23(6), 64–7.

Conway, J. 2008. Getting boards on board: Engaging governing boards in quality and safety. *Joint Commission Journal on Quality and Patient Safety*, 34(4), 214–20.

Cook, R.I. 2003. Lessons from the war on cancer: The need for basic research on safety. *Journal of Patient Safety*, 1(1), 7–8.

Cook, R. 2003. Seeing is believing. *Annals of Surgery*, 237(4), 472–3.

Cook, R.I. 2013. Resilience, the second story, and progress on patient safety, in E. Hollnagel, J. Braithwaite and R.L. Wears (eds), *Resilient Health Care*. Farnham: Ashgate, 19–26.

Cook, R.I. and Woods, D.D. 1994. Operating at the sharp end, in *Human Error in Medicine*, edited by M.S. Bogner. Hillsdale, NJ: Lawrence Erlbaum Associates, 264.

Cook, R.I., Woods, D.D. and Miller, C. 1998. *A Tale of Two Stories: Contrasting Views of Patient Safety – Report from a Workshop on Assembling the Scientific Basis for Progress on Patient Safety.* Chicago, IL: National Patient Safety Foundation.

Cooper, I.D. 2011. Is the informationist a new role? A logic model analysis. *Journal of the Medical Library Association*, 99(3), 189–92.

Cooper, J.B., Newbower, R.S., Long, C.D. and McPeek, B. Preventable anesthesia mishaps: A study of human factors. *Anesthesiology*, December 1978, 49(6), 399–406.

Cooper, J.D. and Feder, H.M., Jr. 2004. Inaccurate information about Lyme disease on the internet. *Pediatric Infectious Disease Journal*, 23(12), 1105–8.

Cordell, T. 2007. Chasing the monster. *North Carolina Medical Journal*, 68, 331–2.

Creaser, C. and White, S. 2008. Trends in journal prices: An analysis of selected journals, 2000–2006. *Learned Publishing*, 21(3), 214–24.

Credo Reference. 2003. Communications and the Arts – Sports – Athletes and Players. *Simpson's Contemporary Quotations*. Boston, MA: Houghton Mifflin, 1988. N. pag. Credo Reference, May 9, 2003.

CRICO. 2009. *Healing the Healer.* [Film]. Cambridge, MA: CRICO.

Croskerry, P. 2000. The cognitive imperative: Thinking about how we think. *Academic Emergency Medicine*, 7, 1223–31.

Croskerry, P. 2009. Context is everything or how could I have been that stupid? *Healthcare Quarterly*, 12(sp), e171–6.

Cross, R. and Prusak, L. 2002. The people who make organizations go – or stop. *Harvard Business Review*, 80(6), 104–12, 106.

Curfman, G.D., Morrissey, A. and Drazen, J.M. 2006. Expression of concern reaffirmed. *The New England Journal of Medicine*, 354(11), 1193.

Curry, L.A., et al. 2011. What distinguishes top-performing hospitals in acute myocardial infarction mortality rates? A qualitative study. *Annals of Internal Medicine*, 154(6), 384–90.

Dalrymple, P.W., et al. 2010. Applying evidence in practice: A qualitative case study of the factors affecting residents' decisions. *Health Informatics Journal*, 16(3), 177–88.

Dana Farber Cancer Institute. 2012. Patient safety rounding toolkit. *Patient Safety Resources*. [Online]. Available at: http://www.dana-farber.org/Adult-Care/Treatment-and-Support/Care-Quality-and-Safety/Patient-Safety-Resources.aspx [accessed: March 16, 2012].

Davenport, T.H. and Prusak, L. 1998. *Working Knowledge: How Organizations Manage What They Know.* Boston, MA: Harvard Business School Press.

Davidoff, F. and Florance, V. 2000. The informationist: A new health profession? *Annals of Internal Medicine*, 132(12), 996–8.

Davidoff, F. and Miglus, J. 2011. Delivering clinical evidence where it's needed: Building an information system worthy of the profession. *Journal of the American Medical Association* [Online], 305(18), 1906–7.

Davies, J.M. 2001. Painful inquiries: Lessons from Winnipeg. *Canadian Medical Association Journal*, 165(11), 1503–4.

Davis, N.M. 2011. *Medical Abbreviations: 32,000 Conveniences at the Expense of Communication and Safety*. 15th edition. Warminster, PA: Neil M. Davis Associates.

Day, C. 2010. Judging journal prices. *Journal of Scholarly Publishing*, 41(2), 145–62.

Deffenbaugh, J.L. 1997. Don't throw out the customer. *International Journal of Health Care Quality Assurance*, 10(1), 35–41.

Degani, A. and Wiener, E.L. 1993. Cockpit checklists: Concepts, design and use. *Human Factors*, 35(2), 28–43.

Dekker, S. 2002. *The Field Guide to Human Error Investigations*. Aldershot: Ashgate Publishing.

Dekker, S.W.A. 2011. *Patient Safety: A Human Factors Approach*. Boca Raton, FL: CRC Press.

De Mestral, C. et al. 2011. Impact of a specialized multidisciplinary tracheostomy team on tracheostomy care in critically ill patients. *Canadian Journal of Surgery*, 54(3), 167–72.

Del Fiol, G. et al. 2012. Implementations of the HL7 context-aware knowledge retrieval ("infobutton") standard: Challenges, strengths, limitations, and uptake. *Journal of Biomedical Informatics*, 45(4), 726–35.

DeLemos, D. et al. 2010. Building trust through communication in the intensive care unit: HICCC. *Pediatric Critical Care Medicine*, 11, 378–84.

Della, M., Lin, M.D. and Kumar, S. 2012. We can all define patient safety … or can we? *Patient Safety and Quality Healthcare* [Online], 9(2), 46–9.

Delong, D.W. 2004. *Lost Knowledge: Confronting the Threat of an Aging Workforce*. New York and Oxford: Oxford University Press.

Denham, C.R. et al. 2008. Are you listening … Are you really listening? *Journal of Patient Safety*, 4(3), 148–61.

Denning, S. 2004. Telling tales. *Harvard Business Review*, 82(5), 122–9, 152.

Department of Health. 2000. *An Organisation With a Memory* [Online: Department of Health]. Available at: http://www.dh.gov.uk/prod_consum_dh/groups/dh_digitalassets/@dh/@en/documents/digitalasset/dh_4065086.pdf [accessed: June 24, 2012].

Department of Health, National Health Service. 2001. *Building a Safer NHS for Patients: Implementing an Organisation with a Memory*. London: Crown Publishing. Available at: http://www.dh.gov.uk/prod_consum_dh/groups/dh_digitalassets/@dh/@en/documents/digitalasset/dh_4058094.pdf

Department of Defense and the Agency for Healthcare Research and Quality. *TeamSTEPPS, Team Strategies and Tool to Enhance Patient and Provider Safety.* [Online]. Available at: http://teamstepps.ahrq.gov/.

Department of Defense. 1981. *Definitions of Terms for Reliability and Maintainability* (MIL-STD-721C). Washington, DC: Department of Defense.

DeRosier, J. et al. 2002. Using health care failure mode and effect analysis: The VA National Center for Patient Safety's Prospective Risk Analysis System. *The Joint Commission Journal on Quality and Patient Safety*, 28(5), 248–67.

Dervin, B. 2003. Audience as listener and learner, in *Sense-Making Methodology Reader: Selected Writings of Brenda Dervin*, edited by B. Dervin, L. Foreman-Wernet and E. Lauterbach. Cresskill, NJ: Hampton Press.

DeWalt, D.A. 2007. Low health literacy: Epidemiology and interventions. *North Carolina Medical Journal*, 68(5), 327–30.

Diamond, C. 2011. Data and information hub requirements, in *Learning What Works*, edited by L. Olsen, C. Grossmann and J. Michael McGinnis. Washington, DC: The National Academies Press, 163–72.

Dixon, B.E. and Zafar, A. 2009. *Inpatient Computerized Provider Order Entry: Findings from the AHRQ Health IT Portfolio* (AHRQ Publication No. 09-0031-EF). Rockville, MD: Agency for Healthcare Research and Quality.

Dixon, N.M. and Shofer, M. 2006. Struggling to invent high-reliability organizations in health care settings: Insights from the field. *Health Services Research*, 41(4 pt. 2), 1618–32.

Dixon-Woods, M., Bosk, C.L., Aveling, E.L., Goeschel, C.A. and Pronovost, P.J. 2011. Explaining Michigan: Developing an ex post theory of a quality improvement program. *Milbank Quarterly*, 89(2), 167–205. Available at: http://psnet.ahrq.gov/resource.aspx?resourceID=22646

Dixon-Woods, M., Leslie, M., Tarrant, C. and Bion, J. 2013. Explaining matching Michigan: An ethnographic study of a patient safety program. *Implementation Science*, 8, 70.

Dhaliwal, G. 2013. Known unknowns and unknown unknowns at the point of care. JAMA Internal Medicine, 173(21), 1959–61.

Dogan, R. et al. 2009. Understanding PubMed® user search behavior through log analysis. *Database – The Journal of Biological Databases and Curation*, bap018.

Doms, A. and Schroeder, M. 2005. GoPubMed: Exploring PubMed® with the Gene Ontology. *Nucleic Acids Research* [Online], 33, w783-6. Available at: http://www.ncbi.nlm.nih.gov/pmc/articles/PMC1160231/pdf/gki470.pdf [accessed: April 28, 2012].

Dominguez, C. et al. 2005. *Studying and Supporting Collaborative Care Processes.* Paper presented at the Human Factors and Ergonomics Society, June 13, 2005. Available at: http://idea.library.drexel.edu/bitstream/1860/1720/1/2006150058.pdf.

Donahue, A. et al. (2012). Consumer health outreach as a sum of parts: Individual and collective approaches of a health care system's libraries. *Journal of Hospital Librarianship*, 12(1), 6168.

Donchin, Y. 2002. Resuscitation trolleys: Human factors engineering. *Quality and Safety in Health Care*. 11(4), 393.

Donchin, Y. et al. 1995. A look into the nature and causes of human errors in the intensive care unit. *Critical Care Medicine*, 23(2), 294–300.

Dovey, S.M. et al. 2002. A preliminary taxonomy of medical errors in family practice. *Quality and Safety in Health Care*, 11(3), 233–38.

Drucker, P. 1995. "Management science" and the manager. *Management Science*, 1(2), 115–26.

Drucker, P.F. and Wartzman, R. 2010. *The Drucker Lectures*. New York, NY: McGraw Hill.

Duffy, F.D. et al. 2004. Assessing competence in communication and interpersonal skills: The Kalamazoo II report. *Academic Medicine*, 79(6), 495–507.

Duran-Nelson, A., Gladding, S,. Beattie, J. and Nixon, L.J. 2013. Should we Google it? Resource use by internal medicine residents for point-of-care clinical decision making. *Academic Medicine*, 88(6), 788–94.

Dwyer, J. 2012. An infection, unnoticed, turns unstoppable. *New York Times*, July 11, A15.

Dy, C.J. et al. 2011. Does a multidisciplinary team decrease complications in male patients with hip fractures? *Clinical Orthopedics and Related Research*, 469(7), 1919–24.

Edmondson, A. 1999. Psychological safety and learning behavior in work teams. *Administrative Science Quarterly*, 44(2), 350–83.

Edmonson, A. 2003. Managing the risk of learning: Psychological safety in work teams, in *International Handbook of Organizational Teamwork*, edited by M. West, D. Tjosvold and K.G. Smith. Hoboken, NJ: John Wiley & Sons Inc.

Edmondson, A.C. 2011. Strategies for learning from failure. *Harvard Business Review*, Special Failure Issue, 89(4), 48–55.

Edmondson, A.C. 2012. Teamwork on the fly. *Harvard Business Review*, 90(4), 72–80.

Edmondson, A.C., Deillon, J.R. and Roloff, K. 2007. Three perspectives of team learning: Outcomes improvement, task mastery, and group process, in *The Academy of Management Annals*, edited by J.P. Walsh and A.P. Brief. Hillsdale, NY: Psychology Press, 269–314.

Egghe, L. 2011. The single publication H-index and the indirect H-index of a researcher. *Scientometrics*, 88(3), 1003–4.

Eichhorn, J.H. 2010. The APSF at 25: Pioneering success in safety, but challenges remain. *Anaesthesia Patient Safety Foundation Newsletter*, 25(2), 21–44.

Eisenberg, B. and Romero, L. 2010. Restoring the health of scholarly publishing. *Academe*, 96(5), 38–43.

Ely, J.W. et al. 2002. Obstacles to answering doctors' questions about patient care with evidence: Qualitative study. *British Medical Journal*, 324(7339), 710.

Ely, J.W. et al. 2007. Patient-care questions that physicians are unable to answer. *Journal of the American Medical Informatics Association*, 14(4), 407–14.

Emont, S. 2011. *Measuring the Impact of Patient Portals: What the Literature Tells Us*. Oakland, CA: California Healthcare Foundation.

Entwistle, V.A., Mello, M.M. and Brennan, T.A. 2005. Advising patients about patient safety: Current initiatives risk shifting responsibility. *Joint Commission Journal on Quality and Patient Safety*, 31(9), 483–94.

Epstein, R. and Street, R.J. 2007. *Patient-Centered Communication in Cancer Care: Promoting Healing and Reducing Suffering* (NIH Publication No. 07-6225). Bethesda, MD: National Cancer Institute.

Esparza, J. 2010. Clinical library services: outreach to enhance patient care. *Journal of Hospital Librarianship*, 10(2), 170–80.

Evidence-Based Medicine Working Group. 1992. Evidence-based medicine. A new approach to teaching the practice of medicine. *Journal of the American Medical Association*, 268(17), 2420–25.

Eysenbach, G. et al. 2002. Empirical studies assessing the quality of health information for consumers on the World Wide Web: A systematic review. *Journal of the American Medical Association*, 287(20), 2691–700.

Fine, J. 2002. *Harrison*. New York, NY: Simon & Schuster.

Fisher, E.S. and Welch, H.G. 2000. Is this issue a mistake? *Effective Clinical Practice*, 3(6), 290–91.

Fitzpatrick, M. et al. 2011. A novel educational programme to improve knowledge regarding health care-associated infection and hand hygiene. *International Journal of Nursing Practice*, 17(3), 269–74.

Fletcher, K.E. et al. 2004. Systematic review: Effects of resident work hours on patient safety. *Annals of Internal Medicine*, 141(11), 851–7.

Florance, V., Giuse, N.B. and Ketchell, D.S. 2002. Information in context: Integrating information specialists into practice settings. *Journal of the Medical Library Association*, 90(1), 49–58.

Foley, M. 2004. Caring for those who care: A tribute to nurses and their safety. *Online Journal for Issues in Nursing* [Online], 9(3). Available at: http://www.nursingworld.org/MainMenuCategories/ANAMarketplace/ANA Periodicals/OJIN/TableofContents/Volume92004/No3Sept04/Tributeto NursesSafety.html [accessed: March 30, 2013].

Ford, D. 2006. Patient safety: The patient's role. *World Hospitals and Health Services*, 42, 45–8.

Fox, S. 2011. *The Social Life of Health Information, Pew Research Center's Internet and American Life Project*. Washington, DC: Pew Research Center.

Frankel, A. et al. 2003. Patient safety leadership walkrounds. *Joint Commission Journal on Quality and Patient Safety*, 29(1), 16–26.

Frankel, A.S., Leonard, M.W. and Denham, C.R. 2006. Fair and just culture, team behavior, and leadership engagement: The tools to achieve high reliability. *Health Services Research*, 41(4 pt. 2), 1690–709.

Gaba, D.M. 2000. Structural and organizational issues in patient safety: A comparison of health care to other high-hazard industries. *California Management Review*, 43, 1–20.

Gawande, A. 2007. *Better: A Surgeon's Notes on Performance*. New York, NY: Metropolitan Books.

Gawande, A. 2010. *The Checklist Manifesto: How to Get Things Right*. New York, NY: Metropolitan Books.

Gawande, A. 2012. Big med: Should hospitals be more like chain restaurants? *New Yorker*, 88(24), 52–63.

Geerts, W.H., Bergqvist, D., Pineo, G.F., Heit, J.A., Samama, C.M., Lassen, M.R. and Colwell, C.W. and American College of Chest Physicians. 2008. Prevention of venous thromboembolism: American College of Chest Physicians Evidence-Based Clinical Practice Guidelines (8th Edition). *Chest*, 133(6 Suppl), 381S–453S.

Gentile, D.A. 1987. Severe methemoglobinemia induced by a topical teething preparation. *Pediatric Emergency Care*, 3(3), 176–8.

Geary, J. 2007. *Geary's Guide to the World's Great Aphorists*. New York, NY: Bloomsbury.

Gibson, C.B. and Vermeulen, F. 2003. A healthy divide: Subgroups as a stimulus for team learning behaviours. *Administrative Science Quarterly*, 48, 202–39.

Gilk, T. and Latino, R.J. 2011. MRI safety 10 years later. *Patient Safety and Quality Healthcare*, 8(November/December), 22–3, 26–9.

Gillespie, U. et al. 2009. A comprehensive pharmacist intervention to reduce morbidity in patients 80 years or older: A randomized controlled trial. *Archives Internal Medicine*, 1699(9), 894–900.

Ginsburg, L. et al. 2005. An educational intervention to enhance nurse leaders' perceptions of patient safety culture. *Health Services Research*, 40(4), 997–1020.

Glasziou, P., Ogrinc, G. and Goodman, S. 2011. Can evidence-based medicine and clinical quality improvement learn from each other? *BMJ Quality and Safety* [Online] (April 20), Supplement 1, i1–17.

Gleick, J. 1987. *Chaos: Making a New Science*. New York, NY: Viking, 255–56.

Goeschel, C.A., Wachter, R.M and Pronovost, P.J. 2010. Responsibility for quality improvement and patient safety: Hospital board and medical staff leadership challenges. *Chest*, 138(1), 171–8.

Goldacre, B. 2009. *Bad Science*. London: Fourth Estate.

Golder, S. and Loke, Y. 2009. Search strategies to identify information on adverse effects: A systematic review. *Journal of the Medical Library Association*, 97(2), 84–92.

Goldfarb, M., Scheulen, J. and Patch, M. 2012. *Partners in Patient Safety: MCIC Emergency Department Patient Safety Collaborative*. Presented at the 2nd Annual Emergency Care Patient Safety Summit, San Antonio, Texas, March 22, 2012.

Goldstein, M.K. et al. 2004. Translating research into practice: Organizational issues in implementing automated decision support for hypertension in three medical centers. *Journal of the American Medical Informatics Association*, 11(5), 368–76.

Google Inc. *Annual Report 2011*. 2011;000-50726. Available at: http://www.sec.gov/Archives/edgar/data/1288776/000119312512025336/d260164d10k.htm [accessed: March 20, 2013].

Gosbee, J.W. and Gosbee, L.L. 2010. *Using Human Factors Engineering to Improve Patient Safety: Problem Solving on the Front Line*. 2nd Edition. Oakbrook Terrace, IL: Joint Commission Resources.

Gosbee, L.L. 2006. *Exploration of Two Double-check Methods*. Toronto: ISMP Canada. Available at: http://www.ismp-canada.org/download/ISMP%20Canada-Usability%20Test%20Report-Independent%20Double%20Check%20%20June06.pdf [accessed: April 10, 2013].

Governor's Press Office. 2013. Governor Cuomo announces New York state to lead the nation in fighting sepsis – the #1 killer in hospitals – and make major improvements in pediatric care through "Rory's Regulations." Available at: http://www.governor.ny.gov/press/012913-nys-lead-nation-fighting-sepsis

Graber, M. 2007. Diagnostic errors in medicine: What do doctors and umpires have in common? *AHRQ Web M&M* [Online]. Available at: http://webmm.ahrq.gov/perspective.aspx?perspectiveID=36 [accessed: January 27, 2013].

Graber, M.A., Randles, B.D., Ely, J.W. and Monnahan, J. 2008. Answering clinical questions in the ED. *American Journal of Emergency Medicine*, 26(2), 144–7.

Graber, M.A., et al. 2007. What questions about patient care do physicians have during and after patient contact in the ED? The taxonomy of gaps in physician knowledge. *Emergency Medical Journal*, 24(10), 703–6.

Graber, M.L. et al. 2012. Cognitive interventions to reduce diagnostic error: A narrative review. *BMJ Quality and Safety*, 21(7), 535–57.

Graham, J.M. et al. 2009. Virtual patient safety rounds: One hospital system's approach to sharing knowledge. *Journal of Healthcare Quality*, 31(5), 48–52.

Graham, S. et al. 2008. Implementation of a high-alert medication program. *Permanente Journal*, 12(2), 15–22.

Graham, S. et al. 2012. Medication safety: Reducing error through improvement programs, in *The Nurses Role in Medication Safety*, edited by L. Cima and S. Clark. Oakbrook Terrace, IL: Joint Commission Resources, 5–34.

Green, M.L., Ciampi, M.A. and Ellis, P.J. 2000. Residents' medical information needs in clinic: Are they being met? *American Journal of Medicine*, 109(3), 218–23.

Grant, M. 2010. Dennis Quaid's Quest. *AARP The Magazine*. 53(September/October), 48–51, 90–91.

Greenhalgh, T. 1997. How to read a paper: The Medline database. *British Medical Journal*, 315(7101), 180–83.

Greenhalgh, T. 2010. *How to Read a Paper: The Basics of Evidence-Based Medicine*. 4th Edition. London: BMJ Books.

Greenhalgh, T. et al. 2011. Why national ehealth programs need dead philosophers: Wittgensteinian reflections on policymakers' reluctance to learn from history. *Milbank Quarterly*, 89(4), 533–63.

Greenhalgh, T., Russell, J. and Swinglehurst, D. 2005. Narrative methods in quality improvement research. *Quality and Safety in Health Care*, 14(6), 443–9.

Greenhow, C, and Gleason, B. 2012. Twitteracy: Tweeting as a new literacy practice. *The Educational Forum*, 76(4), 463–77.

Grenzeback, M. 2009. Google @ Your Library. *Nebraska Library Association Quarterly*, 40(1), 4.

Griffin, F.A. and Resar, R.K. 2009. *IHI Global Trigger Tool for Measuring Adverse Events*. 2nd Edition. (IHI Innovation Series white paper). Cambridge, MA: Institute for Healthcare Improvement.

Groopman, J. 2007. *How Doctors Think*. Boston, MA: Houghton Mifflin.

Grout, J. 2007. *Mistake-Proofing the Design of Health Care Processes* [Online]. Rockville, MD: Agency for Healthcare Research and Quality. Available at: http://www.ahrq.gov/qual/mistakeproof/mistakeproofing.pdf [accessed: April 10, 2013].

Gurses, A.P. et al. 2010. Using an interdisciplinary approach to identify factors that affect clinicians' compliance with evidence-based guidelines. *Critical Care Medicine*, 38(8 Suppl.), S282–91.

Gurses, A.P., Ozok, A.A. and Pronovost, P.J. 2012. Time to accelerate integration of human factors and ergonomics in patient safety. *BMJ Quality and Safety*, 21, 347–51.

Haig, A. and Dozier, M. 2003. BEME Guide no 3: Systematic searching for evidence in medical education – Part 1: Sources of information. *Medical Teacher*, 25(4), 352–63.

Hamm, M.P. et al. 2013a. Social media use among patients and caregivers: A scoping review. *BMJ Open*, May 9, 3(5), e002819.

Hamm, M.P. et al. 2013b. Social media use by health care professionals and trainees: A scoping review. *Academic Medicine*, 88(9), 1376–83.

Hansson, S.O. 2012. Safety is an inherently inconsistent concept. *Safety Science*, 50(7), 1522–27.

Hara, N, and Hew, K.F. 2007. Knowledge-sharing in an online community of health-care professionals. *Information Technology & People*, 20(3), 235–61.

Hardy, L.K., Segatore, M. and Edge, D.S. 1993. Illiteracy: Implications for nursing education. *Nurse Education Today*, 13(1), 24–9.

Harrison, M.I., Henriksen, K. and Hughes, R.G. 2007. Improving the health care work environment: Implications for research, practice, and policy. *Joint Commission Journal Quality in Patient Safety*, 33(11 Suppl), 81–4.

Harrison, M.I., Koppel, R. and Bar-Lev, S. 2007. Unintended consequences of information technologies in health care – an interactive sociotechnical analysis. *Journal of the American Medical Informatics Association*, 14(5), 542–9.

Hart, S.R. et al. 2011. Operating room fire safety. *Ochsner Journal*, 11(1), 37–42.

Hasley, S.K. 2011. Decision support and patient safety: The time has come. *American Journal of Obstetrics and Gynecology*, 204(6), 461–5.

Hausner, E. et al. 2012. Routine development of objectively derived search strategies. *Systematic Reviews* [Online], 1(1), 19. Available at: http://www.systematicreviewsjournal.com/content/1/1/19/ [accessed: October 7, 2012].

Haynes, A.B., et al. 2009. A surgical safety checklist to reduce morbidity and mortality in a global population. *The New England Journal of Medicine*, 360(5), 491–9.

Haynes, R. et al. 1994. Developing optimal search strategies for detecting clinically sound studies in MEDLINE. *Journal of the American Medical Informatics Association*, 1(6), 447–58.

Hayrinen, K., Saranto, K. and Nykanen, P. 2008. Definition, structure, content, use and impacts of electronic health records: A review of the research literature. *International Journal of Medical Informatics*, 77(5), 291–304.

Healthcare Information and Management Systems Society (HIMSS), Health Information Exchange Steering Committee. 2010. HHE implications in meaningful use stage 1 requirements. [Online.] Available at: http://hie.az.gov/docs/tech_infra/AZHIE_HIMSS_HIEMeaningfulUse.pdf [accessed: March 26, 2013].

Healthcare Information Management Systems Society (HIMSS). 2009. *Overview of CDS Five Rights: Chapter 1 – Approaching Clinical Decision Support in Medication Management*. [Online]. Available at: http://healthit.ahrq.gov/images/mar09_cds_book_chapter/CDS_MedMgmnt_ch_1_sec_2_five_rights.htm [accessed: April 8, 2012].

HealthWorks Collective. 2012. *Can Healthcare Providers Afford to Ignore Social Media?* [Online]. Archived webinar. Available at: http://healthworkscollective.

com/28656/audio-archive-can-healthcare-providers-afford-ignore-social-media [accessed: March 16, 2012].

Heifetz, R.A, and Laurie, D.L. 1997. The work of leadership. *Harvard Business Review*, 75(1), 124–34.

Heintz, B.H., Halilovic, J. and Christensen, C.L. 2011. Impact of a multidisciplinary team review of potential outpatient parenteral antimicrobial therapy prior to discharge from an academic medical center. *Annals of Pharmacotherapy*, 45(11), 1329–37.

Heit, J.A. et al. 2002. Relative impact of risk factors for deep vein thrombosis and pulmonary embolism. *Archives of Internal Medicine*, 162, 1245–8.

Heinrich, H.W. 1931. *Industrial Accident Prevention: A Scientific Approach*. New York, NY: McGraw-Hill.

Heintz, B.H., Halilovic, J. and Christensen, C.L. 2011. Impact of a multidisciplinary team review of potential outpatient parenteral antimicrobial therapy prior to discharge from an academic medical center. *Annals of Pharmacotherapy*, 45(11), 1329–37.

Helmreich, R.L. and Merritt A.C. 1998. *Culture at Work in Aviation and Medicine: National, Organizational, and Professional Influences*. Aldershot: Ashgate Publishing.

Helmreich, R.L. and Wilhelm, J.A. 1999. The evolution of crew resource management training in commercial aviation. *International Journal of Aviation Psychology*, 9 (1), 19–32.

Helmreich, R.L. 2000. On error management: Lessons from aviation. *British Medical Journal*, 320(7237), 781–5.

Herskovic, J.R. et al. 2007. A day in the life of PubMed®: Analysis of a typical day's query log. *Journal of the American Medical Informatics Association*, 14(2), 212–20.

Hendrich, A.L., Fay, J. and Sorrells, A.K. 2004. Effects of acuity-adaptable rooms on flow of patients and delivery of care. *American Journal of Critical Care*, 13(1), 35–45.

Henriksen, K. et al. 2007. The role of the physical environment in crossing the quality chasm. *The Joint Commission Journal on Quality and Patient Safety*, 33(11 Suppl.), 68–80.

Hersh, W.R. et al. 2002. Factors associated with success in searching MEDLINE and applying evidence to answer clinical questions. *Journal of the American Medical Informatics Association*, 9(3), 283–93.

Heyworth, L. et al. 2014. Engaging patients in medication reconciliation via a patient portal following hospital discharge. *Journal of the American Medical Informatics Association*, 21(e1), e157–62.

Hibbard, J.H., et al. 2005. Can patients be part of the solution? Views on their role in preventing medical errors. *Medical Care Research and Review*, 62(5), 601–16.

Hickson, G.B. et al. 2002. Patient complaints and malpractice risk. *Journal of the American Medical Association*, 287(22), 2951–7.

Hignett, S. and Lu, J. 2007. Evaluation of critical care space requirements for 3 frequent and high-risk tasks. *Critical Care Nursing Clinics of North America*, 19(2), 167–75.

Hildebrand, E.A. et al. 2010. Exploring human factors in endoscope reprocessing. *Human Factors and Ergonomics Society Annual Meeting Proceedings, Health Care*, 5, 894–8.

Hilficker, D. 1984. Facing our mistakes. *New England Journal of Medicine*, 310(2), 118–22.

Hilgartner, S. and Bosk, C.L. 1988. The rise and fall of social problems: A public arenas model. *American Journal of Sociology*, 94(1), 53–78.

Hillel, G. and Vicente, K.J. 2003. Nursing interruptions in a post anesthetic care unit: A field study. *Proceedings of the Human Factors and Ergonomics Society 47th Annual Meeting*, 1443–7.

Hobson, K. 2010. Joint Commission-Hospital Collaboration Targets Hand-Offs. *WSJ Health Blog* [Online]. Available at: http://blogs.wsj.com/health/2010/10/21/joint-commission-hospital-collaboration-targets-hand-offs [accessed: April 4, 2012].

Hofer, T.P., Kerr, E.A. and Hayward, R.A. 2000. What is an error? *Effective Clinical Practice*, 3(6), 261–9.

Hoff, T.J. and Sutcliffe, K.M. 2006. Studying patient safety in health care organizations: Accentuate the qualitative. *Joint Commission Journal on Quality and Patient Safety*, 32(1), 5–15.

Holden, R.J. et al. 2008. A change management framework for macroergonomic field research. *Applied Ergonomics*, 39(4), 459–74.

Hollnagel, E. 1991. Does human error exist?, in *Human Error: Cause, Prediction, and Reduction*, edited by J.W. Senders and N.P. Moray. Hillsdale, NJ: Lawrence Erlbaum Associates, 153.

Hollnagel, E., Woods, D.D. and Leveson, N.G. 2006. *Resilience Engineering: Concepts and Precepts*. Aldershot: Ashgate.

Humphrey, G.F. 1992. Scientific fraud: The McBride case. *Medicine, Science and the Law*, 32(3), 199–203.

Illich, I. 1977. *Limits to Medicine: Medical Nemesis: The Expropriation of Health*. London: Pelican Books.

Institute for Healthcare Improvement. 2002. *The Breakthrough Series: IHI's Collaborative Model for Achieving Breakthrough Improvement*. [Online]. Available

at: http://www.ihi.org/knowledge/Pages/IHIWhitePapers/TheBreakthrough
SeriesIHIsCollaborativeModelforAchievingBreakthroughImprovement.aspx
[accessed: February 17, 2012].

Institute for Healthcare Improvement. 2007. Trigger tool for measuring ADEs
[Online]. Available at: www.ihi.org/ihi/workspace/tools/trigger/ [accessed:
November 17, 2012].

Institute for Patient- and Family-Centered Care (IPFCC). 2012. *IPFCC Homepage.*
[Online]. Available at: http://www.ipfcc.org/.

Institute for Safe Medical Practices (ISMP). 2005. Fatal misadministration of IV
vincristine. *ISMP Medication Safety Alert! Acute Care Edition,* 10(December 1),
1–2, 4.

Institute for Safe Medication Practices (ISMP). 2005. High-reliability organizations
(HROs): What they know that we don't (Part 1). *ISMP Medication Safety Alert,
Acute Care Edition,* 10(July 14), 1–2.

Institute for Safe Medication Practices (ISMP). 2005. High-reliability organizations
(HROs): What they know that we don't (Part 2). *ISMP Medication Safety Alert,
Acute Care Edition,* 10(July 28), 1–3.

Institute for Safe Medication Practice. 2005. *Example of a Health Care Failure
Mode and Effects Analysis for IV Patient Controlled Analgesia (PCA)* [Online].
Available at: http://www.ismp.org/tools/FMEAofPCA.pdf [assessed: April
18, 2013].

Institute for Safe Medication Practices (ISMP). 2006. IV vincristine survey
shows safety improvements needed. *ISMP Medication Safety Alert! Acute Care
Edition,* 11(February 23), 1–2.

Institute for Safe Medication Practices (ISMP). 2008. Benefits and risks of
including patients on RCA teams. *ISMP Medication Safety Alert! Acute Care
Edition,* 13(June 5), 1–3.

Institute for Safe Medication Practices (ISMP). 2010 Latest heparin fatality
speaks loudly – what have you done to stop the bleeding? *ISMP Medication
Safety Alert! Acute Care Edition,* 15(April 8), 1–3.

Institute for Safe Medication Practices (ISMP). 2011. Telling true stories is an
ISMP hallmark: Here's why you should tell stories, too. *ISMP Medication
Safety Alert! Acute Care Edition,* 16(September 8), 1–3.

Institute for Safe Medication Practice (ISMP). 2011. *ISMP's List of Confused
Drug Names* [Online]. Available at: http://www.ismp.org/tools/confused
drugnames.pdf [assessed: April 18, 2013].

Institute for Safe Medication Practice Canada/ISMP. 2004. *Event Analysis Report:
Hydomorphone/Morphine Event.* [Online]. Available at: http://www.ismp-
canada.org/download/Hydromorphone_Morphine_RCA_Report_final12.
pdf [accessed: April 17, 2013].

Institute of Medicine (US), Committee on Quality of Health Care in America. 2001. *Crossing the Quality Chasm a New Health System for the 21st Century.* Washington, DC: National Academy Press.

Institute of Medicine. 2011. *Health IT and Patient Safety: Building Safer Systems for Better Care.* Washington, DC: Institute of Medicine.

Institute of Medicine. 2011. Learning what works: Infrastructure required for comparative effectiveness research – Workshop summary. *The Learning Health System Series.* [Online]. Washington, DC: National Academy Press, 28. Available at: http://www.ncbi.nlm.nih.gov/books/NBK64787/pdf/TOC.pdf [accessed: September 24, 2012].

Isaac, T. et al. 2009. Overrides of medication alerts in ambulatory care. *Archives of Internal Medicine,* 169(3), 305–11.

Isaac, T. et al. 2010. The relationship between patients' perception of care and measures of hospital quality and safety. *Health Services Research,* 45(4), 1024–40.

Isaac, T., Zheng, J. and Jha, A. 2012. Use of UpToDate and outcomes in US hospitals. *Journal of Hospital Medicine,* 7(2), 85–90.

Isaacs, W. 1999. *Dialogue and the Art of Thinking Together: A Pioneering Approach to Communicating in Business and in Life.* New York, NY: Currency/Doubleday.

Jacsó, P. 2008. Google scholar revisited. *Online Information Review,* 32(1), 102–14. Available at: http://www.cs.unibo.it/~cianca/wwwpages/dd/08Jacso.pdf [accessed: March 20, 2013].

Joanna Briggs Institute. 2011. *Joanna Briggs Institute Reviewers' Manual.* 2011 edition. Adelaide: Joanna Briggs Institute.

Johnson, J., Haskell, H. and Barach, P. 2012. The Lewis Blackman Hospital Patient Safety Act: It's hard to kill a healthy 15-year-old, in *Implementing Continuous Quality Improvement in Health Care,* edited by C.P. McLaughlin, J.K. Johnson and W.A. Sollecito. Sudbury, MA: Jones and Bartlett, 303–12.

Joint Commission. *Universal Protocol* [web site]. Available at: http://www.jointcommission.org/standards_information/up.aspx [accessed: January 15, 2013].

Joint Commission. 2005. Preventing vincristine administration errors. *Sentinel Event Alert,* 34, 1–3.

Joint Commission. 2009. *Comprehensive Accreditation Manual for Hospitals.* Oakbrook Terrace, IL: The Joint Commission.

Joint Commission. 2011. *2011 National Patient Safety Goal 15.01.01: Identifying individuals at risk for suicide.* Oakbrook Terrace, IL: The Joint Commission.

Joint Commission. 2011. Health care worker fatigue and patient safety. *Sentinel Event Alert,* 48, 1–4.

Joint Commission. 2011. National Patient Safety Goals Effective January 1, 2012. Hospital Accreditation Program. UP.01.01.01 - UP.01.03.01.

Joint Commission. 2012. *Hospital Accreditation Standards 2012*. Oakbrook Terrace, IL: Joint Commission Resources, p.PC-18.

Joint Commission. 2013 *Sentinel Event Data Root Causes by Event Type 2004 – June 2013. September 20, 2013* [Online]. Oakbrook Terrace, IL: Joint Commission. Available at: http://www.jointcommission.org/assets/1/18/Root_Causes_by_Event_Type_2004-2Q2013.pdff [accessed: January 24, 2013].

Joint Commission International. 2008. *Understanding and Preventing Sentinel and Adverse Events in Your Health Care Organization*. Oakbrook Terrace IL: Joint Commission Resources.

Jones, M. et al. 2011. The stories behind the data. *Patient Safety and Quality Healthcare*, 8(6), 30–34.

Joseph, A. and Rashid, M. 2007. The architecture of safety: Hospital design. *Current Opinion in Critical Care*, 13(6), 714–19.

Kannry, J., Kushniruk, A. and Koppel, R. 2011. Meaningful usability: Health information for the rest of us, in *Medical Informatics: An Executive Primer* (2nd Edition), edited by K. Ong. Chicago, IL: Healthcare Information and Management Systems Society.

Keiger, D. and De Pasquale, S. 2002. Trials and tribulations. *Johns Hopkins Magazine* [Online], 54(1). Available at: http://www.jhu.edu/jhumag/0202web/trials.html [accessed: October 7, 2012].

Kelly, M.M. and Penney, E.D. 2011. Collaboration of hospital case managers and home care liaisons when transitioning patients. *Professional Case Management*, 16(3), 128–36, quiz 137–8.

Kennedy, D. 2001. Death at Johns Hopkins. *Science*, 293(5532), 1013.

Kenagy, J. 2009. *Designed to Adapt – Leading Healthcare in Challenging Times*. Bozeman, MT: Second River Healthcare Press.

Kennedy, J.F. 1962. Yale University Commencement. Available at: http://millercenter.org/president/speeches/detail/3370 [accessed: April 5, 2013].

Kenney, C. 2008. *The Best Practice: How the New Quality Movement is Transforming Medicine*. New York, NY: Public Affairs.

Kenney, L.K. 2011. More victims than meet the eye. *AAOS Now*. [Online] (November). Available at: http://www.aaos.org/news/aaosnow/nov11/managing5.asp [accessed: April 14, 2013].

Ketchum, A.M., Saleh, A.A. and Jeong, K. 2011. Type of evidence behind point-of-care clinical information products: A bibliometric analysis. *Journal of Medical Internet Research* [Online], 13(1), e21. Available at: http://www.jmir.org/2011/1/e21/ [accessed: April 28, 2012].

Kim, J.J. and Rebholz-Schuhmann, D. 2008. Categorization of services for seeking information in biomedical literature: A typology for improvement of practice. *Briefings in Bioinformatics*, 9(6), 452–65.

Kim, K. 2005. *Clinical Data Standards in Health Care: Five Case Studies California HealthCare Foundation* [Online]. Available at: http://www.chcf. org/~/media/MEDIA%20LIBRARY%20Files/PDF/C/PDF%20Clinical DataStandardsInHealthCare.pdf [accessed: March 29, 2012].

Kim, M.M. et al. The effect of multidisciplinary care teams on intensive care unit mortality. *Archives of Internal Medicine*, 170(4), 369–76.

King, S. 2009. *Josie's Story.* New York, NY: Atlantic Monthly Press.

Kinnersley, P. et al. 2009. Interventions before consultations for helping patients address their information needs. *Cochrane Database of Systematic Reviews*, CD004565.

Kinnersley, P. et al., 2008. Interventions before consultations to help patients address their information needs by encouraging question asking: Systematic review. *British Medical Journal*, 337, a485.

Klein, G., Orasanu, J., Calderwood, R. and Zsambok, C.E. (eds). 1993. *Decision Making in Action: Models and Methods.* Norwood, NJ: Ablex Publishing Company.

Klein, G., Wiggins, S. and Dominguez, C.O. 2010. Team sensemaking. *Theoretical Issues in Ergonomics Science*, 11(4), 304–20.

Klein, M.S. et al. 1994. Effect of online literature searching on length of stay and patient care costs. *Academic Medicine*, 69(6), 489–95.

Knaus, W.A., Draper, E.A., Wagner, D.P. and Zimmerman, J.E. 1986. An evaluation of outcome from intensive care in major medical centers. *Annals of Internal Medicine*, 104, 410–18.

Kneebone, R. 2002. Total internal reflection: An essay on paradigms. *Medical Education*, 36(6), 514–18.

Kneebone, R.L. 2006. Crossing the line: Simulation and boundary areas. *Simulation in Healthcare*, 1(3), 160–63.

Knox, R.A. 1995. Doctor's orders killed cancer patient: Dana-Farber admits drug overdose caused death of Globe columnist, damage to second woman. *The Boston Globe*, March 23 (Metro/Region section: 1).

Koch, S.H. et al. 2012. Intensive care unit nurses' information needs and recommendations for integrated displays to improve nurses' situation awareness. *Journal of the American Medical Informatics Association*, 19(4), 583–90.

Kohn, L.T., Corrigan, J.M. and Donaldson, M.S. (eds). 2000. *To Err Is Human: Building a Safer Health System.* Washington, DC: National Academy Press.

Kolata, G. 2001. Johns Hopkins admits fault in fatal experiment. *New York Times* (July 17), A16.

Koppel, R. 2009. Commentary on EMR Mistaken Identity Case, in *AHRQ Morbidity and Mortality Reports*, edited by R. Wachter.

Koppel, R. 2013. March. Personal communication. Unpublished study at The Hospital of the University of Pennsylvania.

Koppel, R. and Gordon, S. 2012. *First, Do Less Harm: Confronting The Inconvenient Problems of Patient Safety*. Ithaca, NY: Cornell University Press.

Koppel, R. and Kreda, D. 2010. Healthcare IT usability and suitability for clinical needs: Challenges of design, workflow, and contractual relations, in *Information Technology in Health Care: Socio-Technical Approaches: From Safe Systems to Patient Safety*, edited by C. Nohr and J. Aarts. Amsterdam: IOS Press.

Koppel, R. et al. 2008. Identifying and quantifying medication errors: Evaluation of rapidly discontinued medication orders submitted to a computerized physician order entry system. *Journal of the American Medical Informatics Association*, 15(4), 461–5.

Koppel, R. et al. 2005. Role of computerized physician order entry systems in facilitating medication errors. *Journal of the American Medical Association*, 293(10), 1197–203.

Koppel, R. et al. 2008. Workarounds to barcode medication administration systems: Their occurrences, causes, and threats to patient safety. *Journal of the American Medical Informatics Association*, 15, 408–23.

Kothari, A., et al. Lessons from the business sector for successful knowledge management in health care: a systematic review B*iomed Central, BMC Health Services Research* [Online], 11(2), 173. Available at: http://www.biomedcentral.com/1472-6963/11/173 [accessed 1 July 2012].

Kozer, E. et al. 2005. Using a preprinted order sheet to reduce prescription errors in a pediatric emergency department: A randomized, controlled trial. *Pediatrics*, 116(6), 1299–302.

Kripalani, S., et al. 2007. Deficits in communication and information transfer between hospital-based and primary care physicians: implications for patient safety and continuity of care. *Journal of the American Medical Association*, 297(8), 831–41.

Kronenfeld, M.R. Trends in academic health sciences libraries and their emergence as the "knowledge nexus" for their academic health centers. *Journal of the Medical Library Association*, 93(1), 32–9.

Kruger, J. and Dunning, D. 1999. Unskilled and unaware of it: how difficulties in recognising one's own incompetence lead to inflated self-assessments. *Journal of Personality and Social Psychology* [Online], 77(6), 1121–34. Available at: http://www.steamfantasy.it/blog/manuali/unskilled_unaware_of_it.pdf [accessed: 7 October 2012].

Kuperman, G.J. et al. 2007. Medication-related clinical decision support in computerized order entry systems: A review. *Journal of the American Medical Informatics Association*, 14(1), 29–40.

Lampel, J., Shamsie, J. and Shapira, Z. 2009. Experiencing the improbable: rare events and organizational learning. *Organization Science*, 20(5), 835–45.

La Porte, T.R. 1996. High reliability organizations: Unlikely, demanding and at risk. *Journal of Contingencies and Crisis Management*, 4(2), 60–71.

La Porte, T.R. and Frederickson, H.G. 2002. Airport security, high reliability, and the problem of rationality. *Public Administration Review*, 62(suppl), 34–44.

Landrigan, C.P., et al. 2010. Temporal trends in rates of patient harm resulting from medical care. *New England Journal of Medicine*, 363(22), 2124–34.

Lashoher, A. and Pronovost, P. 2010. Creating a more efficient healthcare knowledge market: using communities of practice to create checklists. *Quality and Safety in Health Care*, 19(6), 471–2.

Latour, B. 1987. *Science in Action*. Milton Keynes: Open University Press.

Lau, A.Y. and Coiera, E.W. 2007. Do people experience cognitive biases while searching for information? *Journal of the American Medical Informatics Association*, 14(5), 599–608.

Lawrence, D.W. 2008. What is lost when searching only one literature database for articles relevant to injury prevention and safety promotion? *Injury Prevention*, 14(6), 401–4.

Leape, L. 1994. Error in medicine. *Journal of the American Medical Association*, 272, 1851–7.

Leape, L.L. 2000. Institute of Medicine medical error figures are not exaggerated. *Journal of the American Medical Association*, 284(1), 95–7.

Leape, L.L. 2009. Errors in medicine. *Clinica Chimica Acta; International Journal of Clinical Chemistry*, 404(1), 2–5.

Leape, L.L. and Berwick, D.M. 2005. Five years after 'To Err is Human': what have we learned? *Journal of the American Medical Association*, 293, 2384–90.

Leape, L.L., Berwick, D.M. and Bates, D.W. 2002. What practices will most improve safety? Evidence-based medicine meets patient safety. *Journal of the American Medical Association*, 288(4), 501–7.

Leape, L.L. et al. 1991. The nature of adverse events in hospitalized patients. Results of the Harvard Medical Practice Study II. *New England Journal of Medicine*, 324(6), 377–84.

Leape, L.L., et al. 1999. Pharmacist participation on physician rounds and adverse drug events in the intensive care unit. *Journal of the American Medical Association*, 282(3), 267–70.

Leape, L. et al. 2009. Transforming healthcare: A safety imperative. *Quality and Safety in Health Care*, 18(6), 424–8.

Leibiger, C. and Aldrich, A. 2010. *"Doctor, Doctor, My Students Have Googlitis!": Faculty Intervention via Information Literacy Instruction*. Paper to the Great Plains Conference on Teaching in the Social Sciences, Vermillion, SD,

9 October 2010. Available at: orgs.usd.edu/gpctss/Submissions2010/LeibigerAldrich2010.pdf [accessed: April 28, 2012].

Leistikow, I.P., Kalkman, C.J. and Bruijn, H. 2011. Why patient safety is such a tough nut to crack. *British Medical Journal*, 342, d3447.

Lembitz, A. and Clarke, T.J. 2009. Clarifying "never events and introducing" always events. *Patient Safety in Surgery* [Online], 3, 26. Available at: http://www.ncbi.nlm.nih.gov/pmc/articles/PMC2814808/ [assessed: April 13, 2013].

Leonard, M., et al. (eds). 2013. *The Essential Guide for Patient Safety Officers*. Second edition. Oakbrook Terrace, IL: Joint Commission Resources, Institute for Healthcare Improvement.

Leonhardt, K.K., Bonin, D. and Pagel, P. 2006. Partners in safety: Implementing a community-based patient safety advisory council. *Wisconsin Medical Journal*, 105(8), 54–9.

Leonhardt, K.K. et al. 2008. Creating an accurate medication list in the outpatient setting through a patient-centered approach, in *Advances in Patient Safety: New Directions and Alternative Approaches, Advances in Patient Safety*, edited by K.K. Henriksen, J.B. Battles, M.A. Keyes and M.L. Grady. Rockville, MD: Agency for Healthcare Research and Quality.

Leva, M.C., et al. 2010. The advancement of a new human factors report –'The Unique Report'– facilitating flight crew auditing of performance/operations as part of an airline's safety management system. *Ergonomics*, 53(2), 164–83.

Levinson, W., Lesser, C.S. and Epstein, R.M. 2010. Developing physician communication skills for patient-centered care. *Health Affairs*, 29(7), 1310–18.

Lewis, G.H. et al. 2011. Counterheroism, common knowledge, and ergonomics: Concepts from aviation that could improve patient safety. *Milbank Quarterly*, 89(1), 4–38.

Li, L.C. et al. 2009. Use of communities of practice in business and health care sectors: A systematic review. *Implementation Science* [Online], 4, 27. Available at: http://www.implementationscience.com/content/4/1/27 [assessed: April 13, 2013].

Liang, L. 2007. The gap between evidence and practice. *Health Affairs (Project Hope)*, 26(2), w119–21.

Lightizer, B. and Thurlo-Walsh, B. 2012. Mitigate risk and drive organizational change with just culture. *Patient Safety and Quality Healthcare*. 9(May/June 3), 34–6, 38.

Lim, M. 2012. Clicks, cabs, and coffee houses: Social media and oppositional movements in Egypt, 2004–2011. *Journal of Communication*, 62(2), 231–48.

Lin, D.M. and Kumar, S. 2012. We can all define patient safety … or can we? *Patient Safety and Quality Healthcare*, 9(2), 46–9.

Lin, L. et al. 1998. Applying human factors to the design of medical equipment: Patient-controlled analgesia. *Journal of Clinical Monitoring and Computing*, 14(4), 253–63.

Lindberg, C., Nash, S. and Lindberg, C. 2008. *On the Edge: Nursing in the Age of Complexity*. Bordentown, NJ: PlexusPress.

Lindenauer, P.K. et al. 1999. Hospitalists and the practice of inpatient medicine: Results of a survey of the National Association of Inpatient Physicians. *Annals of Internal Medicine*, 130(4 pt. 2), 343–9.

Lingard, L. 2012. Productive complications: Emergent ideas in team communication and patient safety. *Healthcare Quarterly*, 15, 18–23.

Localio, A.R. et al. 1991. Relation between malpractice claims and adverse events due to negligence: Results of the Harvard Medical Practice Study III. *New England Journal of Medicine*, 325(4), 245–51.

Lockley, S.W. et al. 2007. Effects of health care provider work hours and sleep deprivation on safety and performance. *Joint Commission Journal on Quality and Patient Safety*, 33(11 Suppl.), 7–18. Available at: http://www.jointcommission.org/JQPS_11_07/ [accessed: April 11, 2012].

Lowe, C.M. 2006. Accidents waiting to happen: The contribution of latent conditions to patient safety. *Quality and Safety in Health Care*, 15(Suppl 1), i72–5.

Luther, K. and Resar, R.K. 2013. Tapping front-line knowledge. *Healthcare Executive*, 28(1), 84–7.

MacIntosh-Murray, A. and Choo, C.W. 2005. Information behavior in the context of improving patient safety. *Journal of the American Society for Information Science and Technology*, 56 (12), 1332–45.

Macintosh-Murray, A. and Choo, C.W. 2002. Information failures and catastrophes: What can we learn by linking information studies and disaster research? *Proceedings of the American Society for Information Science and Technology*, 39(1), 239–49.

Macedo-Rouet, M., et al. 2012. How do scientists select articles in the PubMed® database? An empirical study of criteria and strategies. *European Review of Applied Psychology-Revue Europeenne De Psychologie Appliquee*, 62(2), 63–72.

MacLachlan, M. 2006. *Culture and Health*. 2nd edition. Chichester: John Wiley & Sons.

Maclean, N. 1992. *Young Men and Fire*. 1st edition. Chicago IL: University of Chicago Press.

Maguire, P. and Pitceathly, C. 2002. Key communication skills and how to acquire them. *British Medical Journal*, 325(7366), 697–700.

Manojlovich, M. 2010. Nurse/physician communication through a sensemaking lens: Shifting the paradigm to improve patient safety. *Medical Care*, 48(11), 941–6.

Manser, T. 2009. Teamwork and patient safety in dynamic domains of healthcare: A review of the literature. *Acta Anaesthesiologica Scandinavica*, 53(2), 143–51.

March, J.G., Sproull, L.S. and Tamuz, M. 2003. Learning from samples of one or fewer. *Quality & Safety in Health Care*, 12(6), 465–71; discussion 471–2.

Mark, B.A. et al. 2013. California's minimum nurse staffing legislation: Results from a natural experiment. *Health Services Research*, 48(2 Pt. 1), 435–54.

Markey, K. 2007. Twenty-five years of end-user searching, Part 1: Research findings. *Journal of the American Society for Information Science and Technology*, 58(8), 1071–81.

Marshall, J.G. 1992. Impact of the hospital library on clinical decision making: The Rochester study. *Bulletin of the Medical Library Association*, 80(2), 169–78.

Marshall, J.G. et al. 2013. The value of library and information services in patient care: Results of a multisite study. *Journal of the Medical Library Association*, 101(1), 38–46.

Martin, G.P. and Finn, R. 2011. Patients as team members: Opportunities, challenges, and paradoxes of including patients in multi-professional healthcare teams. *Sociology of Health and Illness*, 33(7), 1050–65.

Mastrangelo, G. et al. 2010. Literature search on risk factors for sarcoma: PubMed® and Google Scholar may be complementary sources. *BioMedCentral Research Notes* [Online], (3), 121 Available at: http://www.biomedcentral.com/1756-0500/3/131 [assessed: April 14, 2013].

Marx, D. 2001. *Patient Safety and the "Just Culture": A Primer for Health Care Executives*. New York, NY: Columbia University.

Mason, K.P., Green, S.M., Piacevoli, Q. and The International Sedation Task Force. 2012. Adverse event reporting tool to standardize the reporting and tracking of adverse events during procedural sedation: A consensus document from the World SIVA International Sedation Task Force. *British Journal of Anaesthesia*, 108, 13–20.

Mayo Clinic. 2013. Hospital social network list. *Social Media Health Network*. [Online]. Available at: http://network.socialmedia.mayoclinic.org/hcsml-grid/ [accessed: March 19, 2013].

Mayo Clinic. n.d. Personal health record: A tool for managing your health. [Online]. Available at: http://www.mayoclinic.com/health/personal-health-record/my00665

Maynard, G. and Stein, J. August 2008. *Preventing Hospital-Acquired Venous Thromboembolism: A Guide for Effective Quality Improvement*. AHRQ Publication No. 08-0075. Rockville, MD: Agency for Healthcare Research and Quality. Available at: http://www.ahrq.gov/qual/vtguide/

McDonald, C.J., Weiner, M. and Hui, S.L. 2000. Deaths due to medical errors are exaggerated in institute of medicine report. *Journal of the American Medical Association*, 284(1), 93–5.

McFadden, K., Henagan, S.C. and Gowen III, C.R. 2009. The patient safety chain: Transformational leadership's effect on patient safety culture, initiatives, and outcomes. *Journal of Operations Management*, 27(5), 390–404.

McGowan, J. and Sampson, M. 2005. Systematic reviews need systematic searchers. *Journal of the Medical Library Association*, 93(1), 74–80.

McGowan, J., Sampson, M. and Lefebvre, C. 2010. An evidence based checklist for the peer review of electronic search strategies. *Evidence Based Library and Information Practice* [Online], 5(1). Available at: http://ejournals.library. ualberta.ca/index.php/EBLIP/article/download/7402/6436 [accessed: October 7, 2012].

McGowan, J., Hogg, W., Campbell, C. and Rowan, M. 2008. Just-in-time information improved decision-making in primary care: A randomized controlled trial. *PLoS ONE*, 3(11), e3785.

McIntyre, N. and Popper, K. 1983. The critical attitude in medicine: The need for a new ethics. *British Medical Journal*, 287(6409), 1919–23.

McKeon, L.M., Oswaks, J.D. and Cunningham, P.D. 2006. Safeguarding patients: Complexity science, high reliability organizations, and implications for team training in healthcare. *Clinical Nurse Specialist*, 20(6), 298–304, quiz 305–6.

McKibbon, K.A. and Fridsma, D.B. 2006. Effectiveness of clinician-selected electronic information resources for answering primary care physicians' information needs. *Journal of the American Medical Informatics Association*, 13(6), 653–9.

McLaughlin, R.C. 2003. Hospital extra: Redesigning the crash cart. *American Journal of Nursing*, 103(4), 64a–f.

McLellan, F. 2001. 1966 and all that-when is a literature search done? *Lancet*, 25, 358(9282), 646.

Meade, C.M., Bursell, A.L. and Ketelsen, L. 2006. Effects of nursing rounds on patients' call light use, satisfaction, and safety. *American Journal of Nursing*, 106(9), 58–70.

Meadows-Oliver, M. and Banasiak, N.C. 2010. Accuracy of asthma information on the World Wide Web. *Journal for Specialists in Pediatric Nursing*, 15(3), 211–16.

d.l. Mehrabian, A. and Ferris, S.R. 1967. Inference of attitudes from nonverbal communication in two channels. *Journal of Consulting and Clinical Psychology*, 31, 248–52.

Mehrabian, A. and Wiener, M. 1967. Decoding of inconsistent communications. *Journal of Personality and Social Psychology*, 6, 109–14.

Meisel, Z.F. and Karlawish, J. 2011. Narrative vs. evidence-based medicine – And, not or. *Journal of the American Medical Association*, 306(18), 2022–3.

Merry, M.D. 2005. *Hospital-Medical Staff Culture Clash: Is it Inevitable or Preventable? Health Trustees of New York State: The Challenge of Governance.*

[Online]. Available at: http://www.dynamichs.org/articles/2-Challenge-of-GovMMerry-May2005.pdf

Merry, M.D. and Crago, M.G. 2001. The past, present and future of health care quality: Urgent need for innovative, external review processes to protect patients. *Physician Executive*, 27(5), 30–5.

Miller, G.A. 1956. The magical number seven plus or minus two: Some limits on our capacity for processing information. *Psychological Review*, 63(2), 81–97.

Mills, D.H. 1978. Medical insurance feasibility study: A technical summary. *The Western Journal of Medicine*, 128(4), 360–65.

Mills, D.H., Boyden, J.S. and Rubamen, D.S. (eds). 1977. *Report on the Medical Insurance Study*. San Francisco, CA: Sutter Publications.

Mitchell, J.A., Johnson, E.D., Hewett, J.E. and Proud, V.K. 1992. Medical students using Grateful Med: Analysis of failed searches and a six-month follow-up study. *Computers and Biomedical Research*, 25(1), 43–55.

Mitka, M. 2009. Joint commission offers warnings, and advice on adopting new health care IT systems. *Journal of the American Medical Association*, 307(4), 587–9.

Molloy, G.J. and O'Boyle, C.A. 2005. The SHEL model: a useful tool for analyzing and teaching the contribution of Human Factors to medical error. *Academic Medicine*, 80, 152–5.

Moore, M.S. 2014. Appendix X: Investing in knowledge management – Internal vs. external investment, in *Knowledge Management in Healthcare*, edited by L. Zipperer. London: Gower.

Morello, R.T. et al. 2013. Strategies for improving patient safety culture in hospitals: A systematic review. *BMJ Quality and Safety*, 22, 11–18.

Morath, J.M. and Turnbull, J.E. 2005. *To Do No Harm: Ensuring Patient Safety in Health Care Organizations*. San Francisco, CA: Jossey-Bass.

Moser, R.H. 1959. *Diseases of Medical Progress*. Springfield, IL: C. C. Thomas.

Moser, R.H. 1969. *Diseases of Medical Progress: A Study of Iatrogenic Disease – A Contemporary Analysis of Illness Produced by Drugs and Other Therapeutic Procedures*. 3rd edition. Springfield, IL: C. C. Thomas.

Most, S.B., et al. 2001. How not to be seen: The contribution of similarity and selective ignoring to sustained inattentional blindness. *Psychological Science*, 12(1), 9–17.

Mudge, G.W. 1998. Airline safety: Can we break the old CRM paradigm? *Transportation Law Journal*, 25(2), 231–89.

Mueller, S.K. et al. 2012. Hospital-based medication reconciliation practices: A systematic review. *JAMA Internal Medicine*, 172, 1057–69.

Mueller, S.K. et al. 2012. Impact of resident workload and handoff training on patient outcomes. *American Journal of Medicine*, 125(1), 105–10.

Nabhan, M. et al. 2012. What is preventable harm in healthcare? A systematic review of definitions. *BMC Health Services Research* [Online], 12, 128. Available at: http://www.biomedcentral.com/1472-6963/12/128 [accessed: May 25, 2012].

Nance, J.J. 2008. *Why Hospitals Should Fly: The Ultimate Flight Plan to Patient Safety and Quality Care.* Boseman, MT: Second River Healthcare Press.

Naisbitt, J. 1982. *Megatrends: Ten New Directions for Transforming our Lives.* New York, NY: Warner Books.

Nagpal, K., Arora, S., Abboudi, M. et al. 2010. Postoperative handover: Problems, pitfalls, and prevention of error. *Annals of Surgery*, 252, 171–6.

National Center for Patient Safety. 2011. *Actions & Outcomes: NCPS Root Cause Analysis Tools.* Ann Arbor, MI: National Center for Patient Safety. Available at: http://www.patientsafety.gov/CogAids/RCA/index.html#page=page-14

National Institute for Occupational Safety and Health. 2010. *Engineering Controls* [Online]. Available at: http://www.cdc.gov/niosh/topics/engcontrols/.

National Library of Medicine. 2011. Patient Safety: Medical Subject Headings, MeSH. [Online]. Available at: http://www.ncbi.nlm.nih.gov/mesh?term=patient%20safety [accessed: October 7, 2012].

National Patient Safety Agency. 2004. NHS Root Cause Analysis (RCA) toolkit Reference number 1079 01. [Online]. Available at: http://www.nrls.npsa.nhs.uk/resources/?entryid45=59901 [accessed: October 7, 2012].

National Patient Safety Foundation. 2008. *What You Can Do to Make Healthcare Safer.* [Online]. The National Patient Safety Foundation. Available at: http://www.npsf.org/wp-content/uploads/2011/10/WhatYouCanDo.pdf.

National Quality Forum (NQF). 2009. *Safe Practices for Better Healthcare – 2009 Update: A Consensus Report.* Washington, DC: National Quality Forum.

National Quality Forum. (NQF). 2011. *Serious Reportable Events in Healthcare – 2011 Update: A Consensus Report.* Washington DC: National Quality Forum.

National Transportation Safety Board (NTSB). 1988. Northwest Airlines. DC-9-82 N312RC, Detroit Metropolitan Wayne County Airport. Romulus, Michigan. August 16, 1987 (Aircraft accident report, NTSB/AAR-88/05). Washington, DC.

Neily, J. et al. 2010. Association between implementation of a medical team training program and surgical mortality. *Journal of the American Medical Association*, 304, 1693–700.

Nembhard, I.M. and Edmonson, A.C. 2006. Making it safe: The effects of leader inclusiveness and professional status on psychological safety and improvement efforts in health care teams. *Journal of Organizational Behavior*, 27, 941–66.

Nembhard, I.M. et al. 2012. Understanding the use and impact of the online community in a national quality improvement campaign. *BMJ Quality and Safety*, 20, 68–75.

Nemeth, C.P. 2008. *Improving Healthcare Team Communication: Lessons from Aviation and Aerospace*. Aldershot: Ashgate Publishing Group.

NHS Wales. 2010. *Learning to Use Patient Stories* (1000 Lives: Making Patient Safety a Priority; Tools for Improvement, 6) [Online]. Cardiff: NHS Wales. Available at: http://www.1000livesplus.wales.nhs.uk/sitesplus/documents/1011/T4I%20%286%29%20Learning%20to%20use%20Patient%20stories%20%28Feb%202011%29%20Web.pdf. [accessed: September 24, 2012].

Nissen, M.E. 2002. An extended model of knowledge-flow dynamics. *Communications of the Association for Information Science*, 8, 251–66.

Nissen, M.E., Kamel, M.N. and Sengupta, K.C. 2000. Integrated analysis and design of knowledge systems and processes. *Information Resources Management Journal*, 13(1), 24–43.

Noble, D.J. and Donaldson, L.J. 2011. Republished paper: The quest to eliminate intrathecal vincristine errors: A 40-year journey. *Postgraduate Medicine Journal*, (87), 71–4.

Nolan, T. et al. 2004. *Improving the Reliability of Health Care*. IHI Innovation Series white paper. Boston, MA: The Institute for Healthcare Improvement.

Nonaka, I. 1994. A dynamic theory of organizational knowledge creation. *Organization Science*, 5(1), 14–37.

North, D.C. 1990. *Institutions, Institutional Change and Economic Performance*. New York, NY: Cambridge University Press.

Novak, L.L. 2010. Improving health IT through understanding the cultural production of safety in clinical settings. *Studies in Health Technology and Informatics*, 157, 175–80.

Nunamaker, J.F., Jr., Romano, N.C., Jr. and Briggs, R.O. 2001. *A Framework for Collaboration and Knowledge Management*. Proceedings of the 34th Annual Hawaii International Conference on System Sciences, January 3–6, 2001.

O'Daniel, M., and Rosenstein, A.H. 2008. Professional communication and team collaboration, in *Patient Safety and Quality: An Evidence-Based Handbook for Nurses*, edited by R.G. Hughes (AHRQ Publication No. 08-0043, 2008) [Online]. Rockville, MD: Agency for Healthcare Research and Quality. Available at: http://www.ahrq.gov/qual/nurseshdbk/ [accessed: September 24, 2012].

Ohno, T. 1988. *Toyota Production System – Beyond Large Scale Production*. Portland, OR: Productivity Press.

Oliver, K.B. and Roderer, N.K. 2006. Working towards the informationist. *Health Informatics Journal*, 12(1), 41–8.

Ong, L.M. et al. 1995. Doctor-patient communication: A review of the literature. *Social Science and Medicine*, 40, 903–18.

Ong, M.S. and Coiera, E. 2010. Safety through redundancy: A case study of in-hospital patient transfers. *Quality and Safety in Health Care*, 19 (5), e32.

Oppenheim, M.I., Rand, D., Barone, C. and Hom, R. 2009. ClinRefLink: Implementation of infobutton-like functionality in a commercial clinical information system incorporating concepts from textual documents. *American Medical Informatics Association Annual Symposium Proceedings 2009*, 487–91.

Osheroff, J.A. 2009. *Improving Medication Use and Outcomes with Clinical Decision Support: A Step-by-Step Guide*. Chicago, IL: Healthcare Information and Management Systems Society.

Osheroff, J.A., Teich, J.M., Middleton, B., Steen, E.B., Wright, A. and Detmer, D.E. 2007. A roadmap for national action on clinical decision support. *Journal of the American Medical Informatics Association*, 14(2), 141–5. [Erratum in: *Journal of the American Medical Informatics Association*, 14(3), 389].

Ovretveit, J.C. et al. 2011. How does context affect interventions to improve patient safety? An assessment of evidence from studies of five patient safety practices and proposals for research. *BMJ Quality and Safety*, 20(7), 604–10.

Paget, M. 1988. *The Unity of Mistakes: A Phenomenological Interpretation of Medical Work*. Philadelphia, PA: Temple University Press.

Page, S.E. 2009. *Understanding Complexity*. Chantilly, VA: The Teaching Company.

Page, A., (ed.) 2004. *Committee on the Work Environment for Nurses and Patient Safety, Board on Health Care Services. Keeping Patients Safe: Transforming the Work Environment of Nurses*. Washington, DC: National Academies Press.

Palmieri, P.A., Peterson, L.T. and Corazzo, L.B. 2011. Technological iatrogenesis: The manifestation of inadequate organizational planning and the integration of health information technology. *Advances in Health Care Management*, 10, 287–312.

Pape, T.M. et al. 2005. Innovative approaches to reducing nurses' distractions during medication administration. *Journal of Continuing Education in Nursing*, 36, 108–16.

Pariser, E. 2011. *The Filter Bubble: What the Internet is Hiding from You*. New York, NY: Penguin Press.

Parmelli, E. et al. 2011. The effectiveness of strategies to change organisational culture to improve healthcare performance. *Cochrane Database of Systematic Reviews* [Online], (1), CD008315. doi:10.1002/14651858.CD008315.pub2 [accessed: 7 October 2012].

Patankar, M.S. and Taylor, J.C. 1999. Corporate aviation on the leading edge: Systemic implementation of macro-human factors in aviation maintenance (Technical paper no. 1999-01-1596). *SAE Transactions*, 108(1), 305–10.

Patankar, M.S., Brown, J.P., Sabin, E.J. and Bigda-Peyton, T.G. 2012. *Safety Culture: Building and Sustaining a Cultural Change in Aviation and Healthcare*. Burlington, VT: Ashgate.

Patterson, K. et al. 2002. *Crucial Conversations: Tools for Talking when Stakes are High*. New York, NY: McGraw-Hill.

Paull, D.E. and Mazzia, L.M. 2013. Lessons learned from the VHA Medical Team Training Program, in *Improving Patient Safety Through Teamwork and Team Training*, edited by E. Salas and K. Frush. New York, NY: Oxford University Press.

Perkins, E. 2001. Johns Hopkins' tragedy: Could librarians have prevented a death? [Online]. Available at: http://newsbreaks.infotoday.com/nbreader. asp?ArticleID=17534 [accessed: January 23, 2012].

Perrow, C. 1999. *Normal Accidents: Living with High-Risk Technologies*. Princeton, NJ: Princeton University Press.

Peters, T. and Waterman R.H. 1982. *In Search of Excellence*. Philadelphia, PA: Harper and Row.

Pintor-Mármol, A., et al. 2012. Terms used in patient safety related to medication: A literature review. *Pharmacoepidemiol Drug Safety*, 21(8), 799–809.

Pirnejad, H. et al. 2008. Impact of a computerized physician order entry system on nurse-physician collaboration in the medication process. *International Journal of Medical Informatics*, 77(11), 735–44.

Pitkin, R.M., Branagan, M.A. and Burmeister, L.F. 1999. Accuracy of data in abstracts of published research articles. *Journal of the American Medical Association*, 281(12), 1110–11.

Plake, C., Schiemann, T., Pankalla, M., Hakenberg, J. and Lesser U. 2006. AliBaba: PubMed as a graph. *Bioinformatics*, 22(19), 2444–5.

Pongudom, S. and Chinthammitr, Y. 2011. Inadvertent intrathecal vincristine administration: Report of a fatal case despite cerebrospinal fluid lavage and a review of the literature. *Journal of the Medical Association of Thailand*. (February 94 Suppl 1), S258–63.

Ponte, P.R. et al. 2003. Making patient-centered care come alive: Achieving full integration of the patient's perspective. *Journal of Nursing Administration*, 33, 82–90.

President's Council of Advisors on Science and Technology. 2010. *Realizing the Full Potential of Health Information Technology to Improve Healthcare for Americans: The Path Forward*. Washington, DC: Executive Office of the President of the United States.

Pronovost, P.J. and Freischlag, J.A. 2010. Improving teamwork to reduce surgical mortality. *Journal of the American Medical Association*, 304(15), 1721–2.

Pronovost, P. et al. 2006. An intervention to decrease catheter-related bloodstream infections in the ICU. *New England Journal of Medicine*, 355(26), 2725–32.

Pronovost, P. and Vohr, E. 2010. *Safe Patients, Smart Hospitals: How One Doctor's Checklist Can Help Us Change Health Care from the Inside Out*. New York, NY: Hudson Street Press.

Pronovost, P.J. et al. 2004. Senior executive adopt-a-work unit: a model for safety improvement. *Joint Commission Journal of Quality and Patient Safety*, 30(2), 59–68.

Pronovost, P.J. et al. 2006. An intervention to decrease catheter-related bloodstream infections in the ICU. *New England Journal of Medicine*, 355(26), 2725–32.

Pronovost, P.J. et al. 2008. Improving patient safety in intensive care units in Michigan. *Journal of Critical Care*, 23(2), 207–21.

Pronovost, P.J. et al. 2010. Sustaining reductions in catheter related bloodstream infections in Michigan intensive care units: Observational study. *British Medical Journal*, 340, c309.

Quality Interagency Coordination (QuIC) Task Force. 2000. National Summit on Medical Errors and Patient Safety. [online] Available at: http://www.quic.gov/summit/index.htm

Rabb, S.S., et al. 2006. Double slide viewing as a cytology quality improvement initiative. *American Journal of Clinical Pathology*, 125, 526–33.

Ramos, K., Linscheid, R. and Schafer, S. 2003. Real-time information-seeking behavior of residency physicians. *Family Medicine*, 35(4), 257–60.

Ramsey, S. 2001. Johns Hopkins takes responsibility for volunteer's death. *The Lancet*, 2001 July 21; 348, 231.

Rana, G.K., et al. A validated search assessment tool: Assessing practice-based learning and improvement in a residency program. *Journal of the Medical Library Association*, 99(1), 77–81.

Rasmussen, J. 1990. The role of error in organizing behaviour. *Ergonomics*, 33, 1185–190.

Rasmussen, J., Duncan, K. and Leplat, J. (eds). 1987. *New Technology and Human Error*. Chichester: John Wiley & Sons.

Rasmussen, J. 2000. The concept of human error: Is it useful for the design of safe systems in healthcare, in *Safety in Medicine*, edited by C. Vincent and B. de Mol. Kiddington: Elsevier Science.

Rashid, M. 2006. A decade of adult ICU design: A study of the physical design – best-practice examples. *Critical Care Nursing Quarterly*, 29(4), 282–311.

Rathert, C., May, D.R. and Williams, E.S. 2011. Beyond service quality: The mediating role of patient safety perceptions in the patient experience-satisfaction relationship. *Health Care Management Review*, 36, 359–68.

Reader, T.W. Flin, R. and Cuthbertson, B.H. 2007 Communication skills and error in the intensive care unit. *Current Opinions in Critical Care*, 13(6), 732–6.

Reason, J. 1990. *Human Error*. Cambridge: Cambridge University Press.

Reason, J. 1997. *Managing the Risks of Organizational Accidents*. Burlington, VT: Ashgate.

Reason, J. 2000. Human error: Models and management. *Western Journal of Medicine*, 172(6), 393–6.

Reason, J. 2004. Beyond the organisational accident: The need for "error wisdom" on the frontline. *BMJ Quality and Safety*, (13)Suppl 2), ii28–33.

Resar, R.K. 2006. Making noncatastrophic health care processes reliable: Learning to walk before running in creating high-reliability organizations. *Health Services Research*, 41(4 pt. 2), 1677–89.

Rhiner, M. 2004. The American Pain Foundation TARGET Chronic Pain Initiative: Better patient/clinician communication to improve pain management. *Journal of Pain and Palliative Care Pharmacotherapy*, 18, 55–63.

Riesenberg, L.A., Leisch, J. and Cunningham, J.M. 2010. Nursing handoffs: A systematic review of the literature. *American Journal of Nursing*, 110(4), 24–34.

Robert Woods Johnson Foundation. 2008. *Developing a Patient/Family-Activated Rapid Response Team*. [Online]. Available at: http://www.rwjf.org/qualityequality/product.jsp?id=30391.

Robert Wood Johnson Foundation. *The Transforming Care at the Bedside (TCAB) Toolkit*. [online]. 06/04/2008. Available at: http://www.rwjf.org/content/rwjf/en/research-publications/find-rwjf-research/2008/06/the-transforming-care-at-the-bedside-tcab-toolkit.html

Roberts, N.K., and Klamen, D.L. 2010. The case for teaching explicit reading strategies to medical students. *Medical Education*, 44(4), 328–9.

Robins, N.S. 1995. *The Girl Who Died Twice: Every Patient's Nightmare: The Libby Zion Case and the Hidden Hazards of Hospitals*. New York, NY: Delacorte Press.

Rochlin, G.I., La Porte, T.R. and Roberts, K.H. 1987. Self-designing high reliability: aircraft carrier flight operations at sea. *Naval War College Review*, 40(4), 76–90.

Roderer, N. 2012. Policy and practice changes at Welch Library resulting from the Ellen Roche tragedy. [Email/personal communication].

Ross, C., Nelson, K. and Radford, M. 2009. *Conducting the Reference Interview: A How-to-Do-It Manual for Librarians*. 2nd edition. New York: Neal-Schuman Publishers, Inc.

Rowley, E. and Waring, J., eds. 2011. *A Socio-Cultural Perspective on Patient Safety*. Farnham, UK: Ashgate.

Rudin, R.S., Salzberg, C.A. and Bates, D.W. 2011. Care transitions as opportunities for clinicians to use data exchange services: How often do they occur? *Journal of the American Informatics Association*, 18(6), 853–8.

Runciman, W.B., et al. and the Methods & Measures Working Group of the World Health Organization World Alliance for Patient Safety. 2012. Tracing the foundations of a conceptual framework for a patient safety ontology. *Quality and Safety in Health Care* [Online], 19, e56.

Rydenfält C, Ek A, Larsson PA. Safety checklist compliance and a false sense of safety: new directions for research. *BMJ Quality and Safety*. 2013 Oct 3; [Epub ahead of print].

Sackett, D.L., et al. 2000. *Evidence-Based Medicine: How to Practice and Teach EBM*. 2nd edition. Edinburgh; New York: Churchill Livingstone.

Sackett, D.L., et al. 1996. Evidence based medicine: What it is and what it isn't. *British Medical Journal*, 312(7023):71–2.

Saimbert, M.K., et al. 2010. Medical librarians possess expertise to navigate various search resources and can investigate inquiries during IS project lifecycles. *Journal of Healthcare Information Management*, 24(1), 52–6.

Salanitro, A.H., et al. 2012. Effect of patient- and medication-related factors on inpatient medication reconciliation errors. *Journal of General Internal Medicine*, 27(8), 924–32.

Salas, E., Rhodenizer, L. and Bowers, C.A. 2000. The design and delivery of crew resource management training: Exploiting available resources. *Human Factors*, 42(3), 490–511.

Salas, E, Frush, K eds. 2013. Improving Patient Safety Through Teamwork and Team Training. Oxford University Press.

Salas, E., Lazzara, E.H., Benishek, L.E. and King, H. 2013. On being a team player: evidence-based heuristic for teamwork in interprofessional education. *Medical Science and Education*, 23(3S), 524–31

Saleem, J.J., Patterson, E.S., Russ, A.L. and Wears, R.L. 2011. The need for a broader view of human factors in the surgical domain. *Archives of Surgery*, 146(5), 631–2.

Salinas, G.D., et al. 2011. Barriers to adherence to chronic obstructive pulmonary disease guidelines by primary care physicians. *International Journal of Chronic Obstructive Pulmonary Disease*, 6, 171–9.

Sampson, M., et al. 2009. An evidence-based practice guideline for the peer review of electronic search strategies. *Journal of Clinical Epidemiology* 62(9), 944–52.

Sampson, M., et al. 2008. *PRESS: Peer Review of Electronic Search Strategies*. Ottawa: Canadian Agency for Drugs and Technologies in Health.

Savulescu, J. and Spriggs, M. 2002. The hexamethonium asthma study and the death of a normal volunteer in research. *Journal of Medical Ethics*, 28(1), 3–4.

Scheffler, A. and Zipperer, L.A., eds. 1999. *Enhancing Patient Safety and Reducing Errors in Health Care*. Chicago, IL: National Patient Safety Foundation.

Schein, E.H. 2004. *Organizational Culture and Leadership*. The Jossey-Bass Business and Management Series. Edition 3; John Wiley & Sons.

Scherer, R.W., Langenberg, P. and von Elm, E. 2007. Full publication of results initially presented in abstracts. *Cochrane Database of Systematic Reviews* [Online]. Available at: http://dx.doi.org/10.1002/14651858.MR000005.pub3 [accessed: 28 April 2012].

Schiff, G.D., Kim, S., Abrams, R. et al. 2004. Diagnosing diagnosis errors: Lessons from a multi-institutional collaborative project for the diagnostic error evaluation and research project investigators, in *Advances in Patient Safety: From Research to Implementation*. Rockville, MD: Agency for Healthcare Research and Quality.

Schillinger, D. et al. 2003. Closing the loop: Physician communication with diabetic patients who have low health literacy. *Archives of Internal Medicine*, 163, 83–90.

Schimmel, E.M. 1964. The hazards of hospitalization. *Annals of Internal Medicine*, 60, 100–110. As reprinted in: *Quality and Safety in Health Care*, 2003,12, 58–64; 63.

Schnipper, J.L. et al. 2006. Role of pharmacist counseling in preventing adverse drug events after hospitalization. *JAMA Internal Medicine*, 166, 565–71.

Schon, D.A. 1963. *Displacement of Concepts*. London: Tavistock.

Schultz, S. 2001. Trial patients need to ask questions after Hopkins death. *US News & World Report*, 131(5), 50.

Schwing, L.J. and Coldsmith, E.E. 2005. Librarians as hidden gems in a clinical team. *Medical Reference Services Quarterly*, 24(1), 29–39.

Scobie, A.C. and Persaud, D.D. 2010. Patient engagement in patient safety: Barriers and facilitators. *Patient Safety and Quality Healthcare*, 7(March/April), 42–7.

Scott, S.D., Hirschinger, L.E. and Cox, K.R. 2008. Sharing the load of a nurse "second victim." *RN*, 71(12), 38–43.

Seifert, P.C. 2012. Implementing AORN recommended practices for transfer of patient care information. *AORN Journal*, 96(5), 475–93.

Senders, J.W. 1994. Medical devices, medical errors, and medical accidents, in *Human Error in Medicine*, edited by M.S. Bogner. Hillsdale, NJ: Lawrence Erlbaum Associates, 159–77.

Senders, J.W. and Moray, N.P. 1991. *Human Error: Cause, Prediction, and Reduction*. Hillsdale, NJ: Lawrence Erlbaum Associates.

Senge, P. 1990. *The Fifth Discipline: The Art and Practice of the Learning Organization*. New York, NY: Doubleday.

Senge, P.M. et al. 1994. *The Fifth Discipline Fieldbook: Strategies and Tools for Building a Learning Organization*. New York, NY: Doubleday/Currency.

Shafir, R.S. 2003. *The Zen of Listening: Mindful Communication in the Age of Distraction*. Wheaton, IL: Quest Books.

Sharpe, V.A. and Faden, A.I. 1998. *Medical Harm: Historical, Conceptual and Ethical Dimensions of Iatrogenic Illness*. New York, NY: Cambridge University Press.

Shaughnessy, A. 2009. Keeping up with the medical literature: How to set up a system. *American Family Physician January*, 79(1), 25–6.

Shekelle, P.G. et al. 2011. Advancing the science of patient safety. *Annals of Internal Medicine* [Online], 154(10), 693–6.

Shekelle, P., Eccles, M.P., Grimshaw, J.M. and Woolf, S.H. 2001. When should clinical guidelines be updated? *British Medical Journal*, 323(7305), 155–7.

Shekelle, P.G., Pronovost, P.J., Wachter, R.M., the PSP Technical Expert Panel, et al. 2010. *Assessing the Evidence for Context-Sensitive Effectiveness and Safety of Patient Safety Practices: Developing Criteria*. (AHRQ Publication No. 11-0006-EF). Rockville, MD: Agency for Healthcare Research and Quality. Available at: http://www.ahrq.gov/qual/contextsensitive/context14.htm [accessed: July 5, 2012].

Shekelle, P.G., Pronovost, P.J., Wachter, R.M., Rao, J.K. and Mulrow, C.D. (eds). 2013. Making health care safer: A critical review of modern evidence supporting strategies to improve patient safety. *Annals of Internal Medicine*, 158(5 Pt. 2), 365–440.

Shekelle, P.G., Wachter, R.M. and Pronovost, P.J. (eds). 2013. *Making Health Care Safer II: An Updated Critical Analysis of the Evidence for Patient Safety Practices*. Rockville, MD: Agency for Healthcare Research and Quality. AHRQ Publication No. 13-E001-EF. Available at: http://www.ahrq.gov/research/findings/evidence-based-reports/ptsafetyuptp.html#Report [accessed: March 19, 2013].

Sheridan, S. 2011. *Sue Sheridan: My Story*. [Online]. Available at: http://www.youtube.com/watch?v=Di9epzNFC3s&feature=relmfu [accessed: April 4, 2012].

Sheridan, T.B. 2003. Human error. *Quality and Safety in Health Care* [Online], 12(5), 383–5.

Shiner, B., et al. 2009. Access to what? An evaluation of the key ingredients to effective advanced mental health access at a VA medical center and its affiliated community-based outreach clinics. *Military Medicine*, 174(10), 1024–32.

Shojania, K.G., Wachter, R.M. and Hartman, E.E. n.d. *AHRQ Patient Safety Network Glossary*. Available at: http://psnet.ahrq.gov/glossary.aspx.

Shojania, K.G. et al. 2001. Making healthcare safer: A critical analysis of patient safety practices. *Evidence Report: Technology Assessment* [Online], 43, i–x, 1–668.

Shojania, K.G. et al. 2002. Safe but sound: Patient safety meets evidence-based medicine. *Journal of the American Medical Association*, 288(4), 508–13.

Shojania, K.G., Burton, E.C., McDonald, K.M. and Goldman, L. 2003. Changes in rates of autopsy-detected diagnostic errors over time: A systematic review. *Journal of the American Medical Association*, 289, 2849–56.

Shojania, K.G., Wachter, R.M. and Hartman, E.E. n.d. *AHRQ Patient Safety Network Glossary*. Available at: http://psnet.ahrq.gov/glossary.aspx.

Shortell, S.M., Rundall, T.G. and Hsu, J. 2007. Improving patient care by linking evidence-based medicine and evidence-based management. *Journal of the American Medical Association*, 298(6), 673–6.

Siebens, H. and Randall, P. 2005. The patient care notebook: From pilot phase to successful hospital wide dissemination. *Joint Commission Journal on Quality and Patient Safety*, 31, 398–405.

Sinclair, M. 1998. *The Report of the Manitoba Pediatric Cardiac Surgery Inquest.* [Online: Winnipeg, Manitoba, Canada: Provincial Court of Manitoba]. Available at: http://www.pediatriccardiacinquest.mb.ca/ [accessed: June 24, 2012].

Singer, N. 2009. Merck paid for medical 'journal' without disclosure. *The New York Times*. [Online]. Available at: http://www.nytimes.com/2009/05/14/business/14vioxxside.html? [accessed: March 26, 2013].

Singh, H., Giardina, T.D. and Forjuoh, S.N. et al. 2012. Electronic health record-based surveillance of diagnostic errors in primary care. *BMJ Quality and Safety*, 22, 93–100.

Singh, H. et al. 2010. Notification of abnormal lab test results in an electronic medical record: Do any safety concerns remain? *American Journal of Medicine*, 123, 238–44.

Singh, H. and Sittig, D. 2009. Eight rights of safe electronic health record use. *Journal of the American Medical Association*, 302, 1111–13.

Sinsky, C.A. 2008. E-nirvana: Are we there yet? *Family Practice Management*, 15, 6–8.

Sismondo, S. 2008. Pharmaceutical company funding and its consequences: A qualitative systematic review. *Contemporary Clinical Trials*, 29(2), 109–13.

Smetzer, J.L. 1998. Lesson from Colorado: Beyond blaming individuals. *Nursing*, 28(5), 48–51.

Smetzer, J.L. and Cohen, M.R. 1998. Lessons from the Denver medication error/criminal negligence case: Look beyond blaming individuals. *Hospital Pharmacy*, 33, 640–57.

Smith, R. 1998a. All changed, changed utterly: British medicine will be transformed by the Bristol case. *British Medical Journal*, 316(7149), 1917–18.

Smith, M. et al. (eds). 2012. Committee on the learning health care system in America, Institute of Medicine. *Best Care at Lower Cost: The Path to Continuously Learning Health Care in America*. Washington, DC: National Academies Press.

Smith, R. 1998b. Regulation of doctors and the Bristol inquiry. *BMJ: British Medical Journal*, 317(7172), 1539–40.

Smith, R. 2006. *The Trouble with Medical Journals*. London: The Royal Society of Medicine Press.

Snowden, D.J. and Boone, M. 2007. A leader's framework for decision making. *Harvard Business Review*, 85(11), 69–76.

Snowden, D. 2002. Complex acts of knowing: Paradox and descriptive self-awareness. *Journal of Knowledge Management*, 6(2), 100–11.

Solberg, L., et al. 2008. Can patient safety be measured by surveys of patient experiences? *Joint Commission Journal on Quality and Patient Safety*, 34, 266–74.

Sollenberger, J.F. and Holloway, R.G. Jr. 2013. The evolving role and value of libraries and librarians in health care. *Journal of the American Medical Association*, 310(12), 1231–2.

Soong, C. et al. 2013. Development of a checklist of safe discharge practices for hospital patients. *Journal of Hospital Medicine*, 8(8), 444–9.

Sorensen, A.V. and Bernard, S.L. 2012. Accelerating what works: Using qualitative research methods in developing a change package for a learning collaborative. *Joint Commission Journal on Quality and Patient Safety*, 38(2), 89–95.

Sorra, J.S. and Dyer, N. 2010. Multilevel psychometric properties of the AHRQ hospital survey on patient safety culture. *BMC Health Services Research*, [Online], 10, 199. Available at: doi:10.1186/1472-6963-10-199.

Stahel, P.F., Mehler, P.S., Clarke, T.J. and Varnell, J. 2009. The 5th anniversary of the "Universal Protocol": Pitfalls and pearls revisited. *Patient Safety in Surgery*, [Online] 3, 14. Available at: http://www.pssjournal.com/content/3/1/14 [accessed: March 23, 2013].

Starr, P. 1982. *The Social Transformation of American Medicine*. New York, NY: Basic Books.

Steel, K., Gertman, P.M., Crescenzi, C. and Anderson, J. 1981. Iatrogenic illness on a general medical service at a university hospital. *New England Journal of Medicine* [Online], 304(11), 638–42.

Steen, R.G. 2011a. Retractions in the medical literature: How many patients are put at risk by flawed research? *Journal of Medical Ethics* [Online]. Available at: http://dx.doi.org/10.1136/jme.2011.043133 [accessed: April 28, 2012].

Steen, R.G. 2011b. Misinformation in the medical literature: What role do error and fraud play? *Journal of Medical Ethics*. [Online]. Available at: http://dx.doi.org/10.1136/jme.2010.041830 [accessed: April 28, 2012].

Steinbrook, R. 2002. Protecting research subjects – The crisis at Johns Hopkins. *New England Journal of Medicine*, 346(9), 716–20.

Steinbrook, R. 2006. Searching for the right search – reaching the medical literature. *New England Journal of Medicine*, 354(1), 4–7.

Stephens, R.J. and Fairbanks, R.J. 2012. Humans and multitask performance: Let's give credit where credit is due. *Academic Emergency Medicine*, 19(2), 232–4.

Stevens, P., Matlow, A. and Laxer, R. 2005. Building from the blueprint for patient safety at the Hospital for Sick Children. *Healthcare Quarterly*, 8(sp.), 132–9.

Straus, S. and Haynes, R.B. 2009. Managing evidence-based knowledge: The need for reliable, relevant and readable resources. *Canadian Medical Association Journal*, 180(9), 942–5.

Sturmberg, J.P., Martin, C.M. and Katerndahl, D.A. 2014. Systems and complexity thinking in the general practice literature: An integrative, historical narrative review. *Annals of Family Medicine*, 12(1), 66–74.

Studer, Q. 2003. *Hardwiring Excellence*. Gulf Breeze, FL: Firestarter Publishing.

Suchetka, D. 2010. Burn victim hopes her story calls attention to dangers of surgical fires. *The Plain Dealer*. Available at: http://blog.cleveland.com/metro/2010/05/burn_victim_hopes_her_story_wi.html [accessed: March 17, 2013].

Szulanski, G. 1996. Exploring internal stickiness: Impediments to the transfer of best practice within the firm. *Strategic Management Journal*, 17(Winter 1996), 27–43.

Tamuz, M. and Harrison, M.I. 2006. Improving patient safety in hospitals: Contributions of high-reliability theory and normal accident theory. *Health Services Research*, 41:4 Part II, August 2006.

Tamuz, M., Giardina, T.D., Thomas, E.J., Menon, S. and Singh, H. 2011. Rethinking resident supervision to improve safety: From hierarchical to interprofessional models. *Journal of Hospital Medicine*, 6(8), 445–52.

Tanon, A.A. et al. 2010. Patient safety and systematic reviews: Finding papers indexed in MEDLINE, EMBASE and CINAHL. *Quality and Safety in Healthcare*, 19(5), 452–61.

Tavris, C. and Aronson, E. 2008. *Mistakes Were Made (But Not by Me): Why We Justify Foolish Beliefs, Bad Decisions, and Hurtful Acts*. Boston, MA: Houghton Mifflin Harcourt.

Taylor, B.B., et al. 2008. Do medical inpatients who report poor service quality experience more adverse events and medical errors? *Medical Care*, 46, 224–8.

Thibodeau, P.L. and Funk, C.J. 2009. Trends in hospital librarianship and hospital library services: 1989 to 2006. *Journal of the Medical Library Association*, 97(4), 273–9.

Thomassen, Ø., Storesund, A., Søfteland, E. and Brattebø, G. 2014. The effects of safety checklists in medicine: A systematic review. *Acta Anaesthesiologica Scandinavica*, 58(1), 5–18.

Thompson, D.N., Wolf, G.A. and Spear, S.J. 2003. Driving improvement in patient care: lessons from Toyota. *Journal of Nursing Administration*, 33(11), 585–95.

Timmel, J. et al. 2010. Impact of the comprehensive unit-based safety program (CUSP) on safety culture in a surgical inpatient unit. *Joint Commission Journal on Quality and Patient Safety*, 36, 252–60.

Timmermans, S. and Berg, M. 2003. *The Gold Standard: The Challenge of Evidence-Based Medicine and Standardization in Health Care*. Philadelphia, PA: Temple University Press.

Tod, A.M. et al. 2007. Exploring the contribution of the Clinical Librarian to facilitating evidence-based nursing. *Journal of Clinical Nursing*, 16(4), 621–9.

Toft, B. 2001. *External Inquiry into the adverse incident that occurred at Queen's Medical Centre, Nottingham, 4th January 2001*. London: Department of Health.

Tomlin, A. 2002. Hospital librarians and the Johns Hopkins tragedy. *Journal of Hospital Librarianship*, 2(4), 89–96.

Tompson, S.R. and Zipperer, L. 2011. Systems thinking for success, in *Best Practices in Corporate Libraries*, edited by M. Porter and S. Kelsey. Santa Barbara, CA: CLIO Press, 129–50.

Trafton, J.G. and Monk, C.A. 2008. Task interruptions, in *Reviews of Human Factors and Ergonomics, Vol. 3*, edited by D.A. Boehm-Davis. Santa Monica, CA: Human Factors and Ergonomics Society, 111–26.

Tucker, A., Edmondson, A. and Spear, S. 2011. *Why Your Organization isn't Learning All it Should: Working Knowledge*. [Online]. Available at: http://hbswk.hbs.edu/archive/2397.html [Assessed 17 March 2013].

Turner, B. and Pidgeon, N. 1997. *Man-Made Disasters*. New York, NY: Butterworth-Heinemann.

Tyler, L.S. et al. 2008. American Society of Health-System Pharmacists-ASHP Guidelines on the Pharmacy and Therapeutics Committee and the Formulary System. *American Journal of Health-System Pharmacy*, 65, 1272–83.

Uhlig, P.N., et al. 2002. John M. Eisenberg Patient Safety Awards. System innovation: Concord Hospital. *Joint Commission Journal of Quality Improvement*. 28, 666–72.

Ulmer, C., Wolman, D.M. and Johns, M.M.E. (eds). 2008. Committee on optimizing graduate medical trainee (resident) hours and work schedule to improve patient safety, Institute of Medicine. *Resident Duty Hours: Enhancing Sleep, Supervision, and Safety*. Washington, DC: The National Academies Press.

US Centers for Medicare and Medicaid Services (CMS). n.d. *CMS EHR Meaningful Use Overview.* [Online]. Available at: https://www.cms.gov/ EHRIncentivePrograms/Downloads/Hosp_CAH_MU-TOC.pdf [accessed: March 26, 2012].

US Centers for Medicare and Medicaid Services (CMS), HHS. 2012. Medicare and Medicaid programs; electronic health record incentive program – stage 2. Final rule. HHS. *Federal Register.* Sep 4;77(171):53967-4162

US Centers for Medicare and Medicaid Services (CMS). US Department of Health and Human Services. NIH Report. NIH Awards by Location and Organization. [Online]. Available at: http://report.nih.gov/award/index.cfm [accessed: January 24, 2014].

US Federal Aviation Administration. 2004 FAA advisory circular: AC 120-51E – Crew Resource Management Training. Available at: http://www.faa. gov/documentLibrary/media/Advisory_Circular/AC120-51e.pdf [accessed: January 30, 2014].

US Federal Aviation Administration 2014. Responsibility and authority of the pilot in command. *US Code of Federal Regulations.* 14 CFR 91.3. Available at: http://www.gpo.gov/fdsys/pkg/CFR-2014-title14-vol2/pdf/CFR-2014-title 14-vol2-sec91-3.pdf [accessed: March 16, 2014].

US Food and Drug Administration. 2011. Draft Guidance for Industry and Food and Drug Administration Staff – Applying Human Factors and Usability Engineering to Optimize Medical Device Design. [Online]. Available at: http:// www.fda.gov/downloads/MedicalDevices/DeviceRegulationandGuidance/ GuidanceDocuments/UCM259760.pdf [assessed: January 24, 2014].

US Department of Veteran's Affairs. National Center for Patient Safety. NCPS Root Cause Analysis Tools. [Online]. Available at: http://www.patientsafety. gov/CogAids/RCA/index.html [accessed: March 31, 2013].

US Department of Veteran's Affairs. National Center for Patient Safety. 2001. *The Basics of Healthcare Failure Mode and Effect Analysis.* Videoconference Course Materials. Ann Arbor, MI: US Veterans Administration National Center for Patient Safety. Available at: http://www.patientsafety.gov/SafetyTopics/ HFMEA/HFMEAIntro.pdf [accessed: March 15, 2013].

Uttal, B. 1983. The corporate culture vultures. *Fortune,* 66–72.

Van Beurden, E.K., Kia, A.M., Zask, A., Dietrick, U. and Rose, L. 2011. Making sense in a complex landscape: How the Cynefin framework from complex adaptive systems theory can inform health promotion practice. *Health Promotion International.* [Online]. Available at: doi:10.1093/heapro/dar089 [accessed: September 24, 2012].

Van Rite, E. 2011. *The Challenge of Patient Safety and the Remaking of American Medicine.* PhD Thesis. San Diego, CA: University of California San Diego.

Vaughan, D. 1997. *The Challenger Launch Decision: Risky Technology, Culture, and Deviance at NASA*. Chicago, IL: University of Chicago Press.

Veillette, P.R. 2012. Give E-Checklists an A+. *Business & Commercial Aviation*, 108(1), 36–9.

Versel, N. 2012. Meaningful use Stage 3 emphasizes better decision support. *Information Week/Healthcare Analytics*. [Online]. http://www.informationweek. com/regulations/meaningful-use-stage-3-emphasizes-better-decision-support/d/d-id/1105660 [accessed: January 22, 2014].

Vincent, C. 2010. *Patient Safety*. 2nd edition. West Sussex: Wiley-Blackwell.

Vincent, C., Batalden, P. and Davidoff, F. 2011. Multidisciplinary centres for safety and quality improvement: Learning from climate change science. *BMJ Quality and Safety* [Online], 20(Suppl 1), i73–i78.

Vincent, C., Young, M. and Phillips, A. 1994. Why do people sue doctors? A study of patients and relatives taking legal action. *Lancet*, 343, 1609–13.

Vine, R. 2004. Going beyond Google for faster and smarter web searching. *Teacher Librarian*, 32(1), 19.

Vinge, V. 1992. *A Fire Upon the Deep*. New York, NY: Tom Doherty Associates.

Von Hippel, E. 1994. Sticky information and the locus of problem solving: Implications for innovation. *Management Science*, 40(4), 429–39.

Wachter, R.M. 2010. Patient safety at ten: Unmistakable progress, troubling gaps. *Health Affairs*, 29(1), 165–73.

Wachter, R.M. 2012. *Understanding Patient Safety*. 2nd edition. New York, NY: McGraw-Hill Professional.

Wachter, R.M. 2013. Personal accountability in healthcare: Searching for the right balance. *BMJ Quality and Safety*, 22, 176–80.

Wachter, R.M., Flanders, S.A., Fee, C. and Pronovost, P.J. 2008. Public reporting of antibiotic timing in patients with pneumonia: Lessons from a flawed performance measure. *Annals of Internal Medicine*, 149(1), 29–32.

Wachter, R.M. and Shojania, K. 2004. *Internal Bleeding: The Truth Behind America's Terrifying Epidemic of Medical Mistakes*. New York, NY: Rugged Land.

Wagner, D.P., Noel, M.M., Barry, H.C. and Reznich, C.B. 2011 Safe expectations. *Academic Medicine*, 86, e17.

Walker, B. 2010. Selig won't overturn call that cost perfect game. *NBC Sports: Baseball*. [Online]. Available at: http://nbcsports.msnbc.com/id/37479309/ns/ sports-baseball/ [accessed: October 7, 2012].

Wallace, D.P. 2007. *Knowledge Management: Historical and Cross-Disciplinary Themes*. Westport, CT: Libraries Unlimited.

Wallace, J., Nwosu, B. and Clarke, M. 2012. Barriers to the uptake of evidence from systematic reviews and meta analyses: A systematic review of decision makers' perceptions. *BMJ Open* [Online], e001220. Available at:

http://bmjopen.bmj.com/content/2/5/e001220.full.pdf [accessed: November 18, 2012].

Walshe, K. and Offen, N. 2001. A very public failure: Lessons for quality improvement in healthcare organisations from the Bristol Royal Infirmary. *Quality in Health Care*, 10(4), 250–56.

Ward, L.G., Kendrach, M.G. and Price, S.O. 2004. Accuracy of abstracts for original research articles in pharmacy journals. *Annals of Pharmacotherapy*, 38 (7–8), 1173–7.

Waring, J.J. and Bishop, S. 2010. "Water cooler" learning: Knowledge sharing at the clinical "backstage" and its contribution to patient safety. *Journal of Health Organization and Management*, 24(4), 325–42.

Watts, B.V., Young-Xu, Y., Mills, P.D. et al. 2012. An examination of the effectiveness of a mental health environment of care checklist in reducing suicide on inpatient mental health units. *Archives of General Psychiatry*, 69(6), 588–92.

Wear, S., Bono, J.J., Logue, G. and McEvoy, A. (eds). 2000. *Ethical Issues in Health Care on the Frontiers of the Twenty-First Century*, Springer, FIND

Wears, R.L. and Nemeth, C.P. 2007. Replacing hindsight with insight: Towards a better understanding of diagnostic failures. *Annals of Emergency Medicine*, 49(2), 206–9.

Wears, R.L., Perry, S.J. and Sutcliffe, K.M. 2005. The medicalization of patient safety. *Journal of Patient Safety*, 1(1), 4–6.

Weaver, S.J. et al. 2013. Promoting a culture of safety as a patient safety strategy: A systematic review. *Annals of Internal Medicine*, 158(5 Pt. 2), 369–74.

Weaver, S.J. et al. 2010. The anatomy of health care team training and the state of practice: A critical review. *Academic Medicine*, 85(11), 1746–60.

Weick, K.E. 1987. Organizational culture as a source of high reliability. *California Management Review*, 29(2), 112–27.

Weick, K.E. 1990. The vulnerable system: an analysis of the Tenerife air disaster. *Journal of Management*, 16(3), 571–96.

Weick, K.E. and Sutcliffe, K.M. 2007. *Managing the Unexpected*. 2nd edition. San Francisco, CA: Jossey-Bass.

Weick, K.E., Sutcliffe, K.M. and Obstfeld, D. (2005). Organizing and the process of sensemaking. *Organization Science*, 16(4), 409–21.

Weiner, J.P., Kfuri, T., Chan, K. and Fowles, J.B. 2007. E-Iatrogenesis: The most critical unintended consequence of CPOE and other HIT. *Journal of the American Medical Informatics Association*, 14(3), 387–8.

Weinfeld, J. and Finkelstein, K. 2005. How to answer your clinical questions more efficiently. *Family Practice Management*, 12(7), 37–41.

Weingart, S.N. 2011. Engaging patients in patient safety, in *From Front Office to Front Line: Issues for Healthcare Leaders*, edited by S. Berman. *Joint Commission Resource*, 109–26.

Weingart, S.N. et al. 2005. What can hospitalized patients tell us about adverse events? Learning from patient-reported incidents. *Journal of General Internal Medicine*, 20, 830–36.

Weingart, S.N. et al. 2007. Patient-reported safety and quality of care in outpatient oncology. *Joint Commission Journal on Quality and Patient Safety*, 33, 83–94.

Weingart, S.N. et al. 2011. Hospitalized patients' participation and its impact on quality of care and patient safety. *International Journal for Quality in Health Care*, 23, 269–77.

Weiss, B. 2007. *Health Literacy and Patient Safety: Help Patients Understand*. Chicago, IL: American Medical Association.

Weiser, T.G. et al. 2010. Effect of a 19-item surgical safety checklist during urgent operations in a global patient population. *Annals of Surgery*, 251, 976–80.

Weissman, J.S. et al. 2008. Comparing patient-reported hospital adverse events with medical record review: Do patients know something that hospitals do not? *Annals of Internal Medicine*, 149, 100–108.

Weller, J., Boyd, M., and Cumin, D. 2014. Teams, tribes and patient safety: Overcoming barriers to effective teamwork in healthcare. *Postgraduate Medical Journal*. doi:10.1136/postgradmedj-2012-131168. [Epub ahead of print] PubMed PMID: 24398594.

Wenger, E. 2006. *Communities of Practice: A Brief Introduction*. [Online]. Available at: http://www.ewenger.com/theory/ [accessed: March 16, 2011].

Wenger, E., McDermott, R. and Snyder, W.M. 2002. Cultivating communities of practice: A guide to managing knowledge – Seven principles for cultivating communities of practice. *Working Knowledge for Business Leaders*. [Online]. Available at: http://hbswk.hbs.edu/archive/2855.html [accessed: February 17, 2012].

Wennberg, J. et al. 2009. Inpatient care and patients' ratings of their hospital experiences. *Health Affairs*, 28, 103–12.

Westrum, R. 1993. Thinking by groups, organizations, and networks: A sociologist's view of the social psychology of science and technology, in *The Social Psychology of Science*, edited by W. Shadish and S. Fuller. New York, NY: Guilford, 329–42.

Westrum, R. 2004. A typology of organisational cultures. *Quality and Safety in Health Care*, 13(suppl 2), ii22–ii27.

Westley, F., Patton, M.Q. and Zimmerman, B. 2006. *Getting to Maybe*. Toronto: Random House Canada.

Wheatley, M.J. 2006. *Leadership and the New Science: Discovering Order in a Chaotic World*. 3rd edition. San Francisco, CA: Berrett-Koehler Publishing.

White, D. et al. 2008. Communities of practice: Creating opportunities to enhance quality of care and safe practices. *Healthcare Quarterly*, 11(3), 80–84.

Wickens, C.D. and Hollands, J.G. 2000. *Engineering Psychology and Human Performance*. 3rd edition. Upper Saddle River, NJ: Prentice-Hall.

Wieringa, D., Moore, C. and Barnes, V. 1999. *Procedure Writing: Principles and Practices*. Piscataway, NJ: IEEE Computer Society Press.

Wilf-Miron, R., Lewenhoof, I., Benyamini, Z. and Aviram, A. 2003. From aviation to medicine: Applying concepts of aviation safety to risk management in ambulatory care. *Quality and Safety in Health Care*, 12, 35–9.

Wiklund, M.E. 1995. *Medical Device and Equipment Design: Usability Engineering and Ergonomics*. Buffalo Grove, IL: Interpharm Press.

Wiklund, M.E., Kendler, J. and Strochlic, A.Y. 2011. *Usability Testing of Medical Devices*. Boca Raton, FL: CRC Press.

Wilczynski, N.L., Morgan, D., Haynes, R.B. and Hedges Team. 2005. An overview of the design and methods for retrieving high-quality studies for clinical care. *BioMedCentral Medical Informatics and Decisionmaking*, 21(5), 20. Available at: http://www.ncbi.nlm.nih.gov/pmc/articles/PMC1183213/pdf/1472-6947-5-20.pdf [accessed: April 14, 2013]

Williams, L.C. 2012. Using magic to throw light on tricky healthcare systems: Patient safety problem solving. *Human Factors and Ergonomics in Manufacturing and Service Industries*, 22(1), 87–95.

Williams, L.C. and Bagian, J.P. 2010. Patient safety problem solving: Finding solutions that last. *Focus on Patient Safety: A Newsletter from the National Patient Safety Foundation*, 13(4).

Wilson, T.D. 2005. The nonsense of knowledge management revisited, in *Introducing Information Management: An Information Research Reader*, edited by E. Maceviciute and T.D. Wilson. London: Facet Publishing, 151–64.

Wilson, T., Holt, T. and Greenhalgh, T. 2001. Complexity and clinical care. *British Medical Journal*, 22(323), 685–8.

Wofford, M.M. et al. 2004. Patient complaints about physician behaviors: A qualitative study. *Academic Medicine*, 79, 134–8.

Wogalter, M.S., Conzola, V.C. and Smith-Jackson, T.L. 2002. Research-based guidelines for warning design/evaluation. *Applied Ergonomics*, 33(3), 219–30.

Wolper, L.F. 2010. *Health Care Administration: Planning Implementing and Managing Organized Delivery Systems*. 5th edition. Sudbury, MA: Jones and Bartlett Publishers.

Woodcock, K., Drury, C.G., Smiley, A. and Mad, J. 2005. Using simulated investigations for accident investigation studies. *Applied Ergonomics*, 36(1), 1–12.

Woods, D.D. and Hollnagel, E. 2006. *Joint Cognitive Systems: Patterns in Cognitive Systems Engineering.* Amazon Kindle Edition.

Woodward, S. 2011. Can Twitter lead to safer care? *Suzette's Blog. Patient Safety First!* [Online]. Available at: http://www.patientsafetyfirst.nhs.uk/Content. aspx?path=/Campaign-news/suzettes-blog/can-twitter-lead-to-safer-care/ [accessed: February 5, 2012].

World Alliance for Patient Safety. 2009. *Conceptual Framework for the International Classification for Patient Safety Version 1.1. Final Technical Report, January 2009* [Online]. Geneva, Switzerland: World Health Organization. Available at: http://www.who.int/patientsafety/taxonomy/icps_full_report.pdf [accessed: July 5, 2012].

World Alliance for Patient Safety. 2008. *WHO Surgical Safety Checklist and Implementation Manual.* [Online]. Geneva, Switzerland: World Health Organization Available at: [accessed: September 23, 2012].

World Health Organization. 2007. Information Exchange System. *Alert No. 115. HONG KONG* [Online]. Available at: http://www.who.int/patientsafety/ highlights/PS_alert_115_vincristine.pdf [accessed: November 18, 2012].

World Health Organization. 2010. *International Classification of Diseases (ICD) 10.* [Online]. Available at: http://www.who.int/classifications/icd/en/ [accessed: December 25, 2011].

World Health Organization. 2012. *Patients for Patient Safety Champions.* [Online]. Available at: http://www.who.int/patientsafety/patients_for_patient/regional _champions/en/index.html [accessed: April 5, 2012].

World Health Organization and The Joint Commission. 2007. *Improved Hand Hygiene to Prevent Health Care-Associated Infections.* [Online]. Available at: http://www.ccforpatientsafety.org/common/pdfs/fpdf/presskit/PS-Solution 9.pdf [accessed: February 1, 2012].

Wright, K., and McDaid, C. 2011. Reporting of article retractions in bibliographic databases and online journals. *Journal of the Medical Library Association*, 99(2), 164–7.

Wu, A.W. 2000. Medical error: The second victim. *British Medical Journal*, 320, 726–7.

Wu, A. and Zipperer, L. 2014. The healthcare environment and knowledge, blunt-end experience, in *Knowledge Management in Healthcare*, edited by L. Zipperer. Farnham: Gower.

Yackel, T.R. and Embi, P.J. 2010. Unintended errors with EHR-based result management: A case series. *Journal of the American Medical Informatics Association*, 17(1), 104–7.

Youngberg, B.J. (ed.) 2011. *Principles of Risk Management and Patient Safety.* Sudbury, MA: Jones Bartlett.

Younger, P. 2010. Internet-based information seeking behavior amongst doctors and nurses: A short review of the literature. *Health Information Libraries Journal*, 27(1), 2–10.

Zhu, J. et al. 2011. Can we rely on patients' reports of adverse events? *Medical Care*, 49, 948–55.

Zimmerman, B., Lindberg, C. and Plsek, P. 2001. *Edgeware: Insights from Complexity Science for Health Care Leaders*. Irving, TX: VHA, Inc.

Zipperer, L. 2004. Clinicians, librarians and patient safety: Opportunities for partnership. *Quality & Safety of Health Care*, 13(3), 218–22.

Zipperer, L. 2006. High reliability, information work and patient safety. *National Network*, 31(4–5), 7.

Zipperer, L. 2011. Knowledge services, in *The Medical Library Association Guide to Managing Health Care Libraries*, 2nd edition, edited by M.M. Bandy and R.F. Dudden. New York, NY: Neal-Schuman.

Zipperer, L. and Amori, G. 2011. Knowledge management: an innovative risk management strategy. *Journal of Healthcare Risk Management*, 30(4), 8–14.

Zipperer, L. and Sykes, J. 2009. Engaging as partners in patient safety: The experience of librarians. *Patient Safety & Quality Healthcare*, 6(28–30), 32–3.

Zipperer, L. and Tokarski, C. 2014. Tacit knowledge: Insights from the frontline, in *Knowledge Management in Healthcare*, edited by L. Zipperer. Farnham: Gower.

Zipperer, L., Gillaspy, M. and Goeltz, R. 2005. Facilitating patient centeredness through information work: Seeing librarians as guests in the lives of patients. *Journal of Hospital Librarianship*, 5, 1–15.

Zipperer, L., Gluck, J. and Anderson, S. 2002. Knowledge maps for patient safety. *Journal of Hospital Librarianship*, 2(4), 17–35.

Zipperer, L. et al. 2010. Diagnostic errors: Teamwork to solve tough diagnostic puzzles includes librarians. *National Network* [Newsletter of the Hospital Libraries Section of the Medical Library Association], 34(3), 6–9.

Zorzela, L. et al. 2014. Quality of reporting in systematic reviews of adverse events: Systematic review. *British Medical Journal*, January 8, 348:f7668.

Zucker, M. 2001. A brief history of Hexamethonium. *Respiratory Reviews*, 6(9). Available at: http://www.respiratoryreviews.com/sep01/rr_sep01_johnshop.html [accessed: 7 October 2012].

Zulman, D.M. et al. 2011. Patient interest in sharing personal health record information: A web-based survey. *Annals of Internal Medicine*, 155, 805–10.

Glossary

Adaptive challenges: Persistent murky problems that are systemic in nature and require that an organization and its leadership adjust to radical changes in their environment and processes through sharp end/blunt end knowledge exchange (Heifetz and Laurie 1997).

Blunt-blunt end: Organizations that affect hospital functionality through their rules, standards and policies. Hospital administration operationalizes decisions made by these external entities to create regulations, policies, and procedures that impact the sharp end and the delivery of care. These policy-making bodies make up the blunt-blunt end of the healthcare system (Wu and Zipperer 2014).

Boolean logic/Boolean operators: Boolean is a logic system that refers to relationships between terms and concepts. "Using the 'AND' operator between terms retrieves documents containing both terms. 'OR' retrieves documents containing either term. 'NOT' excludes the retrieval of terms from your search. Use 'NOT' with caution."[1]

Clinical hedges: Optimal search strategies to improve the retrieval of clinically relevant and scientifically sound study reports from large, general purpose, biomedical research bibliographic databases (Wilczynski 2005). Also referred to as clinical queries or search filters.

Computerized provider order entry (CPOE): "A networked system that allows a healthcare professional to enter orders via computer. Uses of CPOE include but are not limited to orders for medications and diagnostic tests (clinical laboratory, imaging, nursing orders, and special types of orders (dietary, for example). Sometimes called 'computerized physician order entry' or 'computerized practitioner order entry'" (Morath and Turnbull 2005: 260).

---

1   See http://www.nlm.nih.gov/bsd/disted/pubmedtutorial/020_350.html

Computers on Wheels (COWs): A small table on wheels with a laptop that is mobile enough to accompany frontline staff to address information and data seeking at the point of need.

Continuous improvement: A method of drawing from data on how a system works over time to design, revise and ultimately enhances processes over time (Berwick 1989).

Controlled vocabulary: A standard set of terms to be applied to describe resource items to retain consistency over time.

Crew Resource Management (CRM): "A process of training, used in the airline industry, that considers human performance limitations (such as fatigue and stress and designs countermeasure to combat them (for example, briefings, monitoring and cross-checking, decision-making, and review and modifications of plans along with instruction in confronting the authority gradient (Helmrich 2000)" (Morath and Turnbull 2005: 261).

Deep Web: The portion of the Web that is not necessarily accessible by standard search tools such as Google. It lies beyond reach of surface level search algorithms and tools, and instead is a discoverable but more direct and pointed method of searching. For example: specific reports of incidents of harm included in a state reporting archive could be considered the Deep Web.

Error: "An act of commission (doing something wrong) or omission (failing to do the right thing) that leads to an undesirable outcome or significant potential for such an outcome … Errors of omission are more difficult to recognize than errors of commission but likely represent a larger problem … In addition to commission vs. omission, three other dichotomies commonly appear in the literature on errors: active failures vs. latent conditions, errors at the sharp end vs. errors at the blunt end, and slips vs. mistakes" (AHRQ PSNet Glossary).

Evidence-based medicine (EBM): "The conscientious explicit and judicious use of current best evidence in making decisions about the care of individual patients" (Sackett et al. 1996: 71).

Forcing functions: "Technical or physical obstacles designed to decrease the probability of error in error-prone circumstances or environments. Forcing functions are designed to anticipate common human errors and make harm from them impossible by blocking either the error or its consequences" (Wachter 2012: 63–4).

Hierarchy of actions: A set of actions that vary in strength to result in reducing system and behavioral potential for failure. "Stronger actions [at the top of the hierarchy] are viewed as those that are more likely to be successful in accomplishing the desired changes, rendering greater utility for the effort expended" (National Center for Patient Safety 2011: n.p.).

High-consequence or high-risk organizations: Industries or organizations where "the potential for loss of human life in the event of an error" is a regular state (Patankar et al. 2012: 16).

H-Index: "The h-index is an index that attempts to measure both the productivity and impact of the published work of a scientist or scholar. The index is based on the set of the scientist's most cited papers and the number of citations that they have received in other publications. The index can also be applied to the productivity and impact of a group of scientists, such as a department or university or country, as well as a scholarly journal."[2]

Human factors: "A field concerned with understanding and enhancing human performance in the workplace, especially in complex systems" (Morath and Turnbull 2005: 265).

Human factors engineering: "A hybrid field that mixes various engineering disciplines, design and cognitive psychology that is concerned with the interplay between humans, machines and their work environments" (Wachter 2012: 113).

Informationist: An extended role for clinical librarians. "Informationists are cross-trained in reference library skills and the essentials of specific biomedical disciplines. They work as full-time members of clinical and some research teams while maintaining formal relationships with their home libraries. They search the literature in response to questions, critically appraise the findings, and summarize them in concise written reports" (Davidoff and Miglus 2011: 1906).

Knowledge map: A knowledge map is not a repository of information, but a tool that points to where it might reside in an organization or community (Davenport and Prusak 1998).

Latent condition: "Conditions such as poor design ... unworkable procedures ... clumsy automation ... that may be present for many years before they

---

2   See http://en.wikipedia.org/wiki/H-index

combine with local circumstances and active failures to penetrate the system's many layers of [safety] defenses" (Reason 1997: 10).

Near misses: "An event or situation that might have resulted in an accident, injure or illness but did not, either by change or through timely intervention (Quality Interagency Coordination Task Force 2000)." Sometimes referred to as "close calls" or good catches, "Near misses are valuable tools for learning about systems vulnerability and resilience" (Morath and Turnbull 2005: 268).

Never events: Formally referred to as serious preventable events, never events are patient safety events that are "unambiguous, largely preventable, and serious as well as adverse, indicative of a problem in a healthcare's safety systems, or important for public credibility or public accountability. Some SREs are universally preventable and should never occur. Others are largely preventable and may be reduced to zero as knowledge and improved presentation strategies evolve" (National Quality Forum 2011: 2).

Normal accident theory: Sociologist Charles Perrow's Normal Accident Theory grew out of his understanding of the disaster at Three Mile Island (Perrow 1984). The technology at Three Mile Island was tightly coupled (i.e., it had time-dependent processes, invariant sequences) and interactively complex (i.e., different elements could affect each other in unforeseen ways). Perrow hypothesized that the combination of these two factors allowed events to spread throughout the system by way of connections that were impossible to anticipate, and with a speed that precluded understanding, much less response. Thus, regardless of the effectiveness of management and operations, accidents in these systems will be "normal" or inevitable.

Normalization of Deviance: "This expression describes the gradual shift in what is regarded as normal after repeated exposures to 'deviant behavior' (behavior straying from correct [or safe] operating procedure). Corners get cut, safety checks bypassed, and alarms ignored or turned off, and these behaviors become normal – not just common, but stripped of their significance as warnings of impending danger … Providers in the system become inured to malfunction. In such a system, what should be regarded as a major warning of impending danger is ignored as a normal operating procedure" (AHRQ PSNet Glossary).

Production pressure: "Represents the pressure to put quantity of output – for a product or a service – ahead of safety … production pressure refers to delivery of services – the pressure to run hospitals at 100 percent capacity, with each bed filled with the sickest possible patients who are discharged at the first sign that they are stable, or the pressure to leave no operating room unused and to keep moving through the schedule for each room as fast as possible ... Production pressure produces an organizational culture in which frontline personnel (and often managers) are reluctant to suggest any course of action that compromises productivity, even temporarily" (AHRQ PSNet Glossary).

Rapid Response Team: "A team of providers is summoned to the bedside to immediately assess and treat the patient with the goal of preventing" (AHRQ PSNet).[3]

Sensemaking: Sensemaking is what happens when participants in a communication attempt to make sense of the inherent gaps. Sensemaking is integral to making the progression from scattered bits of data into information and then into the knowledge that results in understanding (Ans and Tricot 2009). Sensemaking as a systematic construct to describe communication, particularly in organizations has been described as: "The core construct of sensemaking is the ideas of the gap – how people define and bridge gaps in their everyday lives" (Dervin 2003: 223).

Sentinel event(s): "A sentinel event is an unanticipated occurrence involving death or major permanent loss of function unrelated to the natural course of the patient's illness of underlying condition. ... Such events are called sentinel because they signal a need for immediate investigation and response. The terms sentinel event and medical error are not synonymous; not all sentinel event occurs because of an error and not all errors result in sentinel events" (Joint Commission International 2008: 15).

Serious reportable events: See never events.

Situation awareness (sometimes termed "situational awareness"): "Situational awareness refers to the degree to which one's perception of a situation matches reality. In the context of crisis management, where the phrase is most often used, situational awareness includes awareness of fatigue and stress among team members (including oneself), environmental threats to safety, appropriate immediate goals, and the deteriorating status of the crisis (or patient). Failure to

---

3   Adapted with permission from AHRQ Patient Safety Network: Ranji, S., Wachter, R.M. and Hartman, E.E. *Patient Safety Primer: Rapid Response Systems.* AHRQ Patient Safety Network. Available at: http://psnet.ahrq.gov/primer.aspx?primerID=4 [updated October 2012].

maintain situational awareness can result in various problems that compound the crisis" (AHRQ PSNet Glossary).

Surface Web: Website content that is retrievable through standard search activities, functions and tools such as Google. PubMed® and AHRQ PSNet are considered to be surface Web patient safety evidence and information resources.

Tacit knowledge: Knowledge gained from action: it is developed and matures through experience and difficult to transfer to materials that traditionally result in information and evidence.

Note, glossary entries referenced to AHRQ PSNet Glossary were adapted with permission from AHRQ Patient Safety Network: Shojania, K.G., Wachter, R.M. and Hartman, E.E. *AHRQ Patient Safety Network Glossary*. Available at: http://psnet.ahrq.gov/glossary.aspx

Appendix 1
Timeline of Significant Events in the Evolution of Patient Safety

Year	Event
Sporadic Period	
1700	Rush "heroic medicine"
1847	Semelweiss, origin of puerperal sepsis
1860	Nightingale, hospital hygiene and nursing education
1867	Lister and surgical asepsis
1905	Ernst Mach, *Knowledge and Error*
1910	Flexner, *Medical Education in the United States and Canada*
1915	Codman, classification of reporting of surgical errors
1924	First use of term "iatrogenic"
Cult Period	
1956	Barr paper, Hazards of modern diagnosis and therapy, *Journal of the American Medical Association*
1959	Moser, *Diseases of Medical Progress*
1962	Ellison Pierce assigned lecture topic of anesthesia accidents
1964	Schimmel, Hazards of Hospitalisation
1975	Fischoff, hindsight and outcome bias
1977	Mills, *Medical Insurance Feasibility Study*
1977	Ivan Illich, *Medical Nemesis*
1977	Tenerife disaster
1978	Cooper et al., *Preventable Anesthesia Mishaps*
1979	Charles Bosk, *Forgive and Remember: Managing Medical Failure*
1979	Three Mile Island
1980	Clambake Conference on the Nature and Source of Human Error
1981	Steel et al., replicate Schimmel

1982	ABC *20/20* special "The Deep Sleep"
1983	Ellison Pierce becomes president of the American Society for Anesthesiology
1983	McIntyre and Popper, The Critical Attitude in Medicine
1983	NATO/Rockefeller Foundation Conference on the Nature and Source of Human Error
1984	Perrow, *Normal Accidents*
1984	Libby Zion death at New York Hospital
1984	Bhopal disaster in India
1985	Anesthesia Patient Safety Foundation founded
1985	First death from software (THERAC-25)
1986	Chernobyl
1986	JAMA, Anesthesia standards
1988	Marianne Paget, *A Unity of Mistakes*
1987	Rochlin et al., *Self-designing High Reliability*
1989	First Conference on Naturalistic Decision Making
1989	Bell Commission, Libby Zion law
1990	Reason, *Human Error*
1991	Harvard Medical Practice Study published
1991	Institute for Healthcare Improvement founded
1991	Caplan et al., *JAMA*; Hindsight and outcome bias in appropriateness of care judgments
1992	First issue of *Quality in Health Care*
1994	Leape, JAMA, *Error in Medicine*
1994	Bogner, *Human Error in Medicine*
1994	Betsy Lehman dies during treatment for breast cancer
1995	Willie King, wrong leg amputation in Florida
1995	Seven-year-old Ben Kolb dies during routine ear surgery
1995	Extensive media reports on Lehman's death and other errors
1996	First Annenberg Conference *Examining Errors in Healthcare*
1996	Weeramanthri, *Quality in Australian Health Care Study*
1996	Denver nurses medication error
1997	National Patient Safety Foundation founded by the AMA
1998	Second Annenberg conference, *Enhancing Patient Safety and Reducing Errors in Health Care*
1998	NPSF Patient Safety Listserv™ established
1998	First NPSF patient safety research grants awarded
1998	Woods, Cook and Miller, *A Tale of Two Stories*
1999	Woods and Cook, *The New Look at Error, Safety and Failure*
Breakout Period	
2000	IOM's *To Err is Human* published
2000	Studdert et al., Utah-Colorado replication of HMPS
2001	IOM's *Crossing the Quality Chasm* published

2001	Official report on Bristol Royal Infirmary released
2001	New Zealand *Review of Processes Concerning Adverse Medical Events*
2001	Josie King dies at Johns Hopkins Hospital
2001	Healthy research volunteer Ellen Roche dies at Johns Hopkins Hospital
2002	Josie King Foundation started by Sorrel King
2002	*Quality in Health Care* renamed to become *Quality and Safety in Health Care*
2003	Jésica Santillán wrong heart transplant
2004	IOM's *Patient Safety Achieving a New Standard of Care* published
2004	Betsy Lehman Center founded by Mass. Government
2004	Baker, *Canadian Adverse Event Study*
2004	World Alliance for Patient Safety Founded by the World Health Organization
2006	Indianapolis, heparin overdoses injure six newborns, three die
2007	Dennis Quaid's twins suffer heparin overdoses
2011	"Patient Safety" added as a MeSH heading

Appendix 2
Expanded Selected EI&K Tools and Mechanisms by Primary Function

Susan Carr, Barbara Olsen and Lorri Zipperer

Each resource has characteristic strengths and weaknesses, and all should be considered for inclusion in safety improvement strategies. To ignore any of these categories will result in gaps that may invite failure.

General considerations:

- The potential for bias and flaws in reasoning is present in all resources (see Chapter 6).

- Some hospitals block the use of Web-based tools by prohibiting access to the Internet while at work and/or prohibiting the use of personal devices (smartphones) for hospital business.

- This table does not distinguish between digital and printed formats of the various tools and mechanisms. Most are now available digitally, offering the same content as print editions, when print is the original format.

Tool/Mechanism	Characteristics	Examples
Evidence		
Peer-reviewed journals.	• Rigor of review. • Reported results supported with data. • Transparency of content development process.	• *Journal of Patient Safety.* • *BMJ Quality & Safety.* • *Joint Commission Journal on Quality and Patient Safety.*
Consolidation (or point-of-care) resources.	• Compilations of evidence designed to be actionable at the point-of-care. • Process of selection not always transparent.	• UpToDate™. • Micromedex. • Nursing Reference Center. • Dynamed.
Information		
Newspapers, magazines and newsletters .	• Not evidence-based, may be highly influential via investigation, reporting and storytelling. • Not listed in PubMed® or other medical databases (see below)	• *New York Times.* • *Wall Street Journal.* • *Patient Safety and Quality Healthcare.* • *Trustee Magazine.* • ISMP medication safety alerts. • Local newspapers and hospital newsletters.
Literature databases.	• Searchable access to the published literature. • Compiled for use. • Utilize taxonomies/thesauri. • Some (e.g., PubMed®) have free interfaces).	• PubMed®. • Web of Science™. • CINAHL™.
Intranet, local file-sharing, shared directories.	• Only as effective as the process to build and maintain them.	• SharePoint™ .
Books.	• In-depth exploration of central concepts by recognized experts. • First-person storytelling.	• *To Err Is Human* (Institute of Medicine 2000). • *Understanding Patient Safety,* 2nd edition (Wachter 2012). • *Human Error* (Reason 1990). • *Escape Fire* (Berwick 2004). • *Josie's Story* (King 2009).

Tool/Mechanism	Characteristics	Examples
Movies/Video resources.	• Effective for use in orientation, group training. • Some are produced by hospitals in-house in response to patient harm.	• *Beyond Blame* (1997). • *First Do No Harm* video series (Partnership for Patient Safety 2000). • *The Faces of Medical Error...from Tears to Transparency* (Transparent Learning 2010). • *When Things Go Wrong* (CRICO 2011).
Webinars, webcasts, and podcasts.	• Efficient access to information, evidence and data. • Not always designed to share knowledge, though possibilities exist. • Free programs often are sponsored by vendors.	• Partnership for Patients. • Institute for Family- and Patient-Centered Care. • *Health Affairs* "Narrative Matters" podcasts. • *Journal of the American Medical Association* "Author in the Room."
Web-based user-generated content.	• Tremendous variation in quality. • Lack of transparency and explicitness regarding authority.	• Blogs. • Twitter. • YouTube. • Wikipedia. • Subject-focused Wikis.
Online networking groups.	• Registration can be required for access to the group and participation. • Firewall and access restrictions can limit use.	• Facebook. • LinkedIn. • Email discussion lists.
Websites/Portals.	• Content designed for specific audiences, including the public. • Focused audience/editorial oversight can improve applicability of the content.	• AHRQ Patient Safety Network. • Organization awareness sites. • Informational sites. • Commercial/marketing sites.
Search engines.	• Range from universal to specialized search. • Criteria for displayed results are not transparent.	• Google. • Yahoo. • Bing.

Tool/Mechanism	Characteristics	Examples
Knowledge		
Communities of practice.	• Facilitate seeking and sharing of individual expertise to a pre-defined project with a distinct goal in mind. • Can often reside behind security passwords to keep engagement focused and participation manageable and purposeful.	Examples discussed in: • Creating a more efficient healthcare knowledge market: using communities of practice to create checklists (Lashoher and Pronovost 2010). • Participating in communities of practice (Bandy, Condon, and Graves 2008).
Collaboratives.	• Facilitate sharing of frontline team-based experience. • Focus on a pre-defined project with a distinct goal in mind keeps sharing on-point.	• Institute for Healthcare 100,000 and 5-million Lives Campaigns. • Keystone Project. • MCIC Emergency Department Patient Safety Collaborative.
Person to person interaction (mentors, coaches, peers, conference attendance etc.).	• Dynamic opportunities for rapid learning.	• National Patient Safety Foundation annual Patient Safety Congress. • Institute for Healthcare Improvement National Forum. • *British Medical Journal*/Institute for Healthcare Improvement International Forum.

Appendix 3
Full Hierarchy of Actions

Stronger Actions

Type	Information Centric/Library Example	Clinical (Healthcare) Example	References
Architectural/ Physical plant changes	Situate information expertise at the point of need. Librarian is present for patient rounds.	Suicide-resistant door set for mental health patient room; acuity-adaptive patient rooms; shock absorbing flooring to reduce harm from patient falls.	(Hignett and Lu 2007; Rashid 2006; Henriksen et al. 2007; Hendrich et al. 2004; Joseph and Rashid, 2007)
New devices with usability testing prior to purchase	Test new webpage with real users for intuitiveness and ease of use; iterative redesign based upon findings.	Automated defibrillator; site scrub uses natural scrubbing motion to prepare for connection of IV and medication lines.	(Wiklund 2011; Anderson et al. 2011; Donchin 2002; Lin et al. 1998)
Engineering control – forcing function	On-line information request form includes *date-filled* to be completed before submit button is clicked.	IV tubing auto-clamp when pump door opens; drive bar on portable x-ray machine.	(Grout 2007; Carayon 2007)
Simplify the process	Make access available through desktop link; with easy print for e-materials. Eliminate multiple log-in screens and sites. Librarian attends Morbidity and Mortality conferences.	Remove unnecessary steps for LP preparation; include information needed, and bundle supplies for procedures; required programming for patient controlled analgesia has fewer decision points, errors are clear and recoverable.	(Lin et al. 1998; Pronovost et al. 2006)
Standardize equipment or process	Standardize log-in and portal for access.	Standard defibrillator on all code carts; standard arrangement of code cart drawers.	(Gosbee and Gosbee 2010; Mosenkis 1994; Wiklund 1995; McLaughlin 2003)
Tangible involvement by leadership	Director recognizes librarian as active partner in patient safety and information and knowledge transfer in the organization. Librarian authorized as participani on RCA and FMEA teams.	Supporting purchase of standard central venous catheters. Leadership involved and supportive of RCA and HFMEA processes.	(Ginsburg et al. 2005)

Intermediate Actions

Type	Information Centric/Library Example	Clinical (Healthcare) Example	References
Redundancy.	Formulary listings for high-alert medications are researched independently by more than one person with differing expertise.	Abnormal x-ray follow up to both general medicine and subspecialty physicians; and separately to technician, with confirmation that report was received.	(Choksi et al. 2006; Gosbee and Gosbee 2010).
Increase in staffing/Decrease workload.	Hire paraprofessional staff to handle routine tasks, for example, document delivery.	Staffing increased from two to three House Officers (physicians) per ward with staggered shifts allowing fewer hand-offs.	(Mueller et al. 2012; Fletcher et al. 2004).
Software enhancements/ Modifications.	Create a Google search application for clinicians and/or patients. Create computer interface/form for diagnostic error reporting.	Computer alerts for drug-drug interactions.	(Weiner 2007).
Eliminate/Reduce distractions.	Barrier tape to prevent interruptions during intense research work. Use sound canceling covers for printers.	Quiet rooms for programming patient-controlled analgesia (PCA) pumps.	(Trafton and Monk 2008; Pape et al. 2005; Hillel and Vicente 2003).
Checklist/Cognitive aid improved with usability testing and iterative redesign.	New staff have pocket-sized "lab book". Reference interview form to guide complete search question development. Listing of databases available. Time out pocket card for "Why doctors make mistakes."	Ensure all anesthesia equipment is operational through use of a read and verify checklist. Involve anesthesiologists in design and usability testing.	(Arbous and Meursing 2005; Kozer et al. 2005; Guwande 2009).
Eliminate look and sound-alikes.	Eliminate out of date reference materials (electronic or hard copy) or boldly mark previous editions.	Similar named medications (ie Losec and Lasix) not stored near each other; that is, store medications by category of use rather than alphabetically.	(ISMP 2011).
Standardized communication tools.	Develop SBAR (Situation, Background, Assessment, Recommendation) for reference interview.	Read back critical lab value. Pre-procedure briefings.	(Paull and Mazzia 2011).
Enhanced documentation and communication.	Clean and clear version of citation list. Iterative process for search. Use of feedback.	Improved labeling: Medication name and dose highlighted on IV bag. Clinical teams use structured communication for care transitions.	(Rudin 2011; Mueller et al. 2012).
Education.	Knowing cognitive biases decreases misdiagnoses and omissions.	Knowing cognitive biases decreases risk of misdiagnoses.	(Tamuz et al. 2011; Crosskerry 2000).

	Type	Information Centric/Library Example	Clinical (Healthcare) Example	References
Weaker Actions	Double checks.	One person completes search, another person reviews their search.	One person calculates dosage, another person reviews their calculation. Pathologists independently view frozen section slides.	(Gosbee 2006, Raab et al. 2006).
	Warnings.	Copyright signs over copy machines. Sign near search terminal "Got questions?" with contact information.	Adding audio alarms or caution labels. Ensure the labeling is clear (ie easy to see and read).	(Wogalter et al. 2002; Bix 2002).
	Procedure, memoran-dum, or policy.	Draft a new policy. After three lab tests and no substantial diagnostic results, call librarian. "If you spend more than 10 minutes looking call the librarian."	Policy/procedure directing improvement: • Nurses check IV sites every 2 hours. • Instructing placement of green adapters only on compressed gas oxygen wall outlets.	(Wiklund 2011; Hildebrand et al. 2011; Wieringa et al. 1999).
	Training.	EBM training for physicians, nurses and/or librarians.	In-service on hard-to-use defibrillator with hidden door; training is necessary for complex endoscope cleaning process, and also requires support of cognitive aids. Training efficacy is improved with usability testing of device to precisely target training to problematic steps.	(Anderson et al. 2010; Hildebrand et al. 2011).

Note: Adapted from Alligood, E., Jones, B., Williams, L. and Zipperer, L. "Hierarchy of Actions – Librarian/Information-centric Examples." [presentation handouts]. *Diagnostic Error Team Up and Tackle It*, 2011, May 13, Medical Library Association Annual Conference, Minneapolis.

Appendix 4
Doctors, Umpires, and EI&K Seekers

Adapted with permission of *AHRQ WebM&M*. Graber, M.L. Diagostic errors in medicine: What do doctors and umpires have in common [Perspective]? *AHRQ WebM&M* [serial online]. February 2007. Available at:http://www.webmm.ahrq.gov/perspective.aspx?perspectiveID=36.

Issue	Umpires	Doctors	EI&K Seekers
What is the complexity of the decision?	Binary – It's a strike or a ball.	There are thousands of diseases and syndromes, but typically the number of reasonable choices is less than 10.	Multiple choices of terms, resources, cost and timing considerations, scope and applicability of identified resources. Librarians also need to diagnose the MDs thinking.
How well do we do? What is the ACTUAL error rate?	The stated accuracy rate for Major League Baseball umpires is 92–94 percent.	10 percent or more of autopsies disclose important discrepancies that would have changed the clinical care or prognosis (Shojana et al. 2003). Studies looking at specific clinical conditions find an error rate of approximately 10 percent (Schiff et al. 2004).	Unknown, unexplored. Task: Develop a feedback and improvement process engage a teamwork-oriented sensitivity to failure in EI&K. Task: Design a process to work with clinicians to assess quality of EI&K seeking. Task: Confirm lack of studies.
How well do we THINK we do? What is the perceived accuracy rate?	Anecdotally, better than the truth would support.	Much better than reality. Most clinicians can't recall a diagnostic error they themselves have made. While they are keenly aware that diagnostic error exists, they believe errors are made by other physicians, less careful or skilled than themselves.	Better than reality. Overconfidence in term selection; lack of dialogue due to time pressure, non-team sensitivity, in security, etc.

Issue	Umpires	Doctors	EI&K Seekers
What are the consequences of error?	Typically, no impact. Rarely, errors lead to lost games, a losing series, or career changes.	Typically, no impact. The error is inconsequential or is not discovered. Rarely, the error may cause injury or death.	Unknown, unexplored. Lack of organizational concern for its importance and lack of overall personnel commitment to the exploring and defining the reliability of the research process.
What types of cognitive processes are used to make the decision?	The umpire integrates his perception of the ball's path in the context of his knowledge of the strike zone, all interpreted automatically (subconsciously).	Most patient problems are very familiar to clinicians. Physicians integrate their perception of the facts in the context of their medical knowledge base. This occurs automatically (subconsciously) and involves recognizing patterns (schema) they have seen before.	Heuristics, self-satisfaction bias [glossary]. Premature closure and reliance on colleagues can block awareness of the need to seek information to confirm decision-making.
What factors detract from perfection?	Stress, fatigue, distractions, affective factors and the inherent shortcomings of automatic processing (bias).	Stress, fatigue, distractions, affective factors and the inherent shortcomings of automatic processing (bias).	Same as above. Other considerations are operational limitations for resources and training. The burden of what is free detracts from the realization that more is needed.
Can the error rate be reduced?	Possibly. The [performance tracking] system is providing feedback to umpires to improve performance and calibration.	Possibly. Avenues for improvement exist but are unproven (decision support, feedback, "cognitive de-biasing").	Possibly (see how well above). (Decision support, feedback, "cognitive de-biasing"). Tools should be developed to enable improvement.

Note: Original adapted by Zipperer and Williams 2011 from: Graber, M. 2007. Diagnostic errors in medicine: What do doctors and umpires have in common? *AHRQ WebM&M* [Online]. Reproduced with permission of the authors.

Index